Beginning Irish Studies

Manchester University Press

Beginnings
Series editor: William Hughes

'Beginnings' is a series of books designed to give practical help to students beginning to tackle recent developments in English, Literary Studies and Cultural Studies. The books in the series

- demonstrate and encourage a questioning engagement with the new;
- give essential information about the context and history of each topic covered;
- show how to develop a practice which is up-to-date and informed by theory.

Each book focuses uncompromisingly upon the needs of its readers, who have the right to expect clarity to be the distinctive feature of a book which includes the word 'beginning' in its title.

Each aims to lay a firm foundation of well-understood initial principles as a basis for further study and is committed to explaining new aspects of the discipline without oversimplification, but in a manner appropriate to the needs of beginners.

Each book, finally, aims to be both an introduction and a contribution to the topic area it discusses.

To buy or to find out more about the books currently available in this series, please go to: https://manchesteruniversitypress.co.uk/series/beginnings/

Beginning Irish Studies

Graham Price

MANCHESTER UNIVERSITY PRESS

Published by Manchester University Press
Oxford Road, Manchester, M13 9PL

www.manchesteruniversitypress.co.uk

British Library Cataloguing-in-Publication Data
A catalogue record for this book is available from the British Library

ISBN 978 1 5261 9142 7 paperback
ISBN 978 1 5261 9139 7 hardback

First published 2026

EU authorised representative for GPSR:
Easy Access System Europe, Mustamäe tee 50, 10621 Tallinn, Estonia
gpsr.requests@easproject.com

Typeset
by New Best-set Typesetters Ltd

Contents

Biography

Graham Price lectures in the Department of English Language and Literature at Mary Immaculate College Limerick. He previously taught in the School of English, Drama and Film at University College Dublin, the English Department at NUI Maynooth, and Modern Irish and British literature at the University of Limerick. His monograph, *Oscar Wilde and Contemporary Irish Drama: Learning to be Oscar's Contemporary*, was published in 2018 and is the first book-length examination of the Wildean strand in contemporary Irish theatre. Price's co-written book (with Darragh Greene), *Film Directors and Emotion: An Affective Turn in Contemporary American Cinema*, was published in 2020.

Acknowledgements

The layout of this book has its origins in an MA seminar course I took as part of my postgraduate degree in Anglo-Irish Literature and Drama at University College Dublin in 2004. The module title was 'Theorising Ireland' and the convener was Dr P.J. Mathews. When it came to deciding how to structure *Beginning Irish Studies* I got a lot of inspiration from how that module was laid out, particularly the first two chapters, which benefitted greatly from the readings that were assigned for 'Theorising Ireland'.

During the writing of the book, I was greatly helped by a number of very generous friends and colleagues who agreed to read and to give advice on individual chapters. They are David Clare, Margaret Kelleher, Jose Lanters, Ellen McWilliams, Neil Sammells, Moynagh Sullivan and Feargal Whelan. I also owe another debt of gratitude to Neil Sammells for recommending to Manchester University Press that I be approached to submit a proposal for this text.

Over the years I have gained great knowledge and inspiration from my PhD supervisor, Declan Kiberd. His international reputation for being a great scholar and teacher is entirely justified. I am also extremely grateful for the fifteen-year friendship I have had with Frank McGuinness, from which I have gained much knowledge and support: long may it continue.

As the Coda to *Beginning Irish Studies* will make clear, I also owe Michael O'Rourke much thanks for broadening my intellectual horizons immensely over many years. The the(e)ories seminars that he organised with Noreen Giffney and Anne Mulhall, which I attended regularly for nearly ten years from 2005, have contributed greatly to the breadth of knowledge that I hope is apparent in this book.

Ever since I began teaching in 2007, it has been my good fortune to encounter many amazing students in University College Dublin, St Patrick's College Drumcondra, the University of Limerick and NUI Maynooth. To have worked with and learnt from them has been a pleasure and a privilege. I am also glad to have made friends with many of them and that those friendships have endured to this day. I have also been lucky to have worked with a number of inspiring scholars down through the years.

Sections of this book comprise republished articles and book chapters. These works have been republished with the kind permission of Palgrave Macmillan and *Irish University Review*. For their cooperation, they have my sincerest gratitude.

My being able to pursue a career in academia would not have been possible without the support and guidance of my parents, Alvin and Margaret. My two grandmothers, Norah Price and Mary McStay (who is sadly no longer with us) have been sources of inspiration for me throughout my life. The other members of my immediate family – my two sisters (Julie and Laura) and all my uncles and aunts – have helped me in a myriad of ways down through the years. I also want to thank my father for his invaluable proofreading of the final draft of the manuscript.

I want to thank Esther Ryley for being a constant source of support and encouragement. Our regular messaging helped me greatly during the year it took me to write *Beginning Irish Studies*.

Finally, I want to thank all the writers and thinkers (dead and alive) for producing the texts with which I have been lucky enough to engage during course of writing *Beginning Irish Studies*. The Irish nation is truly lucky to have produced such individuals who have, through the centuries, borne witness to the complex and multiform creature that is Irishness. With this book, I hope to have, in some small way, played my part in this ongoing enterprise.

Introduction

Beginning Irish Studies: a summary

Irish Studies is taught in many academic institutions across the English-speaking world and that number is growing at a steady pace. *Beginning Irish Studies* provides a comprehensive introduction not merely to the history and development of this influential academic discipline but will further acknowledge its importance as a dynamic and constantly evolving method for analysing drama, literature, film and poetry in Ireland. The book will further guide the reader to an understanding of the contextual underpinnings of this academic discipline – including gender, empire, ecocriticism, memory studies and intersectionality – as well as the interpretation of these in cultural and critical theory. *Beginning Irish Studies* is both an introduction to the current debate and an invitation to its readers to consider its further developments from various theoretical perspectives. It shall also attempt to envisage the future intersectional alliances that Irish Studies might make in the coming years.

Beginning Irish Studies follows the established pattern of the series, outlining the history and development of the genre and its criticism in discrete chapters, which may be read in any order, and encouraging the reader to explore further by way of provocative invitations to think and reconsider key issues at the end of each chapter. In terms of methodology and structure, this text adheres to *Beginning Theory* to a large extent but without slavishly adhering to its example. The purpose of *Beginning Irish Studies* is thus both to instruct and to encourage the student reader to build upon existing and new knowledge in order to engage in the ongoing debate. The source texts will range from Irish literary and theoretical texts to political and historical. The methodology is wide ranging as each chapter focusses on Irish Studies' engagement with different literary and cultural thinkers and theories. The literary analysis will comprise an amalgam of summarising influential readings of specific texts by established scholars and original insights offered by the author on other works of Irish literature that have received less scholarly attention.

The book is divided into six core chapters and a substantial Coda. Chapter 1 focusses on the period of the Irish Revival, which roughly spans the late nineteenth century until the advent of Irish independence in 1922. Chapter 2 encompasses the cultural period in Irish history that can be called the Counter-Revival, which last approximately from Irish independence until the early 1960s, and the economic expansion that was brought into being by the programme for economic recovery commissioned by T.K. Whitacker in 1958. Chapter 3 looks at the rise of postcolonial theory in Ireland during the late 1970s and which continued to be the dominant theoretical methodology for examining Ireland and Irishness for the rest of the twentieth century. Chapter 4 considers how gender, sex and sexuality in an Irish context have been productively examined and critiqued via the various theoretical lenses contained in the forms of feminist theory and queer theory. Chapter 5 views the way that Irish memory and forms of commemoration can be explored through memory and trauma theory. Chapter 6 looks at the ever expanding use of ecocriticism in an Irish context and how Irish texts of various genres have for centuries considered the relationship between humanity and ecology and how that relationship has undergone massive change over the last thirty years to the extent that we are now living in the age of the Anthropocene in which humans and human-made culture are now impacting upon the natural world. The Coda, 'Waiting for the "Irish Studies to come"', considers an undecidable, democratic future for Irish Studies that can be theorised using Jacques Derrida's theory of the *avenir* (the 'to come').

Beginning Irish Studies has several notable features and strengths:

1. It provides an accessible and structured introduction to an academic discipline taught across the English-speaking world.

2. It considers Irish literature in a way that will be useful for a wide variety of College literature, regardless of whether Irish Studies is the course's main focus.
3. It is grounded in the theoretical conceptions of Irish Studies, but aware of its importance as a means of creating nuanced analyses of literature, cinema, television and drama in Ireland.
4. It offers a coherent vision of the discipline of Irish Studies as a whole that also takes cognisance of theoretical developments across the humanities and social sciences more generally.
5. It is written in a style that is accessible for postgraduate students, which will enable them to gain an understanding of complex theoretical ideas and concepts. These ideas will be rendered understandable without having any of their nuance sacrificed.
6. Whilst intended as an introduction to those who are new to the field of Irish Studies, it does offer new approaches to the discipline that will be of benefit to more established scholars who have a greater familiarity with Irish Studies.

Derridean undecidability

Beginning Irish Studies utilises a lot of the ideas and concepts of the French continental philosopher Jacques Derrida (1930–2004) as a means of framing and clarifying a number of the debates and developments in Irish Studies over a number of decades. The reasons for this are as follows. Derrida's writing offers ways of thinking about possible alliances between individual freedom and communal responsibility, which is a key challenge within Irish Studies. Derrida also advocates modes of ethicality such as hospitality and openness to the Other, which again is a core principle in various sections of the discipline of Irish Studies. Derrida is not slavishly adhered to nor is there a constant Derridean strand running through this text. However, his work offers various productive ways of thinking about the 'nows', 'thens' and 'futures' of Irish Studies.

Equally, Derrida's admiration for James Joyce (as examined in greater detail in Chapter 3), shows how important writers and ideas connected to Irish Studies are to the development of work in the philosophical field of what is nebulously termed Deconstruction – a strand of continental philosophy with which Derrida is intimately connected. Derrida himself once famously asserted that, without James Joyce, Deconstruction would never have come into being. Derrida also spoke of his intimate connection with Samuel Becket during an interview with fellow practitioner of Deconstruction, Derek Attridge. Derrida said that his feeling of closeness to Beckett and his work was the reason why he felt he could not write on the work of the great Irish writer.[1] The implication being that Beckett was already obviously deconstructing language in his literature just as Derrida was doing in his theoretical/philosophical writings. Through thinkers such as Derrida, it is made apparent that Irish literature and the academic discipline partially devoted to its study are as much global as locally specific.

As Derrida's biographer, Benoît Peeters, has noted: 'Throughout his [Derrida's] life, he would consider *Ulysses* and *Finnegans Wake* to be the most grandiose attempt ever to bring together in one oeuvre "the *potential* memory of mankind" [my italics]'.[2] The word 'provisional', with its openness and refusal of any totalisation and absolutism, is one of which Derrida would be very fond, just as he (and Beckett) are both devotees of the word 'perhaps'. Equally, the word 'undecidable' is one that is constantly used in and about the Derridean theoretical corpus and shall be used quite frequently during the course of *Beginning Irish Studies*.

It is important to clearly define 'undecidable' in negative relation to a word with which it is often confused: indeterminate. Unlike 'indeterminate', which suggests something's complete lack of discernible meaning, 'undecidable' is a call to decision making because it implies that something (whether that be a text, a future, an event, an act or many other things) contains within itself numerous *potential* interpretations and/or outcomes that are potentially valid or conceivable and yet none of them can be final. Interpretative and predictive decisions must be made by those who encounter these undecidable entities. It is not, I would argue, too glib an assertion that indeterminate could be considered (as Derridean scholar Nicholas Royle implicitly suggests[3]) as being the 'lazy person's undecidable' because that word absolves individuals from the need to make any attempt to interpret or give an account of that with which they have been confronted.

Another way perhaps to think of 'the undecidable' could be in terms of what was termed by German physicist and Nobel Laureate Werner Heisenberg, 'the uncertainty principle'. In her essay on Brian Friel, Jose Lanters argues for the uncertainty principle being very much at work in Friel's drama and quotes his assertion that all great art should have uncertainty at its core:

> Flux is their [works of art] only constant; the crossroads their only home; impermanence their only yardstick [...] This is the only pattern of their existence: the persistence of the search; the discovery of a new concept; the analysis, exploration, exposition of that concept; the preaching of that gospel to reluctant ears; and then, when the first converts are made, the inevitable disillusion and dissatisfaction because the theory is already out of date or was simply a false dawn. And then the moving on; the continuing of the search; the flux. Impermanence is the only constant.[4]

Lanters argues that the uncertainty principle permeates all Friel's dramatic texts[5] and Friel essentially makes that claim concerning works of great – because inherently democratic – works of art in general. Any discipline that aspires to democratic openness must have the element of undecidability within it and *Beginning Irish Studies* demonstrates the existence of undecidability within many of the strands of Irish Studies that have developed over the years, and some whose future coming would be extremely desirable.

Notes

1 See Jacques Derrida, *Acts of Literature*, ed. Derek Attridge (New York: Routledge, 1992), p. 47.
2 Benoît Peeters, *Derrida: A Biography* (Malden: Polity Press, 2010), p. 84.
3 See Nicholas Royle, *After Derrida* (Manchester: Manchester University Press, 1995).
4 Brian Friel, 'The Theatre of Hope and Despair', *Everyman*, 1 (1968), p. 18.
5 See Jose Lanters, 'Brian Friel's Uncertainty Principle', *Irish University Review: Special Issue – Brian Friel* 29:1 (1999), pp. 162–175.

1
The Irish Revival: the birth of a discipline?

Introduction

This chapter will consider the cultural and historical flashpoint of the Irish Literary and Cultural Revival of the late nineteenth and early twentieth century as being a key moment in the development of Irish Studies. Drawing upon the representative writings and speeches of thinkers, writers and essayists such as Douglas Hyde, D.P. Moran, Arthur Griffith, James Joyce, W.B. Yeats and John Millington Synge, this chapter will examine how the Revival set the terms for various debates that would become of central importance to the emerging discipline of Irish Studies in the coming century. Debates such as tradition vs modernity, Ireland vs England, nationalism vs multiculturalism, rural vs urban Ireland, and Abbey Theatre's role in providing a site for the staging of new visions of Ireland and Irishness will be examined.

The nuanced nature of the Revival will be examined in terms of how it influenced some representative texts from that period: Joyce's *Dubliners*, selected poems by Yeats, selected plays by Lady Gregory, and Synge's *The Playboy of the Western World*. The literary analysis shall be concise but shall clearly show how these texts have been shaped by debates that were to the fore during this exciting period in Irish history. Edward Hirsch's essay 'The Imaginary Irish Peasant' will be foregrounded as one important example of Revival literature having been analysed from a theoretical perspective.

There shall be a certain element of novelty in this chapter because it is relatively rare to find a consideration of the Revival in relation to literary theory. The literary texts that were produced during this period receive far greater attention than the more theoretical works. This chapter shall bring both literature and theory into productive dialogue. A consistent consideration shall be how the Irish Literary and Cultural Revival was a movement that 'sought in various ways to counter the Enlightenment's apparent "disenchantment with the world", and to assert the Irish as a race equipped to oppose the spread of Anglicized modernity'.[1]

The reasoning behind why this book begins with a chapter on the Revival is because I regard this historical, literary and cultural period as being the flashpoint event when Ireland and Irishness began to be self-consciously constructed and imagined by various writers and thinkers. However, because Celtic and Anglo-Irish cultures are so important to the Revivalist project, a large section of this chapter will be devoted to an examination of those pre-Revival periods and cultures. Lady Gregory's translated collection *Cuchulainn of Muirthemne* will be considered as a good source for pre-Revival Celtic culture. Attention shall also be paid to works from earlier in the nineteenth century such as Maria Edgeworth's *Castle Rackrent* and William Carleton's *Traits and Stories of the Irish Peasantry*. These works give a valuable insight into some of the influences that shaped Revivalist conceptions of Anglo and Peasant Ireland. The political career of Charles Stewart Parnell and the transition from the Home Rule movement to demands for complete Irish independence and separation from Britain, and how this turbulent political period influenced Irish literary and cultural production, shall also be considered.

The publication in 2023 of a collection of essays edited by Joseph Valente and Marjorie Howes titled *The Irish Revival: A Complex Vision* has led to a renewed and even more nuanced consideration of this important moment in the literary, cultural and political history of Ireland. This contains insightful chapters on a diverse group of distinguished Irish Studies scholars such as Gregory Castle, Marjorie Howes, Joseph Valente, Anne Fogarty, Tina O'Toole and Paige Reynolds (to name but a few). The collection as a whole demonstrates through a variety of theoretical approaches such as postcolonialism, cultural materialism, and ecofeminism how the Irish Revival was a complex, multiform movement with many different approaches to theorising an independent Ireland to come. Some of these new ways of looking at the Revival shall be examined during the course of this chapter. The chapter shall also elucidate the complexity of Irish Revivalism and suggest that it was in no way a uniform collection of artists, thinkers and ideas.

Key revival tropes and influences

Celticism and Celtic mythology

The Irish Revival was essentially about writing works of literature (whether prose, drama or poetry) that spoke to an old Gaelic and Celtic Irish past. The works had a very strong grounding in myth and legend as the Revivalists felt that they needed to give to the Irish people a sense of a heroic past that they could be proud of. Thus, a lot of plays were written by these authors that dealt with the myth of Cuchulainn (such as Yeats' *On Baille's Strand*) and *Deirdre of the Sorrows* (as written about by Synge in his great drama *Deirdre of the Sorrows*). Lady Gregory's play *Grania* is another notable example of an Irish Revival play that dealt with Celtic mythology.

An important moment in the Revival of Celtic mythology in Ireland occurred in 1902 when Lady Gregory published an English translation of the Cuchulainn mythic cycle titled *Cuchulainn of Muirthemne*. This volume brilliantly combines written versions of the myths with orally transmitted ones that Gregory had heard. Declan Kiberd has argued that this project allowed Gregory to write in the voice of ordinary Irish people and also to explore hidden aspects of her own psyche: 'It was as if the Celtic hero were her own undiscovered animus, a secret self that had lain dormant for years beneath the exterior of the Coole wife [...] [He] also reconciled for her the visionary and secular dimensions, for he saw no distinction between this world and the next'.[2]

W.B. Yeats has written about the importance of mythology for the establishment of a new and authentic Irish culture and how the publications of English language versions of Celtic mythology had been invaluable in terms of making those stories available to a wider, non-Irish speaking audience:

> Literature dwindles to a mere chronicle of circumstance, or passionless phantasies, and passionless meditations, unless it is constantly flooded with the passions and beliefs of ancient times [...] now a new fountain of legends, and I think, a more abundant fountain than any in Europe, is being opened, the fountain of Gaelic legends ... 'The Celtic movement,' as I understand it, is principally the opening of this fountain, and none can measure of how great importance it may be to coming times, for every new fountain of legends is a new intoxication for the imagination of the world.[3]

This quote from the essay 'On the Study of Celtic Literature' (1898) makes clear that Yeats believes that Celtic mythology will be of value, not just for the Ireland of now, but also for an as yet undecidable Ireland to come.

Emer Nolan has described Yeats, and the Revival project of modernisation in general, in the following terms:

> The modern, in colonial conditions, is associated with 'foreignness', domination and violence; it is in no sense naturalised in the course of a long process of economic and social development. It is precisely in such a situation that the culturally 'old' appears most intensely valuable [...] Yeats and his friends who would keep 'Gaelic habits of mind' (even if not themselves 'Gaels') are engaged in a salvage mission which ideally would transform an entire society.[4]

The Revival project of modernisation was essentially founded on the belief that one's past should not dictate who you are, but you should let it be a part of who you are going to be. Whether or not this project also contained an excess of nostalgia and desire the realities of present day Ireland is obviously a question that has been debated for more than a century after the Revival period came to an end.

The Irish rebel and Easter 1916 martyr Patrick Pearse was also inspired by the legend of Cuchulainn who he regarded as being an ancient Celtic version of a Christian martyr. Pearse described Cuchulainn thus: 'A love and a sense of service so excessive as to annihilate all thought of self, a recognition that one must give all [...] this is the inspiration alike of the Story of Colmcille, the inspiration that made one a hero and the other a saint'.[5] When Pearse entered the post office on that fateful Easter week, the ghost and inspiration of Cuchulainn went with him. This is one famous example of the political radicalism that was inspired by aspects of the Revival and what influenced its modernising project. As Gregory Castle asserts: 'Ireland reimagined never loses its ambiguous relation to legend, a relation immortalized in Oliver Sheppard's great statue of Cuchulainn, mounted in 1937 in the General Post Office in O'Connell St'.[6]

One of the most significant events in literary history and cultural criticism that occurred during the Revival period was the publication of a study by future Easter 1916 martyr Thomas McDonagh titled *Literature in Ireland*. This book was published in 1916, a month after McDonagh's execution. The study contains detailed examinations of Anglo-Irish as well as Irish authors, which is evidence of how important their literature was considered in the development of an Irish/Celtic literary canon. Equally, considering McDonagh's political radicalism, the fact that he wrote such a literary history proves how interlinked literature and politics were in the minds of many rebellious individuals at this time. McDonagh's stated aim in writing literature in Ireland is made very clear in his Preface to the work: 'To show the value of the old literature, the prospects of the new'.[7] This ambition to show the importance of old literary traditions to the creation of new forms makes McDonagh connected with at least certain aspects of the Revival project.

The Anglo-Irish Ascendancy

The Irish Revival as an artistic movement was largely comprised of members of the Anglo-Irish Protestant Ascendancy. This identity category refers to descendants of English planters who settled in Ireland and became the Ascendancy in terms of controlling the land and the Big Houses, which is the term used to describe an Anglo-Irish dwelling. One of the last examples of such a house was Bowen's Court in county Cork, which was demolished in 1960 and had been the home of the great author Elizabeth Bowen. Seamus Deane's big concern with much of the writing that emerged from the Irish Revival was that it was produced largely by Protestant Anglo-Irish who would have been looked upon by the Catholic Irish as being colonial imperialists. As Deane himself wrote in a famous pamphlet titled 'Heroic Styles':

> Irish culture became the new property of those who were losing their grip on the Irish land. The effect of these re-writings was to transform the blame for the drastic condition of the country from the Ascendancy to the Catholic middle-classes or to their English counterparts. From Lecky to Yeats and forward to F.S.L. Lyons we witness the conversion of Irish History into a tragic theatre in which the great Anglo-Irish protagonist – Swift, Burke, Parnell – are destroyed in their heroic attempts to unite culture of intellect with the emotion of the multitude.[8]

Deane's position is quite clear. He regarded the cultural and literary work that was produced by Irish Revivalists as being largely an attempt to portray the Irish colonists as tragic figures who were worthy of both sympathy and admiration, despite the fact that Yeats was clearly of the opinion that the Revival should be a movement that would give voice to those who had never expressed themselves in artful English such as the Irish peasant.

In contrast to Deane's position, W.B. Yeats, one of the Revival's most celebrated Anglo-Irish literary figures and cultural commentators, viewed the Revival as an attempt to create new forms and futures for Ireland out of past histories and traditions:

> I think that our Irish movements have always interested me in part because I see in them the quarrel of two traditions of life, one old and noble, one new and ignoble: One undying because it satisfies our conscience though it seemed dying and one about to die because it is hateful to our conscience, although it seemed triumphant throughout the world.[9]

Although Yeats exhibits his characteristic fear and sometimes disdain for the direction that modern Ireland appeared to be taking, he does at least acknowledge that cultural and political change must have a place in the dialectical conversation that Ireland was having with itself during the late nineteenth and early twentieth century about what form its future would take. Yeats' desire to chart a middle course in respect of most vitally important issues and debates is well encapsulated in the following assertion from his *Autobiographies*:

'No mind can engender till divided in two'.[10] This claim also illustrates the influence that the German philosopher Georg Wilhelm Hegel had on Yeats' artistic and critical vision because the dialectical method is regarded as Hegel's great contribution to philosophical thought.

Regardless of whether they were Gaelic or Anglo-Irish, the members of the Irish Revival felt the loss of one famous Anglo-Irish politician: Charles Stewart Parnell. This man, who was known as the 'uncrowned king of Ireland', had been on the verge of securing Home Rule (an Irish parliament with responsibility for home affairs) for Ireland before his career was brought to end as a result of the revelations that he had been having an affair with a married woman, Kitty O'Shea. His political downfall and death in 1891 left what many felt was a cultural and political vacuum in Ireland, which writers and thinkers, whether they identified as Revivalists or not, would struggle to fill over the next three decades. One of the most powerful representations of the schism that Parnell's downfall created in all walks of Irish life is contained in the 'Christmas Dinner Scene' in James Joyce's first completed novel, *Portrait of the Artist as Young Man* (1916), during which pro-Parnell and pro-Catholic members of the same family engage in a violent verbal confrontation. The Ghost of Parnell also haunts the story 'Ivy Day in the Committee Room' in Joyce's *Dubliners* and he is an implicit presence in Synge's article 'A Landlord's Garden in County Wicklow'. Many Anglo-Irish writers at this time would have regarded Parnell's personal and political downfall as being a microcosmic version of what they felt was their impending decline in power and influence in Ireland. As Paul Bew argues: '[Parnell's] ideal of an autonomous, peaceful, pluralistic country eluded him totally, it has also eluded later generations'.[11] Despite Parnell's attempt to ensure that Anglo-Irish Protestants would continue to have a place in the new, more Catholic-centric Ireland, this was not to be the case and it would fall to writers such as Yeats and Synge to bear witness to their people's decline and eventual fall in Ireland.

One of the great influences on some of the Irish Revival's representations of Anglo-Ireland and their Big Houses is Maria Edgeworth's *Castle Rackrent* (1800), the so called 'first historical novel'. *Castle Rackrent* is a text that follows four generations of a landlord family (the Rackrents, formerly the O'Shaughlins). The story is narrated by their native Irish servant (Thady). Throughout the course of this work, we see how this family squander and gradually destroy their fortune and estate. Each member of the family has a particular weakness: Sir Patrick is a drunkard, next is Sir Murtagh who is very fond of suing people but never seems to have much success with his cases. Then we have Sir Kit who is an absentee landlord who likes to take the money that the estate generates and loses it gambling in London. The theme of mismanagement and misrule continues with Sir Condy who drinks, gambles and pays no attention to his personal finances. Eventually, Thady's son Jason takes over the house and thus usurps the Rackrent's privilege.

The work is specifically set before 1782, the year when Ireland gained its own parliament, known as Grattan's Parliament, which gave Ireland a certain amount of control over its own affairs. Thus, Edgeworth is setting the book in a bygone age in Ireland which the readers can view, if they wish, with a certain amount of nostalgia. Edgeworth's stated intention, according to the Preface to *Castle Rackrent*, was to offer insight into a people via their private actions and conversations as opposed to their public behaviour or persona: 'We cannot judge either of the feeling or of the characters of men with perfect accuracy from their actions or their appearance in public; it is from their careless conversations, their half finished sentences, that we may hope with the greatest probability of success to discover their real characters'.[12] Thus, the book is an intimate National Tale where the focus is on the private and the domestic as opposed to public individuals leading grand and epic lives. For this reason, in addition to the episodic nature of its narrative construction, *Castle Rackrent* can also be read as having been an influence on James Joyce's depiction of the culture of decay and paralysis in Ireland's capital city in his short story collection *Dubliners* (1914). Equally, the above quote from Edgeworth could be referring to the sly way in which Thady subtly hints that he is aware of his son Jason's eventual plans to take over Castle Rackrent – an event that Thady protests against – at least out loud.

The narrator of *Castle Rackrent*, Thady Quirke, certainly does represent the stage Irish figure that was very well known to the British as a result of the satiric cartoons and plays. What we have to consider is whether Thady really is a stage Irish character or is just pretending to be. What is certainly true is that there is a high degree of performance in Thady's narrative. He is thoroughly aware that he is speaking to an audience. What is also radical in terms of the narrative is the fact that Edgeworth is allowing the colonised Irish subject to look at and interpret his masters rather than the reverse.

It may indeed be true to say that Edgeworth was aiming for irony when she wrote in the preface to *Castle Rackrent*: 'The author of the following Memoirs has upon these grounds fair claims to the public favour and attention; he was an illiterate old steward, whose partiality to *the family*, in which he was bred and born, must be obvious to the reader' (3, italic in original). It seems that Edgeworth is trying to be as forceful in her endorsement of Thady's honesty as he will be himself. All of these protestations are very likely to have the opposite effect on the reader.

What is important to note about the Rackrent family is that they were not Anglo-Irish but were descended from the native Irish and their original name was O'Shaughlin. It is implied that they converted to Protestantism in order to rise up the Irish social and economic ladder. The portrayal of the Rackrent family members is certainly not in the least bit positive. They are incapable of looking after their own affairs, they drink and gamble their money away and refuse to take any real responsibility for their tenants. One of the great ironies in the book is the supposed affection that Thady has for his masters regardless of their flaws. He constantly tells the reader that he found all of his masters to be admirable men and that they all only had one vice. This constant assertion of his masters' virtues is what makes Thady's status as a narrator totally untenable. At best he is unreliable, at worst he is absolutely duplicitous. The book concludes with Thady's son Jason taking over the Rackrent estate and the reader is left to wonder whether Thady is genuinely as distressed by this as he appears to be.

One of the notable features of this work is how the story is supported by explanatory notes and a glossary, provided by an unidentified editor. These are meant to give background and explanation for the English reader concerning this bygone world in Ireland. However, it is important to consider the editor as a character as opposed to merely a detached individual who has no stake in how these people and events are depicted. Derek Hand has made the following assertion concerning the editor's relationship to this work:

> The editor of *Castle Rackrent* does possess a distinct character and must be thought of as a distinct character within the novel [...] He/she shifts roles throughout: one moment being a folklore collector and then transforming into a liberal commentator explaining the need for the application of Enlightenment values to the Irish scene.[13]

Many readers may have not actually read over the notes or the glossary to *Castle Rackrent* because it certainly does distract one from the work they are reading if they have to constantly switch between it and the back pages. Indeed, it is arguable that Edgeworth wants us to think of this lecturing English voice as a distraction from the vibrancy of the tale being told. Perhaps it is meant to be as big an intrusion as the English presence in Ireland? However, the relationship between Thady and the editor, whether that be a complementary or adversarial one, needs to be considered as part of the challenge of analysing this novel. The editor at the beginning of the work certainly did themselves no favours when they asserted that parts of Thady's speech are not translatable into English since that is exactly what he/she is supposed to be doing. Thus, it is possible to judge this editor as being just as unreliable as Thady himself.

Whilst the notes do spend a lot of time explaining old Irish folklore and issues to do with Enlightenment thought, as Hand has observed, there are no references to the history of the British occupation of Ireland and the results of that occupation. This is an omission that may be due to the fact that the editor wishes those facts to be written out of history and thus can be regarded as attempting an act of forced historical amnesia. It is worth noting that an even more playful attitude towards the insertion of footnotes into a literary text will be taken by Flann O'Brien over a hundred and fifty years later in his novel *The Third Policeman* in which the notes assume the status of a counter-text existing alongside the main narrative. What Edgeworth has achieved in *Castle Rackrent* is to craft a text that functions as both novel and self-aware cultural commentary, something that many works of the Revival would also endeavour to do a hundred years later.

At the conclusion of *Castle Rackrent*, the editor makes the same assertion of reliability as Thady has many times during the work: 'The Editor could have readily made the catastrophe of Sir Condy's history more pathetic if he thought it allowable to varnish the plain round tale of faithful Thady' (96). As with Thady, this protestation of honesty by the editor might well have the opposite effect on a reader.

In 1834, Maria Edgeworth told a correspondent:

> It is impossible to draw Ireland as she now is in a book of fiction – realities are too strong, party passions too violent to bear to see or to look at their faces in a looking-glass. The people would only break the glass and curse the fool who held the mirror up to nature – distorted nature, in a fever.[14]

What Edgeworth seems to be implying in this passage is that the balance of power has shifted and that the wild and savage native Irish now have control of the mirror and the modes of representation which that implies. It also seems to suggest that the Irish are truly Gothic Others who cannot be captured by the conventional means of literary representation. The literary forms available would fail to do them justice and therefore no attempt at drawing them should be made. Thus, Edgeworth was never to write another work like *Castle Rackrent*. It is possible that she realised that any effort (even a self-consciously flawed effort) to encapsulate the new Ireland and the Irish would be totally futile. It is also important to note that this metaphor of the mirror as a symbol for artistic representation is used by several Irish authors in the succeeding century (such as Oscar Wilde and James Joyce) as a means of describing various versions of identity (national, personal etc.) in works of Irish art.

Many of the writers of the Irish Revival followed Edgeworth's example and wrote works of art in various genres to depict the vexed relationship that existed then and in the past between the native Catholic Irish and the Anglo-Irish. These works, particularly the poetry by Yeats in his middle and later periods, display an anxiety concerning the Anglo-Irish legacy that had been left on the land, people and culture of Ireland and a fear that their time of dominance in that country was now coming to an end. Such a fear can also be discerned in works of *fin de siècle* Anglo-Irish Gothic writing by writers such as Oscar Wilde and, certainly most famously, Bram

Stoker in *Dracula* (1897). Luke Gibbons has diagnosed a link between the paranoia exhibited in (Anglo-)Irish Gothic and some of the more fearful motives inherent in the Irish Revival:

> Though strongly associated with modernity, 'the great modern ailment' in the eyes of one nineteenth-century physician, the figure of hysteria (in Anglo-Irish Gothic writing) testified ultimately to the persistence of a troubled past, whether it be secreted in the body or in the petrified violence of the landscape. The Literary Revival may be seen to be an attempt to give a cultural voice to this mute condition, but whether it effected a talking cure remains to be seen.[15]

Gibbons' argument in this passage is that the Irish Revival was an attempt by several Anglo-Irish writers to diagnose what James Joyce would call 'the nightmare of history', to admit to their involvement in this traumatic past, and attempt to at least partly purge their guilt through a national catharsis. In this respect, the Revival can certainly be said to contain Gothic echoes deriving from the work of writers such as Edgeworth and Stoker.

Irish rurality

One key feature of the Revival's conceptualising of modern Ireland was its general tendency to privilege the Irish countryside and its peasant inhabitants. The reason for this was because the Revivalists were strongly of the opinion that it was in the rural West of Ireland that the 'pure' and uncorrupted Irish identity and culture could be found, as opposed to in the urban areas, especially Dublin, which many Revivalists felt were bastions of colonial impurity and West Britonism. For this reason, the Revival and succeeding Irish movements and artists were extremely invested in what Edward Hirsch has called 'the imaginary Irish peasant'. As Hirsch has argued in his essay 'The Imaginary Irish Peasant':

> Yeats, Synge, Joyce, O'Brien, and Kavanagh formulated, destroyed and reformulated the character of Irish peasant life. Since to reconceptualize the peasant was to control and rewrite the essential Irish image, the source of all authentic Irish culture, each revisionary portrait of the peasant privileged itself and tried to establish its own empirical authenticity by turning culture into nature.[16]

Hirsch's argument here centres on how Irish rurality is essentially an artistic invention and numerous generations of Irish writers, from the Revival onward, have imagined their own versions of Irish rurality and its inhabitants. Frank Shovlin makes a similar point, specifically in relation to Revivalist writing: '"The West" [of Ireland] was the Revivalists' Utopia, location of Yeats' Inisfree, Synge's Aran and Lady Gregory's Kiltartan'.[17] It is certainly true that, for Irish Revivalists, the Irish West represented a pure prelapsarian world that was largely uncorrupted by colonial influences and language. Thus, it was viewed in their eyes as a kind of Irish Garden of Eden.

An important influence on Revivalist representations of Irish rurality is William Carleton's multi-volume collection of short stories, *Traits and Stories of the Irish Peasantry* (1842–1844). These stories/tales vary from description of communal rituals in a rural context such as weddings, funerals and wakes, to intimate individual portraits of specific peasants. In her foreword to Volume 1 of the Colin Smythe edition, Barbara Hayley makes the point that the first five stories in the collection draw attention to the act of narration itself.[18] This marks *Traits and Stories* out as an important precursor to the self-consciously imaginative quality of many Revivalist portrayals of the rural West and its inhabitants. Equally, the copious amounts of explanatory footnotes contained in the stories are comparable to those contained in *Castle Rackrent*. Thus, both works can be regarded as literary texts and also examples of cultural commentary intended to educate Anglo-Irish people.

Significantly, Carleton came across and read *Castle Rackrent* in a peasant's cottage whilst travelling to Dublin in 1818 to earn a living. He became enthralled by Edgeworth's style and decided to take inspiration from her adoption of the Irish peasant narrative voice in his own stories.[19] However, whilst Edgeworth's ventriloquised peasant voice (put into the mouth of Thady Quirk) is used to represent the Anglo-Irish Ascendancy, Carleton would adopt the peasant perspective for the purposes of representing their identity and way of life. The fact that Carleton did originally come from a poor Catholic background means that what he was doing with the Irish vernacular can be regarded as being different to what an Anglo-Irish author like Maria Edgeworth was engaged in when it came to using the Irish peasant dialect.

In Carleton's introduction to *Traits and Stories*, he describes the Irish as being a people for whom humour and tragedy coexist in their identity and psyche.[20] Revivalist portrayals of the Irish peasantry also have a tendency to emphasise either the tragic or humorous qualities of these rural Irish people. In some cases, such as Synge's *The Playboy of the Western World* (1907) a balance between comedy and tragedy will be struck.

Yeats highlighted the Revivalist preoccupation with the rural in his later period poem 'The Municipal Gallery Revisited':

> John Synge, I and Augusta Gregory, thought
> All that we did, all that we said or sang
> Must come from contact with the soil, from that
> Contact everything Antaeus-like grew strong.
> We three alone in modern times had brought
> Everything down to that sole test again,
> Dream of the noble and the beggarman.[21]

Yeats believed that the production of an Irish art had to be linked with Ireland's land and the poor people who lived on it since those peasants were the true Irish. Equally, he felt that the Irish Revival should be a democratically open project that embraced both aristocratic and peasant peoples. Yeats was also of the opinion, one that he shared with Synge, that the Irish peasantry shared many qualities with the old Gaelic aristocracy such as a love of the land and of storytelling. This quotation can also be read as Yeats' coded hatred of the new, rising, Catholic middle classes in Free State Ireland.

Perhaps the most famous and celebrated representer of Irish rurality in the Revival period was the writer and playwright John Millington Synge. His fascination with the rural West of Ireland dates back to 1896 when he met W.B. Yeats in Paris and Yeats gave him the following piece of advice: 'Give up Paris. You will never create anything by reading Racine, and Arthur Symons will always be a better critic of French literature. Go to the Aran Islands. Live there as if you were one of the people themselves; express a life that has never found expression'.[22] Synge was to take this advice and would spend five summers (1898–1903) on the Aran Islands, primarily on Inishmore as that was the Island where Irish (a language in which Synge was almost entirely fluent) was primarily spoken.

From Synge's time on Aran was to come his fascinatingly intergeneric text *The Aran Islands* (1901), which is his account of those summers spent on Aran. This book is an amalgam of the genres of travel novel and sociological tract. It is both literature and cultural commentary. That is something that can be said about many Revivalist works. One of the most significant passages in that text concerning Synge's conception of the Aran peasants is the following:

> The absence of the heavy boot of Europe has preserved to these people the agile walk of the wild animal, while the general simplicity of their lives has given them many other points of physical perfection. Their way of life has never been acted on by anything much more artificial than the nests and burrows of the creatures that live round them, and they seem, in a certain sense, to approach more nearly to the finer types of our aristocracies – who are bred artificially to a natural ideal – than to the labourer or citizen.[23]

Here, Synge is painting a picture of the West of Ireland peasantry as being a mixture of sub-human, purely natural and animalistic, but also a throwback to the old Celtic aristocrats whose downfall had occurred as a result of English colonialism. Thus, these people provide a link with the Irish past even as they are rooted in the earthiness of its present. Whilst modern critics feel that Carleton could sometimes seem a little uncertain about how authentic his depiction of Irish peasant life actually was, it is generally accepted that Synge writes with total confidence in the validity of his representation.

Another famous work of Synge's that delivers a powerful picture of Aran Island life is his play *Riders to the Sea* (1904). The play was first performed in 1903 at Molesworth Hall in Dublin by the Irish National Theatre Society (which was what the Irish Literary Theatre was then called and would soon become the Abbey Theatre). It concerns the tragedy of Maurya, a woman who lives on one of the Aran Islands and whose family has been gradually taken away by the sea. Her son Michael is presumed dead for most of the play and is confirmed dead at the play's conclusion. Her last remaining son, Bartley, is going to Connemara, against his mother's urgings, to sell a horse. His mother refuses to give him her blessing and he too dies by drowning.

Oona Frawley has provided the following assessment of *Riders to the Sea* as a Revival play concerned with representing Irish rurality:

> The sublime tragedy of *Riders to the Sea* … renovated notions of the dramatic in Irish theatre with a social realism that altered the perception and function of women on-stage, while highlighting expectations placed on women off-stage; it also granted new dramatic importance to landscape and place by refusing simple idealisations of rural Ireland.[24]

Frawley is correct in saying that this play refuses any romanticisation of rural Ireland since the landscape in which this play is set is very harsh and unforgiving and seems to be eternally hostile to those who inhabit it. We are certainly far from the idealisations created by Yeats in his early career in poems such as 'The Lake Isle of Innisfree'. The social malaise referred to above is powerfully evoked by Synge as he portrays a dying land and people for whom there seems to be no future.

Riders to the Sea is structured around the conflict between inside and outside. In this play, the central female character is trying to keep her son from leaving home and going out into the wide world, an action that Bartley regards as necessary for the family's survival. Synge takes a very stark and realistic view of heroism. Bartley's choice to brave the sea is one born out of the human need for survival rather than any patriotic dreams of glory. Synge makes no effort to depict the death of the men-folk as anything other than a tragedy and does not endeavour to imply that they will be immortalised by story and song. Maurya's urgings to Bartley to stay at home show that his death will achieve nothing but ruination to the already harsh world of the living: 'It's hard set we'll be surely the day you're drowned with the rest. What way will I live and the girls with me, and I an old woman looking for the grave'.[25] Synge essentially has staged a bleak vision of the traditional conception of Irish women as mother and guarantor of the next generation. If the Irish woman is symbolically linked with the Irish nation, then the nation as it is portrayed in this play is one without a future.

The removal of the last male family member symbolises the impending destruction of that family and, allegorically, the end of their whole way of life. Maurya verbalises the impending destruction of their culture in one very powerful speech: ‘In the big world the old people do be leaving things after them for their sons and children, but in this place it is the young men do be leaving things behind them for them that do be old’ (6). What these words encapsulate is the tragic absurdity of a world where, to invoke Hamlet, ‘time is out of joint’ and the natural order is disrupted.

Synge uses old traditions and beliefs in this play that was designed to help give shape and a sense of identity to a modern Ireland. The powers that most strongly affect the people in this island world seem to pre-date Christianity whose representative in this work, the young priest, seems very ineffective. The sea is the primary god in this work and it does not matter that the Christian deity would not want Maurya to be left without a living son.

Riders to the Sea has been described as a pure example of the genre of tragedy. Certainly, the seeming inevitability of the catastrophic end is something that links the drama with classic tragedies from Aeschylus onwards. Maurya might be described as a tragic heroine since it is implied that (like typical tragic figures) she helped propel the tragic events forward by not giving her son Bartley her blessing before he left. This could be termed the moment of tragic action (or inaction) in the drama.

The most powerful moment in *Riders to the Sea* (and the one which strengthens its tragic credentials) comes at the very end when Maurya (as opposed to the priest) is speaking over the dead body of Bartley. The speech she gives has ensured Maurya’s status as an enduring figure in the Irish dramatic cannon:

> MAURYA: (*raising her head and speaking as if she did not see the people around her)* They’re all gone now, and there isn’t anything more the sea can do to me … I’ll have no call now to be up crying and praying when the wind breaks from the south, and you can hear the surf is in the east, and the surf is in the west, making a great stir with the two noises, and they hitting one on the other. I’ll have no call now to be going down and getting Holy Water in the dark nights after Samhain, and I won’t care what way the sea is when the other women will be keening. *(To Nora)* Give me the Holy Water, Nora; there’s a small sup still on the dresser … No man at all can be living for ever, and we must be satisfied. (12)

This monologue incorporates acceptance and a sense of relief in a manner that is experienced by many tragic heroes and heroines at the end of the stories. It is a state that gives these characters a sense and air of dignity. In the case of *Riders*, this moment firmly banishes even the faintest whiff of easy sentiment from the text.

One can compare this speech to one that appears near the end of that iconic tragedy, *Hamlet*. Hamlet is speaking in response to Horatio's wish that he not fight Laertes because he will be risking his life: 'We defy augury. There is special providence in the fall of a sparrow, If it be now, tis not to come; if it be not to come, it will be now; if it be not now, yet it will come. The readiness is all. Let be'.[26] Like Maurya, Hamlet admits of the inevitability of death and achieves a real calmness as a result. Also, another comparison between these two characters is the fact that their inaction at key moments propels the tragic events forward in their respective plays. Interestingly, Synge took some of this speech from a letter written by an Islander that he befriended so there exists a fusion of the artistic and the ordinary in its words.

The key difference between *Riders* and traditional tragedies is that, while the dramatic predecessors in this genre were primarily concerned with higher-class people such as kings, princes and other members of the aristocracy, Synge wishes to ennoble the ordinary Irish peasant. This is where the radical nature of *Riders* comes to the fore; Synge is using a literary genre that is identified with so-called noble people and is applying it to the story of very simple people. In this way, Synge anticipates James Joyce's *Ulysses*, which tells of an ordinary day in the lives of ordinary people using the structure of that elevated ancient epic, *The Odyssey*. It is certainly true that Joyce was an admirer of this play and even went so far as to translate it into Italian. It is in the 'Scylla and Charybdis' episode of *Ulysses* that Joyce acknowledges the connection between Shakespeare and Synge when the character of Buck Mulligan (somewhat pithily) refers to Shakespeare as being the one who 'writes like Synge'.[27]

Although initially hostile to the Revival's privileging of Irish rurality and ignoring his fellow Dubliners, Joyce did become more sympathetic towards rural Ireland and its inhabitants. This can be observed in a passage near the end of his novel *A Portrait of the Artist as a Young Man* in which Stephen Dedalus, the central protagonist, is talking about a man from the West of Ireland that his friend, Mulrennan, had described to him. Although Stephen had never personally met this man, his status as a representative of an Ireland that is uncannily Other to Stephen frightens him:

> I fear him. I fear his redrimmed horny eyes. It is with him I must struggle all through this night till day comes, till he or I lie dead, gripping him by the sinewy throat till … Till what? Till he yield to me? No. I mean him no harm.[28]

This passage conveys a sense of benign aggression on the part of Stephen (and possibly Joyce). While there is no overt connection between the two Irelands as represented by these two men, there is at least the admission of the possibility of peaceful coexistence.

The Revival's interest in imagining Irish rurality was to continue in later texts throughout the twentieth century. The film *Man of Aran* (1936) depicted the Aran Islanders with the same epic and tragic dignity that is discernible in *Riders to the Sea*. Near the end of the twentieth century, Martin McDonagh would stage a version of the Irish peasantry in the play *The Cripple of Inishmaan* (1997), which was intended to mock the Revivalist desire to celebrate that people and version of Irishness. McDonagh was to return to that iconoclastic vision of Irish rurality in his film *The Banshees of Inisherin* (2022). Yeats was probably the most honest imaginer of Irish rurality because he acknowledges that the Irish peasant he celebrates in his poem 'The Fisherman' never existed and was purely a figment of his poetic imagination (97). Some of the most powerful representations of the 'Irish West' written during the Revival are contained in the travel writings/essays of Emily Lawless (whose work shall be examined in greater detail in Chapter 6 below). For further reading on the topic of Irish rurality and its textual representations, a very extensive study of the travel writing of the Revival period is Giulia Bruna's *J.M. Synge and the Travel Writing of the Irish Revival*.

The battle of civilisations/cultures

An important starting point for a study of the Irish Revival and its aims and objectives is a quotation from W.B. Yeats' *Autobiographies*:

> The modern literature of Ireland, and indeed all that stir of thought which prepared for the Anglo-Irish war, began when Parnell fell from power in 1891. A disillusioned and embittered Ireland turned from parliamentary politics; an event was conceived; and the race began, as I think, to be troubled by that event's long gestation; Dr. Hyde founded the Gaelic League, which was for many years to substitute for political argument a Gaelic grammar, and for political meetings village gatherings, where songs were sung and stories told in the Gaelic language [...] But the great mass of our people, accustomed to interminable political speeches, read little, and so from the very start we felt that we must have a theatre of our own. (559–560)

This lengthy quote captures the popular perception of the Revival. It was a multi-organisational movement in which literature, culture, and politics coexisted in a desire to imagine a new Ireland and new ways of seeing and thinking about a politically and culturally independent nation that still did not exist but which could be said to have had the beginnings of its birth during this dynamic period in Irish history.

The rallying call that would be answered by many Irish Revivalists emanated from Douglas Hyde (founder of the Gaelic League and future president of Ireland) in a speech he made in 1982 to the Dublin Literary society titled 'The Necessity for De-Anglicising Ireland':

> It has always been very curious to me how Irish sentiment sticks in this half-way house – how it continues to apparently hate the English, and at the same time continues to imitate them; how it continues to clamour for recognition as a distinct nationality, and at the same time throws away with both hands what would make it so. If Irishmen only went a little farther they would become good Englishmen in sentiment also. But – illogical as it appears – there seems not the slightest sign or probability of their taking that step. It is the curious certainty that come what may. Irishmen will continue to resist English rule, even though it should be for their good, which prevents many of our nation from becoming Unionists upon the spot ... It is just because there appears no earthly chance of their becoming good members of the Empire that I urge that they should not remain in the anomalous position they are in, but since they absolutely refuse to become the one thing, that they become the other; cultivate what they have rejected, and build up an Irish nation on Irish lines.[29]

Irish Revivalists would attempt – via the cultural tools of literature, drama, language and dancing to meet Hyde's challenge of building an Irish nation along Irish lines.

One of the earliest attempts (following Douglas Hyde's diagnosis of the necessity for de-anglicising Ireland), to theorise Ireland and its possible future was D.P. Moran's 1900 essay 'The Battle of Two Civilisations', published in *New Ireland Review*. Significantly, Moran prefers to talk about 'civilisations' rather than 'nations' because he reads the terms civilisations and cultures interchangeably and regards the cultural rather than the physical independence of the Irish nation as being more important. The reason for this is that a distinct culture will give the Irish a sense of authenticity and national separateness – something that could not be achieved by force of arms. In this respect, Moran agrees with Hyde's arguments in 'The Necessity for De-Anglicising Ireland'. Moran makes this point in the first paragraph of his essay: 'We are sick of "Irish National" make believe and frauds; sick of shouting nation when there is no nation; and the much abused national consciousness of the Irish people, and cries for truth and light, and death to shame and impostures'.[30] For Moran, there is no real Irish nation and the first steps to creating one have to be in the form of a cultural revolution rather than one that simply consists of violent uprisings that have historically resulted in failure for Ireland.

Moran felt instinctively that 'Society without conventions is necessarily vulgar and chaotic, and much of the social life of Ireland was driven to prove itself by kicking against convention altogether' (332). It was not enough any longer, as far as Moran and Hyde were concerned, for the Irish to define themselves as being not English. Some affirmative sense of Irish cultural distinctiveness had to be fostered.

Essentially, Moran argues in this essay for an 'Irish Ireland' in which the preservation and rejuvenation of the national language will ensure an authentic Celtic/Irish culture. He was always instinctively hostile to Anglo-Irish Revivalists such as W.B. Yeats who he believed were writing an Irish identity from an outsider's perspective. Their outsider status is made abundantly clear to Moran by the fact that they cannot write or speak Irish, the guarantor of a pure Irishness as far as Moran is concerned. In 'The Battle of Two Civilisations',

Moran goes so far as to castigate Yeats for writing elitist poetry that no ordinary Irish person could possibly understand. Ironically, Moran was also quite sectarian, so religion was definitely a factor for him (as it would be for Daniel Corkery, too). It was Moran's anti-Protestantism that resulted in his falling out with the writer George Moore.

One of Moran's primary issues with individuals such as Yeats taking the lead in defining Irishness and imagining Ireland's future was that Moran felt that this would result in the survival of Anglo-Ireland and its Ascendancy ethos in the Ireland that was to come. Moran argues: 'Even those who shouted most about Irish Parliaments and Irish Republics were swayed by the general desire common to all aspiring men, to be gentlemen of some kind, to be socially "superior"' (332). This culture of social divisions was one that Moran did not wish to survive in the Ireland he imagined as being the Irish national ideal.

The conclusion of the essay, however, does echo how many Revivalists viewed their project of cultural revolution:

> The prospect of such a new Ireland rising out of the foundations of the old with love and not hate as its inspirations, has already sent a great thrill through the land. It is a new and unlooked for situation full with fate, not only for Ireland, but for the world. (336)

These lines could certainly have been written by Yeats and appeared in his essay 'On the Study of Celtic Literature' because both works do desire Ireland's future to be one that embraces old traditions, incorporates them into the present, and uses them to forge an as yet undecidable future to come.

Another important voice (but now largely forgotten) in the battle for a preferred Irish identity during the Revival was that of the journalist William Rooney. 'William Rooney was undoubtedly the most prolific writer for the *United Irishman* [journal] until illness struck him down in March 1901 [...] Rooney stands out in this period as the voice of civic-minded republicanism, very much at odds with the racial ideas of bourgeois cultural nationalism espoused by Moran'.[31]

Unlike Moran who wished to ignore politics completely in favour of a totally cultural revolution, Rooney wished to combine all public elements of Irish society together in a single, modernising, revolutionary project. Rooney outlined his vision for a postcolonial Ireland thus:

> An Irish State self-supporting, self-defending, her flag respected in every port, her shores and her sympathy for the oppressed of every race and colour. Her voice in the councils of the nations; her language, her laws, and her achievements of all her people. Such is a national ideal and to [Wolfe] Tone do we owe the fact that any of its most militant features still recommend themselves to the vast bulk of our countrymen.[32]

As P.J. Mathews, argues: 'One of the great innovations of Rooney's thinking was his realisation of the extent to which culture and politics are inextricably bound up'.[33] Because of Rooney's vision of an all-inclusive civic Irish society, it is understandable that he was more sympathetic to an Anglo-Irish Revivalist such as Yeats than Moran would have been.

James Joyce can be said to have contributed to the battle of civilisations/cultures that was so much in vogue during the Revival period when he gave a lecture in Trieste in 1907 titled 'Ireland: Island of Saints and Sages'. The following is probably the most famous section of the talk:

> Our civilisation is a vast fabric, in which the most diverse elements are mingled, in which Nordic aggressiveness and Roman law, the new bourgeois conventions and the remnant of a Syriac religion are reconciled. In such a fabric, it is useless to look for a thread that may have remained pure and virgin and without having undergone the influence of a neighbouring thread. What race, or what language … can boast of being pure today? And no race has less right to utter such a boast than the race now living in Ireland. Nationality (if it is not a convenient fiction like so many others to which the scalpels of present-day scientists have given the coup de grâce) must find its reason for being rooted in something that surpasses and transcends and informs changing things like blood and the human word […] And, although the present race in Ireland is backward and inferior, it is worth taking into account the fact that it is the only race of the entire Celtic family that has not been willing to sell its birthright for a mess of pottage.[34]

Joyce's vision of Ireland and the Irish national identity embraces multicultural racial and national mixing rather than a purer vision that was expounded by commentators such as D.P. Moran. Given this embracing of racial impurity and liminality, it should come as no surprise that one of Joyce's most celebrated characters was an Irish Jew: Leopold Bloom in *Ulysses* (1922). It should be noted, however, that the final lines of the above quote expresses a certain admiration for the Irish peoples' unwillingness to give up its old traditions and embrace a purely colonial-inspired version of modernity. For this reason, it can be argued that Joyce was not as totally hostile to the Revival project as some have assumed.

These different visions for Ireland's future, as espoused by commentators such as Moran, Rooney and Joyce, testify to the fact that the Revival period was one of rich political, cultural and literary debate during which various public and more private individuals responded to Lady Gregory's assertion in her 1898 essay 'Ireland Real and Ideal': 'We [the Irish] have worn the mask thrust upon us for too long […] we are more likely to win at least respect when we appear in our own form'.[35] Various artists and thinkers of this period had their own ideas concerning what 'our own form' looked like and they were prepared to passionately debate it in the public realms of journals, lectures, literature and theatre. It is arguable that the Irish Literary and Cultural Revival was a period during which debates and sometimes battles between various civilisations/cultures were staged: English, Anglo-Ireland, Irish-Ireland, Multicultural-Ireland and so on.

Staging the nation

Although Yeats is perhaps more famous for his poems than for his plays, he himself decided to focus his Revivalist energies on drama rather than on fiction because he believed that 'in the theatre, the mob becomes a people'.[36] P.J. Mathews has noted how the founding of the Irish Literary Theatre in 1899 'represents not only an important cultural moment but also a significant political juncture in Irish history, when the battle for the control of cultural discourse within nationalism was recognized as a vital concomitant to the wielding of political power'. Mathews is here adding his voice to the many Irish Studies scholars who share Yeats' opinion that the Revival represents an alliance of literary, political and cultural discourse to the extent that one becomes indistinguishable from the others.

When discussing plays that were written during the Revival period, it is important to consider them in light of the Irish Literary Theatre manifesto that Yeats, Lady Gregory and Edward Martyn wrote in 1897:

> We propose to have performed in Dublin, in the spring of every year certain Celtic and Irish plays, which whatever be their degree of excellence will be written with a high ambition and so to build up a Celtic and Irish school of dramatic literature We hope to find in Ireland an uncorrupted and imaginative audience trained to listen by its passion for oratory, and believe that our desire to bring upon the stage the deeper thoughts and emotions of Ireland will ensure for us a tolerant welcome, and that freedom to experiment which is not found in theatres of England, and without which no new movement in art or literature can succeed. We will show that Ireland is not the home of buffoonery and of easy sentiment, as it has been represented, but the home of an ancient idealism. We are confident of the support of the Irish people, who are weary of misrepresentation, in carrying out a work that is outside of all political concerns that divide us.[37]

This document sets out the grand plans that Yeats and others attempted to implement in Irish drama in the late nineteenth and early twentieth century – a drama that would set itself against English literary texts and represent the Irish people as they really were rather than how they were perceived by others. The reference to buffoonery and easy sentiment refers to the caricatures of the Irish that were to be found in magazines such as *Punch* or plays such as Dion Boucicault's *The Shaughraun*. The 'freedom to experiment' implies that these Irish dramas will be more attuned to the modernist movement in literature that was beginning to gather momentum at this time. It is ironic that the document says that these texts will be apolitical since the Revival is considered to be a movement that sought to merge art and politics together and to endeavour, through art, in a paraphrase of James Joyce, to forge the uncreated conscience of the Irish nation and race. This literature is thus meant to be actively creative as opposed to merely passively descriptive and thus conforms to the movement known as cultural nationalism.

One of the most famous plays to be produced by the Irish Literary Theatre was *Cathleen ni Houlihan*, which was co-written by Lady Gregory and W.B. Yeats and staged in 1902. While *Cathleen ni Houlihan* achieves many of the goals set out in the manifesto, it certainly is not an apolitical play. On the contrary, it is one of the most iconic nationalist texts to have ever come out of Ireland. In order to understand why Yeats and Gregory wrote such a play, it is worth considering the controversy that had occurred a few years earlier in 1899 concerning the production of Yeats' *The Countess Cathleen*. This play was regarded by some as being blasphemous for its depiction of Irish peasants willing to sell their souls rather than die of starvation during the famine. It is possible that Yeats wished to atone for this perceived slight against the Irish nation by writing a play that would demonstrate his solidarity with the nationalist cause in Ireland. If this seems a little overly sensitive on Yeats' part, it must be remembered that he (like the majority of notable Irish authors of this period) was a member of the Anglo-Irish class who were doomed to be considered as being forever Irish in England and forever English in Ireland. This feeling of not really belonging anywhere may have been what spurred Yeats and Lady Gregory in their attempts to curry favour with the so-called 'pure Irish' and thus achieve for themselves a sense of acceptance.

The plot of *Cathleen ni Houlihan* is extremely simple. It is set during the 1798 uprising in Ireland (specifically Killala in the northern part of the country), and Michael Gillane is due to be married the next day to Delia Cahel. An old woman comes in and tells of how her four fields (which represent the four provinces of Ireland) have been stolen from her and she needs men to fight for her so she can reclaim them. Michael is enchanted by this story and leaves with her. The play concludes with the old woman being transformed into a beautiful young woman as a result of the men who are willing to sacrifice themselves for her.

It is no secret that the character of Cathleen ni Houlihan represents Ireland. This use of the figure of woman as metaphor for Ireland and the Irish landscape did not originate with this play but rather dates back to the aisling poetry of the late seventeenth and eighteenth century. In these poems, Ireland was represented as either a young or old woman, sometimes being raped by an English man. In *Cathleen ni Houlihan*, the playwrights add a twist to this poetic trope by having the woman appear as old and then become young at the end.

The time and setting of the play (Killala in 1798) would have been very significant for the Irish audiences at the time of the play's first production since Killala was where the French landed on 22 August, 1792, in support of the Irish rebellion. Both the French and the Irish surrendered on 8 September that year. Thus, from the very outset, Yeats and Gregory were signalling that this play was going to have the struggle for Irish independence at its heart.

The Irish characters in this play certainly are lacking in the kind of buffoonery and easy sentiment that the Irish Literary Theatre manifesto bemoaned. The primary reason behind the impending marriage between Michael and Delia seems to be the dowry that Delia's father will pay rather than any romantic impulses. This anti-sentimental portrayal of the Irish anticipates Yeats' famous observation in his poem 'September 1913' that Ireland was now populated by those who 'fumble in the greasy till and add the half pence to the pence' (25). That poem's chorus: 'Romantic Ireland's dead and gone, it's with O'Leary in the grave' (25), is something that Yeats is fighting against in this poem. He wishes to give his Irish audience a sense of the glory and heroism of Ireland's past in order that he might inspire a revival of the past in the more banal present. It is important to note that Lady Gregory wrote almost all of the peasant dialogue in this play – a fact that has only been acknowledged comparatively recently.

One of the central conflicts in *Cathleen ni Houlihan* is between the domestic, inside space of the Gillanne house and the outside world of heroism that the old woman is offering Michael. While the old woman tempts Michael with promises of glory and immortality through legend, his family attempt to coax him back to the world of marriage, domesticity and familial duty. It is one of the potentially radical aspects of this play that it is the woman who is intimately associated with the public sphere considering that, traditionally, female identity is linked with the domestic realm of the house. That is the space away from which Cathleen ni Houlihan is trying to lure Michael.

Despite this progressive reading of *Cathleen ni Houlihan*, it has to be acknowledged that this is a play which poses many problems with regards to its attitude to gender politics. The old woman is totally dependent on men to fight for her land and to return her beauty to her, which suggests an inherent incapacity to act on her part. Woman as object that men have to fight for is an old stereotype that is enforced in this play as it had been in the old aisling poems. There are also misogynistic undertones in Cathleen's character since she is portrayed as a quasi-vampiric figure who regains her youth and beauty by sucking the life out of men in a manner that is reminiscent of the character of Dracula in Bram Stoker's great novel. This creepy aspect of the woman's character is emphasised in the following lines:

> OLD WOMAN: It is a hard service they take that help me. Many that are red-cheeked now will be pale cheeked; many that have been free to walk the hills and the bogs and the rushes will be sent to walk hard streets in far countries ... They that have red cheeks will have pale cheeks for my sake.[38]

The repetition of the red cheeks turning pale might possibly be an attempt by Yeats and Gregory to imply the comparison with a vampire referred to above and certainly paints the old woman as a parasitic figure who drains the life force out of all the men who devote their lives to her. Because of its controversial treatment of women and heroism, this play remains one that succeeding Irish authors such as John Millington Synge and James Joyce have felt compelled to engage with.

Returning to the issue of Irish drama being inherently experimental as mentioned in the Irish Literary Theatre manifesto, *Cathleen ni Houlihan* certainly breaks with the dominant dramatic style of naturalism that was pioneered at this time by Henrick Ibsen and was very popular in Europe. Yeats chose to write a modern play that broke with the realist impulse of naturalism and instead utilised anti-realist myth and harked back to an older form of poetry. Thus, Yeats sought to highlight the capacity of the past to give shape and meaning to the present.

The play concludes with Michael and other Mayo men departing the stage to fight for Cathleen. Their departure is to the sound of people chanting:

> They shall be remembered for ever,
> They shall be alive for ever,
> They shall be speaking for ever,
> The people shall hear them for ever. (10)

This equation of immortality, martyrdom and violence is the most important message that Yeats and Lady Gregory wished to be taken from the play.

This play is also important as a classic example of the so-called 'early Yeats' because of its uncomplicated depiction of the glory of blood sacrifice and its romantic view of Ireland as a mystical place where ghosts and supernatural beings walk. As his career progressed, Yeats was to radically alter his view on heroism, sacrifice and violence as is evident in poems such as 'Easter 1916' and 'Nineteen Hundred and Nineteen'. Yeats' changing attitude towards this play in particular is clearly demonstrated in his late poem 'The Man and the Echo', which asks the famous question: 'Did that play of mine send out/ Certain men the English shot?' This is a reference to the Easter Rising and Yeats is wondering whether his overly romantic depiction of armed struggle in some way inspired some of the rebels to go out and fight.

The version of Ireland and Irishness that this play depicts, and also its fairly unproblematic depiction of the heroism of violence, was not shared by all Revivalist dramatists. This is apparent from the above discussion of *Riders to the Sea* and it will be clear from the analysis below of tragicomic masterpiece *The Playboy of the Western World*. As Nicholas Grene observes: 'Every dramatic movement claims that they can deliver the true Ireland which has previously been misrepresented, travestied, rendered in sentimental cliché or political caricature'.[39] Even within the so-called Revival dramatic movement, there was no unified vision of what Ireland and Irishness should be in a totalising sense. From the point of view of how well individual Irish plays conformed to the Irish Literary Theatre Manifesto, *Riders* is probably the best example of a 'successful Revival play' since it does portray the Irish as being in possession of a noble and ancient heroism and does so without being in anyway politically motivated.

Whilst *Cathleen ni Houlihan* found favour with its first Irish audience, Synge's first play, *The Shadow of the Glen* (1903) caused huge controversy when it was first staged because of its depiction of marital betrayal and its conclusion, which see the main character leaving her husband for another man. Catholic Ireland, as was predictable, reacted very negatively to that dramatic content. Arthur Griffith (founder of Sinn Féin in 1904) issued the following denunciation of the play: 'The play has an Irish name, but it is no more Irish than the Decameron. It is a staging of a corrupt version of the old-world libel on womankind – the widow of Ephesus, which was made current in Ireland by the hedge-schoolmaster'.[40] Griffiths' response to *The Shadow of the Glen* perfectly illustrates how Irish Theatre at this time was viewed by many as being a vehicle for the staging of authentic and proper versions of Irishness. Griffith does not merely criticise *Shadow* as being a bad play, he critiques it as being a staging of Irishness which disqualifies it from being regarded as an Irish play in the slightest degree. An even more extreme version of a play being viewed as 'not Irish' is examined below. It is important to note that the play is a fusion of a story Synge was told on the Aran Islands and Ibsen's *A Doll's House* (the name Nora being the clue there). This shows Synge's mixed Irish/continental European sensibilities.

Significantly, when Yeats received the Nobel Prize for Literature in 1923, the speech he gave was entirely devoted to discussing the Abbey Theatre and the Revival plays that were performed on its stage. This choice of topic would have surprised some people since it was Yeats' poetry for which he was most esteemed at this time. The fact that he chose to discuss his drama and that of other Revival playwrights on this momentous night shows how highly he regarded both his drama and that of the Revival more generally.

One of the most politically subversive plays from the Irish Revival period was Lady Gregory's *The Rising of the Moon* (1907). The radicality of the play resided in its plot, which concerned a native Irish sergeant's conversion to Irish nationalism at the behest of an escaped republican rebel. The policeman had been tempted into the service of the British Crown because of monetary inducements and he comes to regret this turn to the colonial dark side during the course of the drama. The title of the play symbolises both the symbolic rebirth into radicalism of the warder and the potential emergence of Ireland into an as yet unrealised postcolonial future. The undecidability of this future is signalled by the play's final moment, during which the newly converted nationalist ponders whether or not he should have turned in the nationalist rebel in exchange for the reward that was on offer.

The Rising of the Moon was a great favourite of the legendary Irish Republican hero Michael Collins and his spy in Dublin Castle, Ned Broy. This testifies to the political, as well as cultural, commitment that existed in a number of Revival dramas, a major example of which was *The Rising of the Moon*. The play testifies to the truth of the assertion contained within the 'Irish Literary Theatre Manifesto' that Ireland is the home of an ancient idealism and that idealism can be resilient even in the face of the pernicious influences of British colonialism.

What Irish literary and cultural revivalists do:

1. **They use past Irish traditions and mythologies to create a sense of a present and a postcolonial future for Ireland.**
2. **They create literary works for political ends.**
3. **They very often represent the Irish West as a space of pre-colonial Irish purity in which the truth of Irishness can be discerned.**
4. **The Anglo-Irish are generally treated more sympathetically by this movement than was often the case in representations of Ireland by the Irish at this time.**
5. **Whether or not there was a stable and 'authentic' version of Irishness that should be privileged was a major debate among thinkers and artists in this movement.**
6. **They privileged Irish self-sufficiency and self-reliance as opposed to looking to England for support.**
7. **Irish music, language, dancing and sport were revived during the course of this movement.**

Representative textual analyses

W.B. Yeats: early and middle period poetry

Joe Cleary has encapsulated W.B. Yeats' importance as an Irish Revivalist and also as an Irish modernist:

> During the Irish Revival in the late nineteenth century, the cultural nationalist note was ascendant as Yeats tried to conjure into being a new Ireland that would blend the simplicity and responsiveness to the supernatural and the esoteric that he associated with the West of Ireland peasantry and the elegant refinement he identified with the Anglo-Irish Ascendancy ... In sum, Yeats forged from the raw materials of Irish Romanticism an esoteric vision of a sufficiently powerful aesthetic quality to make him one of the twentieth century's most influential poets.[41]

The significance of Yeats' poetry, generally speaking, is its deployment of a very personal, individual poetic voice to the representation of Ireland, Irishness and the Irish people. It is not too hyperbolic to assert that Yeats used his poems to portray himself as representing the 'I' in Ireland. The later works of Yeats shall be examined in Chapter 3 on postcolonial theory. The focus in this section is on the earlier, more obviously Revivalist poems of Yeats.

'The Lake Isle of Innisfree'

This iconic poem was written by Yeats whilst he was living in London and recounts his mental journey back to rural Ireland where he hopes to find the peace that has eluded him in the urban space of London:

> I will arise and go now and go to Innisfree,
> And a small cabin build there, of clay and wattles
> made:
> Nine bean-rows will I have there, a hive for the honey bee,
> And live alone in the bee-loud glade.[42]

The opening line contains the active, present tense statement that the poet will take the initiative and take himself back to the Irish idyll of Innisfree. The depiction of Irish rurality in this poem places it firmly in the genre of Romantic pastoral poetry in which the countryside is associated with peace, serenity and solitude.

The end of the poem acknowledges that this will be a mental journey rather an actual, physical one: 'While I stand on the roadway, or on the pavements grey, I hear it [the lake water] in the deep heart's core' (29). The poet associates rural Ireland with idyllic beauty, and urbanity with greyness and dullness. Through his artistic imagination, he is able to leave the latter and travel to the former landscape.

'To Ireland in the Coming Times'

This poem is Yeats' personal manifesto for his poetic Revivalist project and also an attempt to articulate his vision for a postcolonial Irish future: a future that will embrace past traditions and poetic examples and use them to forge an Ireland to come. It is in this poem that Yeats most obviously representatively fuses the personal with the national. 'To Ireland in the Coming Times' begins with the poet's assertion that he wishes to embrace the inspiration of various older national poets and become the modern version of Bard of Éireann:

> Know that I would accounted be
> True brother of a company
> That sang to sweeten Ireland's wrong
> Ballad and story, rann and song. (38)

Later in the poem the poets who are alluded to in these opening lines are named as Davis, Mangan and Ferguson. The inclusion of Samuel Ferguson is significant because his interest in Irish Celtic mythology would have been viewed as an important precursor to the Celtic character of Irish Revivalism.

The concluding stanza consists of the poet asserting:

> While I may, I write for you
> The love I lived, the dream I knew [...]
> I cast my heart into my rhymes,
> That you in the dim coming times,
> May know my heart went with them. (39)

These lines communicate that the poet will write poems that are deeply personal to him but shall also help imagine an Ireland to come. One that shall be desirable to the poet in the present moment and also for future generations. This poem therefore encapsulates both the private and the public appeal that Yeats wished his poems to possess.

'Easter 1916'

'Easter 1916' is a poem describing the poet's torn emotions regarding the events of the Easter Rising staged in Ireland against British rule on Easter Monday, 24 April, 1916. The uprising was unsuccessful, and most of the Irish Republican leaders involved were executed for treason. The poem was written between May and September 1916, which implies that Yeats composed it after allowing himself a certain degree of temporal and emotional distance from the rawness of the events that occurred during that Easter week.

The poem opens thus: 'I have met them at close of day/ Coming with vivid faces/ From counter or desk among grey Eighteenth-century houses/I have passed with a nod of the head or polite meaningless words,/ Or have lingered awhile and said polite meaningless words' (119). In these lines, Yeats is telling his readers about his knowledge of the Easter 1916 rebels as being ordinary people living ordinary lives. These individuals were not originally intended to be martyrs. Their existences were fairly uninteresting and their conversations, much like those in Eliot's 'Love Song of J. Alfred Prufrock', were not very exciting since the world they lived in was fairly mundane.

However, by beginning the poem with a description of life before the Rising, Yeats is allowing us, his readers, to consider what has been lost as well as what has been gained by this rebellion and thus is refusing to allow this work to descend into mere jingoistic celebration of the event that cost the lives of so many Irish people.

The principal characters in the drama of the rebellion are referred to (although not by name) in the second stanza:

> That woman's days were spent
> in ignorant good will
> Her nights in argument
> Until her voice grew shrill
> [...]

This man had kept a school;
And rode our winged horse
...
This other man I had dreamed
A drunken vain glorious lout.
He had done most bitter wrong
To some who are near my heart.
Yet I number him in the song (120)

The woman whose loss of femininity through involvement in public affairs Yeats laments is Constance Markievicz, a major figure in the struggle for Irish independence and who Yeats knew during her formative years in Sligo. The school master is Patrick H. Pearse, and the drunken vain glorious lout is John MacBride who married Maude Gonne and was very abusive towards her. Although Yeats disliked MacBride personally, he reluctantly recognises his part in the Rising and pays tribute to the patriot rather than the man, as Yeats feels he must do as national Bard of Éireann.

We now turn to one of the most famous lines in this poem and in Irish poetry in general: 'All changed, changed utterly:/ A terrible beauty is born' (119–120).[43] These lines, repeated throughout the poem as a refrain, emphasise Yeats' conflicted attitude towards the Easter Rising. The concept of a 'terrible beauty', while seemingly contradictory, encapsulates this moment in Irish history: it helped to bring about Irish independence (as Yeats foresaw that it would) while also giving birth to a cycle of death and destruction in Ireland. If this view of the Rising sounds a little undecided, I think it is because Yeats himself was unsure about how he felt about it.

It is worth comparing those lines from 'Easter 1916' with the poem called 'The Second Coming', which also considers processes of historical change: 'Turning and turning in the widening gyre, The falcon cannot hear the falconer; Things fall apart; the centre cannot hold; Mere anarchy is loosed upon the world'. In this poem, Yeats is calling attention to what he thinks is the central process of history: that of ever increasing destruction and chaos. In both this poem and 'Easter 1916', Yeats is situating specific historical moments in the context of wider, more universal movements in nature.

The third stanza in 'Easter 1916' executes this strategy most overtly: 'Hearts with one purpose alone/ Through summer and winter seem/ Enchanted to a stone/ To trouble the living stream/ The horse that comes from the road/ The rider, the birds that range/ From cloud to tumbling cloud' (120). In this section Yeats seems to be alluding to the natural world that is more alive and more humane as opposed to the cold, violent world that the rebels are embracing. The stone acts a symbol for the inhumanity of warlike violence that opposes nature and disrupts the flow of existence. This idea is further developed in the final stanza when Yeats observes that 'too long a sacrifice can make a stone of the heart'.

In the final stanza of the poem, Yeats finds himself seriously questioning whether the Rising was worth the cost in human lives: 'Was it needless death after all?/ For England may keep faith/ For all that is done and said./ We know their dream; enough/ To know they dreamed and are dead' (120). The reference to keeping faith refers to England's promise to grant Ireland a parliament of her own after World War I had ended and therefore, maybe the Rising did not need to happen. When Yeats refers to the rebels as dreamers, he is trying to make the point that those who died in the Rising were more interested in the romantic, idealised vision of war rather than the harsh actuality. It also points out the waste of life when it is sacrificed for a dream rather than a reality.

The final lines of the poem do something that has not happened in the poem thus far and that is the naming of the people who were executed after the rebellion: 'I write it out in a verse–/ MacDonagh and MacBride/ And Connolly and Pearse/ Now and in time to be,/ Whenever green is worn,/ Are changed, changed utterly:/ A terrible beauty is born' (121). Yeats almost seems to be naming these martyrs under duress, as if the pressure being exerted upon him by his role as national poet finally gets the better of him and he is forced at the end to reduce the 1916 Rising to a naming of facts rather than the more nuanced, subjective account we have had up to this point. Yeats did not wish to simply offer a limiting, concrete account of the Rising that would fail to take account of its complexities. He wished to write a poem rather than simply a piece of journalese but he knew that the Irish people would wish for some amount of factual recounting of a significant national event from their bard. The role of national poet is thus portrayed as one which is a heavy burden that carries certain responsibilities that cannot be shirked and Yeats faced up to them (albeit reluctantly) in these final lines of the poem.

Easter 1916 was an event that shocked Yeats out of his somewhat romantic view of rebellion and violence that is discernible in *Cathleen ni Houlihan*. His view of Ireland and the possibility of its violently created postcolonial future was greatly altered and this will be seen in the works he creates during Ireland's revolutionary period and then in the earlier years of the Irish Free State (which will be considered in Chapter 3). Thus, 'Easter 1916' can be read as poetic testament to Yeats' transition from middle to late artistic stage.

The Playboy of the Western World

One of the most famous/infamous events that occurred during the Revival period was the so-called 'Playboy riots' which occurred on the night of the premier of Synge's *The Playboy of the Western World* at the Abbey Theatre in 1907. As Lady Gregory telegraphed to Yeats who was in Scotland at the time, 'the audience broke up in disorder at the mention of the word "shift"'.[44] This occurs at the end of the play when the main character, Christy Mahon, declares that the only woman he wants is Pegeen Mike and he wouldn't care if a line of women appeared in front of him all standing in their shifts. A shift is a woman's undergarment and the audience were probably incensed by the verbal image of Irish women wearing nothing more than their underclothes.

The depiction of rural Ireland that Synge offers in *Playboy* would also not have been one that Irish 'patriots' at that time would have found very edifying as it can be unfairly interpreted as portraying Mayo peasants as a violent and lawless people, in awe of Christy Mahon because of the story he has told them about how he had killed his father. If this was partly the cause of the riots then it is ironic since what essentially happened was the viewers of the play broke out into violence as a protest against being portrayed onstage as violent. This misrepresentation on Synge's part of the Irish peasantry is ironic considering that Synge took inspiration for this play from a story he heard whilst holidaying on the Aran Islands.

Luke Gibbons has encapsulated the vision of the Irish peasant that Synge wishes to provide via *Playboy* in the following quotation:

> Synge's preoccupation with lawlessness and violence is central to his overall conception of the western world, for in throwing off the shackles of discipline and constraint, he is undermining one of the main requirements of modernization as exemplified in nineteenth-century Ireland – the centralization of law, ideology and the state apparatus.[45]

This vision of the lawless Irish peasant is significantly at variance with the more idealised version portrayed by William Carleton and Yeats in his earlier poetry and plays and is also contrastable with the tragic dignity of the peasantry as staged by Yeats in *Riders to the Sea*. These differing depictions of Irish peasant identity and essence give concrete proof of the contested status of that figure and how the different portrayals contain a definite element of imagination and artistic construction.

In the preface to *Playboy*, Synge admitted that he wished for there to be an element of imaginative artistry in his depiction of the rural Irish:

> In a good play every speech should be as fully flavoured as a nut or apple, and such speeches cannot be written by anyone who shuts their lips on poetry. In Ireland for a few years more, we have a popular imagination that is fiery and magnificent, and tender; so that those of us who wish to write start with a chance that is not given to writers in places where the springtime of the local life has been forgotten, and the harvest is a memory only, and the straw has been turned into bricks.[46]

Thus, Synge is admitting that *Playboy* is not aiming for realism but for a version of Irish rurality that contains beautiful, poetic language and can be interpreted as trying to externalise the richly artistic inner life that Synge believed the Irish to possess.

The love of *Playboy*'s characters of violence and lawlessness is encapsulated by Pegeen Mike early in the drama: 'And where now will you meet the like of Daneen Sullivan knocked the eye from a peeler, or Marcus Quinn, God rest him, got six months for maiming ewes, and he a great warrant to tell stories of holy Ireland till he'd have the old women shedding down tears about their feet' (100).

This piece of dialogue conflates violence with romance and also with a kind of artistic command of language and an ability to tell stories that becomes significant when Christy Mahon arrives onstage soon after this moment. The use of Hiberno-English in this play (as evidenced above) also provides a harshly poetic vocabulary that perfectly mirrors the people and the landscape that appear in *Playboy*.

The way that Christy recounts his act of patricide is as appealing to the onstage audience and listeners as the content of the story itself: 'I just riz the loy and let fall the edge of it on the ridge of his skull, and he went down at my feet like an empty sack, and never let a grunt or groan from him at all' (106). Several times during the play after Christy has repeated this story he is praised for how well he tells it.

The story that inspired *Playboy* was one that was told to Synge on the Aran Islands by one of the islanders. Essentially, Synge had a narrative recounted to him about how the natives of Aran sheltered a man who was on the run for killing his father. This story is told again in Synge's memoir/travel novel *The Aran Islands*.

Playboy is set in 1902 during the second Boer War. This is made clear in one particular piece of dialogue spoken by one of the villagers: 'Maybe he went fighting for the Boers, the like of the man beyond, was judged to be hanged, quartered, and drawn. Were you off east, young fellow, fighting bloody wars for Kruger' (105). This reference to the Boer War is significant because it was a conflict that many Irishmen took part in because the Boers were fighting for independence against the British. This coming together of Irishmen to fight their colonial masters, albeit in a different country, has been judged as a kind of rehearsal for Ireland's own anti-colonial wars, which were to begin a decade later with the 1916 Easter Rising.

The play contains within some of its scenes moments of the Irish Gothic style that had been so prominent in nineteenth-century Irish writing in works by writers such as Edgeworth, Le Fanu, Maturin, Stoker and early Somerville and Ross. Midway through *Playboy* a story is told by one of the villagers that could have come straight out of one of the texts of the aforementioned authors: '[T]here was a graveyard beyond the house with the remnants of a man who had thighs as long as your arm. He was a horrid man, I'm telling you, and there was many a fine Sunday I'd put him together for fun, and he with shiny bones you wouldn't meet the like of these days in the cities of the world' (131). This story is in essence an amalgam of

Gothicism and the graveyard scene from *Hamlet* in which a skull is also a fetishised object.

Playboy is another Irish text in which a mirror is referred to as a metaphor for representation. In this case, it is a personal, individualistic form of representation rather than the national one that Edgeworth (referred to above) mentioned. This occurs at the beginning of the second part of *Playboy*:

> CHRISTY: *(He takes the looking-glass from the wall and puts it on the back of the chair …)* Didn't I know rightly I was handsome, though it was the divil's own mirror we had beyond would twist a squint across an angel's brow. (115)

Whilst Christy was living with his father he had had to endure the demeaning language that Old Mahon constantly used to describe his son. Now that he is with the men and women of this small Mayo village he was been praised and feted constantly and this increased his confidence and made him what Christy himself would later call 'a mighty man by the power of the lie' (144). It ultimately emerges that both mirror images of him, positive and negative, were inaccurate distortions of the authentic and that it is only at the end of the play Christy might possibly begin to play a true version of his internal and external self.

Christy's presence could be said to influence the selfhood of Pegeen Mike as much she helps to shape his. As she says in wonderment to Christy following one of their intimate conversations: 'And to think it's me that's talking sweetly, Christy Mahon, and I the fright of seven townlands on account of my biting tongue. Well the heart's a wonder, and I'm thinking there won't be our like in Mayo for gallant lovers from this hour today' (137). By wooing and winning Pegeen, Christy has become both a strong, masculine figure, but also a sensitive, somewhat 'feminine' lover (certainly according to how gender narratives have constructed such roles). This is also apparent in the earlier scene where Christy is preening in front of a mirror. Equally, Pegeen has become slightly more 'effeminate' without losing her more stereotypically masculine qualities.

The appearance of Old Mahon and the revelation at the play's climax that Christy had not killed him sparks Christy to try and perform the patricide for a second time. However, when the villagers see this act happen in front of their eyes they realise, as Pegeen put it, 'There's a great gap between a gallous story and a dirty deed' (144) and attempt to hang Christy. Like the play's audience on that opening night, the people of Mayo realise that there is only so much radical and rebellious behaviour that they can stomach. This climax can also be interpreted as one of 'mock Gothicism' because Old Mahon seems to have returned from the dead; except, of course, he had never been killed in the first place.

The play's final moments, when the still alive father and Christy Mahon leave the stage whilst vowing to romp around the country and tell tales about the foolish people of Mayo has been interpreted in a variety of ways, perhaps most notably by Declan Kiberd and Gerardine Meaney. According to Kiberd:

> Synge's *Playboy* ... was a sort of blueprint for a new species of Irish artist. In his hands, the meaning of Gaelic tradition changed from something museumized to something modifiable, endlessly open. He sensed that the revivalists' worship of the past was based on their questionable desire to colonize and control it: but his deepest desire was to demonstrate the continuing power of the Gaelic past to disrupt the revivalist present. In the play ... Christy not only fails to kill his father but decides in the end that he doesn't even want to: it is enough to know that the old man is now happily tractable to the son's future designs.[47]

Kiberd's argument is essentially that *Playboy* concludes with a vision of a postcolonial future when the once colonised figure of the son achieves power over and freedom from the colonial figure of the father and that such a future will be a new and authentic one that is free from idealisations or stage Irish performative stereotypes.

Gerardine Meaney takes a more critical view of how truly revolutionary and liberatory the ending of the drama is: 'At the play's end the roles of father and son are reversed, the roles of dominant and dominated persist. The occupier of the position of power may change, but power itself remains and its structure is unaltered'.[48] Meaney contends that the postcolonial future foretold by *Playboy* will represent nothing except new forms of the old misery because forms of inequality and oppression will still exist. All that will have been altered will be the identities of who dominates and who is dominated. One thing that both readings have in common, however, is they both argue that *Playboy* does wish to offer a vision of a postcolonial Irish future to come – whether that future be positive or negative is debatable.

The final word on this play must be given to Pegeen Mike who is left behind and whose lament closes the drama: 'Oh my grief, I've lost him surely. I've lost the only Playboy of the Western World' (146). Unlike the character Nora in Synge's earlier play *The Shadow of the Glen* (1903) who leaves at the story's end with a tramp for what she hopes will be a freer and more hopeful life than the one she had with her husband, Pegeen is abandoned and doomed to live a stifling existence with a timid husband, Shawn Keogh. The promise of something better with Christy has been completely lost.

With *The Playboy of the Western World*, the Revival's preoccupations with Ireland and Irish identity, particularly in relation to Irish rurality, took a particularly iconoclastic and anarchic turn. In essence, the sacred cows of Revival Drama, as outlined in the Irish Literary Theatre Manifesto, were blown asunder by Synge's tragi-comic masterpiece. The Irish theatre-going audience responded accordingly with the Playboy riots of 26 January 1907, which continued to a lesser degree during subsequent nights of the play's run that week.

Dubliners

The question of Joyce's relationship with the Irish Revival has been a very contentious one. The majority view regards Joyce as being quite a stern opponent of the Revival's conception of Ireland as a mystical place that is best represented by past-legends and the Revivalists' insistence on the rural West as the bastion of national purity. In 1904, shortly before Joyce left Ireland, he wrote a poem called 'The Holy Office' and circulated it among his Dublin circle. This work is Joyce's attempt to distance himself from the authors of the Revival in a very wicked and barbed piece of satire: 'But I must not accounted be/One of that mumming company/With him who hies him to appease/His giddy dames' frivolities/While they console him when he whinges/With gold-embroidered Celtic fringes'.[49] In this parody of Yeats' 'To Ireland in the Coming Times', Joyce emphasises his desire to be excluded from that group, which he regards as misguidedly occupying the Celtic fringes, as opposed to Yeats who desired to signal his wish to be counted among that group of national Irish Celtic-inspired poets. With *Dubliners* (which was published in 1904 but the stories were written over the previous ten years) Joyce wishes to move to the centre of Ireland, its capital city rather than remaining on its peripheries. The title of the collection alone represents a challenge to Revival notions of Irishness since Dublin was perceived by the Revivalist mindset as the bastion of colonial impurity. While authors such as Yeats and Lady Gregory preferred to represent the rural West, Joyce artistically immersed himself in the urban world of Dublin.

Joyce, who was certainly never short of arrogance, thought this collection of short stories was so important in terms of performing a national service that he wrote to his publisher Grant Richards in 1906: 'I seriously believe that you will retard the course of civilisation in Ireland by, preventing the Irish people from having one good look at themselves in my nicely polished looking-glass'.[50] This comparison between *Dubliners* and a nicely polished looking-glass can be usefully contrasted with Stephen Dedalus' assertion in *Ulysses* that the true symbol of Irish art is 'the cracked looking glass of a servant'. What Dedalus might be implying is that the art of the Revival gave the Irish people nothing more than a distorted and untruthful view of themselves whereas his work (and Joyce's by extension) provided a true and accurate vision of Irishness.

It can be argued that Joyce, while certainly not being an unqualified supporter of revival, did attempt to appropriate its ideas and tropes for the purpose of expanding on them and thus providing a more complex and inclusive vision of Irishness rather than the simplistic one that Joyce saw as being supplied by the Revival. The three stories that shall be examined are 'A Little Cloud', 'A Mother' and 'The Dead'.

Joyce famously said that he wrote *Dubliners* 'in a style of scrupulous meanness'. This has led many commentators to conclude that the stories are written in a very simplistic style that cannot possibly be compared with the stylistic pyrotechnics of *Ulysses* or *Finnegans Wake*. Upon closer inspection, however, many of these stories do actually break away from the traditional narrative voice of omniscient third person narration. For example, 'A Little Cloud' opens with the following sentences: 'Eight years before he had seen his friend off at the North Wall and wished him God-speed. Gallaher had got on'.[51] In this passage, the non-descript voice of the third-person narrator is interrupted by the more colloquial sounding 'Gallaher had got on'. This sounds like an individual character speaking rather than being spoken for. If it is not him speaking directly then it is the narrator speaking from his perspective which in narrative terms is known as free indirect discourse. The same sophisticated form of narration can also be found in the opening sentence of 'The Dead': 'Lily, the caretaker's daughter, was literally run off her feet' (199). As we know, Lily was not *literally* run off her feet but this does sound like the kind of idiomatic speech that the character of Lily would employ.

The central focus of 'A Little Cloud' is the character Little Chandler. He could not be more removed from your typical Revival character: 'He was under average stature, he gave one the idea of being a little man. His hands were white and small, his frame was fragile, his voice was quiet' (76). We thus are given the impression of a banal and unremarkable person rather than the remarkable, mythical figures that authors such as Yeats and Lady Gregory created for their readers and viewers.

The image of Dublin that Joyce evokes in this story is one that is very often far from attractive:

> A horde of grimy children populated the street. They stood or ran in the roadway, or crawled up the steps before the gaping doors, or squatted like mice upon the thresholds. Little Chandler gave them no thought. He picked his way deftly through all that minute vermin-like life and under the shadow of the gaunt spectral mansions in which the old nobility of Dublin had roistered. No memory of the past touched him, for his mind was too full of present joy. (77)

Joyce here describes Dublin as a Gothic living space where quasi-human life crawls about its existence. Little Chandler's refusal to be touched by the past could be read as Joyce's refusal to create characters who wish to live in the present by means of the past, which the Revival saw as being a valuable state of existence.

Little Chandler, like Joyce, believes that one has to leave Ireland in order to achieve anything worthwhile and envies his friend Ignatius

Gallaher who did go to England and became a journalist. Little Chandler's plan for success in England as an artist betrays him as a poet who wishes to be what Joyce accused Oscar Wilde of being: 'A court jester to the English'. 'The English critics, perhaps, would recognize him [Little Chandler] as one of the Celtic School by reason of the melancholy tone of his poems … It was a pity he was not more Irish looking' (80). Joyce's diagnosis of Irish art in this period was that it sought to invent and package a marketable form of Irishness for consumption abroad. The myths and legends that Standish O'Grady, William Yeats and so on made popular were, from Joyce's perspective, pandering to a foreign view of Ireland.

The opposite extreme to Little Chandler would be his friend Ignatius Gallaher who divorced himself completely from Ireland and any form of Irish culture: 'The Isle of Man [scoffed Gallaher] … Go to London or Paris: Paris for choice. That'd do you good … I've been to the Moulin Rouge … and I've been to all the Bohemian cafes. Hot stuff' (83). These declarations on Gallaher's part about independence from Ireland and a bohemian sensibility do not have the effect on Little Chandler that Gallaher planned: 'There was something vulgar in his friend which he had not observed before. But perhaps it was only the result of living in London amid the bustle and competition of the Press' (83). Chandler believes that Gallaher has lost a quality in himself as a result of forsaking entirely the identity of his country of birth. Joyce, as is very often the case in his writings, is trying to hint at a middle-ground between Revivalism and an Anglicised Ireland as represented by Gallaher and decried by Douglas Hyde.

Little Chandler represents the paralysis that Joyce saw as existing in Ireland in general but Dublin in particular at this time. Little Chandler has many ambitions and romantic hopes but the squalidness of reality refuses to allow him to achieve them. His paralysis is hinted at very early on in the story: 'He remembered the books of poetry upon his shelves at home. He had bought them in his bachelor days and many an evening, as he sat in the little room off the hall, he had been tempted to take one down from the bookshelf and read something to his wife. But shyness had always held him back; and so the books had remained on their shelves' (92). Little Chandler's inability to take down a book and read to his wife is a metaphor for his inability to achieve his desires as a poet and is one of the many microscopic images in *Dubliners* of a paralysed colonial Ireland.

The final words that Little Chandler utters in this story after he has made his little baby cry can be read as Joyce's diagnosis of the inability of Ireland at this time to articulate perfectly their own national identity, even with the help of the Revival: 'It's nothing … He … he began to cry … I couldn't … I didn't do anything … What?' (93). Little Chandler's struggle for articulation symbolises an Ireland which was struggling to authentically represent itself at the beginning of the twentieth century.

The story 'A Mother' paints a picture of the Irish Revival as a chance for self-serving, opportunistic people to make financial gains through promoting the romantic vision of Irishness: 'When the Irish Revival began to be appreciable Mrs Kearney determined to take advantage of her daughter's name [Kathleen] and brought an Irish teacher to the house. Kathleen and her sister sent Irish picture postcards to their friends and these friends sent back other Irish picture postcards' (154). The motives of mother and daughter for getting involved in the Irish music scene are entirely opportunistic and their intention is to promote a picture-postcard version of Ireland.

The opening of this story gives its readers a description of a Revivalist that is far from attractive or ingratiating:

> Mr Holohan, assistant secretary of the Eire Abu Society, had been walking up and down Dublin for nearly a month, with his hands and pockets full of dirty pieces of paper, arranging about the series of concerts. He had a game leg, and for this his friend called him Hoppy Holohan. (153)

Holohan's can be interpreted as a symbolic reference to the paralysis that Joyce saw afflicting Dublin at this time whose cure, in Joyce's opinion, did not entirely reside with the Irish Revival.

The bad treatment of Mrs Kearney and her daughter by the concert organisers represents a coruscating attack by Joyce on the male-centred Revival, which was dominated by men and whose views on women (as far as Joyce was concerned) were certainly not the most progressive: 'They thought they had only a girl to deal with and that, therefore, they could ride roughshod over. But she would show them their mistake. They wouldn't have dared to have treated her like that if she had been a man' (167).

The conclusion of the story shows Mrs Kearney and Kathleen departing the hall and leaving the final word on them and their conduct to a judgemental male perspective: 'Mr Holohan began to pace up and down the room in order to cool himself, for he felt his skin on fire. "That's a nice lady!" he said. "O she's a nice lady". "You did the proper thing, Holohan", said Mr O'Madden Burke, poised upon his umbrella in approval' (168). It is clear that the two men condemn Mrs Kearney entirely for her behaviour purely on the grounds that it is unladylike. Mrs Kearney was almost certainly right when she asserted that how she was viewed and treated would have been very different if she had been a man. Thus, 'A Mother' is as much a story about the misogyny that permeated Dublin in the first decade of the twentieth century as it is a critique of the cynically mercenary streak that could be said to have permeated certain aspects of the Irish Revival.

'The Dead' is probably the most complex example of Joyce's engagement with the Irish Revival. The story centres primarily around Gabriel Conroy who could be regarded as a typical anti-Revivalist given his preference for European influences and holiday destinations over Irish ones. He tells his friend Miss Ivors that he cannot go on a holiday to the 'Aran Isles' because he is going on a cycling holiday around select parts of Europe such as France or Belgium. Upon being reminded that his wife Greta, like Nora Barnacle, comes from Galway, Gabriel replies coldly, 'her people are' (215). Miss Ivors presses Gabriel further about being more embracing of his own home and culture: '"And haven't you your own land to visit", continued Miss Ivors, "that you know nothing of, your own people, and your own country?" "O to tell you the truth" retorted Gabriel suddenly, "I'm sick of my own country, sick of it"' (216). Miss Ivor's final shot at Gabriel is to call him a West Briton, which means someone who is immersed in British cultural influences. Thus, Gabriel's desire for cosmopolitanism marks him out as another version of Ignatius Gallaher in 'A Little Cloud'.

The climax of this story begins with Gabriel seeing his wife on the stairs of his aunt's home listening intently to the song *The Lass of Aughrim* and it is at this moment that Gabriel begins to exhibit a certain amount of Revivalist thought processes: 'He stood still in the gloom of the hall, trying to catch the air that the voice was singing and gazing up at his wife. There was grace and mystery in her attitude as if she were a symbol of something' (240). Through Gabriel's gaze, Gretta becomes less a flesh and blood woman and more of an abstract symbol in much the same way that Revivalists such as Yeats conceived of women as representing the Irish nation in texts such as *Cathleen ni Houlihan*.

However, Joyce does not merely ape Yeatsian Revivalism because, as the above passage makes clear, Gabriel cannot see his wife's face when she is on the stairs, which means that the vision of her that he is interpreting according to his own subjective and objectifying male gaze is a flawed one because he does not have access at that point to the most expressive part of his wife's body which is obviously her face. It is worth noting that the most obvious difference between Joyce's story and the John Houston 1987 film version is that Houston allows Gabriel and the audience full access to Gretta's visage at that exact moment in the narrative. The camera in that scene acts as a stand-in for a human male gaze which successfully objectifies Gretta in a way that Joyce's story did not.

When the Conroys return to their hotel, Gretta retrieves the narrative from the male perspective of Gabriel and gives the readers a sense of her as a suffering human being who has experienced extreme emotions such as grief and loss and we thus apprehend her as being more than purely an abstract symbol. When Gretta says of her former lover Michael Furey, 'I think he died for me', she sounds like a Cathleen ni Houlihan being torn apart by grief because of the memory of someone who had sacrificed themselves for love of her. Gretta thus represents a version of the Revival figure of Cathleen ni Houlihan but a more complex and multi-layered version than the one created by Yeats. It can be argued that Joyce is engaging with Revivalism for the purpose of attempting to rectify many of the inadequacies he perceives in that movement.

Gabriel is so moved by his wife's story of love and loss in Galway that he feels regret at having allowed himself to repress any form of passion and extreme emotion from his soul: 'Better pass boldly into that other world in the full glory of some passion, than fade and wither dismally with age' (255). It is this observation that makes Gabriel sound most like a Revivalist since they wished to revive the passion and epic romances from the Irish past and present them as being integral to the Irish identity. It is also interesting that this passage could be regarded as the central message of Synge's final play *Deirdre of the Sorrows* in which Deirdre and her lover return home to face almost certain execution rather than risk the erosion of their passion by marriage and the tedium of habit and familiarity.

Gabriel's acceptance that 'The time had come for him to set out on his journey westward' (255), is a momentous moment in both his life and Joyce's artistic career because both creator and created are acknowledging, perhaps for the first time, that western Ireland cannot be ignored as part of the Irish identity. Ireland is both rural and urban and to ignore one, as Joyce probably felt the Revivalists had done in relation to the urban world, is to betray the Irish nation.

The final passage of the story can be read as Joyce's attempt to offer an image of Ireland that is open to both Revival and other conceptions of national identity:

> Yes, the newspapers were right: snow was general all over Ireland. It was falling on every part of the dark central plain, on the treeless hills, falling softly into the dark mutinous Shannon waves. It was falling, too, upon every part of the lonely churchyard on the hill where Michael Furey lay buried … His soul swooned slowly as he heard the snow falling faintly through the universe and faintly falling, like the descent of their last end, upon all the living and the dead. (255–256)

Gabriel is lying in bed in his urban home but his mind is imagining the snow that is falling all over Ireland falling on rural areas. Thus, through one mind, the urban is connected with the rural and the Revival vision of Ireland with other versions of national identity in a utopian moment of openness and inclusivity.

The closing moment of 'The Dead' could be regarded as an encapsulation of the majority of Joyce's career since when he was writing the vast bulk of his works he was physically outside of Ireland (either in Trieste, Zurich or Paris) but mentally he was very much in his country of birth and thus acted as a bridge between Ireland and the rest of Europe. One of Joyce's greatest achievements was to help bring European modernism to Ireland and also to give modernism a somewhat Irish feel through his works, which are now regarded as some of the finest examples of that form of literature.

James Fairhall has argued the following in relation to the place 'The Dead' holds in the *Dubliners* collection and also how it exhibits a sympathy towards Revivalism's view of the 'Irish West':

> In 'The Dead', Joyce's coda to *Dubliners*, the pattern of linguistic seduction, thwarted escape, and return to a historically determined paralysis differs somewhat. Gabriel seems to have dealt successfully with the problem of his subject position in a colonized country by choosing a cosmopolitan identity based in part on language – that is, on his disavowal of Irish, his ability to speak French and German, and his writing of book reviews without regard for nationalist politics. Yet the words of two women associated with the West, site of Ireland's severest colonial trauma, undo his cosmopolitanism and his sense of verbal mastery over women and Ireland.[52]

A similar argument concerning Joyce's nuanced and complex relationship with the Revival as evidenced in the collection *Dubliners* is developed at great length in Frank Shovlin's (quoted above) 2012 study *Journey Westward: Joyce, Dubliners, and the Literary Revival* (Liverpool University Press).

Study questions

1. **What is the link between culture and politics?**
2. **What versions of Irish rurality are envisioned in Revival literary works?**
3. **How are heroism and violence viewed in differing Revival texts?**
4. **What are the troubling aspects of the Irish Literary and Cultural Revival's collective vision for postcolonial Ireland?**
5. **In what ways did the Revival respond to Douglas Hyde's call to 'De-Anglicise Ireland'?**
6. **Evaluate James Joyce's engagement with the Irish Revival.**
7. **Assess D.P. Moran's view that: 'there is manifestly no essential difference between first class literary works executed by an English-speaking man born in Ireland, and that executed by an English speaking man born in England'.**

Notes

1 Sean Hewitt, 'Natural History and the Irish Revival', in Kathryn Conrad, Cóilín Parsons, and Julie McCormack (eds), *Science, Technology, and Irish Modernism* (Syracuse: Syracuse University Press, 2019), p. 19.
2 Declan Kiberd, *Irish Classics* (London: Granta Books, 2001), p. 408.
3 W.B. Yeats, 'The Celtic Element in Literature', in *W.B. Yeats: The Major Works*, ed. Edward Larrissy (Oxford: Oxford University Press, 2008), pp. 376–377.
4 Emer Nolan, 'Modernism and the Irish Revival', in Joe Cleary and Claire Connolly (eds), *The Cambridge Companion to Modern Irish Culture* (Cambridge: Cambridge University Press, 2005), p. 160.
5 P.H. Pearse, *Political Writings and Speeches* (Dublin: Talbot Press, 1924), p. 25.
6 Gregory Castle, in Kathryn Conrad, Cóilín Parsons, and Julie McCormack (eds), *Science, Technology, and Irish Modernism* (Syracuse: Syracuse University Press, 2019), p. 112.
7 Thomas McDonagh, *Literature in Ireland* (Dublin: Talbot Press, 1916), p. vii.
8 Seamus Deane, 'Heroic Styles', *Field Day Pamphlets* (Derry: Field Day Publications, 1985), p. 8.
9 W.B. Yeats, 'A Postscript to a Forthcoming Work of Essays by Various Writers', in J. Frayne and C. Johnson (eds), *Uncollected Prose* (London: Macmillan, 1975), vol. II, p. 245.
10 W.B. Yeats, *Autobiographies* (Dublin: Gill & Macmillan, 1955), p. 345.
11 Paul Bew, Charles Stewart, *Charles Stewart Parnell* (Dublin: Gill & Macmillan, 1991), p. 145.
12 Maria Edgeworth, *Castle Rackrent* (Oxford: Oxford World's Classics, 1991), p. 1. All future references refer parenthetically to this edition.
13 Derek Hand, *A History of the Irish Novel* (Cambridge: Cambridge University Press, 2011), p. 64.
14 Edgeworth, Maria, *Chosen Letters*, ed. F.V. Berry (Boston: Houghton Mifflin, 1931), p. 384.
15 Luke Gibbons, '"Some Hysterical Hatred": History, Hysteria and the Literary Revival', *Irish University Review* 27:1 (1997), p. 23.
16 Edward Hirsch, 'The Imaginary Irish Peasant', *PMLA* 106:5 (October 1991), p. 1116.
17 Frank Shovlin, *Journey Westward: Joyce, Dubliners, and the Literary Revival* (Liverpool: Liverpool University Press, 2012), p. 3.
18 See Barbara Hayley, 'Foreword', *Traits and Stories of the Irish Peasantry* (Gerrards Cross, Buckinghamshire: Colin Smythe, 1990), p. 12.

19 See William Carleton, *The Autobiography of William Carleton* (London: White Row, 1968), p. 77.
20 See William Carleton, 'Introduction', *Traits and Stories of the Irish Peasantry* (Gerrards Cross, Buckinghamshire: Colin Smythe, 1990), p. xxii.
21 W.B. Yeats, *Selected Poems* (London: Penguin, 2000), pp. 204–205. All future references to Yeats' poems refer parenthetically to this edition.
22 W.B. Yeats, 'Preface to *Well of the Saints*', in John Millington Synge, *The Playboy of the Western World and Other Plays* (Oxford: Oxford University Press, 2008), p. 52.
23 John Millington Synge, *The Aran Islands*, *Collected Works*, *Prose: II* (Oxford: Oxford University Press, 1966), p. 56.
24 Oona Frawley, '*The Shadow of the Glen* and *Riders to the Sea*', in P.J. Mathews (ed.), *The Cambridge Companion to J.M. Synge* (Cambridge: Cambridge University Press, 2009), p. 17.
25 John Millington Synge, *The Playboy of the Western World and Other Plays* (Oxford: Oxford University Press, 2008), p. 5. All other references refer parenthetically to this edition.
26 William Shakespeare, *Hamlet* (New York, W.W. Norton & Company Inc., 1992), p. 96.
27 James Joyce, *Ulysses*, ed. Declan Kiberd. Students' annotated edition (London: Penguin, 2000), p. 274.
28 James Joyce, *Portrait of the Artist as Young Man* (Oxford: Oxford University Press, 2008), p. 212.
29 Douglas Hyde, 'The Necessity for De-Anglicising Ireland', http://www.gaeilge.org/deanglicising.html (accessed 20 May, 2026).
30 D.P. Moran, 'The Battle of Two Civilisations', *New Ireland Review* xiii (August 1900), p. 323. All future references refer parenthetically to this edition.
31 P.J. Mathews, *Revival: The Abbey Theatre, Sinn Fein, The Gaelic League and the Co-operative Movement* (Cork: Cork University Press, 2000), p. 99.
32 Quoted in ibid., p. 100.
33 Ibid., p. 101.
34 James Joyce, 'Ireland: Island of Saints and Sages', in Ellsworth Mason and Richard Ellmann (eds), *Critical Writings* (New York: Viking Press, 1966), pp. 165–166.
35 Lady Gregory, 'Ireland Real and Ideal', *Nineteenth Century* 44 (November 1898), p. 769.
36 Quoted in Mathews, *Revival: The Abbey Theatre, Sinn Fein, The Gaelic League and the Co-operative Movement*, p. 22.

37 Paige Reynolds, *Modernism Drama and the Audience for Irish Spectacle* (Cambridge: Cambridge University Press, 2007), p. 9.
38 W.B. Yeats, *Cathleen ni Houlihan* (New York: Norton Critical Edition, 1991), p. 10.
39 Nicholas Grene, *The Politics of Irish Drama: Plays in Context from Boucicault to Friel* (Cambridge: Cambridge University Press, 1999), p. 6.
40 Arthur Griffith, *United Irishman* (17 October, 1903), p. 1.
41 Joe Cleary, 'Introduction: Ireland and Modernity', in Joe Cleary and Claire Connolly (eds), *The Cambridge Companion to Modern Irish Culture* (Cambridge: Cambridge University Press, 2005), pp. 12–13.
42 Yeats, *Selected Poems*, 28. All future references to Yeats' poems refer parenthetically to this edition.
43 Originally 'Are' and then became 'All'.
44 Emily Ernst, 'The Playboy Riots', cmuplayboy.wordpress.com/the-playboy-riots/
45 Luke Gibbons, *Transformations in Irish Culture* (Cork: Cork University Press, 1996), p. 33.
46 John Millington Synge, *The Playboy of the Western World and Other Plays* (Oxford: Oxford University Press, 2008), pp. 96–97. All future references refer parenthetically to this edition.
47 Declan Kiberd, *Inventing Ireland* (London: Vintage, 1996), p. 187.
48 Gerardine Meaney, *Gender, Ireland, and Cultural Change* (New York: Routledge, 2010), p. 161.
49 James Joyce, 'The Holy Office', *Poems and Exiles* (London: Penguin Books, 1992), p. 103.
50 James Joyce, *Letters 1*, ed. Stuart Gilbert (New York: Viking Press, 1957), p. 64.
51 James Joyce, *Dubliners* (London: Penguin Books, 1956), p. 76. All future references refer parenthetically to this edition.
52 James Fairhall, *James Joyce and the Question of History* (Cambridge: Cambridge University Press, 1993), p. 250.

2

The Counter-Revival: revising a discipline?

Introduction

This chapter shall examine the cultural zeitgeist of the 1930s–1960s in Ireland, which has now come to be known as the Counter-Revival. This unofficial movement was a literary and cultural move against some of the orthodoxies that had existed in the Irish psyche since the Revival and had endured since the foundation of the Irish state in 1922. The Counter-Revival resulted in the production of some exciting works of literature and drama as well as some stimulating works of journalism that helped to fuel new debates concerning how Ireland and Irishness should be conceived in the post-independence period. Although opinion is divided over whether one should officially refer to the Counter-Revival as a definite movement, there is no doubt that the writers and thinkers during these decades did share certain concerns and sometimes a common vision of what constitutes the various Irish identities that existed at this time. What shall be examined is how the exponents of the Counter-Revival often successfully turned disappointment and disillusionment into great works of literature and cultural commentary. Thus, they played a valuable role in advancing Irish literature and culture.

This chapter shall begin by considering Daniel Corkery's polemical text, *Synge and Anglo-Irish Literature*, as being a catalyst for the birth of a counter movement against official orthodoxies concerning Irish identity. Corkery's absolutist and old-fashioned codifying of the signifiers of Irishness gave a new generation of writers and thinkers something to fight against. This is particularly in evidence in the 'anti-rurality' turn in Irish writing that we shall observe in works such as Flann O'Brien's *An Béal Bocht* (*The Poor Mouth*) and Máirtín Ó Cadhain's *Cre na Cille*.

Attention shall be devoted to the epochal journal *The Bell* which was founded in 1940. Analysis of editorials written by its editor Seán Ó Faoláin show how this publication led to reconsiderations of the role of literature in the imagining of nation, which are significantly different to the Revivalist vision of the role Irish literature should have in cultural production and political action.

How Counter-Revivalist texts represent Irish rurality, grand national narratives and the performative nature of identity can be usefully compared and contrasted with how the previous generation of writers and thinkers had grappled with these themes and issues. Terence Brown's celebrated study *Ireland: A Social and Cultural History* will be used as a vital source for this period in Irish cultural and literary history.

The social conservatism that emerged very quickly in the Irish Free State following its creation is one reason for the growing sense of disillusionment among the Irish people at that time. The Censorship of Publications Act 1929, which sought to ban books considered immoral, and the refusal to legalise divorce are two examples of the repressive atmosphere that was beginning to percolate an Ireland that was supposed to have thrown off colonialist oppression and embraced a more liberal style of governing – the kind of country that was outlined in the 1916 Proclamation of Independence.

Because the growth of Irish conservative politics happened in tandem with the rise of the influence of the Catholic Church on Irish social affairs, a curiously unique Catholic conservatism became the primary political dogma of the Irish Free State and then of the Irish Republic. For example, whilst the politics of the Conservative Right is meant to privilege the individual more so than the group, the opposite is true in the case of Catholic conservatism, even as it retains many other features of right-wing politics such as economic conservatism and free market economics. This persists to the present day in certain sections of Irish public discourse and debate and shall be discussed in more detail in Chapter 4.

Anglo-Irishmen and women were also unhappy about the direction the new state was taking because they felt that laws such as censorship of writing and prohibition of divorce were aimed at their writing and religious beliefs. Yeats himself was moved to make a speech in the Irish senate about such anti-Anglo-Irish legislation or lack thereof on Thursday 11 June, 1925:

> I think it is tragic that within three years of this country gaining its independence we should be discussing a measure which a minority of this nation considers to be grossly oppressive. I am proud to consider myself a typical man of that minority. We against whom you have done this thing, are no petty people. We are one of the great stocks of Europe. We are the people of Burke; we are the people of Grattan; we are the people of Swift, the people of Emmet, the people of Parnell. We have created most of the modern literature of this country. We have created the best of its political intelligence.[1]

Yeats' personal, artistic move away from that of a hopeful Revivalist to a more disillusioned and antagonistic Irish person can be said to mirror the transitional mood of the Irish nation as it moved from a colonial to an independent, postcolonial country. This movement is what shall be tracked and examined during the course of this chapter.

Daniel Corkery and the rise of Counter-Revival literature

The novelist and critic Daniel Corkery made a highly influential contribution to post-independence Ireland's sense of itself with the publication of his study *Synge and Anglo-Irish Literature* in 1931. In this critical text, Corkery makes the argument that there are three key facets of the 'Irish identity': (1) religion (2) nationalism and (3) the land. Unless a writer in Ireland is preoccupied with at least one of these issues, he cannot call himself an 'Irish writer'. Corkery's absolutism can be read as at least partially a revolt against Matthew Arnold's notion of the sentimental Celt who cannot cope with 'the despotism of fact'. In contrast, Corkery writes of the Gaelic poets in his work *Hidden Ireland* as someone who is completely realistic and unsentimental: 'This core of hardness is scarcely ever lacking to the Gaelic poet; it tracks him right down the centuries, and one never finds it missing. It is intellectual in its nature: hard headed and clear sighted, witty at its best'.[2] In contrast to the openness of the original Irish Revival to the inclusion of Anglo-Irish artists,

Corkery wishes to promote a (Gaelic) Revival that will exclude such individuals from being called 'Irish'.

Corkery is also complicit in the romanticising of the Irish peasant and their way of life. He says in *Synge and Anglo-Irish Literature*:

> If one approaches 'Celtic Revival poetry' as exotic, then one is in a mood to appreciate its subtle rhythms, and its quiet tones; but if one continues to live within the Irish seas, travelling the roads of the land, then the white-walled houses, the farming life, the hill-top chapel, the memorial cross above some peasants grave – memorable only because he died for his country – impressing themselves as the living pieties of life must impress themselves, upon the imagination, growing into it, dominating it, all this poetry becomes after a time little else than an impertinence.[3]

Corkery is insisting that no one can appreciate the authenticity and individual qualities of Irish life and literature if one is not immersed in the rural Irish countryside and the life of the peasants who inhabit that landscape.

Terence Brown has argued that, whilst the Irish Revival of the pre-revolutionary period was genuinely radical and largely democratically open, the proponents of a similar Revivalism in the early years of the Free State, 'tended to express the need for revival in terms of conservatism and a despairingly authoritarian control of a society that was becoming increasingly anglicized'.[4] We shall see how several writers in the years following the publication of Corkery's *Synge and Anglo-Irish Literature* began to revolt against the idealisation of rural Ireland and the Irish language as being the repositories of a 'pure Irishness' and by so-doing contributed to the existence of what can broadly be called 'Counter-Revival Irish literature'.

'The Great Hunger'

Patrick Kavanagh is one of the iconic writers of the Counter-Revival – a movement in Irish literature that rejected the idealisation of Ireland in Revival literature. Kavanagh himself made the following diagnosis of the Revival in an essay entitled 'Self Portrait': 'I would say now that the so-called Irish Literary Movement which purported to be so frightfully Irish and racy of the Celtic soil was a thorough-going

English-bred lie'.[5] What Kavanagh is saying, essentially, is that writers such as Yeats and Lady Gregory were only peddling old-fashioned views of Ireland and the Irish, derived from patronising ideas from England that depicted the Irish as sentimental, spiritual and poetic but not very grounded in every day realities.

The time when Kavanagh was writing his poetry, in the 1940s and 1950s, was a very depressing period in which to be living in Ireland. The Free State that had emerged following Irish independence was a very conservative, ultra-Catholic nation and many felt that the Ireland that they were promised by Republican revolutionaries and Revivalist writers had not been delivered. This sense of disillusionment can be discerned in Kavanagh's famous poem 'The Great Hunger'.

'The Great Hunger' was written in 1942, during World War II, a conflict in which Ireland had refused to participate and which encapsulated the isolationist policy that then Taoiseach Eamon De Valera wished Ireland to pursue in relation to its foreign and economic policy. It tells the story of Paddy Maguire, a farmer in county Monaghan, where Kavanagh himself was born. It is a work that offers a picture of rural Ireland as a place of hopelessness and despair. The sense of misery can be discerned very clearly in the title 'The Great Hunger', which is a reference to the great Irish famine of the mid-nineteenth century when the potato crop failed and many Irish people either died or fled to countries such as America. Thus, the title of this poem is reminding the readers of a time when the land failed the Irish people.

The beginning of the 'The Great Hunger' offers an image of the Irish peasants that is very far from romantic: 'Clay is the word and clay is the flesh, Where the potato-gatherers like mechanised scare-crows move, Along the side-fall of the hill – Maguire and his men'.[6] These potato farmers are compared with inhuman entities such as machines and scarecrows so as to offer a counter-image of rural Ireland to that portrayed by Yeats and Synge.

Kavanagh's poem can also be read as a counter-version of Yeats and Lady Gregory's 1902 play *Cathleen ni Houlihan* in which mother Ireland is portrayed as an old woman that needs men to fight for her so that she can recover her four fields (which represent the four provinces of Ireland). In 'The Great Hunger', Maguire is essentially married twice: to his mother with whom he has lived all his life, and also to the land. In both cases, the relationship is parasitic as we can see in this stanza:

> She stayed too long,
> Wife and mother in one.
> When she died
> The knuckle bones were cutting the skin of her son's backside.
> And he was sixty-five.
> O he loved his mother
> Above all others.
> O he loved his ploughs.
> And he loved his cows
> And his happiest dream
> Was to clean his arse
> With perennial grass. (40)

The land and the mother are combined as lovers in this passage and Maguire is portrayed as giving his life in the service of both.

The following lines comprise part of the poem's conclusion:

> Patrick Maguire, the old peasant, can neither be damned nor glorified:
> The graveyard in which he will lie will be just a deep-drilled potato field,
> Where the seed gets no chance to come through
> To the fun of the sun.
> The tongue in his mouth is the roof of the yew.
> Silence, silence. The story is done. (55)

The poetic voice is demanding that no hyperbole be used to describe an ordinary, banal individual such as Maguire because he is neither a hero nor a villain in the life story of which he is a part. By demanding that nothing but silence should follow Maguire's death, the poem insists that no poetic representation could create anything other than a misrepresentation of the harsh and unremarkable facts of the life of such a peasant as Maguire.

An Beal Bocht (*The Poor Mouth*)

An Beal Bocht (*The Poor Mouth*) was described by its author Flann O'Brien (Brian O'Nolan) as being 'an enormous jeer at the Gaelic morons with their bicycle clips and handball medals'.[7] The novel is set in Corca Dhorbha (Corkadorey), which is a thinly concealed, parodic version of the Dingle Peninsula in the West of Ireland. This rural Irish local is far from the idealised version of Irish rurality that Gaelic Revivalists at this time wished to promote. It never stops raining and everyone is as poor as church mice although they revel in speaking their beautiful mother tongue as if that is some kind of spiritual cure for their material poverty. The book is written in the style of memoir, and the narrator whose life he is supposedly selectively recounting is named Bonapart O Cunasa.

Terence Brown has described the book as having 'comprehensively satirized the literary exploitation of the western island, in a hilarious send-up of the island reminiscence, particularly in its translated form. The life evoked in this work is so awful, so miserable, so squalid'.[8] The scenes in the book when tourists visit the island and wax lyrical about the Irish language as they observe the abject poverty of its speakers are the moments of most pointed and biting satire.

In one important passage in *An Beal Bocht*, two possibilities about the Gaelic Irish peasantry are raised together:

> –Are you certain the Gaels are people? Said I.
>
> –They have that reputation anyway, little noble, said he, but no confirmation of it has ever been received. We're not horses nor hens; seals not ghosts; and, in spite of that, it's unbelievable we're humans – but all that is only opinion.[9]

On the one hand, the suggestion here is that the harshness of the life that the Gaelic Irish must endure has made them closer in terms of resemblance to animals than 'civilised' humans. Equally, this passage can be interpreted as an allusion to how the rural Irish peasant is nearly more a figment of the collective Revivalist imagination than a collection of real, flesh and blood human beings.

Declan Kiberd has very aptly described *An Beal Bocht* as a Counter-Revival text:

> *An Beal Bocht* is not only a send up of the scenic landscape, Gothic ruins and romantic music of [Dion] Boucicault's glamorized countryside, it is, even more urgently, an attack on the Dublin revivalists of the twentieth century, who could idealize the saintly simplicity of western life, only by ignoring the awful poverty on which it was

> based. With *The Great Hunger* and *Cre na Cille*, O'Nolan's novel is a subversive anti-pastoral, a characteristic nineteen forties reaction against some pious evasions of the revivalists.[10]

O'Nolan has achieved with *An Beal Bocht* a masterful parodic satire in terms of both style and content. The genre of island reminiscences is sent up as are the assumptions of 1940s Gaelic Revivalists who have no knowledge of the harsh reality of the life that has to be endured by the West of Ireland peasants. Equally, he's also mercilessly (maybe unfairly) satirising the memoirs of Tomas Ó Croithean, Miheál Ó Súilleabháin and so on because he regards these works as misery memoirs. Thus, we can read *An Beal Bocht* as a text that is simultaneously attacking and satirising those who idealise rural Ireland and also those who paint a very bleak picture of that world and its inhabitants.

Cre na Cille (*Dirty Dust*)

Máirtín Ó Cadhain's long poem *Cre na Cille* (1949) is set in an Irish graveyard and centres around the chattering and bickering voices of the dead bodies that reside in the graves. It is important to note that these are not ghosts that are speaking, they are actually talking cadavers. The novel was a cause celebre for many years due to its foul language. For almost seventy years the only readers who could appreciate the work were those who were fluent in the Irish language. It was not until Alan Titley translated it into English in 2016 that the readership of the work expanded.

The poem is set during World War II and the dead voices have left behind them a rural Ireland that is depicted as very similar to the ones represented in 'The Great Hunger' and *An Beal Bocht* – one of great hardship and poverty in which the peasantry attempt to make a living from a land that refuses to support their needs. There is no plot to speak of in the work, just the savage tongues of the dead bodies voicing their anger and grievances repeatedly in a style that calls to mind the style that would later be referred to as 'Beckettian'. As Declan Kiberd notes, '*Cre na Cille* is punctuated not by general conversation but by collections of rival monologues, without interaction of any significant kind, as each speaker seeks to appease his or her monomania and reduce all interlocutors to silence'.[11] Such a description applies to many of the works that Beckett was to write in both prose and drama from the 1950s until the end of his career in the 1980s.

The fact that the monologues in *Cre na Cille* are all voices of the dead means that the novel could be interpreted as a precursor to the moment in *Waiting for Godot* when the two tramps lament being tormented by dead voices who would not stop talking. Ó Cadhain himself was to argue that the later works of Beckett constituted his attempt to solve the problem of living in a linguistically constituted world in which the illusion of meaning is created by possibly meaningless language: 'Beckett looked to answer the question in novels and plays of a kind not written before; and now the words themselves have been left out. Only a kind of mime remains'.[12] In *Cre na Cille*, Ó Cadhain is able to grapple with the death of language whilst at the same time implicitly acknowledging the specific decline and possibly the eventual total destruction of the Irish language in the new Free State.

Significantly, both O'Nolan and Ó Cadhain wrote their 'Counter (Gaelic) Revival works in the Irish language. O'Nolan was a huge supporter of the Irish language and once went so far as to write to Patrick Kavanagh and chided him for not being more supportive of the Irish language: 'Any notion of reviving Irish as the universal language of the country is manifestly impossible and ridiculous but the continued awareness here of the Gaelic norm of word and thought is vital to the preservation of our peculiar and admired methods of handling English'.[13] Thus, it is reasonable to argue that the target of O'Nolan's and Ó Cadhain's anti-pastoral, 'Counter-Revival vision was targeted at the idealising of the Irish language and landscape on the part of the Gaelic Revivalists rather than any real hostility to the authenticity of either language or landscape. This is equally the case with the work of Irish pastoral by Flann O'Brien as discussed above.

The Bell and Irish globalisation

The Bell magazine (1940–1954) was founded in 1940 by the writer Sean Ó Faoláin. Among the writers to contribute to its first edition were Elizabeth Bowen, Flann O'Brien, Patrick Kavanagh, Frank O'Connor and Jack B. Yeats. It also published some of the early prose works of Brendan Behan and John McGahern. *The Bell* comprised a mixture of social and literary commentary. At a time of strident Catholic conservatism and a somewhat debased remnant of Celtic Revivalism that sometimes appeared as a grotesque parody of the great days of the Irish Revival prior to the achievement of independence, *The Bell* provided, particularly under the editorship of Seán Ó Faoláin, a source of liberal and Counter-Revival commentary that helped shape the zeitgeist of this period in Irish literary and cultural history. When Peadar O'Donnell replaced Ó Faoláin as editor in the period from 1946 until the magazine's closure in 1954, editions became less frequent and the quality was somewhat more sporadic. However, *The Bell* was a valuable catalyst for exciting ideas and debate throughout its existence.

Frank O'Connor offered the following diagnosis of the ills facing Free State Ireland and its writers in the 1930s that can be interpreted as providing some of the reasons for the foundation of *The Bell*:

> After the success of the Revolution [...] Irish society began to revert to type. All the forces that had made for national dignity, that had united Catholic and Protestant, aristocrats like Countess Markievicz, Labour revolutionists like Connolly and writers like AE, began to disintegrate rapidly, and Ireland became more than ever sectarian, utilitarian, the two nearly always go together, vulgar and provincial [...] Every year that has passed, particularly since de Valera's rise to power, has strengthened the grip of the gombeen man, of the religious secret societies like the Knights of Columbanus, of the illiterate censorships [...] The significant fact about it is there is no idealistic opposition which would enable us to measure the extent of the damage.[14]

To create just such an 'idealistic opposition' to the prevailing, conservative orthodoxies of the new Ireland was certainly one of the driving ambitions that led to the founding of *The Bell* in 1940.

The editorials written by Sean Ó Faoláin during his editorial tenure were extremely exciting contributions to Irish public discourse and debate. The editorial that he wrote in 1940, 'Tradition and Creation' in vol. 2, no. 1 of *The Bell* constituted a profound demand to the Ireland of his time to be careful not to value the legacy of the past completely at the expense of radical literary experimentation.

This was something which he felt certain strands of the Revival had been guilty of: 'Our dilemma, to-day, is surely this – that we are living in a period of conflict between the definite principles of past achievement and the undefined principles of present ambition [...] The Revival of Gaelic and the Revival of Industry are not happy bedfellows'.[15] For Ó Faoláin, the need to embrace modernity, innovation and experimentation was largely antithetical to the urge to keep aligned with a Gaelic past and language that would frustrate radicality and the ability to create newness in Irish literature, culture and industry.

While Ó Faoláin expresses admiration for Yeats and Synge, he does argue that their radical embracing of tradition and experimentation is lost on those who view Revivalism as being merely an embrace of the past and a refusal to pay enough attention to the present and an undecidable future to come. Such an urge, according to Seán Ó Faoláin, can only lead to conservatism and repression: 'Whenever something backward and exhausted gathers to itself an assortment of men to serve its reactionary purposes we may be sure that it will always reach back for the oldest and deadest traditions to make out of them a crusaders banner' (12). It is not surprising that Ó Faoláin would issue a warning such as this in 1940 when one considers that World War II was raging at the time. This as a conflict that involved fascistic elements such as Mussolini's Italy and Hitler's Germany, two regimes that had come into existence as a result of the aforementioned leaders appealing to the olden times and traditions of their countries to stir up their people's patriotic fervour.

It is arguably to the best of the Revivalist period and cultural impulse that Ó Faoláin is appealing when he writes: 'If there is any distinct cleavage among us to-day it is between those who feel that tradition can explain everything, and those who think that it can explain nothing. And we need to trust in those who say: "Why cannot we use the best of both?"' (6). For Ó Faoláin the radicality of the Revival resided in that embracing of the liminal ground between the past and the present as seen in the writings of those such as Yeats, Lady Gregory, John Millington Synge, and in the best essayistic moments of D.P. Moran. This is the legacy of the Revival that Ó Faoláin was urging his generation of Irish people to embrace and ignore the absolutism and backward looking impulse that some misguided individuals took to be the central message of the Irish Revival. As Ó Faoláin has argued: 'The Irish Literary [Revival] Movement and the 1916 Rebellion killed between them the old wolf-dog and round tower Ireland' (7). Ironically, certain Irish public figures in Ó Faoláin's time sought to invoke Celtic Revivalism as a tool to revive that ancient Ireland to the complete detriment of any hope of a radical and experimental present moment.

Another important editorial written by Seán Ó Faoláin for *The Bell* appeared in vol. 2, no. 5 and was titled 'Our Nasty Novelists'. In this piece Ó Faoláin departs from the belief that was popular with many Revivalists, which was that works of art should be created with the ambition of expressing a race (in this case the Irish race) in its totality:

> What is wrong with this Type idea, this All-art-must be-Representative-of-the-Race idea, is that it is just *not* a critical implement. It does not work. There is no such person as a typical Englishman, or a typical Irishman. The infinite variety of human nature rejects such an intellectual abstraction for what it is, and literature illustrates the depth of its folly. Thus, Hamlet can hardly be a typical Englishman (or Dane) except to those who believe that all Englishman (or Danes) believe in ghosts, behave outrageously to women, kill their uncles and their uncles' employees, and spend their spare time mooning about in graveyards.[16]

Whilst many Revivalist artists and thinkers thought and expressed their ideas concerning Ireland and Irishness in terms of collective nouns and first person plurals, Ó Faoláin is advocating a view of the Irish people and their numerous, individual identities that is more embracing of the first person singular.

Ó Faoláin was living in an Ireland in which Joyce's *Ulysses* was beginning to be regarded by the artistic and critical establishment as being 'the great Irish epic' in which the uncreated conscience of the race had been forged. Ó Faoláin was certainly not of that opinion: 'Of all the people in Ireland who ever have heard of James Joyce, how many have even read a line of him? I remember my long debate with a commercial traveller about *Ulysses* which ended when I found that he thought the author was George Bernard Shaw' (10). Joyce would probably have been in sympathy with Ó Faoláin's view about art's relationship to nation since *Ulysses* is a work that is often in open revolt against absolutist notions of nationality, race, and the possibility of ethically representing a people in any pure, totalising fashion. This is particular apparent in the 'Cyclops' episode of that 'epic' work.

Ó Faoláin makes the radical argument in this editorial that it is in the genre of literary realism that a nation and a people have the best chance of authentic representation. He makes it clear that he is not referring to a form of writing that is totally documentary-like in style and devoid of any literary or artistic qualities. Ó Faoláin says that he thinks that all realists are two thirds Romantics and vice versa for all so-called literary Romantics (9). In Ó Faoláin's opinion, only the Realists can disabuse the Irish people of such unrealistic notions such as the possibility that the Irish language will ever be more than a minority language spoken mainly by elitists in Dublin who do so primarily so they can feel superior to the 'plebian' Dubliners. In essence, embracing realism will show people the impossibility of a totally successful Gaelic Revival in Ireland.

A year before the foundation of *The Bell*, Flann O'Brien's celebrated 'proto-postmodern novel' *At Swim-Two-Birds* was published. This work can be read as the realisation and anticipation of several of Ó Faoláin's points about what an ideal Irish work of literature should look like. O'Brien embraces Celtic mythology in that book but does so in a way that is partly comic rather than wholly referential and deferential. Equally, it is a work that is explicitly on the side of the individual rather than collective. Because of this, Ó Faoláin would almost certainly have described *At Swim-Two-Birds* as a work that is thematically realistic but experimental in style.

Ó Faoláin also wrote numerous editorials in which he took aim at the idealising of Irish rurality in a manner similar to several works by Kavanagh, O'Nolan and Ó Cadhain (as discussed above): 'If there once was an old association of the Peasant with Liberty it is all over. The romantic illusion, fostered by the Celtic Twilight, that the West of Ireland, with its red petticoats and bawneens, is for some reason more Irish than Guinness Brewery or Dwyers' Sunbeam-Wolsey factory, has no longer any basis whatsoever'.[17] It is clear, therefore, that *The Bell* was engaged in, and in some cases helped influence, the zeitgeist of 1940s Counter-Revival Ireland in a way that shaped cultural discourse in the succeeding decades concerning the role of literature and the arts in Irish public discourse and debate over what constituted an 'authentic' vision of Irishness. As Elke D'Hoker and Phylis Boumans have argued in their article on *The Bell*: 'Periodicals do not just reflect or sustain literary consensus, but are active players in the literary field. Through their structure of periodicity and repetition, they have the power to generate and shape readerly expectations, generic conventions and literary taste'.[18] These are certainly achievements for which the periodical *The Bell* can be given credit in the context of Irish literary and cultural discourse.

What Irish Counter-Revivalists do:

1. **They critique the perceived essentialisms of the Irish Literary and Cultural Revival with regards to representations of nation, race and culture in an Irish context.**
2. **They attempt to open post-independence Ireland up to European literary and cultural influences.**
3. **They very often deconstruct easy assumptions concerning the utopian qualities of Irish rurality that certain Revivalists could be accused of promoting.**
4. **The notion of Irish literature producing a stable conception of an 'Irish National Tale' is very often critiqued in Counter-Revival literary and cultural texts.**

Representative textual analyses

Counter-Revival short stories

The short story has a long history in the canon of Irish literature and some of Ireland's most famous authors have contributed to this genre. Frank O'Connor wrote one of the great studies of the Irish short story titled 'The Lonely Voice' (1962) in the aftermath of his great career as a creative writer in that form. In that study O'Connor famously argued: 'Always in the short story there is this sense of outlaw figures wandering around the fringes of society'.[19] These attitudes of rebellion, defiance and alienation that are to be found in the central characters of short stories, as argued by O'Connor, made this literary form a perfect medium to represent the sense of disillusionment and disappointment that constituted the spirit of Counter-Revival Irish culture.

William Trevor has written this assessment of the short story form and why it has been so successful in Irish literature:

> It is occasionally argued that the Irish genius for the short story is related to the fact that when the novel reared its head the Irish were not ready for it. This is certainly true. In England, for instance, the great Victorian novel had been fed by the architecture of a rich, stratified society in which complacency and hypocrisy, accompanied by the ill-treatment of the unfortunate and the poor, provided both fictional material and ground for protest ... In Ireland there was dissatisfaction, repressed religion, the confusion of two languages, and the spectre of the Famine [...] Stories, far more than novels, cast spells, and spells have been nurtured in Ireland for as long as imperial greed has been attempting to hammer its people into a subject class [...] English fiction writers tend to state that their short stories are leavings from their novels. In Ireland, I have heard it put the other way round.[20]

Trevor's argument – which is an echo of Seán Ó Faoláin's and Frank O'Connor's assessments of the short story in Ireland – is that, because of Ireland's colonial and then postcolonial status, it has not really attained the status of a 'made' and stable society that would facilitate the growth of an Irish novelistic tradition. Because the novel is normally a genre associated with knowable and tightly structured nations and societies, Ireland was not very well suited to that genre's styles of representation. Thus, the short story as a form was utilised by many prose writers during the decades following the foundation of the Irish state and then after the official declaration of an Irish Republic in 1949.

What follows shall be an examination of two short stories by major exponents of that literary form, Frank O'Connor and Edna O'Brien. How they use the formal qualities of the short story mode to present a Counter-Revival view of Ireland shall be of primary importance to this analysis.

'Guests of the Nation'

This famous short story by Frank O'Connor offers a critique of the Irish War of independence with the benefit of ten years' temporal distance. It was published in 1931 and focusses on the relationship with individual IRA rebels and their hostages during that three-year conflict. The title is contradictory on several levels. The Irish 'nation' did not actually exist during that conflict, and the 'guests' could refer to either the hostages or the rebels. None of them felt completely connected to the Ireland of this time because they were either English or, in the case of the Irish characters, members of the working class who would not have been respected as being on an equal footing with the more affluent Irish who resided in this 'Irish nation' of the imagination. These are the themes and issues that are dealt with during this ten-page story. Ultimately, it explores how the English and Irish characters felt more of an affinity with each other because they were all of the same class than they word have felt with their fellow countrymen who were class and military superiors. Thus, 'Guests of the Nation' challenges notions of a unified, equal Irish nation and a singular Irish identity that many Irish Revivalists had championed prior to Irish independence.

The story begins with a description of the camaraderie that existed between the rebels and their hostages: 'After the first couple of days we gave up trying to keep an eye on them'.[21] The relationship between the main characters is portrayed from the outset as being as far from that of captor and prisoner as it is possible to be. We are even told at the beginning of the story that the Irish captors have picked up some of the English prisoners' phraseology.

The English prisoner Hawkins is ironically given the dialogue that probably summed up the opinions of many ordinary Irish people in Ireland at that time: 'The capitalists pay the priest to tell you about the next world so that you won't notice what the bastards are up to in this' (344). This causes an argument with the Irish rebel Noble who gives voice to the traditional voice of Catholic conservatism that became the norm in the new Free State: 'Before ever a capitalist was thought of people believed in the next world' (344). Encouraging a focus on the next world and not worrying too much about the problems in this one is considered one of the great strategies used by the Catholic Church and certain politicians to curb social discontent.

Despite the camaraderie between these men, there is still the ever present threat of execution of the prisoners if the English soldiers shoot four of their IRA prisoners. This scenario transpires and Hawkins and Belcher are taken out and shot by the senior officer Jeremiah Donovan and buried by the unnamed narrator and Noble. The description of the moments before the execution is harrowing as the soldiers beg for their lives. Hawkins even goes so far as offering to defect to the Irish side in the war, showing how little affinity he feels with 'his nation' of England.

The narrator says that he does not remember much of the burial, which implies how traumatic he found the experience since he cannot engage with it in the immediate moment of its happening. Noble and the narrator are both clearly psychologically impacted by the executions as evidenced by Noble's subjective perception of the place where the bodies of the English soldiers are buried, which has expanded in his mind's eye so that it is twice the size it was before. In contrast, the narrator perceives the bog that now contains their two prisoners' bodies as having shrunk as if it were a million miles away (353). For both men, the killings are now contained in their minds as traumatically subjective perception rather than as objective, 'real' spaces. The concluding lines of the story have the narrator describing himself as feeling 'very lost and lonely like a child' (353). Thus, this narrator has become a prime example of one of the lonely voices that Frank O'Connor associated with short story narratives.

It is significant that Frank O'Connor wrote a biography of Michael Collins, the celebrated IRA commander and Anglo-Irish Treaty signatory, in 1937. This book, which O'Connor described as a labour of love, signals O'Connor's desire to move away from the prescriptive Republican outlook that was prevalent in Ireland during the aftermath of its bloody Civil War and embrace a more hospitable version of Irishness that would accommodate various political and identitarian outlooks. In O'Connor's foreword to this biography, he describes Collins as being of so great a value to his country because he was 'a realist'. 'It is as a realist that Collins will be remembered, and as a realist he should be an inspiration to the new Ireland. From the Civil War and the despair that followed it sprang a new honesty in

Irish life and thought. The old sentimentalism against which Collins almost unconsciously strove has suffered'.[22] When referring to Irish sentimentalism, O'Connor does not explicitly reference Revivalism and the prescriptive and somewhat idealistic nationalist politics with which it was (sometimes unfairly) associated. It is clear that he regards Collins as being a rebel against sentimental views of Ireland and her postcolonial future to come. Thus, O'Connor's Michael Collins is a perfect encapsulation of both the disillusionment that many writers and thinkers felt following the foundation of the Free State and also an example of how a realistic outlook on postcolonial Ireland could help shape a positive future for that infant nation. In essence, that is what Counter-Revivalists such as O'Connor, Ó Faoláin, Patrick Kavanagh and Flann O'Brien strived to achieve, albeit in often radical and experimental ways.

The importance of the life and legacy of Michael Collins to post-independence Irish literature and culture (as seen in the writings of Frank O'Connor) has been ably demonstrated by Tim Pat Coogan in his definitive biography of The Big Fellow, published in 1991. As Coogan passionately asserts:

> [Collins] did not like The Treaty he signed with England, but he and most of his closest friends and advisors regarded it as a stepping stone to full independence and a united Ireland, and the best he could do for the moment. His death ensured that the moment would be a long one and this generation lives with its consequences. The choices Collins had to make, the tensions and bitterness that led to the creation of modern Ireland, have a bearing on the atrocities of today, and perhaps more importantly, on those of tomorrow. If we wish to understand today's tragedies and perhaps avert them, it is essential to know and learn from the story of Michael Collins.[23]

The conflicted but ultimately realistic feelings that Collins felt about the Treaty he signed with Britain and the Ireland that would emerge from that act are mirrored in the works of the Irish Counter-Revivalists that have been the subject of this chapter, as are the scars of the Civil War that raged as a result of the passing of the Treaty by the Irish parliament by a majority of 64 votes to 57. The Civil War and its terrible results is certainly something that is lamented by O'Connor in his book on Collins in which the death of The Big Fellow is portrayed as one of the greatest tragedies in Irish history. 'Guests of the Nation', although set during the Irish War of Independence and not the Civil War, is written in a coldly realistic style and outlook that portrays the revolutionary period as a supreme tragedy. This was also a reality that Collins came to realise before his tragic death made him a martyr to that tragedy.

'Irish Revel'

Edna O'Brien's 'Irish Revel' (1962) begins, as do most short stories, in the middle of a tale rather than at the beginning of one:

> Mary had hoped that the rotted front tyre would not burst. As it was, the tube had a slow puncture, and twice she had to stop and use the pump … For as long as she could remember she had been pumping bicycles, carting turf, cleaning outhouses, doing man's work … Theirs was a mountainy farm in Ireland, and life was hard.[24]

From the commencement of this story, we are given a picture of Mary as someone who is leading a very unglamorous life. As a woman she is expected to stay at home and look after the family and the farm – an existence that she finds less than satisfying. This is no rural paradise in Ireland and, by the author's own admission, life is tough. The text inserts a subtle and powerful allusion in the story to the fact that Mary is doing 'man's work' at home. This is clever because it undermines the myth that women can keep their feminine identity best in the domestic realm. According to Mary, it is staying at home that is turning her into a manly woman. Thus, conformity can provide unlooked for opportunities for subversion.

Mary is plagued with the memory of a man that she met years ago, and her desire to see him again is what constantly occupies her mind. How she perceives her own body is bound up with thinking about how he would view her: 'Now and then, she smiled at the thought of how she would appear to him – taller and with breasts now, and a dress that could be worn anywhere. She forgot about the rotted tyre, got up and cycled' (497). The thought of this stranger who she met once dictates her mood and the reader is left to infer that this encounter means far more to her than it probably does to the man. The whole story revolves around ideal perception and the disappointing reality. Mary is expecting that she is going to be invited to attend a party and then she finds out that she has been invited for the purpose of being a waitress.

The petty bigotry of Ireland at this time is exposed through the characters of Doris and Eithne who look down on Mary because they do not like shy mountainy people. They also are very quick to label someone a Jew because of the size of one's nose. The snobbery that the town people feel towards the rural dwellers in this book indicates an Ireland that is divided rather than united with all its inhabitants regarded as equal.

Like Joyce's 'The Dead', this story centres on a party, although the characters at this party (predominantly men) are far less attractive. Mary is portrayed as an object for these men to commodify with their leering gazes. The fact that she is from a rural area seems to lend her a certain exotic quality:

> To him [Mr O'Toole] she looked far prettier than those good-for nothing towngirls – she was tall and thin like himself; she had long black hair that some people might think streelish, but not him, he liked long hair and simple minded girls; maybe later on he'd get her into one of the other rooms where they could do it. She had funny eyes when you looked into them, brown and deep, like a bloody bog-hole. (504)

Mary is thus objectified by Mr O'Toole's gaze and considered purely on a superficial level. The contact that Mr O'Toole plans to have with her is entirely physical. The comparison between her eyes and a bog-hole shows how her rural identity is bound up with the attraction that she holds for him. This passage perfectly encapsulates how the male gaze can operate when it is directed at women, just as Gabriel's gaze in 'The Dead' attempted to objectify Gretta but was ultimately thwarted because of his inability to see her face. Equally, Mr O'Toole's treatment of Mary is comparable to Gabriel's patriarchal attitude towards the maid Lily when he thrusts a coin into her hand, thus establishing gender and class advantage over her. In O'Brien's famous novel *Country Girls*, the main character Kate is an avid reader of Joyce's *Dubliners* and this can be interpreted as O'Brien projecting her own admiration of that short story collection onto one of her fictional characters.

Near the story's conclusion, the girls forget their differences in an effort to eject Mr O'Toole from their room. This moment represents an alliance of women against a male threat which (although only fleeting) suggests a feminist allegiance. Of course, by the next morning, Doris and Eithne are back to calling Mary the sneaky one and the old differences have returned.

The story closes with Mary alone and wishing that she had someone to love her. The image of her standing on the side of the road is rendered all the more bleak by the following description: 'Frost was general all over Ireland; frost like a weird blossom on the branches, on the river-bank from which Long John Salmon leaped in the great, hairy nakedness' (514). The image of frost being general all over Ireland is a re-wording of the famous description at the end of 'The Dead', of snow being general all over Ireland. In contrast, Edna O'Brien's vision is much harder and bleaker than Joyce's depiction of an Irish landscape united by picturesque snow. We leave Mary returning to her home and to the domestic realm that was considered the proper place for Irish women at this time.

Like many short stories written during this period, 'Irish Revel' offers a bleak and disappointed representation of post-independence, post-Revival Ireland. Life is dull, depressing, and without a sense of hope for the future that animated the texts of various genres that were produced during the Revival and prior to the establishment of the Irish Free State, particularly a story like Joyce's 'The Dead'. Edna O'Brien is also committed in this story and in many of her other writings to show how independent Ireland was particularly hard for the women who inhabited that postcolonial nation. This is a topic that shall be examined in greater detail in Chapter 4.

Waiting for Godot and *The Quare Fellow*: the Irish dramatic counter-tradition?

Waiting for Godot is regarded as one of the most influential plays of the twentieth century and a defining example of what the critic Martin Esslin has called 'Theatre of the Absurd'. This type of theatre has various distinguishing elements. It has its roots in the experimental drama of the 1920s and 1930s and also the horrors of World War

II. The plays are generally concerned with language breakdown, the absence of a traditional, linear theatrical plot, and many of the characters feature as double acts, often appearing as caricatures with no sign of depth or inner life; time and history are rendered as problematic concepts. This chapter's consideration of *Godot* shall examine how Beckett's (Anglo-)Irishness can be regarded as being intrinsic to his postmodern and absurdist dramatic vision.

Despite the fact that Beckett never surrendered his Irish passport and that when he was asked by a French journalist whether he regarded himself as being English his response was 'au contraire', the Irishness of Beckett and especially the presence of Ireland in his work has been a vexed question for generations of Beckett scholars. Former UCD English Professor J.C.C. Mays gave the following account of the evolution of the study of the 'Irish Beckett' in an article he wrote in 1984, explaining how long it took for Beckett to be accepted as an Irish writer within the corridors and publishing houses of academia:

> The fact is, Beckett's incorporation into the Irish tradition is recent. You could sum up the change that has taken place by looking at the syllabus for the MA in Anglo-Irish Studies at University College. Fifteen years ago, he was nowhere mentioned: it was all Synge, Yeats, Lady Gregory, O'Casey. The year he won the Nobel Prize (1969), two lectures were slipped-in halfway through the academic year. This was regularized in 1970, and the next year again (1971) Beckett began to share the tail-end of a course with Joyce. Three years later (1974), he was taught separately, at last getting a course to himself, like Yeats and Joyce. Another way to sum up the change is to notice that Maurice Harmon's *Modern Irish Literature 1800–1967: A Reader's Guide* (Dolmen Press 1967), which was a standard introduction and survey of the subject as it was then understood in Ireland, contains no mention of Beckett: the assumption was that Beckett was not an Irish writer. By contrast, the updated version published by Wolfhound Press in 1977, a decade later, includes Beckett along with Yeats and Joyce.[25]

Professor Mays has highlighted the cultural myopia that existed until quite recently in Beckett studies regarding his relationship to his country of birth. Many critics will cite Beckett's observation that he would rather be in France at war than Ireland at peace as evidence that he saw himself as more of a European writer than an Irish one.

This could conceivably have been as a result of Irish academia's instinct at the time when this essay was written (in the mid-1980s) to ignore Irish Counter-Revival literature more generally.

In recent times, however, academic attention has turned increasingly towards Beckett's Irishness and the impact that he had on Irish literature in the twentieth century. Anthony Roche has gone so far as to affirm that: 'the presiding genius of contemporary Irish drama, the ghostly founding father, is Samuel Beckett'. John P. Harrington, in his essay 'Samuel Beckett and the Countertradition', speaks of Beckett's Irishness but primarily in relation to Harrington's perception of Beckett as forging a more international and open dramatic tradition than the one pioneered by the Irish Revivalists. Harrington said in relation to the bleak and bare setting of waiting for Godot: 'This certainly was not so recognisably "Irish" as the countryside setting of Synge's *The Playboy of the Western World* (1907) or the tenement of O'Casey's *Juno and the Paycock*'.[26]

For Harrington, Beckett's Irishness rests on his attempts to make Irish more European and thus allow for a new conception of Irishness, post-World War II. Harrington concludes his essay with his assertion of the value of the dual traditions in Irish drama: 'Irish drama, by incorporation of both its tradition, as represented by Synge and O'Casey, and its countertradition, as epitomised by Beckett and his younger admirers, establishes its national identity in an international context and so claims its place in the history of the twentieth century.[27] Arguably, both *Waiting for Godot* and Brendan Behan's *The Quare Fellow* are examples of Irish drama that works against the dramatic traditions that had become concretised during the Irish Revival. These plays can be regarded as being both in and out of the prevalent Irish dramatic tradition, in much the same way as Joyce's relationship with the Revival consisted of both rejection and acceptance. Anthony Roche has provided the most thorough comparative analysis of *Waiting for Godot* and *The Quare Fellow* in his influential study *Contemporary Irish Drama: From Beckett to McGuinness*.

As Roche has written about extensively, both plays premiered at the Pike Theatre in Dublin in the 1950s, *The Quare Fellow* in 1954 and *Waiting for Godot* in 1955. The fifty-seat theatre was perfectly suited to enhance the sense of incarceration and surveillance that is prevalent in both dramas.

It is important at this point to outline what are the similarities between these two superficially very different plays. The importance of waiting is paramount in both plays; neither have a central character/hero/heroine; a sense of imprisonment pervades both works, the influence of music hall farce is apparent in their dramatic styles; and the story that is contained on their stages can be characterised as black and tragi-comedies. Although *The Quare Fellow* can be described as being the more obvious 'Irish play' of the two, close examination of *Godot* reveals its debt to earlier Irish dramatic works by playwrights such as Yeats.

Waiting for Godot's opening stage directions, far from being utterly different from those of any other Irish play, actually bear striking similarities to those of Yeats' 1938 drama, *Purgatory*:

> [*Purgatory*:] A ruined house and a bare tree in the background.[28]
> [*Waiting for Godot*:] A country road. A tree. Evening.[29]

The themes of exile, nomadism and the treacherousness of history unite *Purgatory* and *Godot*, and this comparison between their opening stage directions links Beckett very definitely with one of the founders of twentieth-century drama in Ireland.

Equally, Synge's *Well of the Saints*, with its two tramps who forsake realism and insight for blindness and faith in a god they do not really believe in, also serves as an important intertext, or silent presence, in *Waiting for Godot*. Beckett voiced his admiration for Irish Revival drama when he was asked to write a greeting for a tribute to George Bernard Shaw on the centenary of his birth in 1956. Beckett declined, preferring to praise O'Casey's *Juno and the Paycock*, Synge's *Well of the Saints* and Yeats' *At the Hawk's Well*: 'I wouldn't suggest that G.B.S. is not a great playwright, whatever that is when it's at home. What I would do is give the whole unupsettable applecart for a sup of the *Hawk's Well*, or the *Saints*, or a whiff of *Juno*, to go no further'.[30] What this suggests is that Beckett prefers recognisably Irish dramas to those of Shaw, which were primarily set in England. Also, Beckett's reference to Shaw's 'unupsettable apple cart' implies that he is not a huge fan of the highly regimented style of realism and naturalism that Shavian drama uses and prefers instead a less traditional, more experimental and modernist drama such as Yeats' *At the Hawks Well.*

Unlike *Waiting for Godot*, *The Quare Fellow* is explicitly set in Ireland, specifically 1950s Ireland. The version of post-independence Ireland is far from idealised or utopian. What we are presented with onstage is a country riven with class inequality and one that has retained capital punishment from colonial British law. As John Brannigan argues: 'The prison setting of the play is an obvious dystopian site, and, like the various representations of emigration and poverty in writings contemporaneous with *The Quare Fellow*, serves as a strong counter-point to the self-serving narrative of progress and contentment proffered in post-independence political discourse'.[31] This description of the setting and the plot of *The Quare Fellow* highlights how it is a text that fits well into the Counter-Revival vision of Ireland that was common in literary, cultural and dramatic works at this time.

Anthony Roche has made a similar argument concerning how the setting and story of *The Quare Fellow* helped provide a political message that was cutting edge at the time the play was first staged: 'Part of *The Quare Fellow*'s socialist design is to bring its bourgeois audience beyond the public façade inside the prison, to chart in excruciating detail the processes involved in the hanging of a man'.[32]

The representation of post-independence Ireland in *The Quare Fellow* highlights the disappointment that the new Irish state was for many people in Ireland at this time. It takes the story of the impending execution of a prisoner and uses it to show how little has changed in Ireland since independence had been achieved. As the character of Dunlavin pithily observes: 'When the Free State came in, we were afraid they were going to change the mattresses for feather beds […] But sure, thanks to God, the Free State didn't change anything more than the badge on the warders' caps'.[33] The implication was that colonial Ireland was a prison and post-colonial Ireland essentially just another style of prison.

Although *The Quare Fellow* is set in urban Dublin, references to rural Ireland and its inhabitants appear several times in the dialogue and paint an Anti-Revivalist view of Irish rurality, particularly in relation to how non-rural Irish people feel about their fellow countrymen and women. Dunlavin distinguishes between two different prisoners on the basis of their background more than the facts of their crimes:

> Yes, and then of course the other fellow used a meat chopper. Real bog man act. Nearly as bad as a shotgun, or getting the weed-killer mixed up in the stirabout. But a man with a silver topped cane, that's a man that's a cut above meat-choppers whichever way you look at it. (52)

This assertion shows Dunlavin's urban prejudice against rural 'bog men' and also admiration for those who are more demonstrably upper class. This shows how class distinction was still rife in Ireland despite the hopes of Republican Rebels and Socialists such as James Connolly.

The continuing decline of the Irish language, something that many Revivalists such as Synge and D.P. Moran wished to combat, is mockingly alluded to in one line from *The Quare Fellow* spoken by the prison Governor: 'We advertised for a native hangman during the Economic War. Must be fluent Irish speaker [...] There were no suitable applicants' (112). Although Behan was a highly proficient Irish speaker, unlike an Anglo-Irishman like Beckett, he was sufficiently realistic to realise that not even independence could revive the Irish language on a large scale.

Beckett's and Behan's experiences during World War II may have contributed to their disillusionment with the Irish state. Beckett fought for the French resistance against Nazism whilst the country of his birth chose neutrality and refused to contribute to the struggle against totalitarian dictatorship. Behan spent most of the war interned in the Curragh detention camp because of the Irish government's determination to negate the threat of Republican terrorism. Thus, we can see why they might not feel a great affinity with the government of Ireland even as they still took inspiration from its dramatic examples and techniques.

The lack of a leading man is a common feature in Irish drama and this is certainly the case in *Waiting for Godot* and *The Quare Fellow* where we have various characters attempting to seize control of the stage whilst constantly being undercut by their fellow stage participants. Vladimir and Estragon represent a common trope of Irish theatre: the all-male duo. Whether that is Jack and Algy in Wilde's *The Importance of Being Earnest*, Joxer and the Captain in O'Casey's *Juno and the Paycock*, or Gar Public and Private in Brian Friel's *Philadelphia Here I Come*, the last hundred years have seen the theatres of Ireland filled with homosocial pairs playing off each other in Laurel and Hardy-like fashion. These characters that exist in an almost symbiotic relationship of interdependence may represent the split mindset of colonial Ireland where the people have to live in the knowledge of being divided between two cultures: a colonial one and a native one that is constantly being invented and re-invented:

> ESTRAGON: What exactly did we ask him [Godot] for?
> VLADIMIR: Were you not there?
> ESTRAGON: I can't have been listening.
> VLADIMIR: Oh … nothing very definite.
> ESTRAGON: A kind of prayer.
> VLADIMIR: Precisely.
> ESTRAGON: A vague supplication.
> VLADIMIR: Exactly …
> VLADIMIR: Consult his family.
> ESTRAGON: His friends.
> VLADIMIR: His agents (18)

What exchanges of dialogue like this one give us is the impression of two psyches that need each other to form a whole. What one of them says would not be complete without the other one to respond.

Anthony Roche has also observed that both *Godot* and *The Quare Fellow* have characters in their titles that are referred to constantly in their plots but are never seen onstage. This frustrating of audience expectations is a key facet of modern and contemporary drama. It allows for the subversion of traditional notions of dramatic plot and facilitates new forms of postmodern dramaturgy.

One of the most important versions of *Waiting for Godot* from an Irish perspective was Walter Asmus' production, which opened in October 1991 at the Gate Theatre and has been revived many times since. Vladimir was played by Barry McGovern and Estragon by Johnny Murphy. The casting of these two actors in the main roles was important owing to the fact that they both had recognisably Irish (and specifically Dublin) accents. As Brian Singleton has observed: 'But this [Asmus' Godot] was no stage-Irish comic accretion … This was the siting of Beckett's tramp poets amid the wanderers of Synge and Yeats, their displacement made all the more poignant and, indeed, political by the locating nature of their accents'.[34] Singleton's assessment of this version of Beckett's play also highlights the element of his work that unites him with less problematically Irish writers like Synge and Yeats and that is the presence of the figure of the peasant and tramp.

In an introduction to the Selected plays of Brian Friel, Seamus Deane anticipated Singleton's observations concerning some of the primary features of modern Irish drama: 'Since the beginning of this [the twentieth] century, Irish drama has been heavily populated by people for whom vagrancy and exile have become inescapable conditions about which they can do nothing but talk, endlessly and eloquently and usually to themselves. The tramps of Yeats and Synge *and Beckett* [my italics], the stationless slum dwellers of O'Casey or Behan, bear a striking resemblance to Friel's exiles.[35]

While the works of Yeats and other Revival dramatists in the earlier part of the twentieth century had a more certain attitude regarding identity and history as stable entities, *Waiting for Godot* and *The Quare Fellow* celebrate the unnatural and the instability inherent in such categories. The characters in *Waiting for Godot* seem to inhabit roles that they are not entirely comfortable with and which they seem to be almost coerced into playing by an unseen force:

> *(Enter Vladimir agitatedly. He halts and looks long at the tree, then suddenly begins to move feverishly about the stage. He halts before the boots, picks one up, examines it, sniffs it, manifests disgust, put it back carefully. Comes and goes … Halts suddenly and begins to sing loudly.)*
>
> VLADIMIR: A dog came in – *(Having begun too high he stops, clears his throat, resumes).* A dog came in the kitchen and stole a crust of bread. Then cook up with a ladle. And beat him until he was dead. (57)

Vladimir's agitated manner on the stage seems to indicate his being flustered by the fact that he knows he must perform for an audience but his not sure what pose or position on stage to adopt. His bursting into song represents his fulfilling the assigned role of performer however inappropriate his actions may seem. The fact that he is singing at this moment when there is no reason for him to be doing so highlights the unnatural and overly theatrical performance he is being forced to play. The numerous stage directions contain regular instructions about how and when the characters should move, which illustrates how controlling this stage is of the characters upon it. In his extended monologue near the conclusion of the drama, Vladimir admits he knows that his identity is an unnatural creation for theatre: 'At me too someone is looking, of me too someone is saying. He is sleeping, he knows nothing, let him sleep on' (91).

The Quare Fellow also revels in the performative nature of personal identity, which is made clear at the beginning and end of each of the play's acts when an unseen prisoner sings the famous song 'The Auld Triangle'. This device emphasises the importance of performance to the play's style, themes and structure. At the conclusion of *The Quare Fellow*, the execution of the titular character is not seen onstage and instead another prisoner provides a humorous, overtly theatrical commentary:

> We're ready for the start, and in good time, and who do I see lined up for the off but the High Sheriff of this ancient city of ours, famous in song and story as the place where the pig ate the whitewash brushes and [*The warders remove their caps.*] We're off, in this order: The Governor, the Chief, two screws Regan and Crimmin, the quare fellow between them. (120)

This piece of pseudo-reportage, which is also a parody of sports commentary, highlights how the characters in this play are constantly having to play roles in this carceral space in which everything and everyone is kept under constant surveillance. The choric figure of Warden Regan gives voice to the dark reality about capital punishment. It is state-sponsored murder that contains all the formal ritualism of a stage performance: 'I think the whole show should be put on in Croke Park; after all, it's at the public expense and they let it go. They should have something more for their money than a bit of paper stuck up on the gate' (114).

In 2023/2024, the Abbey Theatre put on a production of *The Quare Fellow* in which most of the male characters were played by women. The radicality of this casting choice resided in how it reminds its audience that one of the forced performances that is staged in this drama is that of masculinity itself. This is evident in the fact that the machismo that is displayed by many characters in this play does not seem natural but rather a version of camp-masculinity through which the characters come across not as natural but, rather, what Oscar Wilde would call 'painfully natural'.

An Irish reading of *Waiting for Godot* illuminates Beckett's refusal to subscribe to a grand narrative of Irishness and his desire to expose any rigid form of identity category as being a scripted performance imposed on people by sociocultural forces. In Beckettian drama, we very often encounter enactments of Oscar Wilde's assertion that: 'The world is a stage, but the play is badly cast'.[36] While Revival drama was steeped in the so-called history and tradition of Ireland, *Waiting for Godot* seems to lack any concrete sense of the past or any notion of tradition. When Vladimir asks Estragon if he cannot even remember the events of the previous day, Estragon says: 'Either I forget immediately or I never forget' (58). There is no sense of a past (immediate or distant) for these characters to draw on which leaves them living in a cultural vacuum. This is what Declan Kiberd has said about the recurrent amnesia experienced by the characters:

> On the stage of *Waiting for Godot* is enacted the amnesia which afflicts an uprooted people … Such lost souls can, paradoxically, be as deadened by habit as by forgetfulness … As a victim of a history which he does not understand, Gogo must deal with every situation as if it were a wholly new event. In the face of that terror, he enacts – as do all people whose past have been denied them – the invention of traditions.[37]

While the Revivalist writers, albeit in a myriad of different ways, were confident that there was an Irish history and a tradition to be reconnected with, Beckett wishes to demonstrate the impossibility of such an achievement. The repetition that constitutes the structure of this play can be seen as encapsulating George Santayana's famous quote: 'Those who cannot remember the past are doomed to repeat it'.[38] This is somewhat comparable to the repetition of the same song at the beginning of Acts in *The Quare Fellow* as it emphasises the repetitious nature of life in prison and how the same habits and rituals are repeated on a daily basis until you are granted some kind of release, either from the prison or from life itself.

When history or the passage of time is in anyway present in *Waiting for Godot*, it is portrayed as something frightening and nightmarish:

> ESTRAGON: All the dead voices.
> VLADIMIR: They make a noise like wings.

ESTRAGON: Like leaves.
VLADIMIR: Like sand.
ESTRAGON: Like leaves …
VLADIMIR: To have lived is not enough for them.
ESTRAGON: They have to talk about it. (62–63)

The uncertainty of what the dead voices are trying to communicate makes them frighteningly indeterminate and the possibility of the two tramps learning anything from these figures from the past is nil. Pozzo seems also to be a victim of history as he says to Vladimir: 'Have you not done tormenting me with your accursed time! (80)' Near the end, when Vladimir wonders 'was I sleeping whilst the others suffered, am I sleeping now?' (23) he may have been obliquely referring to what his mentor James Joyce had written in *Ulysses*: 'History is a nightmare from which I am trying to awake' because of the shared linkage between sleep and nightmarish suffering (42).

The use of language in *Waiting for Godot* stands in stark contrast to the poetic style of Yeats and Synge. This text concentrates on the evacuation of meaning in speech in an even more extreme way than McDonagh was later to do. The characters' incessant talking to each never seems to allow for any really meaningful moment of communication and language fails in its goal of connecting people. Nowhere is this more evident than in Lucky's famous monologue near the close of Act 1:

> Given the existence as uttered forth in the public works of Puncher and Wattman of a personal God quaquaquaqua with white beard quaquaquaqua outside time without extension who from the heights of divine apathia divine athambia divine aphasia loves us dearly with some exceptions for reasons unknown but time will tell. (42–43)

This speech, with its lack of organising grammatical structures such as full stops, echoes the final episode of *Ulysses*, which contains only eight full stops over sixty odd pages. It also enacts Stephen Dedalus' observations on Joyce's *Portrait of the Artist* about the potential strangeness of the English language to an Irish person: 'The language in which we are speaking is his [the English dean of studies] before it is mine. How different are the words *home*, *Christ*, *ale*, *master*, on his lips and one mine! I cannot speak or write these words without unrest of spirit'.[39] On Lucky's lips, words that we habitually utter seem very strange and this can be linked to the anxiety of a colonial people who know that they are speaking a language not their own and thus have a right to regard English as a strange language. It was Beckett's desire to escape the traps of speaking an imposed English language from which he felt alienated that led him to write *Godot* and many of his earlier works in French before having them translated into English, mainly by himself. Also, when Beckett said he wrote in French so he could write without style, he added that he wanted to get away from the 'Anglo-Irish exuberance and automatisms' in his language.[40]

One of the inspirations for Beckett's turn towards writing in French is very conceivably Oscar Wilde's symbolist drama *Salome* (1892), which Wilde originally wrote in French. The reason Wilde gave for doing so was as follows:

> I have one instrument that I know I can command, and that is the English language. There was another instrument to which I had listened all my life, and I wanted once to touch this new instrument to see whether I could make any beautiful thing out of it. [...] Of course, there are modes of expression that a Frenchman of letters would not have used, but they give a certain relief or colour to the play. A great deal of the curious effect that Maeterlinck produces comes from the fact that he, a Flamand by grace, writes in an alien language. The same thing is true of Rossetti, who, though he wrote in English, was essentially Latin in temperament.[41]

Wilde saw that he had mastered a language that was in essence foreign to him and had partly been imposed on him and his people by colonial influences, now he wished to turn to another language that was not naturally his but one which he chose of his volition to utilise. Also, like Beckett, Wilde saw the value of writing in a foreign tongue because he could create something new as a result of the language's strangeness to him. This was something that would not be possible for a native speaker of French since such a speaker would have been using the language in a more programmatic fashion.

Beckett's emphasis on language's failure is something that contrasts him with Joyce (and also Wilde). As Beckett himself has written:

> With Joyce the difference is that Joyce was a superb manipulator of material – perhaps the greatest. He was making words do the absolute

> maximum of work. There isn't a syllable that is superfluous. The kind of work I do is one in which I'm not master of my material. The more Joyce knew the more he could. He's tending towards omniscience and omnipotence as an artist. I'm working with impotence and ignorance.[42]

Whilst Joyce manipulated the protean nature of language in works such as *Ulysses* and *Finnegans Wake*, Beckett's work revels in the failure of language to communicate and to stabilise physical reality. For this reason, silences become an essential part of his drama. If language cannot create and facilitate, then it should be scrapped completely. The differing uses of language that we can see in the works of Joyce and Beckett also illuminates why Joyce is regarded as the archetypal modernist wordsmith and Beckett is the master postmodernist because of his revelling in the failure of language.

The drama of Brendan Behan, whilst as humorous as Beckett's, utilises language in a more direct and clearly cutting way than Beckett's does. The use of jokes and verbal word play shows that Behan is the inheritor of the verbal comedic style of Oscar Wilde which is one thing that differentiates his work from Beckett's – despite the fact that Beckett is very often performed onstage in a highly comedic fashion for the purpose of getting laughs out of the audience. It is arguable that later generations of Irish playwrights followed Wilde's and Behan's example and used verbal word play as a means of cutting through the shibboleths of previously revered Irish cultural norms and tropes. Brian Friel could be said to have provided the watch word for the future of Irish drama when he wrote in *Philadelphia Here I Come!* – the first modern Irish play – 'It's the silence that's the enemy', an assertion with which Beckett would certainly not have agreed.

The drama of Samuel Beckett and Brendan Behan, whilst not representing a complete departure from that of the Irish Revival, is sufficiently different from that theatrical movement to warrant referring to their works as representing an Irish Counter-Revival dramatic tradition. The plays of Beckett and Behan, albeit sometimes in very different ways, represent tradition, Irishness, historical narratives, and notions of stable identity categories in a different and often more problematic way than was the case in many Irish Revival plays. The fact that Beckett and Behan were writing during the years after the postcolonial Ireland for which the Revival had sought to prepare is significant because they saw Ireland then as a somewhat disappointing reality whilst the Revivalists viewed it as a hopeful dream that could be realised in a future to come. The Counter-Revival drama of Beckett and Behan can be seen as influencing the postmodern and contemporary plays of Brian Friel, Marina Carr, Conor McPherson, Mark O'Rowe and so on as much as their Revivalist predecessors have done. The fact that there are a substantial number of differences between the dramatic works of Beckett and Behan, just as there are a number of similarities (as has been shown), demonstrates the complex, multiform creature that Irish Counter-Revival Drama, as encapsulated by the representative theatrical texts of these two authors, truly was.

The chosen texts in this section exist as important literary works in their own rights. However, they can also be interpreted as reflecting the views of cultural theorists such as Sean Ó Faoláin and Daniel Corkery, even if their attitudes towards their works are sometimes highly critical. We can thus see that the 1930s to early 1960s in Ireland was a time when the cultural ethos that had been championed in pre-Free State Ireland by the Irish Celtic, Literary and Cultural Revival was being refined and, in some cases, challenged by the preeminent authors and cultural theorists of the day. As was the case with the Irish Revival, many of the architects of the Counter-Revival were both literary artists and cultural commentators and therefore both movements can be seen as producing rich amalgamations of both styles of writings.

Study questions

1. **Consider the roll of *The Bell* in the fuelling of cultural debate during the Counter-Revival period.**
2. **How is Irish rurality represented differently during the Counter-Revival as opposed to during the era of the Irish Revival?**
3. **Compare the representation of Irishness in Revival and Counter-Revival drama.**

4. **In what ways does the literature of the Counter-Revival period interrogate the 'All-Art-must-be Representative-of-the-Race idea' [Sean Ó Faoláin]?**
5. **How do Counter-Revival prose writers engage with the literary legacy of James Joyce?**
6. **How do Counter-Revival poets engage with the legacy of W.B. Yeats?**

Notes

1 W.B. Yeats, 'Senate Speech', Thursday, 11 June, 1925, https://www.oireachtas.ie/en/debates/debate/seanad/1925-06-11/12/#:~:text=YEATS,-Share&text=%22The%20refusal%20to%20legalise%20divorce,justice%20to%20the%20Hindu%20widow (accessed 20 December, 2024).

2 Daniel Corkery, *Hidden Ireland* (Dublin: Gill & Macmillan, 1967), p. 218.

3 Daniel Corkery, *Synge and Anglo-Irish Literature* (Cork: The Mercier Press, fifth impression, 1966), p. 24.

4 Terence Brown, *Ireland: A Social and Cultural History 1922–1985* (London: Fontana Paperbacks, 1985), p. 67.

5 Patrick Kavanagh, 'Self-Portrait', in *Patrick Kavanagh: A Poet's Country. Selected Prose*, ed. Antoinette Quinn *Prose* (Dublin: Lilliput Press, 2003), p. 306.

6 Patrick Kavanagh, 'The Great Hunger', in *Patrick Kavanagh: Selected Poems* (London: Macgibbon and Kee, 1968), p. 34.

7 Anne Clissmann, *Flann O'Brien: A Critical Introduction to His Writings* (Dublin: Gill & Macmillan, 1975), p. 235.

8 Brown, *Ireland: A Social and Cultural History*, pp. 192–193.

9 Flann O'Brien, *The Poor Mouth*, trans. Patrick Power (Dublin: Dalkey Archive Press, 1996), p. 100.

10 Declan Kiberd, *Inventing Ireland: The Literature of the Modern Nation* (London: Vintage, 1996), p. 498.

11 Declan Kiberd, *Irish Classics* (London: Granta Press, 2000), p. 582.

12 Quoted in ibid., p. 582.

13 Brown, *Ireland: A Social and Cultural History*, p. 193.

14 Frank O'Connor, 'The Future of Irish Literature', *Horizon* 5:25 (January 1942), pp. 56–57.

15 Seán Ó Faoláin, 'Tradition and Creation', *The Bell* vol. 2, no. 1 (1940), p. 6.
16 Seán Ó Faoláin, 'Our Nasty Novelists', *The Bell* vol. 2, no. 5 (1940), p. 7. Emphasis in original.
17 Seán Ó Faoláin, 'Silent Ireland', *The Bell*, vol. 6, no. 5 (1943), p. 460.
18 Elke D'Hoker and Phylis Boumans, 'Moulding the Mid-Twentieth-Century Irish Short Story: Seán O'Faoláin and *The Bell*', *Irish Studies Review* 28:3 (2020), p. 288.
19 Frank O'Connor, 'The Lonely Voice', in Charles E. May (ed.), *Short Story Theories* (Ohio: Ohio University Press, 1976), p. 87.
20 William Trevor, 'Introduction', *The Oxford Book of Irish Short Stories*, ed. William Trevor (Oxford: Oxford University Press, 1989), pp. xiv–xv.
21 Frank O'Connor, 'Guests of the Nation', *Oxford Book of Irish Short Stories*, ed. William Trevor (Oxford: Oxford University Press, 2001), p. 343. All future references refer parenthetically to this edition.
22 Frank O'Connor, *The Big Fellow* (Dublin: Poolbeg Press Ltd, 1996), p. 10.
23 Tim Pat Coogan, *Michael Collins* (London: Arrow Books, 1991), pp. xiii–xiv.
24 Edna O'Brien, 'Irish Revel', in *The Oxford Book of Irish Short Stories*, ed. William Trevor (Oxford: Oxford University Press, 1989), p. 495. All future references refer parenthetically to this edition.
25 J.C.C. Mays, 'Young Beckett's Irish Roots', *Irish University Review* 14:1 (1984), pp. 18–19.
26 John P. Harrington, 'Samuel Beckett and the Countertradition', in Shaun Richards (ed.), *The Cambridge Companion to Twentieth-Century Irish Drama* (Cambridge: Cambridge University Press, 2004), p. 164.
27 Ibid., p. 175.
28 William Butler Yeats, *Purgatory*, in *Modern Irish Drama* (New York: Norton Critical Edition, 1991), p. 33.
29 Samuel Beckett, *Waiting for Godot* (London, Faber & Faber, 1968), p. 7. All future references shall refer parenthetically to this edition.
30 James Knowlson, *Samuel Beckett: An Exhibition* (London: Turret Books, 1971), p. 14.
31 John Brannigan, *Brendan Behan: Cultural Nationalism and the Revisionist Writer* (Dublin: Four Courts Press, 2002), p. 88.
32 Anthony Roche, *Contemporary Irish Drama*, second edition (London and New York: Palgrave Macmillan, 2009), p. 26.
33 Brendan Behan, *The Quare Fellow*, in *The Complete Plays* (London: Methuen, 2000), p. 59. All future references refer parenthetically to this edition.

34 Brian Singleton, 'The Revival Revised', in Shaun Richards (ed.), *The Cambridge Companion to Twentieth-Century Irish Drama* (Cambridge: Cambridge University Press, 2004), p. 268.
35 Seamus Deane, 'Introduction', in Brian Friel, *Brian Friel: Plays One* (London: Faber & Faber, 1996) pp. 14–15.
36 Oscar Wilde, 'Lord Arthur Savile's Crime', in *Collins Complete Works of Oscar Wilde*, ed. Merlin Holland, fifth edition (Glasgow: HarperCollins, 2003), p. 165.
37 Declan Kiberd, *Inventing Ireland: The Literature of the Modern Nation* (London: Vintage, 1995), p. 539.
38 George Santayana, *Reason in Common Sense*, volume 1 of *The Life of Reason* (Amherst: Prometheus, 1905).
39 James Joyce, *Portrait of the Artist as a Young Man* (Oxford: Oxford World's Classics, 2008), p. 159.
40 Quoted in Stefan Collini, 'Highlight of Stay So Far', *London Review of Books* 38:23 (December, 2016).
41 Quoted by Archibald Henderson in *Overland Monthly*, no. 1, July 1907, p. 14.
42 Israel Shenker', 'Moody Man of Letters', *New York Times*, 6 May, 1956, pp. 1, 3.

3
Postcolonial theory and Irish Studies

Introduction

The late 1970s and 1980s are considered a key period in the development of Irish Studies. This is due to the rise of postcolonial theory/criticism within academia worldwide. This chapter shall consider how Irish critics, largely from English departments, brought the postcolonial theories of thinkers such as Edward Said, Homi Bhabha and Frantz Fanon into contact with Irish literary and cultural criticism. The question of whether or not Ireland can be regarded as actually being 'postcolonial' shall be of central concern. The relationship between the discipline of modernist and postcolonial studies in an Irish context will also be examined. The importance of the *Field Day Anthology of Irish Writing* and associated theoretical pamphlets by critics such as Seamus Deane, Declan Kiberd and Richard Kearney to the development of Irish postcolonial studies shall be elucidated. Whether the Irish version of postcolonial studies has ever become more than what Colm Tóibín termed 'nationalism in exotic clothes' shall be debated. The arguments that developed around historical revisionism (spearheaded by academics such as Roy Foster) versus nationalism in the 1970s and 1980s shall also be acknowledged as significant in this evolutionary moment for Irish Studies. As Neil Sammells (one of the founders of the journal *Irish Studies Review*) said to this author:

> The debate [between nationalism and revisionism] was bitter and ad hominem and the product of a particular historical moment. It felt at the time like a battle between a desire to modernise thinking about Ireland and a clinging to outdated pieties. It was one of the reasons why Irish Studies felt exciting and 'real' at the time.[1]

This chapter shall argue that postcolonial theory took root in Irish Studies as a liminal position between the two extremes of nationalism and revisionism, without ever becoming a mere compromise between the two extremes.

The chapter will build upon the arguments concerning Ireland's status as postcolonial nation and the producer of postcolonial literature that are to be found in studies such as Seamus Deane's *Celtic Revivals*, David Lloyd's *Anomalous States* and Luke Gibbons' *Transformations in Irish Culture*. Another important critical text to be examined in this chapter shall be *Writing Ireland* by David Cairns and Shaun Richards because it was the first determined effort to apply critical theory to Irish literature. How this work interposed itself between revisionism and nationalism and sparked a culture war in Irish literary studies, which had been bubbling under since the early 1980s will be examined in depth.

The literary texts that shall be examined in this chapter will be Joyce's *Ulysses*, Brian Friel's *Translations* and selections of Yeats' later poetry in conjunction with his play *Purgatory*. The impact of the nationalism vs revisionism debate on the development of post-colonial Irish Studies in the 1980s shall also be questioned. The chapter contains an extensive examination of revisionist and nationalist historical narratives by historians such as Roy Foster and Ronan Fanning because it was out of those debates that Irish postcolonial studies began to take hold in the 1980s.

Unlike the previous two chapters, this one shall deal with a recognisable theoretical discipline in relation to Irish Studies. In contrast, the Revival and Counter-Revival chapters engaged with likeminded writers and thinkers whose work created a zeitgeist for a particular historical moment in Ireland. This means that texts from a variety of different temporal periods in Ireland can be considered together because the analysis is based around theoretical methodology more than historical context.

What is postcolonial theory/studies?

Lance Pettitt provides a succinct and concise general definition of postcolonial theory:

> [Postcolonial theory] is not a single theory but a diverse, interdisciplinary critical discourse, which has been used to explore the economic, social, cultural and psychological relations between coloniser countries and their colonised territories. The 'post' of postcolonial (unhyphenated) is slightly misleading since its area of interest is not just confined to countries after the coloniser has withdrawn and political independence has been achieved, that is, when they have become temporally and spatially post-colonial (hyphenated). A postcolonial consciousness comes into being as the result of a colonised individual critically recognising their place in the historical structure called colonialism.[2]

Many of the academic texts associated with the theoretical writings and cultural commentary that is now postcolonial theory were produced by critics who commented upon the decolonisation of Africa and southern Asia in the 1950s and 1960s. These thinkers include Albert Memmi and Frantz Fanon.

Possibly the most iconic 'postcolonial text' is Edward Said's *Orientalism* (1978). The titular concept at the heart of this book concerns the West's patronising and sometimes contemptuous attitude towards Eastern nations and peoples. Said argues that representations of the colonial Other in texts such as Joseph Conrad's *Heart of Darkness* represent an outsider's inauthentic view of these people. Said refers to Orientalism as a style of thought that marks the distinction between the Eastern 'Orient' and (most of the time) the Western 'Occident'. He points out that most writers and thinkers draw a clear binary opposition between the West and East when they come to write their literary and theoretical texts.[3]

'We can sum up so far by saying that postcolonial theory is a way of analysing the power relations between two countries within the structure of colonialism'.[4] It has been noted that one of its strengths as a form of theoretical inquiry is that it enables the comparing and contrasting of different countries' experience of different types of colonialism. Thus, although Ireland is not a 'typical' example of a colonised nation because of its developed economy and geographical location, postcolonial theory enables comparisons to be made between

Ireland developing nations such as India whose status first as a colonial and then a postcolonial nation was never challenged in the same way as Ireland's was. One of the key arguments put forward by leading Irish postcolonial thinkers is that Ireland's experience of dispossession in terms of land and language by the British means that they should be regarded as having experienced the processes of colonialism. Therefore, independent Ireland should be considered a postcolonial nation regardless of the fact that it is part of Europe and has a robust economy.

One of the main criticisms of postcolonial readings is that they present a potentially dogmatic and overtly nationalist perspective on texts that are meant to have more enriching and universal meanings than the merely political. This chapter shall explore the extent to which Irish postcolonial theorists adopted the view that 'all ideologies – Nationalism included – are susceptible to active reappropriation and unconscious *mis*-appropriation, thus such ideologies, in the passage from the centre to the margins, are liable to unpredictable transformations'.[5] In this respect, postcolonial theory can be regarded as creating a liminal discursive space between the narrow and essentialist dogmatism of both Irish nationalism and revisionism.

Modern/(post)colonial Ireland

The period in Irish history that saw the growth of postcolonial theory as an influential theoretical lens through which to view Ireland and to interrogate questions concerning Irish identity (the 1970s until the early 1990s) was one of great turmoil. The 'Northern Irish Troubles' had begun in 1969 and this resulted in violence between Republican and Loyalist paramilitaries in the Irish Republic and in Northern Ireland. This conflict would result in over a thousand people, many of whom were civilians, being killed over the course of several decades until 1998. Equally, Ireland had gone through a period of economic and (to some extent) cultural modernisation during the 1960s as a result of Sean Lemass' time as Taoiseach and the programmes for economic expansion that he implemented with the Civil Servant TK Whitacker. Thus, we can say that an Ireland of conflict, but also an Ireland that was becoming more open to outside, global influences, provided an intellectual ground that was hospitable to the nuanced views of identity that postcolonial theory can potentially provide.

It should be noted that many of the literary texts discussed during the course of this chapter are often referred to as 'modernist' works. The strange relationship between Ireland and modernity as a result of its colonial experience has been interrogated by many critics and theorists ever since the late 1970s. Joe Cleary has convincingly argued that:

> Ireland did not have to wait – as is too frequently assumed – for the arrival of industrialization or technological modernity to undergo that traumatic sense of breakneck modernization, of rapid cultural transformation or psychic alienation – the shock of the new – conventionally regarded as a constitutive or exemplary experience of the modern. In Ireland, modernization via colonization preceded modernization via industrialization; colonization was at least as devastating and destructive to any idea of stable organic society or to the continuity of tradition as the latter would ever be.[6]

The above passage explains very succinctly why postcolonial Irish Studies is very often bound up with studies of 'Irish modernism' and this shall be explored in considerable depth below. In particular, the chapter considers the contention that Ireland was a modern nation before those of mainland Europe as a result of its experience of colonialism, and therefore it is understandable that Ireland and other postcolonial/periphery nations such as America contributed greatly to the number of major works during the 'high modernist' period of literary and cultural history.

Patrick Bixby has provided a counter-signature to the above argument:

> The history of colonialism in Ireland, with its deprivations, oppressions, and other motives for emigration, helps to explain why these writers spent large portions of their careers abroad in European capitals and so often encountered foreign ideas and artistic movements [...] [It is not] necessary to conceive of modernism, even in its earliest phase, as strictly a Continental and Anglo-American affair, taking place in Paris or Berlin or London or New York, since its emergence was always dependent upon exchanges (of ideas and individuals) between these capitals, the colony, and the so-called peripheries. Conceived in this way, Irish modernism is a category that, despite their differences,

> Joyce and Yeats can coinhabit more comfortably than other literary-historical configurations.[7]

Because of the arguments put forward by critics such as Cleary, Bixby and numerous others, it is now very possible to conceive of Irish colonial and postcolonial literature as also representing supreme examples of Irish modernism. Indeed, modernist and postcolonial literatures, if we think of them as being particular literary genres and styles, are united in their conception of temporality as elastic and their desire to imagine undecidable, and as yet unrealised, futures to come.

Revisionism vs nationalism

The rise of postcolonial theory as a method of interpreting Irish identity, culture and history, it can be argued, happened as a result of the debate between Irish revisionist and nationalist history and historians in the 1970s and 1980s within academia and in public discourse more widely. Revisionist history, broadly speaking, is an attempt to do what Walter Benjamin called 'reading history against the grain'. In the case of Ireland, it represented an attempt by certain historians to interpret the narrative of Irish history as not simply being one of evil coloniser (England) vs victimised colonial subject (Ireland).

In 1986, the eminent historian Roy Foster wrote a famous essay titled 'We are all Revisionists Now' in which he laments how historical revisionism in an Irish context had come to be regarded as something completely negative and was used as a pejorative term rather than as a description of a nuanced academic methodology for historical inquiry:

> To oppose this [nationalist] view of historical study … is not the same thing as an endorsement of British influence in Ireland; it is merely adopting a different focus. Anyone who knows a few Irish historians will have realised that 'revisionism' in scholarship is perfectly compatible with 'nationalism' in politics. It may seem odd that the point needs making. But the trouble is that 'revisionist' has come to be used as a smear-word for those supposedly unsound on the national question.[8]

Foster believed that the embracing of revisionism within Irish public discourse and debate would show a sign of growth, maturity and confidence within the Irish Republic as the years of the revolutionary wars began to fade further into memory: 'The sceptical strengths of the Irish mind should be capable of taking this [Revisionism] on, and questioning everything that needs questioning. In a country that has come of age, history need no longer be a matter of guarding sacred mysteries'.[9] Needless to say, many Irish historians and cultural commentators did not share Foster's assessment of the value of revisionism in cultural and political analysis.

In 1988, University College Dublin held a symposium called 'Nationalist Perspectives on the Past' during which revisionism was hotly debated from various perspectives. Dr Ronan Fanning, speaking on behalf of historical revisionism, argued that 'much of the sound and the fury obfuscating the revisionist debate stems from a national loss of innocence. For national innocence could not survive what has happened in Northern Ireland since 1969' (the beginning of the Troubles).[10] Like Foster, Fanning argues that all historians must be in some way open to revisionist thinking otherwise they will be incapable of revising their view of the past should some new information become available.

Fanning defers to Yeats' poem 'Leaders of the Crowd' at one point in his lecture to give artistic weight to his argument:

> They must to keep their certainty accuse
> All that are different of a base intent.
> Pull down established honour [...]
> How can they know
> Truth flourishes where the student's lamp has shone,
> And there alone, that have no solitude.[11]

Yeats' warning here concerns the dangers of closed-mindedness and a refusal to engage with other opinions for fear of having one's certainties endangered. A mind should socially surround itself with various perspectives and point of view. However, as Fanning asserts, 'historians, like all scholars, can have too much solitude'[12] and this jeopardises their openness to the otherness of new ideas. Fanning's invocation of a poem in support of his academic argument also shows how the discipline of Irish Studies, like other forms of scholarly inquiry, can cross fertilise by using cultural, literary, political and historical allusions to justify arguments and positions.

Opposing Fanning and revisionism at this symposium was historian Desmond Fennell:

> I know that new historical facts are continually being discovered and I welcome that. I am not afraid that any discovery of new facts will shake my belief in the essential tenets of Irish nationalism, for those tenets are not a myth depending on an act of faith, but practical moral convictions that are held mutatis mutandis, by people everywhere – convictions concerning a nation's right to freedom, the wrongness of its being subject to another nation, and the rightness of resisting and rebelling against such oppression.[13]

For Fennel, nationalist historiography represents a total, incontrovertible truth concerning the rights of nations to self-determination and should never be challenged. This opinion represents an idealistic view of the practice of creating historical narratives. Fennell believes that such narratives should always be positive and used to build national unity, coherence and stability.

In contrast, Fennell argues that Revisionism is detrimental to national pride and unity because of its inherent pessimism and bleakness concerning the rights of nations to gain freedom by any means necessary: 'It was as if a counter-revolution, come to power in Moscow, should rewrite Russian history so as to denigrate the October revolution, all that led to it, and all that flowed from it'.[14]

It can also be argued that the Revisionist demand that Ireland rebel against old narratives of nationalism and coloniser/colonised relations represents a very antiquated narrative of progress. The point being that the Irish are being patronisingly told that they are behaving like naive and simple minded remnants of colonial native identity. The nationalist argument would be that postcolonial Ireland should not feel itself beholden to imperialist conceptions and narratives of what 'progress' and 'national maturity' should look like.

Thus, we see that the thesis of nationalist historiography came to be challenged by the antithesis of Revisionism. From these two propositions, this chapter shall argue, came the synthesis of postcolonial theory in the context of Irish Studies. This theoretical methodology can be regarded as occupying a liminal space between those two aforementioned extremes of historical, cultural and literary analysis.

Field Day and Irish cultural debate

One of the major catalysts that led to the widespread adoption of postcolonial theory as a major source of Irish cultural analysis was the foundation of the Field Day Theatre Company by the Northern Irish playwright Brian Friel and the actor Stephen Rea in 1980. Although initially envisaged as a touring theatre company that would take its various production around the whole island of Ireland, Field Day eventually branched out into a publishing house which printed pamphlets that analysed Irish culture, literature and politics from various theoretical perspectives, especially that of postcolonial theory.

Although certain individuals, such as the writer Colm Tóibín, were suspicious of Field Day's political leanings, regarding them as essentially peddling 'nationalism in exotic clothes', in reality many of the pamphlets and essays that they published represented a very nuanced and even-handed approach to conceptions of nation and nationalism in an Irish context. One of the most famous Field Day essays was written by Edward Said in which he argued for Yeats as a (post)colonial writer: 'Yeats is a poet who belongs to a tradition not usually considered his, that of the colonial world ruled by European imperialism now – that is during the late nineteenth and early twentieth centuries – bringing to a climactic insurrectionary stage, the massive upheaval of anti-imperialist resistance in the colonies'.[15] Although Said has been criticised for ignoring Yeats' membership of the Anglo-Irish Protestant Ascendancy, I would argue that his willingness to include such a figure as Yeats in the list of decolonising writers highlights the openness to multiple versions of national races that is a feature of the best versions of postcolonial theory.

The fact that one of the members of the Field Day Board was the eminent academic and postcolonial theorist Seamus Deane meant that many of the pamphlets were written by academics such as Declan Kiberd who were suspicious of what Frantz Fanon in *The Wretched of the Earth* (1961) called the national bourgeoisie and were far more enthusiastic about newer forms of nationalism that could be used by minority, colonised people to gain freedom from the imperial centre.

In the Field Day theatre manifesto, Deane gave voice to that organisation's investment in the power of narrative that was to be so important in the plays and essays they produced:

> If a congealed idea of theatre can be broken, then the audience which experiences this break would be more open to the modifications of other established forms. Almost everything which we believe to be nature or natural is in fact historical; more precisely, is an historical fiction. If Field Day can breed a new fiction of theatre, or of any other area, which is sufficiently successful to be believed in as though it were natural and an outgrowth of the past, then it will have succeeded. At the moment, it is six characters in search of a story that can be believed.[16]

The power of narrative and the relationship between reality and representation are concerns that run through several major Irish postcolonial texts (as shall be discussed in more detail below) – works such as Richard Kearney's *Transitions: Narratives in Modern Irish Culture* and Shaun Richards and David Cairns' *Writing Ireland: Colonialism, Nationalism, and Culture*.

Seamus Deane's pamphlet, 'Heroic Styles', has been discussed briefly in Chapter 1 of this book. Its primary argument is that Irish literature and culture has been somewhat harmed by the dominance of Anglo-Irish writers in its literary and cultural canon. Deane regards the image of the Anglo-Irish writers as triumphant and proud people of culture – as propagated by individuals such as Yeats and Edmund Burke – as having helped to create a national amnesia in Ireland concerning that hyphenated race's involvement in the cycles of injustice that constituted life in colonial Ireland. For Deane, a far more attractive example of a 'true Irish writer' was James Joyce and his new and radical modernist experiments with literary style, which could be contrasted with what Deane regarded as the idealising nostalgia of Yeats' late Romanticism. As a Northern Irishman who had experienced some of the worst moments in the early years of the Troubles, it is perhaps understandable that Deane would write such an essay. However, the fact that he was considered to be representative of Field Day in its totality did leave it open to largely apocryphal accusations of peddling a myopic and absolutist version of Irish nationalism.

Another notable and theoretically sophisticated pamphlet was Richard Kearney's 'Myth and Motherland' in which Kearney examines 'a particular mythic structure, that of sacrificial martyrdom, operating behind the words and actions of both prisoners and poets in Ireland, chiefly the Maze [IRA] hunger strikers and the writers of the Irish Revival'.[17] Kearney is particularly interested in Joyce's modernist experimentations with myth and the mythic in *Ulysses*, which Kearney believes result in a productive dialectic between the individual and the community. Kearney argues that Joyce's 'mythic method' shows that 'myth need not be the suspension of the individual, as Yeats and Joyce believed. For myth can only survive the multiple re-inventions of different individuals and these individuals can best communicate through the universalizing idioms of myth'.[18]

One of the most famous Field Day pamphlets is Declan Kiberd's 'Anglo-Irish Attitudes'. Kiberd begins this essay by outlining his argument, which is also the central thesis of his influential text of Irish postcolonial criticism, 'Inventing Ireland: The Literature of the Modern Nation' (1996):

> The English did not invade Ireland – rather, they seized a neighbouring island and invented the idea of Ireland. The notion 'Ireland' is largely a fiction created by the rulers of England in response to specific needs at a precise moment in British history. The English have always presented themselves to the world as a cold, refined and urban race, so it suited them to see the Irish as hot headed, rude and garrulous.[19]

Kiberd argues that many Anglo-Irish writers, such as Oscar Wilde, George Bernard Shaw and W.B. Yeats, use their lives and works to create dialectics that challenge this British urge to create binary oppositions; whether they be man/woman, English/Irish, Good/Evil and so on.

Kiberd focusses particularly on Wilde as being the prime exponent of Hegelian dialecticism: 'Far from being an exponent of the witty paradox, Wilde is interested in that moment of modernism when the ancient antithesis dissolves to reveal an underlying unity'.[20] Oscar Wilde's studied performance of Englishness during his life in England can be interpreted as an example of his attempting to expose race and nationality as being largely a performative construct. By focussing his pamphlet on Anglo-Irish writers, Kiberd very conceivably could have been trying to explode the myth that Field Day was an organisation composed primarily of nationalist sympathisers.

Richard Rankin Russell has correctly argued that the Field Day Theatre Company enabled Friel to write plays that embraced fluidity and hybridity in order that he might raise questions concerning Northern Irish and Republic of Ireland narratives of identity. 'In the process, it allowed him [Friel] to continue to explore his interrelated concerns of modernity, community, and place through the travelling onstage depictions of local, dynamic communities'.[21] These same goals and achievements can equally be said to have been at the heart of the Field Day pamphlets and major preoccupations of their various authors. Field Day shall also be discussed in relation to Irish feminism in the next chapter because of the outcry regarding the omission of female authors from the first volumes of the *Field Day Anthology of Irish Writing*. This controversy, as shall be discussed in Chapter 4, opens up useful comparisons and contrasts between certain strands of postcolonial theory and those of feminism.

Postcolonial Irish Studies

Irish postcolonial theory, or postcolonial Irish Studies, can be said to have its origins in the anti-colonial writings of Roger Casement, the Irishman who was executed for treason because he attempted to import arms covertly for use in the 1916 Rising. Prior to his involvement in Irish political radicalism, Casement was involved in colonial administration in the Belgian Congo and Latin America in the early 1900s. During this time he wrote articles and diary entries criticising the Belgians' treatment of the Congo natives and the plundering of the African continent.

Richard Kirkland has written about Casement as a proto-postcolonial theorist.

> Casement's own history of deliberate anti-colonial agitation constitutes one of the many possible starting points for such a [theoretical] process within Irish Studies. Just as Prakash, Franz Fanon and Gandhi are

> examples of historical figures located within anti-colonial struggle whose relationships with that struggle provides the precondition for theory, so the dissidence seemingly implicit to the Casement case should be seen as an extension of his own anti-colonial intervention. It is important to recognize that Casement's own writings on Ireland draw heavily on colonial frameworks and analogies with other colonized nations, and in this proposed their own form of ethical critique built around a narrative of decolonization.[22]

Casement openly stated that he never felt more Irish than when he was exposed to the horrific excesses of colonialism in the Belgian Congo. His writings drew many connections between the experience of colonialism in Ireland and in other parts of the world such as the continent of Africa. These types of cross-comparisons are to be found in the writings of many postcolonial thinkers in Ireland.

Despite the long-standing debate concerning whether Ireland can be called a 'colony' in the traditional sense of the word, Edward Said, the great originator of postcolonial theory, has no doubt that Ireland was a colony and its decolonising strategies were inspirational to other nations when it came to achieving physical and cultural independence from their imperial masters: 'I am so grateful to Ireland, especially for its literary and cultural example. You have had many more years of imperialism than we [the Palestinian people] have had, and you have produced a fabulous culture of resistance'.[23] Irish literary and cultural critics have reciprocated Said's gratitude and have produced texts of postcolonial theory that, in varying degrees, draw upon the works of thinkers such as Said, Fanon, Bhabha and Memmi.

Arguably, one of the great literary passages that epitomises a postcolonial mindset is contained in Seamus Heaney's poem 'Punishment', which appears in his celebrated 1975 collection *North*. This poem juxtaposes the execution of a woman in Germany hundreds of years ago, presumably for the crime of adultery, and the tarring and feathering in contemporary Northern Ireland of Catholic women who went out with British soldiers (the German woman's body was excavated, well preserved, from a bog). Heaney admits that he stood by and did nothing when these women were punished for sleeping with their natural enemies and guiltily admits that he would have done the same if he were a witness to the execution of the German woman:

> I who have stood dumb
> when your betraying sisters,
> cauled in tar,
> wept by the railings,
> who would connive
> in civilized outrage
> yet understand the exact
> and tribal, intimate revenge.[24]

In these lines, Heaney represents the divided and conflicted mind that is the inevitable consequence of living as a colonised subject and which is the tone of many works of postcolonial criticism. Heaney acknowledges the horror of the violence inflicted on innocent victims by nationalist fighters, yet he also admits his understanding of the need for the nationalist/tribal individual mindset to seek revenge. Thus, this confession condemns the worst excesses of nationalism and yet expresses understanding of the need for its existence – an attitude that the poet holds in common with many of the thinkers discussed in this chapter.

One of the earliest textual examples of an Irish postcolonial theoretical text was David Cairns' and Shaun Richards' *Writing Ireland: Colonialism, Nationalism and Culture* (1988). This book adopts what is termed a 'cultural materialist' methodology to argue that 'a combination of historical context, theoretical method, political commitment and textual analysis offers the strongest challenge [to colonial powers] and has already contributed substantial work'.[25] This interdisciplinary approach to the analysis of power dynamics within a colonial and postcolonial context has been commonly adopted by other academics who worked at the coalface of what we can term 'postcolonial Irish Studies'.

Cairns and Richards are keen to emphasise the power of discourse when it comes to examining colonial dynamics:

> The process of describing the colonized and inscribing them in discourse as second class citizens in comparison with colonizers commenced with the invocation of the judicial and military power of the State, but subsequently the colonizers attempted to convince the colonized themselves of their irremovable deficiencies and the consequent naturalness and the permanence of their subordination. The wish of the colonizer should be willingly accepted rather than require constant recourse to coercion.[26]

Cairns and Richards' primary thesis, as Eoin Flannery argues, is that 'Hegemony … is inaugurated in the colonial context through processes of discursive, ideological management, which are targeted at obliterating the self-present identities of colonised people and the stealthy imposition of a sanctioned 'otherness'. Equally, in this theoretical matrix we can also hear an echo of Fanon's writings on the necessary liquidation of the colonised's identity.[27]

David Lloyd's *Anomalous States: Irish Writing and the Postcolonial Moment* (1993) represents a radical attempt in postcolonial Irish Studies to think beyond narrow notions of nationalism and analyses how major Irish writers in the twentieth century used their works to think postcolonial nationhood and Irishness outside narrow gauge nationalism. Although considered an important work of Irish postcolonial criticism, Lloyd only briefly references Fanon and does not mention Said at all. Lloyd's primary theoretical point of reference is Antonio Gramsci's conceptualisation of 'the subaltern'. Although the term subaltern is used by Gramsci to denote people who occupy the lower rungs of the social ladder and are constantly seeking to overthrow the governing class, Lloyd argues that one can read Gramsci's definition of subaltern against itself: 'If one defines the subaltern not as that which desires the state but as that which is subaltern because it resists or cannot be represented by or in state formation, its "episodic and fragmentary history" can be read as the sign of another mode of narrative, rather than an incomplete one'.[28] Lloyd wishes to represent the postcolonial Irish as a perpetually subaltern entity rather than the inheritors or those who desire to inherit Fanon's bourgeois nationalist identity. Therefore, stable notions of nationalism and nation formation can be read as being disrupted in Ireland and its postcolonial literature. Appropriately, this book's chapters begin with Heaney and end with a discussion of the nineteenth-century novel, thus disrupting the orderliness of linear temporality which is normally considered as following a line of progression directly from the past, into the present, and forward into the future.

Eoin Flannery assesses one of the strengths of Lloyd's version of postcolonial criticism thus: 'Lloyd's radical appropriation of subaltern reading strategies in an Irish context interrogates the representational synchronicity of the state and its national narrative'.[29]

Like Cairns and Richards, Lloyd is greatly invested in analysing forms and styles of representation and narration and considering their importance for an ethical and authentic depiction of Ireland in the context of its postcolonial moment. For these critics, the act of telling is as important, if not more so, as what is being told.

Declan Kiberd's *Inventing Ireland* is possibly the most ambitious attempt to write a sweeping narrative of Irish history and culture from the late 1800s to the end of the twentieth century, broadly using the methodology of various strands of postcolonial theory. Perhaps the chapter in *Inventing Ireland* that draws most strongly and continuously on postcolonial theory is the one (quoted in Chapter 1 above) that focusses on J.M. Synge's *The Playboy of the Western World*. Kiberd argues that Synge's play enacts Frantz Fanon's three stages of decolonisation: colonisation, nationalism and revolution. Kiberd also argues that Synge unknowingly lived out parts of his own life according to those stages: 'Synge is arguably the most gifted Irish exponent of the three phases of artistic decolonization later described by Fanon. He effortlessly assimilated the culture of the occupying English and then proceeded to immerse himself in the native [Irish] culture'.[30]

Kiberd's theoretical focus is always primarily on literature because he regards a nation's literary works as being one of the main sources of self-realisation and fulfilment for a county and their people. One of the ambitions of *Inventing Ireland* is to show how Irish literature can be productively compared with and read alongside the great works of other postcolonial nations such as India and countries in Africa. This is not to deny national specificities but rather to demonstrate how productive it can be to view a nation as having an identity that was invented by national and transnational influences that are both positive and sometimes negative.

For most of his academic career, Kiberd has viewed the Revival as a progressive and sometimes quasi-utopian movement that was always imagining an as yet undecidable future to come. He truly believes that such a future still remains to be realised by succeeding generations of Irish writers, thinkers and politicians:

> The cultural traditions of the Irish Renaissance [Revival] were not only plural but hugely reconciling and they are still available to be

> tapped by persons of goodwill: whatever happens, culture will be the site and stake of the debate, as politics wanes […] The need is to reopen ourselves to the cultural philosophy of Hyde, Yeats, Hannah Sheehy Skeffington and that whole revivalist generation, whose project is still incomplete.[31]

Although Kiberd, in the early part of his career, held similar views to Deane concerning Yeats being an Anglo-Irish, nostalgic colonialist merely posing as a radical Irish revolutionary artist, Kiberd has openly admitted to that opinion being too harsh.

Like Kiberd, Luke Gibbons has argued for a different, less America-inflected model for thinking about progress, modernisation and modernity when it comes to analysing the 'Irish narrative' and discourses centring around the representation of Ireland. This idea of a kind of colonial temporality can be found in Gibbons' *Transformations in Irish Culture* (1996) and Joyce's *Ghosts: Ireland, Modernism, and Memory* (2015). Equally, Gibbons also shares Kiberd's investment in examining cultural hybridity in relation to the formation of various Irish identities.

In Colin Graham's *Deconstructing Ireland* (2001), Graham expresses a certain unease that postcolonial Irish Studies risks creating definition of Ireland and Irishness that become naturalised and solidified to the extent that alternative definitions are excluded and denied validity. In this respect, Graham subscribes to Oscar Wilde's assertion that 'to define is to limit'. Graham warns that 'giving "Ireland" a meaning which fills out the term comfortably is seemingly the underwriting principle of Irish criticism's existence'.[32] The use of postcolonial theory in discourses of Irishness was originally intended as a radical and troubling act. However, according to Graham, it is now in danger of beginning the stable norm.

Gerry Smyth has also warned of the dangers of an over reliance on theoretical discourse and jargon when it comes to excavating meaning from various texts:

> The present-day shift in emphasis to critical discourse […] signals a [contentious] recognition that there can be no decolonising literature, no national culture of resistance, before prefiguring critical discourse creates a series of social and institutional spaces [such as Universities] in which a culture and its particular cultural effects can function and have meaning.[33]

Without dismissing critical and cultural discourses, Smyth does warn against making them the guarantors of all textual meaning and radicality and also not assuming that the only way you can read 'correctly' is if you go to university and learn from an acknowledged 'master' of textual analysis.

The texts discussed above share a few common features. They are committed to testifying to the power of narrative when it comes to giving a colonial and postcolonial nation and people a sense of themselves. Literature, culture and politics are presented in those works as being productively bound together. Narrow and regressive conceptions of nature and nationalism are deconstructed and new alternatives are proposed for the creation of postcolonial nationhood and citizenry. Fundamentally, these postcolonial critics are perpetually looking to the future in their restless search for a new Ireland to come. In this respect, they can be considered in some respects antithetical to many 'postmodern' thinkers such as Francois Lyotard, Roland Barthes and Jean Baudrillard who have – in their revolt against all perceived forms of essentialism, including national and racial – sometimes been accused of creating modes of thought that blunt the political valency of theories such as postcolonialism.

What Irish postcolonial critics do:

1. **They reject the claims to universalism made on behalf of canonical literature and seek to show its limitations of outlook, especially its general inability to empathise across boundaries of cultural and ethical difference.**
2. **They examine the representations of cultures other than Irish in literature as a way of achieving this end.**
3. **They show how certain works of literature are often evasively and crucially silent on matters concerned with colonisation and imperialism.**
4. **They foreground questions of cultural difference and diversity and examine their treatment in relevant literary (and cultural) works.**
5. **They celebrate hybridity and 'cultural polyvalency', that is, the situation whereby individuals and groups belong**

simultaneously to more than one culture (for instance, that of the coloniser, through the colonial school system, and that of the colonised, through local and oral traditions).

6. **They counter the idea that Ireland, for geographical and economic reasons, was never a 'colony' in the traditional sense of the word and that the Irish therefore cannot be called a 'postcolonial nation'.**
7. **They argue that Ireland experienced the traumatic effects of modernity earlier than many other European nations because of the impact of colonialism and the sense of cultural rupture that it created.**
8. **They develop a perspective, not just applicable to postcolonial literature (and other forms of textuality), whereby states of marginality, plurality and perceived 'otherness' are seen as sources of energy and potential change.**[34]

Representative textual analyses

Ulysses

James Joyce marked himself out for future generations of thinkers and theorists as being an Irish postcolonial writer *par excellence* as soon as he had Stephen Dedalus in *Portrait of the Artist as a Young Man* declare his intention to 'forge within the smithy of my soul the uncreated conscience of my race'.[35] Whilst it is highly unlikely that Dedalus, Joyce's supposed 'alter-ego' would have ever possessed the ability to complete such a grandiose artistic project, critics of Joyce's work have for many a decade attempted to read his literary oeuvre as Joyce's attempt to do just what Stephen asserted he would do. This is particularly true of the textual analysis that has been done on Joyce's modernist masterpiece, *Ulysses*, from approximately the 1980s until the present day.

Declan Kiberd has written the following description of *Ulysses* that clearly marks it out as a postcolonial text of various radical potentialities: '*Ulysses* is an endlessly open book of utopian epiphanies. It holds the mirror up to the colonial capital that was Dublin on June 16th 1904, but it also offers redemptive glimpses of a future that might be made over in terms of these utopian moments'.[36] This appraisal is clearly meant to connect *Ulysses* with the futural orientation that is very much associated with postcolonial theory and asserts that Joyce wished his novel to act as a preparatory work for the day when the 'post' was placed beside Ireland's colonial status.

Kiberd's reading of *Ulysses* in *Inventing Ireland* centres on making the case for *Ulysses* being an example of the literary genre called magical realism, which is associated with postcolonial authors such as Gabriel Garcia Marquez and Salman Rushdie. Referring to the numerous voices and styles that coexist in *Ulysses*' pages, Kiberd argues that 'Joyce produced in *Ulysses* a genuinely multicultural text, which didn't just redraw the boundaries between discourses at some other point. And he provided a model for the magic realists in the refusal of *Ulysses* to ground itself in a narrating subject or an identifiable author: instead, he offered a text without any final authority'.[37] This reading is very much typical of Kiberd's postcolonial reading strategy, which is invested in showing how great works of Irish literature can also be productively linked with other colonies' literary works.

Equally, Kiberd is interested in exploring how *Ulysses* is part of a literary tradition of mythical realism that had been beloved of Irish Revivalists:

> Joyce employs the technique of mythical realism, juxtapositioning [sic] Odyssean marvels against the Irish quotidian. This method has been shown to have been implicit in many texts of the Irish revival, especially in the early days of the Abbey, whose writers were among the first to grasp that fantasy, untouched by any sense of reality, is only a decadent escapism, while reality, unchallenged by any element of fantasy is merely squalid literalism.[38]

Kiberd's argument is that Joyce's Irishness is intrinsic to his modern/modernist style of literary experimentation and, equally, his status as a postcolonial writer also influences the radicality of his formal literary experimentations. Derek Hand has also argued that *Ulysses* was a text that could only have been produced in the cultural and literary period of the Irish Revival: 'The cultural and political fluidity of that period created a unique cultural space, allowing a genius such as Joyce to discover the means of expressing his personal and artistic concerns with the themes of father-son relations, betrayal, love and the civic responsibilities of life in the modern city'.[39]

Vincent Cheng's *Joyce, Race, and Empire* (1995) 'is another critical work, [like Kiberd's] that reads formal difference and multiplicity in Joyce's work, not as depoliticized pluralism, but as being directly engaged in undermining the prevailing ideologies of nation, identity and cultural formation'.[40] In this respect, Cheng was inspired by Lloyd's reading of *Ulysses* in *Anomalous States* in which Lloyd 'directly contrasts Joyce's [stylistic] adulteration with the singular, patriarchal vision of mainstream Irish nationalism that is most vividly represented by the Citizen in the 'Cyclops' episode of *Ulysses*'.[41]

A recent example of a text that reads *Ulysses* in the context of Irish colonialism and revolution is Luke Gibbon's *James Joyce and the Irish Revolution: The Easter Rising as Modern Event* (2023). As the title suggests, this book interrogates the revolutionary and modern aspects of both *Ulysses* and the 1916 Rising, a rebellion that has too often been interpreted as an act of nostalgic folly by dreamy-eyed rebels who wished to recapture the old fashioned heroics of Celtic heroes such as Cuchulainn. Gibbons convincingly argues that the form of *Ulysses* not only resembles that of revolutionary action but also was a text valued by Irish revolutionaries such as Ernie O'Malley who saw within this supposedly impenetrable text a perfect encapsulation of their experience of revolution and the trauma that resulted from those experiences (Chapter 5 of this book shall examine Ernie O'Malley's engagement with *Ulysses* in more detail).

In this lengthy and provocative passage Gibbons perfectly sums up why *Ulysses* is the perfect text of Irish postcolonialism and revolution:

> Many of the formal breakthroughs in *Ulysses* lie in its capturing forces that were eddying in society at the time in which it is set, but which only surfaced at the time of writing. Artistic form, by means of its autonomy, stands back from the present but does not step outside: in what [Theodor] Adorno called 'the recollection of the possible', it transcends the present to point toward alternative pasts, other futures.[42]

Gibbons argues for the problematic temporality that exists in *Ulysses* as a liberating, revolutionary gesture that allows for the freeing of the past from certainty and stasis and suggests the possibility of a variety of undecidable, multiple futures that may one day announce their presence in an unexpected moment that can truly be called an 'event'.

One work that takes a different view of the formal qualities and experimentations at work in *Ulysses* is Enda Duffy's *The Subaltern Ulysses* (1993). Duffy argues that '*Ulysses* distributes the literary effects of modernist defamiliarization on the one hand and almost archaic strand of realist mimeticism on the other to present the reader ultimately with a postcolonial text'.[43] In essence, Duffy's thesis is that *Ulysses* mocks colonial stereotypes of the figure of the native and nationalist discourse, which is portrayed as being a merely thinly veiled version of colonial narrative and dogma.

These anti-colonial formal and stylistic strategies are clearly evident in the 'Cyclops' episode of *Ulysses* in which, according to Duffy, the character of Leopold Bloom 'parallels the Irish and Jewish question as two instances of politically motivated racial injustice. He thereby broadens the questions of Irish independence, looking to the moment when it might make common cause with movements of national liberation everywhere'.[44] The hyperbolic language of nationalism is parodied and taken to extremely ludicrous places. This narrative strategy results in nationalism being seen as an archaic and very intolerant worldview in dire need of revision in the form of a future subaltern, postcolonial subjectivity.

One analytic omission that currently exists concerning *Ulysses* as a postcolonial novel along the lines that have already been discussed concerns the utilisation of the life and work of Oscar Wilde within *Ulysses*. This chapter shall address that gap in scholarship and argue that Joyce's interest in Wilde's work – specifically the poem 'The Harlot's House' contributed to his representation of postcolonial futurity in the 'Circe' episode of *Ulysses*.

The importance of Oscar Wilde's life and work to James Joyce and his writing has by now become an accepted fact within Wildean and Joycean criticism. However, less attention has been paid to how Wilde's writing came to influence the postcolonial, futural strand that runs through Joyce's *Ulysses*. Joyce is certainly known to have been familiar with most of these works by Wilde and admired them. In 1906, Joyce wrote to his brother Stanislaus about the powerful impact that *The Picture of Dorian Gray* had had upon him, particularly because of the implicit hints of male same-sex desire contained within the text.[45] When he was in Trieste, Joyce gave a lecture titled 'Oscar Wilde: The Poet of Salome'. Although Joyce never made any documented reference to 'The Harlot's House', that poem's setting and Gothic imagery of decay and decadence make it a useful piece to compare with certain sections of *Ulysses*.

'The Harlot's House' and 'Circe' also contain spectral presences that symbolise, not traumatic pasts, but potentially redemptive futures to come. In this respect, these two works contain a message about spectral relations that would be powerfully argued for by Jacques Derrida in *Specters of Marx*:

> It is necessary to speak of the ghost, indeed to the ghost and with it, from the moment that no ethics, no politics, whether revolutionary or not, seems possible and thinkable and just that does not recognize in its principle the respect for those others who are no longer, or for those others who are not yet there, presently living, whether they are already dead or not yet born.[46]

For Derrida, the function of ghosts is not to produce terror but rather to represent respect for the past and an openness to the future to come. The fluid nature of ghostly bodies, signifying absent presence, means that ghosts can challenge the ordered linearity of past leading to present leading to future. As David Coughlan outlines, the Derridean ghost is this thing that 'is both living and dead, that is neither living nor dead, that is past and is not past but to come, that looks like a dead father, or husband, or daughter [or son]'.[47] Thus, the ghost is a powerful adversary of the bodily restrictions controlled by what Michel Foucault has termed biopower through which private behaviour is silently policed and controlled by cultural norms.

As well as 'ghost', Derrida also uses the term *monstrous arrivant* in his 2003 text, *Rogues*, to describe the possible arrival of the event of an undecidable future to which all should remain open and be prepared for. For Derrida, the *monstrous arrivant* is that 'which comes, the event of what comes and of who comes, of what arrives or happens by reason and to reason … and at the end of the horizon, of teleology, the calculable programme, foresight, and providence – one no longer sees it coming, no longer horizontally: without prospect or horizon'.[48] A calm, open acceptance must be adopted towards the arrival of the *monstrous arrivant* and oppressive feelings associated with sublimity must be avoided as one receives the event of its presence.

'The Harlot's House' concludes with the appearance of an entity that brings an end to the poem's decadent revelry and signals the dawn of a new era and hope for the future to come: 'Then suddenly the tune went false,/ The dancers wearied of the waltz,/ The shadows ceased to wheel and whirl// And down the long and silent street,/ The dawn, with silver-sandalled feet,/ Crept like a frightened child'.[49] The specificities of this arrival, whether it be corporeal, symbolic or ghostly, is left undecidable. What is clear, from the poetic imagery, is that a momentous event has taken place. Far from symbolising a traumatic past, this arrival is an image of something new, its full nature and import as yet uncertain, but bringing with it the hope of bright new dawn. Like Derrida's ghost, the dawn is that which has come, and will come again in the present and the future.

'Circe' climaxes with the appearance of the spectral figure of Bloom's son, Rudy:

> *(Against the dark wall, a figure appears slowly, a fairy boy of eleven, a changeling, kidnapped, dressed in an Eton suit with glass shoes and a little bronze helmet, holding a book in his hand [...] He has a delicate mauve face. On his suit he has diamond and ruby buttons. In his free left hand he holds a slim ivory cane with a violet bowknot. A white lambkin peeps out of his waistcoat pocket.)*[50]

Bloom's son rising from the grave could arguably be a reference to a line earlier in the novel about the 'Home Rule sun rising up in the northwest' (68),[51] which would mean that Rudy's ghost was prophesising a hopeful future to come for Irish parliamentary politics, as opposed to only representing Bloom's traumatic past. Thus, this ghost performs a more positive symbolic function than Stephen's mother does in *Ulysses*. Significantly, futurity in both Wilde's poem and Joyce's novel is represented by recourse to the image of the coming of the dawn which creates continuity between the two works' climactic events.

The spectre of Rudy fulfils a more positive, future-oriented symbolic function than do other ghosts in Joyce's literary corpus. As Luke Gibbons argues: 'The ghost in Joyce's work appears in moments of crisis where the past slips through the private nets of memory but has not become public history, hovering in a liminal zone between inner and outer life'.[52] Up until this moment in *Ulysses*, ghostly hauntings in the book have symbolised the traumatic haunting of the present by the past. 'Telemachus' contains a moment of pure Gothicism as Stephen Dedalus recalls a dream in which he is visited by the vampiric ghost of his dead mother whose passing was a cause of great guilt for Stephen because he refused to pray over her dying body: 'In a dream, silently, she had come to him, her wasted body within its loose graveclothes giving off an odor of wax and rosewood, her breath bent over him with mute secret words [...] Ghoul! Chewer of corpses. No mother, let me be and let me live' (10–11).

I would argue that this moment of the present being haunted by the traumatic ghost of the past can be contrasted with the conclusion of 'Circe' where the appearance of a ghost represents the possibility of a redemptive future to come. The ghost of Stephen's mother, metamorphosed into a ghoul, symbolises the past that Stephen must awaken from if he is to live in the present and look forward to the future (as is the case for Leopold Bloom when he is plagued by the accusing ghost of his father earlier in 'Circe') – a future that will begin to make itself manifest in the concluding moments of 'Circe'. Significantly, just prior to the event of Rudy's spectral arrival, Stephen had resisted being goaded into a fight with two British soldiers, despite various ghosts from Ireland's rebel past – such as Wolfe Tone – appearing and urging him to do so (695). By refusing to be an active participant in a violent confrontation, Stephen personally rejects the traumatic legacy of Ireland's colonial past and what Bloom would call the destructive powers of 'Force, hatred, history, all that' (432). Unlike *The Picture of Dorian Gray*, which climaxes with Dorian attempting to kill the past by stabbing his portrait, only to be engulfed and destroyed by that past, 'The Harlot's House' and 'Circe' are texts that journey through a landscape of decadence and decay and eventually attain a glimpse of love passing into the house of lust.[53] The vision in 'Circe' of what Derrida calls the *avenir* (the 'to come'), as represented by the spectre of Rudy, is in marked contrast to Stephen's decadent fear of the future consisting of 'the ruin of all space' (28) – something that troubled his consciousness earlier in the novel.

Home Rule had already been granted by the time Joyce came to write 'Circe' and by foreshadowing an event that had already occurred in his lifetime, but not in the timeframe of the novel, Joyce is able to cast himself in the role of a Wildean, future-oriented artist via his use of a post-Gothic Gothicism. One key distinction is that, while the spectre of Rudy foreshadows a specific Irish future, the arrival at the end of 'The Harlot's House' represents something more akin to Derrida's undecidable, non-programmable future to come.[54]

Appropriately, Derrida famously claimed that Joyce was a ghost that haunted his work from the beginning and that there would have been no Deconstruction without Joyce because of the towering example of Joyce's experiments with language and various forms of spectral presence.[55] Thus, Joyce's Gothicism resulted in him becoming a compellingly absent presence who anticipated and helped shape several major literary and philosophical developments in the decades after his death. Paraphrasing Wilde, the future turned out to be what Joyce already was.

Richard Ellmann asserts that modern literature is always searching to be Joyce's contemporary[56] and I would argue that Joyce is equally concerned with being the contemporary of Oscar Wilde. Through the form and content of the 'Circe' episode, Joyce manages to succeed in that endeavour. Joyce used Wilde's complex literary relationship with late Victorian Gothic as an enabling example of how to begin to create an aesthetic that is inextricably linked to *fin de siècle* Gothicism but also offers what Declan Kiberd calls 'redemptive glimpses of a future [to come]'[57]: This is a future in which new forms of relationality – temporal, spatial, gendered, sexual – can be imagined and hopefully realised through the enabling force of art. The examination of both Wilde's and Joyce's complex and nuanced engagement with *fin de siècle* Gothicism adds a new and valuable layer to the familiar argument concerning how vital the importance of being Wildean was for James Joyce. As Joyce's ghost did for Derrida, so too does the ghost of the 'Gothic Oscar Wilde' haunt the works of James Joyce.

To conclude, Neil Sammells' argument concerning the value of the Gothic literary mode for Anglo-Irish writers like Wilde is equally true in relation to an Irish writer such as Joyce who was engaged in writing a literature steeped in liminality and inbetweenness for his postcolonial nation: 'Caught between Englishness and Irishness, divided in their cultural and political allegiances, Anglo-Irish writers were drawn to Gothic fiction as a means of expressing their sense of liminality and to the uncanny as an imagined disruption of prosaic and uncongenial present'.[58] Sammells regards Wilde's *The Picture of Dorian Gray* as an example of Camp Gothic and *The Canterville Ghost* and *Lord Arthur Saville's Crime* as examples of Comic Gothic. The 'Circe' episode of *Ulysses* contains elements of both the aforementioned forms of parodic Gothicism whilst the absent presence of Stephen Dedalus' mother and that of Rudy are example of pure and serious Gothic tropes being present within Joyce's novel just as they are in Wilde's 'Harlot's House'.

Yeats' *Purgatory* and later poems

One of the most significant events in the life of the early William Butler Yeats occurred in 1888 when he spent Christmas Day with Oscar Wilde in his house in Tite Street, Chelsea. Following the dinner, Wilde read to Yeats extracts from his new essay 'The Decay of Lying'. This work, among other things, advocates the creation of new realities and potential futures via the medium of artistic style. Many readers of 'The Decay of Lying' will habitually refer to what they regard as its central message: 'Life imitates art'. Yeats was greatly taken by this essay and he used it as inspiration for his Celtic Revival, proto-modernist project of trying to imagine in his work a postcolonial future for Ireland. What that Ireland looked like in Yeats' work changes considerably as his career progresses. The fact that he was a member of the Anglo-Irish Protestant Ascendancy inevitably meant that his attitude towards the 'new Ireland' was different to that of the native Irish Catholic population. This is apparent in Yeats' later poems that were written during the revolutionary period and post-independence. It is also an influence on his play *Purgatory*.

The plot of *Purgatory* is, on the surface at least, very straightforward. It tells a family saga of decline and fall through its two remaining members: an Old Man (the father) and a Boy (his sixteen-year-old son). It is set outside the former family home, which the

Old Man's father had drunkenly burnt down, leading the Old Man to kill his father as the building perished. The Boy is sceptical about tales of his family's former grandeur, and is repelled by the Old Man's story of losing his own mother as she gave birth to him, and the decline subsequent events wrought on the family. The mother was a member of the Anglo-Irish Ascendancy whilst his father was a native Irish stable hand. Thus, their union represented the contamination of the Anglo-Irish bloodline. Tonight, the Old Man tells the Boy, is the anniversary of the Old Man's mother's wedding night. This was the night on which he was conceived after a bout of drunken carousing by his father, and thus when his mother's fate was sealed. At this point a ghostly figure appears illuminated in a window of the wrecked house. In an attempt to wrest his mother's soul from Purgatory, the Old Man suddenly stabs and kills the Boy. However, this attempt appears to be in vain: the approaching hoof beats of his ghostly father returning to the bridal bed at the play's finale signal that no spirits have left the place, and the grim cycle of death and pollution begins again.

Yeats would have learnt a lot about the concept of Purgatory from stories he heard in the West of Ireland from Irish peasants – stories that he wrote down in a volume of tales called *The Celtic Twilight*. One such story was related to him by an informant from Co. Galway: 'And another time I saw Purgatory. It seemed to be in a level place, and no walls around it, But it all one bright blaze, and the souls standing in it'.[59] The depiction of Purgatory in Yeats' play bears certain similarities to this story since the room where the mother lies is well lit.

The style of *Purgatory* is influenced by Japanese Noh theatre. This is most obvious in its use of ghosts and the sparseness of its stage. The opening stage directions tell us that the play is set around only a ruined house with a bare tree in the background. Samuel Beckett was to make use of that same minimalist set in his play *Waiting for Godot* in which the opening stage directions read: '*A country road. A tree. Evening*'. Recently published papers have revealed that Beckett did see the first staged production of *Purgatory* and admired it greatly. However, Yeats does not slavishly follow Noh drama but rather adopts whatever features of this form he feels are useful to his purposes. For example, the characters in this play do not wear masks, which is very common in Noh theatre. There is also much more emphasis on talk and no dancing.

Like *Waiting for Godot*, *Purgatory* is greatly concerned with seemingly pointless repetition. This is obvious from the opening lines spoken by the Boy: 'Half door, hall door. Hither and thither day and night. Hill or hollow, shouldering this pack. Hearing you talk'.[60] It is clear that it is also the living and not merely the dead who are caught in a purgatorial cycle, hoping against hope that they will be redeemed. The fact that the boy is 16 is significant because he would have been born in 1922, the year that the Irish Free State was founded and the power of the Anglo-Irish began to be severely eroded.

The Big House was a very powerful symbol for the Anglo-Irish as it represented their power and privilege and it functions as a character in many of their works. This is certainly the case in this play where the father's first spoken words are: 'Study that house. I think about its jokes and stories; I try to remember what the butler said to the drunken gamekeeper in mid-October, but I cannot' (255). The decaying home is a metaphor for the decline of the Anglo-Irish family. The Old Man's failure to remember the time he spent in the house symbolises the loss of tradition and history. One of the crimes that the Old Man levels at his father is killing the house, as if the house is a living thing with a life to be snuffed out.

In Yeats' poem, 'Meditations in Time of Civil War', several sections are devoted to describing the Big Houses that he inhabited and which are now being destroyed by a new order in Ireland. Here is one such section describing Thoor Ballylee in Co. Galway: 'An ancient bridge, and a more ancient tower, A farmhouse that is sheltered by its walls, An acre of stony ground, Where the symbolic rose can break in flower'.[61] It was Yeats' hope that this house would survive the changing times and serve as a symbol of continuance. He expressed this desire in his poem 'To be Carved on a Stone at Thoor Ballylee', written in 1921: 'I, the poet William Yeats,/ With old mill boards and sea-green slates,/ And smithy work from the Gort forge,/ Restored this tower for my wife George;/ And may these characters remain./ When all is ruin once again'.

One could argue that, by the end of his life, Yeats had given up such utopian notions of transcending the passage of time and instead embraced a more pessimistic view of the cycle of history. This is reflected in *Purgatory* but also in his lengthy piece of verse, 'Nineteen Hundred and Nineteen':

> We too had many pretty toys when young:
> A law indifferent to blame or praise,
> To bribe or threat; habits that made old wrong
> Melt down, as it were wax in the sun's rays;
> Public opinion ripening for so long
> We thought it would outlive all future days.
> O what fine thought we had because we thought
> That the worst rogues and rascals had died out. (142)

This reference to rogues and rascals anticipates the character of the Old Man's father whose bad behaviour brought down the family of the woman that he married.

The Big House in *Purgatory* is mourned partially because of the history that existed within it and which has now been erased:

> Old Man: Great people lived and died in this house;
> Magistrates, colonels, members of Parliament,
> Captains and Governors, and long ago
> Men that had fought at Aughrim and the Boyne …
> But he killed the house; to kill a house
> Where great men grew up, married, died,
> I here declare a capital offence. (257)

In addition to the house, the tree also serves as a powerful symbol for the themes of memory and the past. Although it is bare in the present, the Old Man recreates it through words as being very beautiful and leafy: 'I saw it a year ago stripped bare as now, I saw it fifty years ago. Before the thunderbolt had riven it, Green leaves, ripe leaves, leaves thick as butter' (257). Thus, the tree symbolises the collision between the past and the present, and between history and memory that is at the core of this drama. The tree as a symbol for tradition and inheritance is a common feature in several of Yeats poems. Here is a quote from 'Coole Park and Ballylee': 'ancestral trees, Or Gardens rich in Memory'.[62] The physical landscape in both works can be read as containing the spirit of Yeats' people.

Although *Purgatory* is concerned with epic issues and debates, they are all handled through the deep focus on a very small number of characters. This is the hallmark of much of Yeats' work as Timothy Webb has noted:

> Although in his earlier years Yeats had identified himself as a Nationalist, he habitually resisted the simplifications of propaganda and of popular rhetoric. The older Yeats was much more open to the receipt of public affairs than his younger self; yet the events of Easter 1916, of the Troubles and the Civil War, and of post-war Europe, were registered almost less, perhaps, as external realities than as part of Yeats's own poetic and psychological life ... [P]ublic events are placed and recorded but the prevailing perspective is a subjective one, and conflicts are internalised.[63]

In *Purgatory*, Yeats examines the collapse of the Anglo-Irish protestant ascendancy through the lens of one particular family's psychological turmoil. This is comparable with his poem 'Easter 1916', which deals less with the epic events of that week in Ireland and far more with his own conflicted reaction to them. The Old Man in *Purgatory* falsely believes that he can save his mother from her suffering but, as the play suggests, this can be achieved by her alone. The image of the Big House in flames may have been suggested to Yeats by the climax of Elizabeth Bowen's 'Big House Novel' *The Last September* (1929), which involves a fictional Anglo-Irish Big House being burnt to the ground by Irish rebels during the War of independence. Bowen's novel has come to be regarded as one of the great novelistic representations of the decline of the Anglo-Irish Ascendency in the same way as *Purgatory* is considered one of the great theatrical representations of that same fall from grace.

The Boy's obsession with getting his fair share of the family money can be seen to reflect Yeats' disillusionment with modern Ireland as a place where people's sole concern is with material gain. This attitude of Yeats' can be most obviously seen in his poem 'September 1913':

> What need you, being come to sense,
> But fumble in a greasy till
> And add the halfpence to the pence
> And prayer to shivering prayer, until
> You have dried the marrow from the bone;
> For men were born to pray and save;
> Romantic Ireland's dead and gone,
> It's with O'Leary in the grave. (73).

The name O'Leary refers to John O'Leary who was an Irish nationalist and poet. O'Leary worked as a financial agent of the Irish Republican Brotherhood and he was also the editor of the publication *The Irish People*. He was arrested on 14 September, 1865 and charged with high treason. He was sentenced to twenty years in an English jail and was exiled to Paris in 1874. He received amnesty in 1885 and returned to Dublin, where he convinced Yeats to join the cause of literary nationalism. By invoking O'Leary's name, Yeats is reflecting on the last of what he regarded as the true Irish heroes. The people left behind in his wake, as far as Yeats was concerned, were a pale reflection of O'Leary's glory. In *Purgatory*, we can also see the remnants of a glorious Ireland that has now faded away.

Purgatory has sometimes been regarded as a work which reflects Yeats' interest in Fascism and the notion of pure-bloodedness that became so associated with Nazi Germany. The Old Man's desire to kill his father and his son seems to be partly inspired by a desire to eradicate the contaminated bloodline that has infected his family: 'I killed that lad for he was growing up, He would soon take some woman's fancy, Beget and pass pollution on' (261). Yeats was certainly very interested in Fascism and even wrote articles on Nazi legislation for the *Irish Independent*. However, it is problematic to assert that *Purgatory* is an endorsement of the theory of eugenics since the Old Man's desire to keep his bloodline unpolluted has led to nothing more than the cannibalising of his entire family and condemned him to a live a fruitless and unfulfilling purgatorial existence. W.J. McCormack has argued that *Purgatory* can be regarded as a play that is critical of both Anglo-Ireland and Fascism:

> Between 'Purgatory' and the Irish Independent pronouncements on Nazi legislation one may find at least one significant resemblance. The Boy and the Old Man in turn give in momentarily to the idea that they are alive, that they go on living; it is the intolerable burden of the play that they do not live and they must yet go on. The beneficiaries of German legislation are allowed the same inert, repetitive existence, they may 'go on living where their fathers lived'. Small comfort to six million Jews in the ovens! Yet no one who has ignored the exposure of his inauthentic tradition in 'Purgatory' has earned the right to call Yeats a fascist.[64]

McCormack is here highlighting how *Purgatory* exposes the destructive results of living according to one set tradition and in accordance to rigid rules of racial purity. The loyalty to a past existence destroys any possibility of living in an evolving present. Also, the reference to going on with a futile existence highlights the similarities between this work and *Godot*.

Purgatory is not the first of Yeats' plays to feature the killing of a son by his father. In *On Baille's Strand*, the hero Cuchulain unknowingly kills his son at the end of the drama – in the same way, obviously, that Oedipus mistakenly kills his father at the end of *Oedipus Rex*. Purgatory can be seen as a reworking of *On Baille's Strand* since the Father very deliberately kills his son and he had also killed his father beforehand. Thus, *Purgatory* is simultaneously intertextually referencing *Oedipus* and *On Baille's Strand*.

Irish art in the twentieth century features many examples of father-and-son conflict. Sometimes the father will kill the son and sometimes the son will kill the father. Depending on which one occurs, the society in which the works are set either shows itself capable or incapable of renewal and growth. Obviously the natural cycle is for the son to take over from the father but that cannot happen if the son has been murdered. In Synge's *Playboy of the Western of World* for example, Christy Mahon symbolically kills his father (although at one point he thinks he has done so literally) and takes his place. That play is referenced implicitly in *Purgatory* when the Old Man says: 'I'll to a distant place, and there, Tell my old jokes to new men' (261). At the conclusion of *Playboy*, the father tells the villagers of Mayo: '[M]y son and myself will be going our own way and we'll have times from this out telling stories of the villainy of Mayo and the fools is there' (146). Unlike the father in the finale of Synge's play, however, Yeats' father is left to roam on his own after having killed his son and is reduced to relaying the same tale over and over again to people who may well not be interested.

Gerardine Meaney's analysis of Yeats' *On Baille's Strand* could be used equally well in relation to *Purgatory*: 'Unable to overcome this feminine power and deprived of his son, Cuchulainn cannot beget the future. He remains warrior, never king. Here heroic masculinity is presented as dependent on a complex set of relationships, which can withdraw as well as endow posterity, fame and identity'.[65] In *Purgatory*, the future seems to be non-existent as the people have cannibalised any hope of begetting one. Although the Old Man partially blames his mother for bringing about the downfall of his family by sleeping with an outsider, it is his masculine urge towards conflict that ultimately destroys the members of his bloodline.

Many recent Irish films have used this Oedipal theme of father-and-son relations in their plots. Jim Sheridan's film *The Field* replicates the climax of *On Baille's Strand* in its final moments when the father drives his son off a cliff and then, overcome by guilt, begins to whip the waves just as Cuchulainn does at the end of Yeats' play. Another of Sheridan's films, *In the Name of the Father*, although based on the true-life case of the Guildford Four and their wrongful imprisonment, focusses specifically on the relationship between Gerry Conlon and his father Giuseppe. In order to do this, the filmmakers broke with historical fact and had the two men in the same cell. It is only with the death of his father that Gerry Conlon begins to find the strength to fight against his wrongful conviction. In essence, the son becomes the father after the father's death. Another example from historical fiction is the film *Michael Collins*, which Elizabeth Butler Cullingford reads as being an allegory of the Cuchulainn myth with De Valera as the Cuchulainn killing his son Michael Collins. Thus, we can see that *Purgatory* represents, in its thematic concerns, some of the major elements of Irish art in the twentieth century.

Jacqueline Genet has succinctly summarised some of the various thematic strands that are present in *Purgatory:*

> A socio-political and national play, a metaphysical drama, *Purgatory* is even more a tragedy of a man inhabited by the instinct of destruction, by guilt and haunting anguish. He is hero and 'villain' at once, a lover of the past but contaminated by the present, dreaming of courtly love but uniting in a ditch with a tinker's daughter … He is guilty of parricide and infanticide, at once Oedipus, Cuchulain and Lear. By its economy and terseness *Purgatory* is perhaps the greatest tragedy in one act of our time. There is nothing so simple or so suggestive as *Purgatory* before *Waiting for Godot*.[66]

What Genet has correctly highlighted is this play's ability to combine opposites into a dialectic unity, which is at the core of *Purgatory*'s appeal. It refuses to simply endorse one side of any argument and reveals Yeats' two-sided approach to life. As he himself once said: 'A mind cannot engender until divided in two'.[67]

The works of Yeats' 'late period' demonstrate his anxiety about what would become of him and the Anglo-Irish people more generally in a postcolonial Ireland that would in all likelihood be hostile to them and their traditions. For this reason, his postcolonial Irish literary texts very often exhibit a pessimism concerning what post-independence, postcolonial Ireland would look like. The final work of Yeats that shall be considered in this chapter, the poem 'Among School Children', offers a somewhat more optimistic view of 'the new Ireland'.

'Among School Children' begins with the old Yeats, now a senator in the Irish Free State, inspecting a school and pondering how the school children of modern Ireland must feel when confronted by this 'sixty-year old-smiling public man' (151). His mind then begins wandering back into his past and his thoughts dwell on the 'Ledean body' of his former muse Maude Gonne and how their 'two natures blent/ Into a sphere from youthful sympathy' (151). This poem contains many images of dialectical synchronicity where seeming opposites blend together into a unity, which was what Yeats had hoped could happen in all walks of life in post-independence Ireland.

The poet ponders on how every present contains vestiges of its past and how present moments can ripple into the future:

> I look upon one child or t'other there
> And wonder if she stood so at that age -
> For even daughters of the swan can share
> Something of every paddler's heritage -
> And had that colour upon cheek or hair,
> And thereupon my heart is driven wild:
> She stands before me as a living child. (152)

Yeats' past with Maude Gonne is being revived by his artist's eyes looking upon this young school child. Thus, rather than merely dwelling on the Maude Gonne of the past, this poetic vision makes her a part of a communal present. In a similar fashion to 'The Lake Isle of Innisfree', 'Among School Children' centres on the poet's mind wandering away from its immediate moment and contemplating other times and places, which are then partially connected with his present time and the physical space in which he currently finds himself; in this case, that space is among school children.

Several of the rhetorical questions that comprise the final stanza of 'Among School Children' suggest the interdependence of various wholes and their constituent parts: 'O chestnut-tree, great-rooted blossomer, Are you the leaf, the blossom or the bole? (153). This can be interpreted as suggesting the importance of the individual to communities, whether they be families, nations or races. The poem concludes with the famous rhetorical question, 'How can we know the dancer from the dance?' (153). This line invokes one of the great goals of most of Yeats' work, the unity of seeming opposites. It may also be a moment in the Yeatsian canon that bears the stamp of the influence of Oscar Wilde because Wilde's work is constantly suggesting that the world in which we live is very much stylistically constituted and that nouns (being words) are very much dependent on verbs (doing words) for their existence.

Yeats' poetic aesthetic and images, which privilege openness and a certain level of undecidability – as can be seen in 'Among School Children' – is something that is clearly in evidence in Yeats' later poems. As David Lloyd has argued: 'Where [Yeats'] earlier writings are devoted to the project of founding and forging a nation, the later writings, in the wake of the Free State's foundation, subject all acts of foundation to the most rigorous examination within a set of aesthetic terms which are profoundly antithetical to any tradition of symbolism' (60). Although Lloyd does not explicitly mention 'Among School Children' in his analysis of Yeats' later work, the argument quoted above is certainly applicable to that poem as the above analysis has shown.

Robert Tracey's analysis of 'Among School Children' highlights its value as a postcolonial Irish poem: 'The [poetic] voice [in 'Among School Children' eventually] breaks free of solipsism, soliloquy, solitude, and enters a vision of shared identity, of community, that is the poem'.[68] The achievement of a vision of unity and connectedness, whether that be in racial, national or colonial terms, is what is at the theoretical heart of the works of many postcolonial thinkers.

John Brannigan has described Yeats' public and artistic life as being that of a distinctly Anglo-Irish postcolonial writer: 'Yeats did write himself and his revival contemporaries into the mythology of the foundation of the Irish Free State in 1922. He took his place in its upper chamber as a senator, and continued to speak of the ways in which the state might give expression to its cultural distinctiveness'.[69] Although sometimes despairing, Yeats never seemed to lose hope that, via art and politics, Ireland could attain a postcolonial future that would be inclusive rather than exclusive in terms of what version(s) of Irishness would be privileged.

Translations[70]

In his introduction to *Brian Friel: Collected Poems*, Seamus Deane refers to the reasons why Friel is so important as an Irish writer: 'No Irish writer since the early days of this [twentieth] century has so sternly and courageously asserted the role of art in the public world without either yielding to that world's pressures or retreating into art's narcissistic alternatives'.[71] In Deane's view, Friel's art is sufficiently aesthetically engaged in contemporary cultural and political realities as to be ethical in their representations of the socio-political realities of Ireland in Friel's time and earlier. This appraisal of Friel links him with early twentieth-century writers such as Yeats and Joyce and also implicitly asserts Friel's value as a postcolonial Irish writer because he is willing to use art as a means to engage in the political act of imagining and staging of moments that theorist Richard Kearney would call carnal and linguistic hospitality.[72] Kearney has argued for the need to think through a form of ethics that unites both word and touch in an act of responsible hospitality. 'What is needed is the more embodied approach of a carnal hospitality that assists in discerning the right ways of touching and not touching, of uniting word and body, teaching us how to incarnate the reconciliation and forgiveness with the stranger'.[73] This command from Kearney clearly has great potential for application in the context of relations between coloniser and colonised, especially in Ireland where colonialism clearly exists in the form of linguistic dispossession.

In *Translations*, Friel triumphantly achieves both hospitable carnal and linguistic encounters between English coloniser and Irish colonised in a manner that puts into dramatic practice the theorisation of ethical encounters between imperial self and colonised other that appears in many influential works of postcolonial theory. Friel's friendship with Richard Kearney and Kearney's involvement in the academic side of the Field Day group (particularly with regard to the conceptualising of Ireland's 'artistic fifth province', which was so beloved by many of the members of Field Day's board of directors who wished to imagine a place in Ireland where political divisions did not exert such a destructive force on its people) may conceivably have shaped some of Friel's philosophical interests in concepts such as hospitality in a colonial and postcolonial context.

The theatre audience who watch *Translations* are made very aware of the need for translation and linguistic hospitality when it becomes clear to them that, despite the fact that they can only hear English being spoken on stage, the reality is that many of the characters are speaking Irish and are not understanding the English being spoken by the non-Irish speakers. The audience are thus forced to imagine the lack of communication on the stage and this makes them even more acutely aware of the need for linguistic accommodation between different nations and national identities. For this reason, when Brian Friel was asked whether an Irish language version of the play could be produced, he insisted that such a version had to be completely in Irish so the same problems concerning hospitality and accommodation could be foregrounded for the viewers of the drama. As Lionel Pilkington argues: 'The exclusion of the Irish vernacular in the play is not merely a convenient theatrical convention, but is crucial to the play's political message'.[74]

The character of Jimmy Jack, the elderly Greek scholar and 'partner in crime' of the schoolmaster Hugh, is introduced via the stage directions as someone for whom hospitality could be regarded as the watch word on which his entire identity and character depends: '*For Jimmy the world of the gods and the ancient myths is as real and as immediate as everyday life in the townland of Baile Beag*'.[75] Jimmy Jack's desire to marry the mythic goddess Pallas Athene also symbolises a carnal hospitality, connecting bodies, languages and temporalities, that is appropriate to his willingness to accommodate the linguistic contours of the present and the past within his own personal lexicon. This reading of Jimmy Jack is confirmed by Hugh near the play's conclusion: 'I look at James and three thoughts occur to me: A – that it is not the literal past, the 'facts' of history, that shape us, but images of the past embodied in language. James has ceased to make that discrimination' (445). Jimmy Jack's home is predicated on the language he uses to view it and this hospitality to a mythic past that is symbolised by how at home he is when he speaks Greek makes his imagined romance with Pallas Athene seem totally appropriate. In Jimmy Jack's mind's eye, the mythical body of Pallas Athene is translated into one of present day carnality.

The return of the prodigal son Owen to his hometown of *Baile Beag* (Ballybeg) is signalled as a foretelling of unwelcome change. As Owen bluntly informs his family and neighbours: 'My job is to translate the quaint, archaic tongue you people persist in speaking into the King's good English' (404). The first moment of an unethical, violent form of translation occurring in the play happens when Owen translates into Irish what his commander, Lancey, says in English:

> LANCEY: And also, so that the entire basis of land valuation can be reassessed for purposes of more equitable taxation.
> OWEN: This new map will take the place of the estate agent's map so that from now on you will know what is yours by law. (406)

Whilst Lancey emphasises the benefits to colonial administration as a result of this Ordnance Survey map and the translating of Irish names into English for the map, Owen misrepresents the English words and tells the villagers how it will be a good thing for them. Owen's brother, Manus, who also speaks English, feels that there is nothing incorrect about their Irish place names and that the form of translation being undertaken by Owen and Yolland represents an unethical form of inhospitality to the native Irish tongue. This opinion is communicated to Owen by his brother in no uncertain terms. Manus goes so far as to compare the acts of translation and cartography being undertaken to a military operation. As far as Manus is concerned, the English visitors are acting as bad, unethical guests and, for that reason, he will refuse to offer them any hospitality.

Perhaps the most memorable moment of colonial hospitality in terms of both bodily and linguistic connectedness in *Translations* occurs during the love scene between Yolland and Maire. Importantly, the stage directions request that, if possible, this scene should take place outside rather than in the hedge school building. This implies that Friel wished a mood of openness and intimacy between the two lovers at this moment in the play. One of the most moving moments in all of Friel's dramatic oeuvre occurs when Yolland and Maire achieve a moment of intimacy and connection that involves the use of words but also transcends them since neither lover understands what the other is saying:

> YOLLAND: Because if you could understand me, I could tell you how I spend my days either thinking about you or gazing up at your house in the hope that you'll appear even for a second.
> MAIRE: Every evening you walk by yourself along the Tra Bhan and every morning you wash yourself in front of your tent.
> YOLLAND: I would tell you how beautiful you are, curly headed Maire. I would so like to tell you how beautiful you are. (429)

Neither Yolland nor Maire demands that their language be privileged. They both speak what they wish to say and yet somehow they manage to communicate their love for the Other because of and yet also in spite of their linguistic choices. They hear and somehow this results in a connection, even though the words used mean nothing to them. Significantly, the stage directions tell us that during parts of this scene, the two characters are speaking '*almost to himself/herself*' (429). As Christopher Murray argues: 'This is a private and secret language [but one which allows for the admittance of the Other also]. As they exchange the words they move across the stage and touch hands. The contact is extremely important. It is the highpoint of the dramatic action. It translates for the audience a love that challenges division'.[76] Thus, an act of linguistic hospitality to the Other's language leads directly to the carnal hospitality that climaxes this scene; when both Maire and Yolland finally kiss one another.

The kiss that occurs between Maire and Yolland can be interpreted directly as an act of pure carnal hospitality. This is the case because, as Adam Philips argues, the kiss blurs the distinction between giving and taking: 'You cannot kiss yourself. Even as you are receiving pleasure, you have opened yourself to the Other and offering them a gift of non-sexual jouissance that cannot be achieved by a person by themselves. The Other's hospitality is always required to achieve this moment of ecstasy that in no way involves the stimulation of sexual organs that can be done by the act of masturbation'.[77] This is the only moment of physical intimacy that is staged between Yolland and Maire. It is one that shows the willingness they both share to engage in carnal hospitality and to open the self unconditionally to the Other's desires.

It is also in this scene that Yolland begins to metamorphose into one of the native Irish characters that he has been spending so much time with recently, Hugh. As Anthony Roche argues: 'Yolland is now "fully native" and, Friel adds, "alcoholic almost" and this aligns him with Hugh'.[78] Thus, linguistic and carnal hospitality are occurring at the same time and result in the becoming other of both languages and bodies, even as both don't appear to be undergoing a direct transition or translation. Like the English character of Tom Broadbent in *John Bull's Other Island* (1904), Yolland's embracing of Irishness is connected with physical intoxication, which symbolically links bodily pleasure with spiritual transformation.

When one thinks of an Irish play in which a female character is fought for by Irish and British males, one inevitably thinks of Yeats' and Lady Gregory's epochal *Cathleen ni Houlihan* (1902) in which Ireland is symbolised by an Old Woman who becomes young as a result of the shedding of virile, masculine Irish blood (see Chapter 1 in this book for a deeper engagement with this play). In *Translations*, however, the woman chooses the British suitor over the Irish one. This choice by Friel represents a version of narrative hospitality because the romance in this play gestures toward an accommodation of national difference rather than a continuation of hostility between nations. Thus, carnal and narrative hospitality are folded together in this moving scene of romance between Maire and Yolland.

In the 2022 Abbey Theatre production of *Translations*, the director, Caitriona McLaughlin asserts that the reason she foregrounded the character of Maire (played by Zara Devlin) on the play's poster was because she saw her as being symbolic of Ireland in the same way as Cathleen ni Houlihan was: 'Kathleen [sic] ni Houlihan represents Ireland. Roisin Dubh represents Ireland. All these dark, unavailable women. So, I thought she [Maire] represents Ireland'.[79]

Translations' concluding moments bring us to its supreme gesture towards linguistic/narrative hospitality on a colonial level. The choric figure of Hugh declares to Maire that they must now bow to the inevitable and begin to incorporate English into their lives and make it part of their modern identity: 'We must learn where we live. We must learn to make them [English words] our own. We must make them our new home' (444). The subtlety of what Hugh is saying needs to be acknowledged. He does not say that they must speak

English as the colonial foreigner speaks it, rather, he wishes the Irish to adapt and to some extent translate the English language into a form that will be appropriate and representative of Irish lives and identities. Thus, Hugh is prophesising the emergence of the dialect of Hiberno-English that will be used so successfully by later writers such as J.M. Synge. Kearney has identified how this moment in *Translations* is intended to serve as an anticipation of Irish literary achievements that have already occurred long before this play was first produced: 'Speaking in his capacity as poet, Hugh bequeaths to his community [...] the challenge of an Irish literature written in English'.[80]

When Hugh tells Maire not to worry about the English word 'always' because 'it is a silly word' (446), he is also telling her that 'always' is a very inhospitable word since it is overly prescriptive and neglectful of nuance and complexity. In order for the Irish to survive as a people and for their language to be preserved, they must embrace provisionality and otherness at a linguistic and carnal level. By opening itself to the weakening of its identity in order to ensure her capacity for renewal, Ireland can ensure her survival and avoid becoming the silent woman struggling in vain to speak, as is the case with the character of Sarah who also functions in this play (Cathleen ni Houlihan-like) as a symbol of Ireland in an age when its language was threatened.

The challenge uttered by Hugh was of course already a retroactive one in the eyes of the play's audience because, at the time of the first staging of *Translations*, authors such as Synge, Yeats, Joyce and Beckett had already engaged in this linguistic hospitality and written towering works of Irish literature in their own versions of English and sometimes Hiberno-English. In the case of Samuel Becket, he also followed the example set by Oscar Wilde through his play *Salome* and extended his linguistic hospitality to the French tongue. It is entirely justifiable to argue that the great works of Anglo-Irish literature have all emerged from individual, artistic acts of linguistic hospitality.

The play climaxes with Hugh's attempt at reciting the story of *The Aeneid* and the fall of Troy as a means of linguistically ennobling Ireland's current tragic moment and attempting to foreshadow a future resurrection from tragedy that can be achieved by linguistic hospitality. Although Greek has been the preferred ancient language throughout the drama's duration, it is the story of the eventual triumph of Troy following the conquering of her by Greece that takes centre stage in the climax of *Translations* via Hugh's Latin recitation. Hugh has to begin his oral performance of *The Aeneid* a second time, which symbolises the break-down of language and his mastery of his chosen linguistic contours. By having the play end before the speech can be completed, Friel suggests the continuation of a story and how its ending is not set in stone. The drama thus concludes with a moment of openness rather than inhospitable, total closure. F.C. McGrath has correctly – albeit implicitly – highlighted conditional linguistic hospitality as being one of the achievements of *Translations*: 'With its experimental representation of Irish [and sometimes Latin] in English, the play revives and renews the old English culture in the image of the hedge school as it translates it into another language and another time. Like Yeats and Synge, Friel translates a Gaelic past into an Anglo-Irish present'.[81]

By ending *Translations* with a partial Latin recitation of Virgil's *Aeneid* by an Irishman living in 1833, which is being viewed originally by an audience in 1980, two generations of Irish people are partaking in the event of seeing the ghosts speaking from the past and seeing a potential for a redemptive present and future. Drawing upon Murray's description of the play's final moments: 'With this liminality, the play fades out rather than concludes. We are left inhabiting two [and possibly even three] time scales simultaneously, sensed through two languages superimposed'.[82] I would argue that there are three languages haunting the end of *Translations* – Irish, English and Latin – and none of them are privileged over the other in this moment of acceptance of a new, linguistically open Ireland in which ghosts of various kinds can be spoken of, to and with.

Translations was famously the first play to be put on by The Field Day Theatre Company and its premiere was in the Derry Guildhall, the then seat of local government in that city. As Marilyn Richtarik correctly observes, Derry was a place in Northern Ireland that was highly significant for both the Catholic/nationalist and Protestant/Unionist communities. For Unionists, Derry's withstanding of a siege by James II in 1689 made the continuation of Protestant rule possible. Thus, Derry signified the Unionists' desire to remain British.

For the nationalists, the electoral gerrymandering in that city had allowed the Unionists to maintain electoral and governmental power over the Catholics.[83] By staging this very political play, which is set in a turbulent past and deals with issues such as a colonialism and racial intolerance – albeit set in a time more than a hundred years ago – in such a location, those involved in Field Day were seeking to make a hospitable gesture towards the individual British/Unionist bodies and also their body politic. This staging choice also states that the play was meant to gesture towards an (already discussed) artistic fifth province on the Island of Ireland in which two religious and racial communities could feel at home and feel willing to extend hospitality to their religious and racial others. Richard Kearney's involvement with Mark P. Hederman in the biannual journal *The Crane Bag*, which ran from 1977 to 1985, was very influential in terms of making popular the concept of the hospitable artistic fifth province on the Island of Ireland, an idea that was to prove very attractive to the Field Day board members when it came to the onerous task of trying to encapsulate a *raison d'etre* for Field Day that would capture the public imagination of Ireland North and South.

Translations was performed in early 2023 in Ukraine's National Academy Drama Theatre in war torn Kyiv. In that version, Ballybeg became Bakhmut. The Director Kylo Kashilkov, in an interview with Raidió Teilifís Éireann (RTÉ), Ireland's national television station, said 'we decided to choose this play because we feel a connection between our situation and the situation in Ireland many years ago'.[84] This is not surprising when one considers that the Russian invasion of Ukraine, whilst it is certainly a conflict over territory, is also at least partly one over competing languages. The Ukrainian version of *Translations* can be interpreted as an example of linguistic and carnal hospitality during which the play's participants speak of, and endeavour to embody, the ghosts of a nightmarish Irish past so that they might envisage their own, post-war future to come. By putting on Friel's *Translations* in this way, Ukraine has also become engaged with Ricoeur's narrative hospitality by attempting to use in an ethical fashion a narrative from and of another nation to speak for their own experiences.

Edward Said has written of *Translations*' capacity to represent and speak for various non-Irish nations and identities such as Indian,

Algerian or Palestinian – people for whom 'the silencing of their voices, the renaming of places and replacement of languages by the imperial outsider, the creation of colonial maps and divisions also implied the attempted reshaping of society'.[85] Without invoking Ricoeur or 'narrative hospitality' directly, Said has described how Ricoeur's concept is very much at play in *Translations* and testifies to its capacities to speak for various victims of unethical linguistic and bodily erasures. The Ukrainian version of Translation testifies to the validity of this assertion.

In *Translations*, Friel uses his dramatic craft to try and imagine a more ethical, more hospitable world in which the Other can be accommodated via linguistic and carnal hospitality. The narratives that are contained within *Translations* are constantly endeavouring to do justice to the traumatic experiences of the self, Others and otherness. In the achievement of these ethical/hospitable moments onstage, forgiveness from the Other can be sought and granted by the various audience members, especially those watching the play in Ireland, North and South. Equally, it is implied that forgiveness for the Other will be accepted if it should be sought. As Friel's fellow Field Day director Seamus Deane has argued: 'the fact that the play has been written is itself an indication of the success of the imagination in dealing with everything that seems opposed to its survival. What is most characteristically tragic in the play is the sense of exhilaration which it transmits to its audience'.[86] The exhilaration and the sensuous desires for linguistic and carnal hospitality that are created onstage are thus communicated to the audience who can then – if they are so moved – leave the imagined community of the theatre both carnally and linguistically stimulated and may now attempt to realise those exhilarating desires in their larger community. *Translations* can thus be read as a dramatic texts that is endeavouring to enact on stage for the purposes of inspiring those in the audience an ethical vision for postcolonial Ireland. Significantly, *Translations* is a text that can be interpreted through the varying prisms of nationalist, revisionist and postcolonial theoretical analyses. It is a play that portrays the harshness of British rule in Ireland, and critiques nationalist violence while also trying to offer a vision of a postcolonial Irish future that transcends national and racial hatred and division.

Study questions

1. **Analyse the revisionism/nationalism debate in Irish culture.**
2. **'It is not the literal past, the "facts" of history, that shape us, but images of the past embodied in language' (*Translations*). Evaluate the contribution of Field Day to the rise of postcolonial theory in Irish theoretical discourse.**
3. **What are the potential problems inherent in analysing a culture and/or literature from a 'political perspective'?**
4. **In what ways is postcolonial theory different from both Revisionism and nationalist theory?**
5. **What similarities exist between postcolonial theory and nationalism and revisionism in terms of how they interrogate conceptions of Ireland and Irishness?**
6. **How is postmodern theory a radical departure from theories such as postcolonialism?**

Notes

1 Personal communication.
2 Lance Pettitt, *Screening Ireland* (Manchester and New York: Manchester University Press, 2000), p. 9.
3 See Edward Said, *Orientalism* (New York: Vintage Books, 1979), p. 2.
4 Ibid., p. 14.
5 Ibid., p. 16. Emphasis in original.
6 Joe Cleary, 'Introduction: Ireland and Modernity', in Joe Cleary and Claire Connolly (eds), *The Cambridge Companion to Modern Irish Culture* (Cambridge: Cambridge University Press, 2005), p. 7.
7 Patrick Bixby, *Nietzsche and Irish Modernism* (Manchester: Manchester University Press, 2025), p. 5.
8 Roy Foster, 'We Are All Revisionists Now', *The Irish Review*, 1 (1986), p. 2.
9 Ibid., p. 5.
10 Ronan Fanning, 'The Meaning of Revisionism', *The Irish Review* 14 (Spring 1988), p. 17.
11 Quoted in ibid., p. 19.
12 Ibid.

13 Desmond Fennell, 'Against Revisionism', *Irish Review* 14 (Spring 1988), p. 20.
14 Ibid., p. 26.
15 Edward Said, 'Yeats and Decolonization', in Dennis Wilder (ed.), *Literature in the Modern World* (Oxford: Oxford University Press, 1990), p. 34.
16 Quoted in Marilynn Richtarik, 'The Field Day Theatre Company', in Shaun Richards (ed.), *The Cambridge Companion to Twentieth-Century Irish Drama* (Cambridge: Cambridge University Press, 2004), p. 192. For an account of the aims, objectives and productions of Field Day, see Marilynn Richtarik, *Acting Between the Lines: The Field Day Theatre Company and Irish Cultural Politics 1980–1984* (Oxford: Oxford University Press, 1995; Washington, DC: Catholic University of America Press, 2001).
17 Richtarik, *Acting Between the Lines*, p. 175.
18 Ibid.
19 Declan Kiberd, 'Anglo-Irish Attitudes', *Field Day* (London: 1985), p. 83.
20 Ibid., p. 86.
21 Richard Rankin Russell, *Modernity, Community, and Place in Brian Friel's Drama*, second edition (Syracuse: Syracuse University Press, 2022), p. 193.
22 Richard Kirkland, 'Frantz Fanon, Roger Casement ad Colonial Commitment', in Colin Graham and Glenn Hooper (eds), *Irish and Postcolonial Writing: History, Theory, Practice* (Basingstoke: Palgrave, 2002), p. 54.
23 Quoted in Eoin Flannery, *Ireland and Postcolonial Studies: Theory, Discourse, Utopia* (Basingstoke and New York: Palgrave Macmillan, 2009), p. 1.
24 Seamus Heaney, 'Punishment', https://allpoetry.com/poem/11645373-Punishment-by-Seamus-Heaney (accessed 20 May, 2026).
25 Richard Cairns and Shaun Richards, *Writing Ireland: Colonialism, Nationalism, Culture* (Manchester: Manchester University Press, 1988), p. viii.
26 Ibid., p. 88.
27 Flannery, *Ireland and Postcolonial Studies*, p. 45.
28 David Lloyd, *Anomalous States: Irish Writing and the Postcolonial Moment* (Dublin: Lilliput Press, 1993), p. 127.
29 Flannery, *Ireland and Postcolonial Studies*, p. 88.
30 Declan Kiberd, *Inventing Ireland: The Literature of the Modern Nation* (London: Vintage Books, 1996), p. 186.
31 Declan Kiberd, 'Republicanism and Culture in the New Millenium', in Robert J. Savage (ed.), *Ireland in the New Century: Politics, Culture, Identity* (Dublin: Four Courts Press), p. 84.

32 Colin Graham, *Deconstructing Ireland: Identity, Theory, Culture* (Edinburgh: Edinburgh University Press, 2001), p. 66.
33 Quoted in Flannery, *Ireland and Postcolonial Studies*, p. 120.
34 Taken from Peter Barry, *Beginning Theory*, third edition (Manchester: Manchester University Press, 2009), p. 192.
35 James Joyce, *Portrait of the Artist as A Young Man* (Oxford: Oxford University Press, 2008), p. 213.
36 Declan Kiberd, 'Introduction', *Ulysses*, ed. Declan Kiberd. Students' annotated edition (London: Penguin Classics, 2000), p. lxxx. All future references refer parenthetically to this edition.
37 Kiberd, *Inventing Ireland*, p. 339.
38 Ibid., p. 338.
39 Derek Hand, *A History of the Irish Novel* (Cambridge: Cambridge University Press, 2011), p. 144.
40 Aaron Kelly, *Twentieth-Century Irish Literature: A Reader's Guide to Essential Criticism* (New York: Palgrave Macmillan, 2008), p. 74.
41 Ibid., p. 73.
42 Luke Gibbons, *James Joyce and the Irish Revolution: The Easter Rising as Modern Event* (London: University of Chicago Press, 2023), p. 6.
43 Enda Duffy, *The Subaltern Ulysses* (Minneapolis: University of Minnesota Press, 1993), p. 4.
44 Ibid., p. 127.
45 James Joyce, *Selected Letters*, ed. Richard Ellmann (London: Faber & Faber, 1975), p. 96.
46 Jacques Derrida, *Specters of Marx* (New York: Routledge, 1994), p. xviii.
47 David Coughlan, *Ghost Writing in Contemporary American Fiction* (London and New York: Palgrave Macmillan, 2016), p. 5.
48 Jacques Derrida, *Rogues: Two Essays on Reason*, trans. Pascale-Anne Brault and Michael Naas (Stanford: Stanford University Press, 2004), p. 135.
49 Oscar Wilde, 'The Harlot's House', in *Collins Complete Works of Oscar Wilde*, ed. Merlin Holland, fifth edition (Glasgow: HarperCollins, 2003), p. 867.
50 James Joyce, *Ulysses*, ed. Declan Kiberd. Students' annotated edition (London: Penguin, 2000), 702–703. All future references refer parenthetically to this edition.
51 For a similar version of this argument, see Harry Blamires, *The New Bloomsday Book: A Guide through Ulysses*, p. 196.
52 Luke Gibbons, *Joyce's Ghosts: Ireland, Modernism, and Memory* (Chicago: University of Chicago Press, 2017), p. xiii.
53 Ibid.
54 See Derrida, *Rogues*, p. 4.

55 See Murray McArthur, 'The Example of Joyce: Derrida Reading Joyce', *James Joyce Quarterly* 32:2 (Winter, 1995), p. 227.
56 See Joyce, *Selected Letters*, p. 3.
57 Declan Kiberd, 'Introduction', in *Ulysses*, ed. Declan Kiberd. Students' annotated edition (London: Penguin Classics, 2000), p. lxxx.
58 Neil Sammells, 'Oscar Wilde: Performing Gothic', in Avril Horner and Sue Zlosnik (eds), *Comic Gothic: An Edinburgh Companion* (Edinburgh: Edinburgh University Press, 2024), p. 96.
59 William Butler Yeats, *Celtic Twilight: Myth, Fantasy, Folklore* (Canada: Prism Press, 1998), p. 95.
60 William Butler Yeats, *Purgatory*, in Richard Allen Cave (ed.), *Selected Plays* (London: Penguin Twentieth Century Classics, 1997), p. 255. All future references refer parenthetically to this edition.
61 William Butler Yeats, *Selected Poems* (London: Penguin Classics, 2000), p. 136. All future references refer parenthetically to this edition.
62 Yeats, *Poetry Drama, Prose* (New York: Norton Critical Edition, 2001), p. 170.
63 Timothy Webb, 'Introduction', in *W.B. Yeats: Selected Poems*, ed. Timothy Webb (London: Penguin Classics, 2000), p. xl.
64 W.J. McCormack, 'Yeats's Purgatory: A Play and a Tradition', in *Crane Bag, Anglo-Irish Perspectives* 3:2 (1979), pp. 33–44.
65 Gerardine Meaney, *Gender, Ireland, and Cultural Change* (New York: Routledge, 2010), p. 159.
66 Jacqueline Genet, 'Yeats's "Purgatory": A Re-Assessment', *Irish University Review* 21:2 (1991), p. 244.
67 *The Collected Works of W.B. Yeats Vol. III: Autobiographies: 03* (Touchstone Press, 1999), p. 263.
68 Robert Tracey, *The Unappeasable Host: Studies in Irish Identities* (Dublin: UCD Press, 1998), p. 106.
69 John Brannigan, *Archipelagic Modernism: Literature in the Irish and British Isles, 1890–1970* (Edinburgh: Edinburgh University Press, 2015), p. 57.
70 Some of the following analysis of *Translations* appears in an article I published in *Irish University Review* in November 2025 titled 'Spectrality and Hospitality in Brian Friel's *Translations*'.
71 Seamus Deane, 'Introduction', *Brian Friel: Plays 1* (London: Faber & Faber, 1996), p. 22.
72 See Richard Kearney, 'Double Hospitality', *Journal for Continental Philosophy of Religion* 1:1 (2019), pp. 71–89.
73 Kearney, 'Double Hospitality', p. 71.
74 Lionel Pilkington, 'Language and Politics in Brian Friel's *Translations*', *Irish University Review* 20:2 (1990), p. 285.

75 Brian Friel, *Translations*, *Plays 1* (London: Faber & Faber, 1996), p. 384. All future references refer parenthetically to this edition.
76 Christopher Murray, 'Palimpsest: Two Languages as One in Brian Friel's *Translations*', *Hungarian Journal of English and American Studies (HJEAS)* 5:1, Special Issue in Honour of Brian Friel (1999), p. 93.
77 See Adam Philips, *On Kissing, Tickling, and Being Bored* (Cambridge, MA: Harvard University Press, 1993), p. 97.
78 Anthony Roche, *Brian Friel: Theatre and Politics* (London and New York: Palgrave Macmillan, 2011), p. 138.
79 Quoted in Maria Gavina-Costero, 'Revisiting Brian Friel's *Translations* Through the Lens of Stage Director Caitríona McLaughlin', *Irish Studies Review* 32:2 (2024), p. 290.
80 Richard Kearney, *Transitions: Narratives in Modern Irish Culture* (Manchester: Manchester University Press, 1988), p. 142.
81 F.C. McGrath, *Brian Friel's (Post)Colonial Drama: Language, Illusion, and Politics* (Syracuse: Syracuse University Press, 1999), p. 195.
82 Murray, 'Palimpsest: Two Languages as One in Brian Friel's *Translations*', p. 95.
83 See Richtarik, *Acting Between the Lines: The Field Day Theatre Company and Irish Cultural Politics 1980–1984*, p. 13.
84 *World*, RTÉ Europe, 26 February, 2023, ed. Tony Connelly.
85 Edward Said, 'Afterword', in Clare Carroll and Patricia King (eds), *Ireland and Postcolonial Theory* (Cork: Cork University Press, 2003), p. 178.
86 Deane, 'Introduction', p. 22.

4
Gender, sex and sexuality

Introduction

Because of the persistent linkage of the Irish nation with femininity as a result of colonial stereotyping and the aisling poetic tradition, it was always inevitable that theories surrounding gender and sexuality should become important within an Irish Studies context. The Irish Constitution of 1937 in which the family was enshrined (in Article 41.1.1.2) as the primary unit of the state, and wives and mothers were named as its primary caregivers, also created a legacy of problematic gender relations and politics for the Irish nation. This chapter shall consider works such Gerardine Meaney's seminal essay 'Sex and Nation' and Kim McMullen's 'Decolonizing Rosaleen' and will explore the burgeoning association that has developed between feminism and queer theory in Irish Studies during the late 1990s and beyond. Attention shall be paid to recent debates and referenda surrounding divorce, contraception and abortion that have raged to greater and lesser degrees in Ireland during the late twentieth and early twenty-first century. These were significant issues because, at their core, what was at stake was Irish women's right to assert their own individual bodily autonomy. It was during these debates and referenda that Irish feminist theory and activism began to grow in strength in terms of their place in public discourse and debate on the Island of Ireland because of the work of pioneers such as Ailbhe Smith. Following on from the previous chapter, an analysis of the controversy surrounding the *Field Day Anthology of Irish Women's Writing* (Field Day volumes IV and V) in 2003 and what their existence says about how the Irish literary canon had previously been constructed and which authors up until then had been privileged.

An examination of the growth in Irish academic interest in the form of theoretical inquiry known as queer theory in the late noughties shall constitute the second part of this chapter. This interest is understandable considering Ireland's long-standing problematic relationship with same-sex desire. This is illustrated by the fact that homosexuality was only made legal in Ireland in the early 1990s. Drawing on the literary and cultural writings of thinkers such as Joseph Valente, Noreen Giffney, Anne Mulhall and Michael O'Rourke, this chapter shall outline how a Queering of Irish Studies helps illuminate why Oscar Wilde always regarded Irishness and otherness as being inextricably linked.[1] Claire Bracken's *Irish Feminist Futures* shall be highlighted as a prime example of a contemporary academic text that utilises both feminism and queer theory in an Irish context. The texts selected for analysis through the lens of feminism and queer theory are Neil Jordan's *The Crying Game*, Eavan Boland's *Outside History*, Frank McGuinness' *Carthaginians* and Louise O'Neill's *Asking for It*. The concluding questions shall ask what is the relationship between gender and sexuality, and how has our understanding of that relationship changed over time as a result of the rise of feminism and queer theory? The political histories of recent Irish referenda such as those on divorce, marriage and abortion, shall also be discussed.

Feminising Irish Studies

The role of women as a unifying force in Ireland has been a constant factor in the country's history, from the short-lived Poblachta Eireann (1916) to the Republic of Ireland (which was proclaimed in 1949 and obviously exists to this day). This role, though central, was never intended to allow for the emancipation of women or to proclaim their status as being equal to men. A major reason for this was the strong influence of the Roman Catholic Church on the Irish people; according to that religion, a woman's only valid role in a traditional Catholic society was Mother.

After Ireland achieved independence, extreme emphasis was placed upon enshrining the nuclear family as a sacred Irish institution. The most powerful weapon used in insuring that this came about was the Constitution of 1937 in which article 41.1.1 read as follows:

> The State recognizes the Family as the natural primary and fundamental unit group of Society, and as a moral institution possessing inalienable and imprescriptible rights, antecedent and superior to all positive law.
>
> The State, therefore, guarantees to protect the Family in its constitution and authority, as the necessary basis of social order and as indispensable to the welfare of the nation and the State.[2]

Essentially, this article linked the nation and the family inextricably; it essentially made the private realm public and the domestic realm political. In Article 41.2, the Constitution made the following proclamation:

> The State recognizes that by her life within the home, woman [sic] gives to the State a support without which the common good cannot be achieved … the State shall, therefore, endeavour to ensure that mothers shall not be obliged by economic necessity to engage in labour to the neglect of their duties in the home.[3]

This document was meant to strike a blow for Irish unity after the Civil War of nearly twenty years previously had left the country bitterly divided. The Constitution essentially tries to present us with an Ireland modelled on the vision of Ireland as envisaged by William Butler Yeats through the play *Cathleen ni Houlihan*. The emphasis on Ireland as Mother is prevalent throughout the document. Two of the main objections that have been consistently raised about the above provisions in the Irish Constitution are the reference to mothers' 'duties' in the home and also the conflation of the identities of 'woman' and 'mother' as if there can be no distinction between the two.

In 1932, Fianna Fáil introduced a ban on women working in the public service when they got married since it was felt that any married woman who had a job was not fulfilling her natural duty as a wife. This law was only repealed in 1973. In fact, so severe were the Irish laws in relation to women that, in 1937, the Geneva Convention blacklisted the Irish Free State.

Abortion had been banned in Ireland in 1893 and the 1937 Irish Constitution also contains prohibitions against divorce. These restrictions can be regarded as an attempt to control women's power over their own bodies: once married, their bodies were meant to belong to their husbands and, once pregnant, their life was meant to become secondary to the life of the unborn child. In 1983, an amendment was introduced to the Irish Constitution which banned abortion. This amendment was not repealed until 2018 when the Irish people voted by a margin of 3–1 to remove it from the Constitution.

In 1943, as part of a St. Patrick's Day speech, Eamon De Valera pronounced his vision of Ireland as being both a rural paradise and a land filled with idealised women:

> That Ireland which we dreamed of would be the home of a people who valued material wealth only as a basis for right living, of a people who were satisfied with frugal comfort and devoted their leisure to the things of the spirit – a land whose countryside would be bright with cosy homesteads, whose fields and villages would be joyous with sounds of industry, with the romping of sturdy children, the contests of athletic youths and the laughter of comely maidens.[4]

That famous speech encapsulates the value of place on Ireland as a rural idyll and on the purity and virtue of the Irish woman.

One of the great tragedies in recent Irish history, the death of fifteen-year-old Anne Lovett and her son whilst giving birth beside a grotto on 31 January, 1984, has often be interpreted as an example of the harsh effects that Catholic doctrine has had on the Irish people's attitude towards, and treatment of, women. Anne Lovett had managed to conceal her pregnancy from everyone in her small village in Granard, Co. Longford. The reason she had done so was because the baby had been conceived out of wedlock. This event has come to be seen as emblematic of Catholic Ireland's (at the time) very repressive attitude towards sexuality and how and when it should be expressed. Fintan O'Toole has correctly asserted that

> the tight intertwining of the Catholic Church with both the institutions of government after Irish independence in 1922 and the moral and ideological underpinnings of independence itself meant that the control of sexuality, reproduction, and childhood could never be marginal to the definition of Irishness, of respectability, of citizenship, of belonging.[5]

Because of the inextricable linkage in Ireland between gender/sex and nation, the country has become a happy hunting ground for both feminist activism and cultural theory. feminist literary criticism of today has roots in the women's movement of the 1960s. This movement was, in important ways, literary from the start, in the sense that it realised the significance of the images of women promulgated by literature, and saw it as vital to combat them and question their authority and their coherence.

One text that played a major role in the evolution of both feminist theory and activism is Simone de Beauvoir's *The Second Sex* (1949). The famous line from that book, 'One is not born, but rather becomes, a woman', serves as a pivotal point for *The Second Sex*. It begins the second half, wherein de Beauvoir redescribes the life of women from birth to adulthood. This part of *The Second Sex* reveals many of the countless constraints inculcated since birth which inhibit a woman's ability to achieve transcendence/freedom. De Beauvoir first takes us through childhood, commenting on such things as the dolls that girls play with, which prepare them for their future role, into adolescence, where girls realise both that they are technically free but oppression sets up a situation in which acting on that freedom is nearly impossible.

For de Beauvoir, women's oppression differs from many other forms of oppression insofar as there appears to be no historical starting-point for it; nor is there any solidarity of economic interest, or even any 'social location' for this oppressed group. Women are oppressed as women, but separated from each other, and often have more in common with men of their own social class than they do with other women from different classes. Significantly, de Beauvoir's theories in relation to the doing rather than the being of womanhood was highly influential on Judith Butler's theory of gender performativity, as shall be examined shortly.

Another important text in the history of feminist theory is Helene Cixous' 'The Laugh of the Medusa'. Cixous is a Jewish Algerian writer, French feminist critic and theorist, novelist and playwright. She was a close friend and translator of the works of Jacques Derrida. She is considered to be one of the first 'post-structuralist feminists'. 'The Laughter of the Medusa' was published in 1975. As the title suggests, the essay argues that we don't have to see certain iconic female images as being purely evil just because we are told that they are. Cixous encourages a feminist reclamation of certain maligned versions of femininity. An Irish author who uses her theatrical texts to force audiences to rethink simplistic versions of 'the good woman' is Marina Carr, especially in *Portia Coughlan* (1997) and *By the Bog of Cats* (1998).

The most influential concept to emerge from 'The Laugh of the Medusa' is that of *ecriture feminine* (female writing). *Ecriture feminine* is the expression of the female body and sexuality in writing, an expression that cannot be coded or theorised. Cixous employs the motif of Medusa as a metaphor for women's multiplicity that opposes patriarchal strictures on women's body and voice. Cixous argues that an authentic *ecriture feminine* should reject patriarchal conceptions of linguistic and narrative order. For Cixous, the domination of the female voice and in turn the absence of a feminine discourse in the past had stagnated and concealed the creative force of the female writers thus chaining them within the barriers of masculine language. She believes that such writing, which is in no way different from the male writing, could only aim at 'obscure[ing] women or reproducing the classic representations of women (as sensitive – intuitive – dreamy etc.)', something which distinctly reminds one of women writers of the Victorian period internalising and imitating the dominant structures of male tradition, their writing reflecting a conflict between 'obedience and resistance'.

To begin with, Cixous contends that *ecriture feminine* could only be manifested in the genre of poetry, as opposed to the 'coded, clichéd, ordinary language' contained in prose. Employing the structure of binary opposition, Cixous asserts that the language of poetry (unlike prose) is not trite, but holds manifold meanings; it is closer to the unconscious and hence closer to female sexuality (female bodies – wherein lies their unconscious repressed by the 'superegoized structure'). For Cixous, novelists are but the 'allies of representationalism'. Poetry, for Cixous, 'condenses, renders opaque, carries great psychic density. It is opposed to the discourse that flattens, systematizes'.[6] The poetry of Eavan Boland, which shall be examined shortly, can be interpreted as an attempt by an Irish feminist writer to create a poetic style that could be termed *ecriture feminine*. Cixous does not believe that all women's writing follows the afore-mentioned path. She is very attuned to the power of style, imagery and symbolism in texts and believes that this style can be appropriated by both men and women.

One of the most famous and contested examples in Irish literature of a man writing in a style that could be described as *ecriture feminine* is the final episode in Joyce's *Ulysses*, titled the 'Penelope' episode or 'Molly's monologue'. In this remarkable piece of 'pseudo-prose', the character of Molly Bloom speaks to the reader in an oral-inflected style in which almost all grammatical structures are abandoned, with the exception of eight full stops over the course of over sixty pages. To begin with, Joyce is clearly rebelling against linguistic order by giving Molly a style that refuses traditional grammatical structures associated with the gendered-male style of the traditional novel. Whether that is radical or an example of male stereotype of a disordered female mind is open to debate. Declan Kiberd makes this radical claim concerning 'Penelope':

> *Ulysses*, judged in retrospect, is a prolonged farewell to written literature and a rejection of its attempts to colonize speech and thought. Its mockery of the hyper-literary Stephen [Dedalus], of the writerly talk of librarians, of the excremental nature of printed magazines, is a preparation for its restoration of the human voice of Molly Bloom; and, in a book where each chapter [episode] is named for a bodily organ, the restoration of her voice becomes a synecdoche for the recovery into art of the whole human body.[7]

Whilst this argument has plenty to recommend it, it also somewhat falls back on the fetishisation of the female voice at the expense of female discourse. As was pointed out above, this privileging of female voice over discourse was something that Cixous bemoaned and wished *ecriture feminine* to rebel against.

Gerardine Meaney also observes that Molly's monologue is not a piece of orality but of oralisation. Thus, Joyce cannot really be said to be authentically providing a version of a female voice in the form of writing. Rather, he is ventriloquising and speaking for a female subjectivity and style that is filtered through his masculine lens. Meaney argues that *Ulysses* is ultimately a combat of binary opposites that are, at least to some extent, gendered: 'Ireland or England, Molly or Bloom, dialogic or adulterative, pure or hybrid, myth or history. [These conflicts] reassert themselves at the novel's end'.[8] I would argue that, by crafting a style that combines some elements of the orderliness of writing but also aspects of the fluidity of orality, Joyce has created a liminal stylistic space that could be described as a version of *ecriture feminine*.

These debates surrounding the radicality or otherwise of the 'Penelope' episode do certainly point towards its status as a remarkable piece of modernist writing that has helped fuel many debates concerning the ethicality or lack thereof of male authors speaking as and for female identities and subjectivities – concerns that have been at the heart of the evolution of feminist theory in an Irish Studies context since the end of the twentieth century.

An important catalyst for the emergence of feminism in Irish Studies was the publication of the first three volumes of the *Field Day Anthology of Irish Writing*, the first being published in 1990. These volumes, whilst lauded as an important intervention in the creation of a history of Irish writing, were also criticised for their lack of focus on female writers. Also, as Kim McMullen argues: 'The problem is not with individual omissions [...] but rather with the monologic tendency that seems implicit in the anthology's construction of "Irishness," especially in the twentieth century.[9] The 'Irishness' that emerges from the first three volumes of the *Field Day Anthologies* can be fairly described as an identity that was primarily male, masculine and demonstrably 'white'. For these reasons, volumes IV and V of the *Field Day Anthology of Irish writing* were devoted entirely to Irish women writers and edited by eminent Irish feminist critics such as Gerardine Meaney and Clair Wills. These volumes were published in 2003 and greatly enhanced the focus of Irish Studies on feminist theory and activism. As Patricia Coughlan asserts:

> The welcome appearance in 2003 of Field Day IV–V has served to keep the troubled relation of gender with canonicity before our minds. Despite the existence of enlightened reviewers and academic critics sympathetic to the feminist project, the whole system of reception of contemporary writing still shows a marginalising of women's work.[10]

Linda Connolly describes the development of feminist criticism in an Irish Studies context thus:

> As was the case in postcolonial criticism, history was a central dynamic in the early formation of Irish women's studies. Until the late 1970s, women were more or less an invisible and marginal category in Irish academic scholarship, in general. However, we now know, for instance, that an active women's movement was one of the most potent (if pervasive) social movements to mobilise in Irish society from the late nineteenth century onwards.[11]

Important women's movements, led by activists such as Nell McCafferty and Nuala O'Faolain, began to develop in earnest in the 1960s and 1970s. Famously, in the early 1970s, prominent Irish feminists made the journey from the Republic of Ireland to Northern Ireland to bulk buy condoms, which were illegal in the Irish Republic, and distribute them south of the border.

Until relatively recently, as Connolly notes,

> analytic certainty about Irish women's lives has frequently been arrived at without any reference to their diverse, often conflicting, voices and agency. Of equal note is a tendency to essentialise or totalise all Irish women as a group. Analysis framed by modernisation theory has particularly purveyed simplistic cultural assumptions about Irish women.[12]

Equally, postcolonial theory very often presented a simplified analysis of the Irish woman in symbolic terms – specifically, how her value to Ireland is primarily a metaphor for that nation.

In the early 2000s, Margaret Kelleher wrote that 'with the exception of some individual critics, Irish Studies as a discipline remains singularly ill-informed of (and by) the debates and concerns that have occupied Irish feminist criticism in the past decade'.[13] For Moynagh Sullivan: 'woman functions as an object through which Irish Studies can mediate its relationship to itself'.[14] What this means is that, in the then very patriarchal world of Irish Studies, the figure of woman existed in purely symbolic relations to an Ireland, and a discipline of Irish Studies, that was male dominated but which saw itself as being in the service of a nation that was symbolically gendered as feminine and sexed as female. This resulted in the physical reality of female lives being given no real consideration in the narrative of the Irish nation and state. Connolly makes a similar claim: 'A narrow reading of Irish feminism through the prism of a coherent nationalism/

Irish identity does not have a neutral effect. 'Irish' feminism in its contradictory manifestations is negated by such an approach, as is the widely documented feminist critique of 'the nation' – articulated both by anti-nationalist and nationalist activists in the Irishwomen's movement (North and South) for over a hundred years and widely discussed in feminist criticism and theory.[15]

Elizabeth Butler Cullingford has described how difficult it is for Irish feminist critics to break away from the traditional, male-centred nationalist approach to Irish Studies:

> In attempting to map an honest and politically responsible course through the minefield that is contemporary Irish Studies, I am often reminded of the moment when a male Irish academic characterised me as a British imperialist bitch ... The problem was that, in a 1991 article on Yeats, Pearse and Heaney, I had criticised the nationalist tendency to use women as icons of the land or of the national struggle. That view, also expressed by the poet Eavan Boland (Scar) and the IRA member Mairead Farrell (Mother Ireland), is by now utterly commonplace; even then it seemed a somewhat belated intervention of feminist ideas into Irish discourse. But a feminist critique of nationalism risks being interpreted as support for British troops on the streets of Belfast.[16]

Thus, we see that, when considering the relationship of feminism and nationalism in Ireland, a blind spot can be discerned in some versions of postcolonial criticism.

In Edna Longley's influential pamphlet, 'From Cathleen to Anorexia' (1990), Longley argues that 'to over-stress the independence of Irish literature from English literature (and vice versa) distorts literary history and does not help contemporary politics'.[17] This was the primary criticism that Longley had of Irish postcolonial theory, and the various Field Day projects specifically. The fact that Field Day had as its official academic face the strident nationalist Seamus Deane made Longley suspicious of Field Day from the outset. In Longley's view, deconstructing the binary oppositions that many saw as existing between Catholics and Protestants was the way to help bring about a possibly lasting peace in Northern Ireland. Longley then goes even further by arguing that 'perhaps the equivalent of an advanced feminist "troubling and subverting" is precisely what our Nationalist and Unionist patriarchal strait-jackets need'.[18] In other words, a radical feminist politics can possibly be a saviour of Irish politics North and South of the border.

In 2001, Alan Finlayson wrote a piece in which he advocated for a new direction in Irish Studies that could be interpreted as being more hospitable to a feminist-inflected strand of Irish Studies:

> Maybe what is needed is indeed another different paradigm for Irish studies … Perhaps something like a kind of radical empiricism that seeks out the facts at the same time as it is aware that a truly empirical mindset undermines the very concepts that allow us to think of facts as speaking for themselves thus forcing us to be inventive with ourselves … Rather than the constructed authenticity of texts and events as the binding frame for Irish studies, we would be faced by the ethical imperative forced on us by the actual. Althusser, a submerged presence in the work of both Graham and Kirkland, suggested in his autobiography that his attachment to materialism came from a desire to have the courage not to tell lies to himself.[19]

The actualisation of Finlayson's proposal would allow for a feminist Irish Studies that takes account of the lived realities of Irish women throughout the history of Ireland. This would allow for the acknowledgement of the nuanced nature and plurality of Irish female identities and free them from the abstraction of '(Irish) woman as nation'. This is part of the feminist project that has been undertaken in Irish Studies by a large number of feminist critics.

In 1991, Gerardine Meaney published her influential pamphlet 'Sex and Nation' in which she offered an outline of the future direction that she believed Irish feminism in its various forms should take. One of the key statements made by Meaney in this publication was the following: '[Irish] Feminism cannot, in attempting to see women outside their traditional role as symbols of the nation, be content to merely impose a revised role on them, a role as victims of the nation or of history'.[20] Meaney goes on to argue that:

> The work of contemporary continental feminist thinkers [such as Helene Cixous and Julia Kristeva], with its emphasis on the way in which we are produced by and produce the dominant culture and the internal complexities of any programme of cultural and psychological change, may offer a way out of the twin stereotypes into which any analysis of women in Irish culture so easily falls. An analysis which emphasises how deeply we are involved in patriarchal culture

> and in our idealisation as symbols of the nation denies us the moral high ground – we are not the innocent victims of Irish or any other kind of historical circumstance.[21]

Meaney's advocacy of the incorporation of continental philosophy into a feminist/Irish Studies discursive context as a means of diagnosing the causes of Irish women's exclusion from empowerment and agency in many aspects of Irish culture, literature and politics has proven influential for many succeeding generations of Irish feminist critics and activists. This approach to feminist criticism also helps to illuminate the points of connection between feminism and postcolonial theory. Such connections are succinctly described by Kim McMullen: 'Postcolonial and feminist analyses share a common interest in the construction of "difference" and in exposing and destabilizing the mechanisms by which domination and subordination are sustained within given a cultural moment'.[22]

An important text in which feminist and ecocriticism (which will be examined in a later chapter) are brought into productive dialogue is Margaret Kelleher's *The Feminization of Famine: Expressions of the Inexpressible* (1997). Kelleher examines the tradition of female representations in Irish famine literature from the nineteenth century to the present day. The texts range from the novels of William Carleton to the writings of Liam O'Flaherty and John Banville. The work also uncovers a significant body of writing on the famine written by women such as Emily Lawless in the nineteenth century. An interesting comparison between Irish and Bengali famine literature is also offered. This reminds us that the Irish and Bengali people used hunger strikes as a form of political protest, which may be intended to remind their colonial masters of what they had suffered as a result of terrible famines.

Kelleher highlights specific feminine gendered motifs that are utilised in famine literature; images of mothers and children, and the almost fetishisation of women's starving bodies. Kelleher argues: 'The female figure has been made, in the course of famine representations to bear various meanings and to disguise others; embodying death and survival, horror and heroism, her form is an important reminder that the most "moving" of images may fail to move understanding'.[23] This analysis is also relevant to the ongoing gender politics of post-independence Ireland in which, for most of its existence, the figure of Woman has been abstracted and rendered symbolic of the Irish nation whilst also largely denying access to state power to individuals on any large scale until relatively recently.

Claire Bracken's *Irish Feminist Futures* (2016) is one notable book that has utilised various thinkers from twentieth-century continental philosophy with a view to analysing recent works of Irish literature and endeavouring to extrapolate from those texts moments during which an undecidable feminist future for Ireland could be envisaged. One powerful analytic example from this text involves an examination of the conclusion of Marina Carr's *Portia Coughlan* (1996) in which Bracken argues that Portia's suicide can be read as 'a figurative gesture towards an affective form of embodied living that requires the death of the separated subject in the birth of the connected self'.[24] What Bracken contends is that Portia, by causing her bodily death in order that she can be reunited with her dead twin brother Gabriel is embracing a new form of embodied subjectivity in a futural, spectral realm that privileges the union of male and female bodies rather than their separation and conflict. Bracken's investment in a theory of spectral futurity in a feminist critical context aligns her and her work with the Derridean concept of the *avenir* (the 'to come'), through which an as yet unprescribed future for Ireland and Irish feminism can at least be partially conceptualised.

What Irish feminists do:

1. **They rethink the canon, aiming at the rediscovery of texts written by women. This is particularly in evidence in the *Field Day Anthology of Irish Women's Writing*.**
2. **They consider how women are represented in Irish literature by both men and women.**
3. **They recognise the role of language in making what is social and constructed seem transparent and 'natural'.**
4. **They critique the trope of woman as nation.**
5. **They explore whether there is a female language, an *ecriture feminine*, existing in Irish literary and cultural discourse, and**

whether this is also available to men. An important example of the latter question is the debate concerning how authentically James Joyce replicated a female voice and writing in the 'Penelope' episode of *Ulysses*.[25]

6. **They view Gayatri Spivak's concept of the subaltern (touched upon in the previous chapter in the discussion of David Lloyd's *Anomalous States*) through the embodied lens of the female as opposed to the more abstract prism of classed and colonial subjects.**

Queering Irish Studies

The term queer theory was first coined by Teresa de Lauretis at a conference in 1990. It emerges from gay/lesbian studies' attention to the social construction of categories of normative and deviant sexual behaviour. But while gay/lesbian studies, as the name implies, focussed largely on questions of homosexuality, queer theory expands its realm of investigation. Queer theory looks at, and has a political critique of, anything that falls into normative and deviant categories, particularly sexual activities and identities. The word 'queer', as it appears in the dictionary, has a primary meaning of 'odd', 'peculiar', 'out of the ordinary'. Major thinkers associated with queer theory, such as Judith Butler, insist that there can be as many acts of queering as there are theorists who wish to engage in that broadly termed act. In other words, queer, in this context, is something you do as opposed to something you are.

Eve Kosofsky Sedgwick, one of the most influential figures in the history of queer theory, makes the following distinction between 'queer' and 'gay/lesbian' subjectivities:

> 'Queer' seems to hinge much more radically and explicitly on a person's undertaking particular, performative acts of experimental self-perception and filiation. A hypothesis worth making explicit: that there are important senses in which 'queer' can signify only when attached to the first person. One possible corollary: that what it takes – all it takes – to make the description 'queer' a true one is the impulsion to use it in the first person.[26]

In essence, what Sedgwick is arguing is that 'Queer' is a form of individuality that is not grounded in any implied group. It evades total inclusion into collective nouns or first person plurals. However, it is certainly the case that queer theory and queer theorists do advocate alliances between different queer individuals.

One of the formative publications for queer theory was Judith Butler's 1988 essay, 'Performative Acts and Gender Constitution' in which Butler argues that 'gender is in no way a stable identity or locus of agency from which various acts proceed; rather, it is an identity tenuously constituted in time – an identity instituted through a stylized repetition of acts'.[27] Butler's radical claim is that gender is not something a person 'is', rather, it is something a person 'does'. When Butler refers to gender as being 'performative', she is distinguishing performativity from performance in that the latter implies the performer pre-existing the performance whereas, in the case of the former, the performance existed prior to the individual performers' attempts to enact the already existing script of gender. One of the reasons why Butler conceived of gender performativity was a means of correcting what she saw as reductive quality in feminist theory and activism at that time – the idea that there was a universal version of 'female' and 'gender'. This notion, in Butler's view, could not help but exclude certain individuals who did not conform to those absolutist and essentialist definitions.

The provisionality and fluidity of 'queer' as an identity category is encapsulated perfectly by Sedgwick when she argues that queer is 'the open mesh of possibilities, gaps, overlaps, dissonances and resonances, lapses and excesses of meaning when the constituent elements of anyone's gender, of anyone's sexuality aren't made (or *can't be* made) to signify monolithically'.[28] Like Butler when it comes to gender, Sedgwick is here privileging the verb-based notion of doing when it comes to something supposedly stable, knowable and noun (being)-based.

In Elizabeth Bowen's *The Last September*, the character of Lois seems to be doomed to perpetually perform society's normative conception of femininity. As Lois laments to herself: 'She hated women, but she didn't know how to be anything else'. Bowen's novel consistently portrays a group of Anglo-Irish people during the Irish War of Independence for whom identity is a series of performative exercises.

The plays and films of Martin McDonagh, from *The Cripple of Inishmaan* (1997) to *The Banshees of Inisherin* (2022) all portray versions of masculinity that are deliberately represented and over the top, exaggerated, and clearly unnatural performances. Invoking both Judith Butler and Susan Sontag, many of the masculinities in Martin McDonagh's dramatic and cinematic oeuvre appear as both performative and overtly camp.

Lloyd (Meadbh) Houston's *Irish Modernism and the Politics of Sexual Health* (1923) has compellingly argued for the politicisation of sexuality and sexual health from the Revival up to the 1960s. How sexual health is narrativised and utilised by Irish writers, activists and essayists as a marker of various versions of Irish identity is of paramount importance in that study. The banning of Kate O'Brien's novel *The Land of the Spices* in 1941 because of the reference to two men engaged in 'the embrace of love'[29] is proof of how valued sexual 'morality' and 'purity' were in Ireland during much of the twentieth century.

Ironically, Ireland's experience of centuries of colonialism meant that its relationship with various identities and subjectivities became extremely problematic and demonstrably 'queer'. When Oscar Wilde was informed that his 1891 symbolist play *Salome* had been rejected by the British censor, his response was to affirm that he should not be held to the standards of British morality for the simple reason that: 'I am not English; I am Irish, which is quite another thing'.[30] I would argue that this assertion by Wilde, albeit unintentionally, emphasises the queerness of Ireland itself. In Wilde's time this definition of Ireland as a 'queer nation' was appropriate because of the fact that its status as a colonial other rendered it perpetually queer and outside the realms of the normative imperial centre. However, over the last twenty years, the growth of the academic discipline of Irish Studies has led to an emphasis on Ireland as a national identity that is in the process of perpetual metamorphosis and thus opens up queer apertures in relation to the study of Irishness.

In her influential text, *Bodies that Matter*, Judith Butler has defined queerness thus:

> If the term 'queer' is to be a site of collective contestation, the point of departure for a set of historical reflections and futural imaginings, it will have to remain that which is, in the present, never fully owned, but always and only redeployed, twisted, queered from the prior usage and in the direction of urgent and expanding political purposes. This also means that it will doubtless have to be yielded in favour of terms that do that political work more effectively. Such a yielding may well become necessary in order to accommodate – without domesticating – democratizing contestations that have and will redraw the contours of the movement in ways that can never be fully anticipated in advance.[31]

For Butler, the queerness of queer resides in its unknowability and unpredictability. Butler does, however, seem to imply that sometimes queer needs to pull back from named political movements such as gay activism or feminism in order that these groups can endeavour to achieve named political objectives and leave queerness to a state of continuing evolution and openness. For critics such as Joseph Valente, Ireland has been in just such a state for several hundred years.

It has been noted by several commentators that there is a very strong interest in non-heteronormative identities in Ireland's activist and academic communities in recent years. Noreen Giffney has highlighted the academic interest in the study of hetero and queer sexuality that has been prevalent in Ireland for some time.[32] Although elements in Irish society have historically been hostile to queer identities (as evidenced in the, until relatively recently, criminal status of homosexuality), the connection between Irishness and queerness is certainly one that is apparent to many, and the presence of such anti-normative identities in the island of Ireland is certainly not a secret. As Eoin O'Broin noted in 1997, Ireland has more lesbian and gay Pride festivals than in any other part of Europe.[33]

Joseph Valente has argued that:

> Just as the colonization of Ireland long predated the historically recognizable geo-political project of colonialism itself, so the queering of Ireland began well in advance of the queer theory/queer studies/queer nationalist project … in advance even of the germinal reappropriation of the term queer itself from sexual slur to affirmative self-designation … I am not just referring to a felt analogy between

> the heritage and marginalization shared by the LGBT and the Irish community, as compelling as that analogy may be. I refer to the felt correlation … between the programmatic contestations of all homogenous identities under the sign of queer and the imposed division and hybridity of the Irish subject under colonialism, metrocolonialism, partition, postcolonialism etc.[34]

Valente is here making the point that Ireland's liminal status in relation to various categories of identity has made it a site of queerness, which goes some way towards explaining the interest in Ireland that queer theory and queer studies has generated.

Robyn Wiegman has succinctly differentiated between queer studies and queer theory:

> Queer Studies reinterprets [queer theory's] … assault on identity by making normative identities as well as the structures in which sexual and gendered normativities are produced and protected its primary disciplinary identity and critical aim. It is for this reason that the term 'queer' can be appended to the very identity markers its critical divergence was cast against, begetting LGBTQ Studies and similar conglomerations, not as contradictions but as elaborations, even proliferations, of the subjects, objects, and sites of the field's interdisciplinary engagements.[35]

Thus, queer studies is prepared to actively work on behalf of named anti-normative groups while queer theory tries to critique the legitimacy of any fixed identitarian category, whether that be straight, gay, transgendered and so on. Many of the works in this review wish to perform a certain amount of affirmative action on behalf of some of the aforenamed groups by highlighting their marginalisation and struggle for affirmation.

Queer Notions, edited by Fintan Walsh, offers a stimulating collection of plays that embrace non-normative sexualities. Theatre, as Frank McGuinness acknowledges in his forward to the volume,[36] is the perfect medium for affecting change in society because you are gathering people into a silent, group space and offering them a chance to be changed by what they see in front of them. How an audience reacts to the spectacle before them obviously varies from person to person and thus the barrier between public and private space is broken. It is for this reason that some of the most influential movements looking for political and cultural change in Ireland during the twentieth century have utilised the medium of drama. The Irish literary revival used the Abbey Theatre to stage plays that depicted new possibilities for Irish identity, and the Field Day theatre group expressly wished to use their plays to create an 'imaginary fifth province' in Ireland.[37]

In his introduction, Fintan Walsh declares the collection's commitment to an as yet unimagined future. He argues that these plays offer glimpses of the possibilities that might lie ahead for a queer world should there be openness on the part of later generations to receive the messages potentially contained in these dramas.[38] Walsh's introduction, with its emphasis on futurity, connects this text with the essays on masculinity already discussed and, by drawing upon Jacques Derrida's *Archive Fever*, aligns itself with one of the major influences on queer theory, that is, Derrida.[39]

The plays contained in *Queer Notions*, whilst exploring practices associated with gay and lesbian identities, generally attempt to deconstruct the notion that any sexual orientation is fixed or fully knowable. This is the case, for instance, in both Loughlin Deegan's *The Queen and the Peacock* and Deirdre Kinahan's *Passage*, where gay and lesbian characters' sexual identifications are destabilised by their engagement with hetero sex. Thus, these two works can be defined as queer, as in their depiction of the flux of desire and its undoing of identity, they challenge any hygienic homo/hetero binary. Walsh, in his introduction, also implies that he sees these plays as being far more than gay or lesbian texts. Rather, he regards them as offering more divergent and nuanced views of sexual relations, the relation between desire and its objects.[40]

Eibhear Walshe's *Oscar's Shadow: Wilde, Homosexuality and Modern Ireland* is an original study of the impact of the Wilde trials on Ireland. Walshe has been involved for many years in publishing books and essays on LGBTQ and queer studies and is one of the pioneering academics who endeavoured to open up Irish Studies to discussions of gender and sexuality. *Oscar's Shadow* represents Walshe's latest effort to further such analyses in an Irish context.

Spanning the hundred years since those trials occurred in 1895, Walshe examines how the Irish reaction to Wilde's imprisonment for two years for the crime of 'acts of gross indecency between men' was originally perceived in Ireland as an example of English victimisation of an Irishman. Walshe perceptively contrasts this reaction with the 1884 Dublin Castle trials, which involved British civil servants being accused of the same crimes. In this case homosexuality was highlighted as a foreign vice and vehemently condemned.[41]

Walshe then considers how Wilde's literary successors engaged with Wilde's legacy, particularly Yeats and Joyce. The conclusion drawn by Walshe is that they continued the Irish trend of focussing in on the rebelliousness of Wilde and not highlighting his non-normative sexual practices. In the case of Joyce, Wilde became the perfect example of the artistic loner that Joyce wished to become.[42] When one considers the numerous references, both implicit and explicit, to Wilde's life and work that appear in *Ulysses*, the importance that Wilde held for Joyce becomes very clear.

The story that Walshe's book essentially tells is of how Ireland began to gradually accept and engage with Wilde's homosexuality over the course of a century. This story is told in microcosm in the chapter devoted to Micheál Mac Liammoir, actor and founder with Hilton Edwards of the Gate Theatre. Mac Liammoir, like Wilde, invented his own persona when he left England and moved to Ireland. Originally, his name was Alfred Wilmore but he changed his name when he moved to Ireland and began to act out the role of the Celticised Irishman. In essence, he was Wilde in reverse. While Mac Liammoir performed several monologues recounting Wilde's life (the most famous of these being *The Importance of Being Oscar*), he carefully edited out references to Wilde's sexuality and thus made Wilde a safe figure for public consumption.

In his later life, Mac Liammoir began to embrace Wilde's, and also his own, sexual preferences in his memoir, *Enter a Goldfish*. As Walshe has observed:

> [T]he ending of the memoir indicated the fact that Mac Liammoir had reached a point in his writings when the public and private discourse could be accommodated … For Mac Liammoir himself as a writer, the lifelong taboo on the love that dare not speak its name had eventually been broken, and the unspeakable was finally made to speak through his writings on Wilde. For public perceptions of Wilde in Ireland, Mac Liammoir had effected a revolution.[43]

The second half of Walshe's book considers how the rest of Ireland gradually began to accept Wilde's homosexuality during the end of the twentieth and the beginning of the twenty-first century. Walshe highlights books such as Colm Tóibín's *The Master* and Jamie O'Neill's *At Swim Two Boys* as literary texts that use Wilde as a means of narrating a version of homosexual identity both in Ireland and abroad.

The books discussed in this chapter highlight the growing use of queer theory in relation to certain topics in Irish Studies. The question that now must be asked is: what does the future hold for the relationship between these two academic disciplines? While queer theory has certainly been used to examine gender and sexual identities in Ireland, it could be argued that more work could be done with queer theory in relation to categories such as race and disability as they pertain to Ireland and the question of Irish identities. The usages of queer theory are potentially manifold and the important thing is to continue to expand that category to include all non-normativities. As Noreen Giffney has argued, there is potential in Ireland for the creation of a 'quare theory' that will be open to many other theoretical discourses. This would be a theoretical being that would neither dominate nor be dominated by others.[44] In essence, 'quare theory' could be regarded as the queering of queer theory. It is certainly important that queer theory not remain stagnant but instead always be moving forward towards an undecidable future. In his essay 'The Soul of Man Under Socialism', Oscar Wilde evoked an image of progression as constant deferral, which is applicable to queer theory: 'A map of the world that does not include Utopia is not even worth glancing at, for it leaves out the one country at which Humanity is always landing. And when Humanity lands there, it looks out, and, seeing a better country, sets sail'.[45] While the notions of humanity and utopia are probably too specific and reductive for queer theory, the metaphor of the never-ending journey to a destination that is not fully known is an apt one for queer theory and queer studies.

The year 2024 saw the publication of a seminal collection of essays edited by Jennifer Redmond and Mary McAuliffe titled *The Politics of Gender and Sexuality in Modern Ireland: A Reader*. There are some excellent studies on lesbian and trans culture in the book, which makes it an excellent source for specific lesbian and trans-queer culture in Ireland. It offers fascinating historical reflections and contemporary analyses of issues related to the contested and often hidden histories of sexual politics and gender identities in Ireland in the nineteenth and twentieth centuries. Sara Philips' essay on the emergence of an Irish trans archive is very important because that has been, until recently, an often neglected area of Irish academic study. The work provides an opportunity for the voices of female queer Irish Studies scholars to be heard, which has been quite rare in the history of the discipline.

In their introduction to *The Politics of Gender and Sexuality in Modern Ireland*, Redmond and McAuliffe quite rightly noted (as this chapter has also been saying) the continuing prevalence of issues concerning gender, sex, and sexuality in public discourse and debate in Ireland:

> Issues of gender and sexuality have occupied the Irish public for decades and this is unlikely to end any time soon [...] As Judith Butler has argued, bodies do matter; the materiality of the body has an intimate connection to the performativity of gender and hence the treatment of those bodies by the law, in the public sphere and in our conceptions of masculinity, femininity and otherness.[46]

The Politics of Gender and Sexuality in Modern Ireland, as the editors observe, performs a valuable act of historical reclamation of many ignored histories and identities in Ireland:

> The book considers gender and sexuality [from a] historical perspective, going beyond the binary of male and female heterosexual experience to explore LGBTQI+ histories, the treatment of intersex persons in Ireland, the history of trans people and activism in Ireland, and strategies used to resist patriarchal, heteronormative constructions of sexual and gender identities. Recent trends in historical research have been emphasising personal experiences that were marginalised, suppressed or ignored [...] The pace of social change in Ireland in recent decades has been fast, marked by the referenda on marriage equality (2015) and abortion (2018) and investigations into the treatment of unmarried mothers and their children captivating the country and bringing old issues into a new light.[47]

Books such as this one, with its commitment to historical reclamation and the creation of more reparative narratives concerning the multiplicity of identities and ways of being that exist in Ireland, suggest that the Irish nation and people might be firmly embarked on the work of awakening from a Joycean nightmare of history.

Another notable book that deals with gender, sex and sexuality in a variety of different ways is Lloyd (Meadbh) Houston's *Irish Modernism and the Politics of Sexual Health* (2023). It is an original and engaging study of how Irish writers from the literary period that can be generally described as 'modernist' responded to the narratives surrounding sexual health that became prevalent from the nineteenth century onwards. Taking 1880 as a starting point, the book explores the politicisation of sexual health in Irish culture up to the 1960s. How sexual health is narrativised and utilised by Irish writers, activists and essayists as a marker of various versions of Irish identity is of paramount importance. Houston draws upon perspectives from various academic discourses such as Irish Studies, modernist studies, and medical humanities as a means of broadly examining how debates over sexual hygiene, venereal disease, birth control, fertility and eugenics were used by various public figure to construct and put into conflict competing conceptions of Irishness. The main authors that are examined are W.B. Yeats, J.M. Synge, James Joyce, Samuel Beckett, Kate O'Brien and Flann O'Brien. The journalistic writings of D.P. Moran, Arthur Griffith and Hanna Sheehy Skeffington are also used to productive effect. Some key events in Irish social and political history, such as the Parnell affair, the Playboy riots, the Limerick Pogrom and the Censorship of Publications Act (1929) are given in-depth analysis. Ultimately, Houston comes to the conclusion that the politicisation of sexual health in Free State Ireland and then the Republic of Ireland has remained 'a nightmare from which modernists were increasingly ill-equipped to help the nation to awake.[48]

Irish Modernism and the Politics of Sexual Health is a valuable text for any scholar who is interested in the intersections between Irish writing and Medical Humanities. The connections between sexual health, bodily autonomy, and the persona of the self-inventing artist (although occasionally a little tenuous) are generally convincing. Considering our contemporary moment's investment in referring to 'Irishness' – both in mainstream media and online – in absolutist terms, the book's investment in considering the plurality of Irish identities all cohabiting the same Island is most welcome.

What Irish queer theorists do:

1. **They critique the notion that gender is something that is noun-based (something you 'are') rather than verb-based (something you do).**
2. **They argue against the notion that heteronormative lives constitute the norm or the 'natural' in society.**
3. **They engage in a 'queering' of so called good or 'liveable' lives and endeavouring to expose the intolerance and monstrosity that allows for the endorsement of such ways of being in the world as 'natural'.**
4. **Queer thinkers will often research the lives of non-heteronormative individuals whose stories have been written out of a society's official narratives about itself.**

Representative textual analyses

Carthaginians

Frank McGuinness' birthplace being county Donegal may possibly have provided him with a keen interest in the Queer preoccupations of liminality and undecidability in relation to life, subjectivity and reality in general, as McGuinness acknowledges in an interview with Anthony Roche:

> [Donegal is] a place of contradiction, a place of ambiguities. It's an isolated place, as well. I think all of those factors contributed to making me into a writer. I am a man who doesn't really know where he stands a lot of the time. These various plays are an attempt to decipher the location of where my head's at. I never found a sense

> of place an easy thing to grasp and I certainly never found it an easy thing to celebrate. I'm not at ease anywhere. But I have no doubt where I absolutely belong and where I come from, and that is Donegal. And I've no doubt where I will go to, and that is Donegal. It has continued to have a very powerful hold on my imagination and it will always be so, I'm certain of that. I find that there's no escaping it, but then I don't think there's any desire to escape from it. That said, I don't think I could live in it, certainly not at this stage in my life.[49]

In this honest admission, McGuinness admits to the same sense of 'home' as problematic for him, possibly because of his sense of always being perpetually Other no matter where he lived because of his queer identity.

David Cregan has made the following argument concerning the 'queerness' of Frank McGuinness' characters:

> More often than not, the conflict of the homosexual character is internal rather than simply external, disrupting a victim-like mentality that can oftentimes be representative of the narrative of marginalized identity. In this sense, McGuinness 'naturalizes' gay identity, often telling his story from the perspective of the protagonist, but never sympathizing in any overtly political way with a particular perspective, and thus repeatedly disrupting the common binaries which keep people and ideas apart. His is a queer theatrical epistemology in that it offers a dramatic vision that questions all reductive notions of identity, gay or straight.[50]

McGuinness' 'queer theatre' is described by Cregan as one in which all binaristic oppositions (national, gendered, sexual etc.) are collapsed in favour of subjectivities that are characterised by fluidity and performance rather than by naturalness and fixity.

At the centre of *Carthaginians* is the demonstrably anti-heteronormative (queer) character of Dido, the almost guardian angel of the three women who are keeping watch in a graveyard for the dead to rise. The play is set during the height of the Northern Irish Troubles and all of the main characters are in some way damaged by that conflict and particularly by the legacy of the tragedy of Bloody Sunday, the day in January 1972 when 14 young Irishmen were shot dead by members of the British Para Troop regiment whilst attending a civil rights march in Derry.

Toxic, nationalist and imperialist masculinity permeate this drama and blight the lives of the characters. The only saviour figure is

Dido and his attempts to craft a counter, queer narrative to the toxically masculinist, heteronormative one that was such a scourge for the people of Northern Ireland during the Troubles. That counter-narrative takes the form of Dido's 'play within the play', *The Burning Balaclava*, which is staged halfway through the drama. The play is written by Dido under the pseudonym Fionnuala McGonigle (F McG) and represents his attempt to offer redemption and humour to the Troubles in the north through dramatically queer art. By giving the author of this play the same initials as himself, Frank McGuinness is arguably connecting himself with that artist's identity and offering an approving assessment of the play's intentions and goals. *The Burning Balaclava* is a clever mixture of comedy and tragedy as Dido implies when he summarises his main character Padraig: 'Padraig is tormented by the troubles of his native land. Should he or should he not take up the gun for Ireland? Should he or should he not speak Gaelic all the time? Should he or should he not screw his girlfriend, a Protestant?'[51]

In a very queer move, several characters in this mini-drama are played by the opposite genders to those expected by the audience and this echoes the metaphorical subverting of gender roles that Wilde played with throughout his career and perfected in *The Importance of Being Earnest*. Equally, *The Burning Balaclava* could be a commentary upon that other Wildean play within another text which is the 'Circe' episode in James Joyce's *Ulysses*. During that play's darkly carnivalesque action, men and women morph into their opposite genders in a manner that Fionnuala McGonigle echoes when she writes male and female characters and casts members of the opposite sex to play them. Joyce and McGuinness are both noted admirers of Wilde's *The Importance of Being Earnest* so it is arguable that Joyce is a mediating presence between Wilde and McGuinness in relation to Wilde's influence upon *The Burning Balaclava*.

The characters in *The Burning Balaclava* openly speak of their utopian aspirations to find a place in which their loves and desire could be achieved:

> MAELA: There's a place for people like us.
> PAUL: Somewhere.
> MAELA: Sometime.
> PAUL: Some place.
> MAELA: A new province.

PAUL: A new province?
MAELA: A province where Catholics and Protestants can go to bed together and talk dirty. (339)

Although McGuinness had openly distanced himself from the Field Day theatre group by the time *Carthaginians* had been written, this reference to a fictional Irish province does echo the aspiration of that organisation to create an 'artistic fifth province'. Via the improvisational use of the lyrics of 'Somewhere' from *West Side Story*, the characters in *The Burning Balaclava* express their desire for a separate plane of existence that can only possibly exist in the realm of art. The pathos of this moment is, in a very Wildean move, slightly undercut by comedic triviality when they reveal that all they want in this new province is a place where both religions on the Island of Ireland can come together and talk dirty.

The final moments of *Carthaginians* sees Dido leaving the stage and his sleeping friends after having endeavoured to act as a transformative influence throughout the drama. His final word 'Play' (370) epitomises his attitude towards life as being an extended performance in which he and those around him must attempt to improvise any freedoms that they are going to attain in this extended dramatic work called life. That Dido is a perfect portrait of the dandy as saviour and that he (like Pyper) is always on the side of life and survival has been testified to by Claire Gleitman in her analysis of the climax of *Carthaginians*: 'Appropriately, he [Dido] is given the last scene to himself. Dido's status as saviour is reinforced by the fact that he stands wakeful vigil over those who sleep around him, whom he blesses. The allusion to Jesus is strengthened by Dido's injunction to "Remember me" (370), words that Christ uttered at the Last Supper. In an affirmation of Derry's continuing life, Dido lists some of its streets and pronounces the city "[s]urviving"'.[52] Dido envisions an exquisite future for the whole island of Ireland in which performance and style trump entrenched positions centring around rigid and black-and-white positions concerning moral, political or any other type of identity.

The unproblematically heteronormative, male characters in Carthaginians, such as Hark and Paul, are those for whom redemption and a hopefully future remain very remote. It is to the women and the queer-male figure of Dido that Northern Ireland must look to if it wishes to be optimistic about the prospects of a better future to come. Thus, *Carthaginians* is a play in which both feminist and queer readings exist simultaneously and can be said to elucidate some of the common theoretical ground that is shared by both forms of cultural theory.

The poetry of Eavan Boland

In 1989, Eavan Boland wrote her pamphlet 'A Kind of Scar: A Woman Poet in the National Tradition' in which she diagnoses some of the problems that existed in modern Irish poetry, particularly those that existed as a result of what she saw as the patriarchal, male-dominated aspects of Irish poetry's prevailing formal and thematic qualities: 'Long after they rejected the politics of Irish nationalism [Irish poets] continued to employ the emblems and enchantments of its culture. It was the culture, not the politics, which informed Irish poetry: not the harsh awakenings, but the old dreams'.[53] As far as Boland was concerned, the Irish poetic aesthetic was stranded in the past and dominated by a masculinist, nationalist vision for poetry even though the problems with political Irish nationalism had long since been diagnosed and largely jettisoned from Irish politics.

Carmen Zamora Llena sums up the attitude that Boland shared with many women Irish poets towards Irish poetry as it existed in the late 1980s and early 1990s: '[Many Female Irish Poets] have as their starting point a similar conflict with a masculine tradition that has doubly estranged them as women and poets. They feel the need to dialogically explore the relationship between their feminine experience and their national past as a way to (re)construct their own national and gender identity, which has been lost in the wounds left by their inherited past'.[54] This ambition was one that was championed and, to some extent, pioneered by Eavan Boland in her poetry collection *Outside History* (1990). As Lucy Collins has argued: 'The importance of a specifically Irish identity is central both to the critical trajectory Eavan Boland has traced for herself as a poet and to the way in which her work has been received and read'.[55] The Irish identity that Boland wished to poetically represent was one that would include both those who had always been inside Irish history and those who had, until then, been outside of its narrative margins.

In her poem 'Outside History', the poet asserts that 'I have chosen: out of myth in history I move to be, part of that ordeal, who darkness is only now reaching me from those fields, those rivers, those roads clotted as firmaments with the dead' (32). The poetic project being described in this work is one that will pay attention to both the concrete reality and the abstract mythology out of which historical and artistic narratives are created. A promise is made in 'Outside History': the dead who have been forgotten and given no proper textual representation will be ethically invoked.

Boland's childhood was largely spent in London, and experience of living in that imperial capital can be read as giving her a sense of what it could sometimes be like to be a woman in Ireland:

> My childhood, certainly in the London years, wasn't happy. That isn't to say it wasn't a privileged childhood, because it was. But it was fictional and desolate in an odd way … there was this huge, compartmentalised house. And I felt thoroughly displaced in it. I never believed I belonged there. I never felt it was my home. Some of the feelings I recognise as having migrated into themes I keep going back to – exile, types of estrangement, a relation to objects – began there.[56]

'Since concepts of home, in particular of the unified family, have been central to the construction of an Irish national imaginary, it is noteworthy that Boland expresses her unease through the metaphor of the compartmentalised house. Her sense of displacement is double: the family of the diplomat is identifiably Irish, yet always at a distance from Ireland, and within this complex dynamic Boland is further displaced by the lack of permanence and intimacy of this life'.[57] Significantly, Boland refers to her childhood as being almost 'fictional'. This suggests that she realised that all experiences can take on the malleability of fiction and thus can be reimagined via a subjective, imaginative consciousness. Whether Boland is remembering accurately is irrelevant, the fact is that, via the process of memory becoming imagination, her representation of her childhood can attain the quality of authentic truth.

In the titular poem from *Outside History*, Boland compares the representative experience of Irish women to that of the stars in the sky: 'There are outsiders, always. These stars – these iron inklings of an Irish January, whose light happened thousands of years before our pain did: they are, they have always been outside history'. Like the stars, the lived experiences of Irish women have been largely neglected by the official, grand narratives of history and literature because the narrative voice that controlled those stories was very much sexed male and gendered masculine. In *Outside History*, Boland endeavours to bring those outsiders inside the representative fold of Irish poetry. By so doing, Boland also tries to create an Irish poetic *ecriture feminine*, following the example of Helene Cixous.

One notable poem of Boland's that implicitly advocates a specific feminine version of Irish poetry in terms of style and themes is 'Mise Eire' ('I am Ireland') (1987), which begins with the following confident assertion: 'I won't go back to it – into old dactyls, oaths made by the animal tallows of the candle, land of the Gulf Stream, the small farm, the scalded memory, the songs that bandage up the history, the words that make a rhythm of the crime'.[58] Boland is demanding that new Irish poetry will be both stylistically and thematically revolutionary. Poetry in Ireland should no longer 'make a rhyme of the crime', which implies that too many Irish poems have either glorified masculine dominance or actively and criminally erased the feminine and female experience from their aesthetic.

Boland does not wish the Irish female identity to be confined to these narrow binaries that have over the years become more symbolic than actually representative of lived female experiences and identities in Ireland. The extent to which this poem resists grand narratives or merely produces another totalising story about Irishness is certainly a debatable issue. Edna Longley was of the opinion that Boland's poetry did not allow itself to break free from the urge that Irish poems seemed to feel to always be writing about the Irish nation and forms of Irish nationalism.[59] Gerardine Meaney argues that, in 'Mise Eire', Boland does not acknowledge the power of poetic language and artistic language more generally to revise old symbols and metaphors in radical ways. Thus, for Meaney, the poem merely replicates old absolutisms in new but equally rigid and stultifying forms.[60]

It is important to note that Eavan Boland has pointed to the radical fluidity of various tropes and signifiers when placed in the correct artistic hands. Boland famously said of Yeats' later poems that he 'feminised the nation and nationalised the feminine'.[61] Whether this was Yeats' intention or not does not really matter. What is important is that Boland sees in the trope of Mother Ireland and Woman as Nation the possibility for the creation of radical and liberating symbols of gender in the context of nation and nationalism.

An important argument concerning the radicalness of the poetic voice in 'Mise Eire' is put forward by Clutterbuck when she asserts that the 'I' in this poem refuses absolute fidelity and subordination to a totalising version of femininity and female identity. By refusing to be either totally of or totally separate from the abstract symbolism of the 'Mother Ireland' version of Irish female identity, 'an invitation is issued to Irish people to know as irretrievably mixed, our concepts, on the one hand, of the foreignness and unacceptability of the construct of Mother Ireland, and on the other, of its familiarity and usefulness'.[62] Such a reading testifies to the nuance and complexity both of Boland's poetic vision and of the possibilities for future conceptualisations of nation, gender, sex and sexuality that her poems potentially can offer.

The poem 'Anorexic' is an example of Boland using her poetry to represent the reality and mythology surrounding the Irish female identity. The poem begins with lines that describe the self-loathing an anorexic can feel concerning her body

> Flesh is heretic.
> My body is a witch.
> I am burning it.
> Yes I am torching
> her curves and paps and wiles.
> They scorch in my self denials.[63]

The poetic voice is describing how alienated she feels towards her body and intends to use starvation as a means of punishing it for sins the poet believes it has committed. Starvation is certainly not unfamiliar to the Irish people. One needs only to think about the stories and images that have been created to represent the Great Famine of the 1840s or the IRA Hunger Strikes in 1980s' Northern Ireland. In 'Anorexic', the trope of the starving Irish person is given a feminist twist and used to explore issues around the bodily control exerted on Irish females via societal and cultural prescriptions.

The second half of the poem focusses on the mythic female figure of Eve and her association with original sin:

> Only a little more,
> only a few more days
> sinless, foodless,
> I will slip
> back into him again
> as if I had never been away.
> Caged so
> I will grow
> angular and holy. (75).

The masculine pronoun 'him' refers to Adam and the story of how Eve was born out of his rib. The poet is yearning for death so she can escape the original sin that Eve committed and that every human being is burdened with as soon as they are born. This 'sin' is of course the eating by Adam and Eve (at Eve's behest) of the fruit from the tree of knowledge that causes them to be banished from the Garden of Eden to which humanity has never been granted entry since.

The poem gives voice to how the Catholic Church has burdened females with a certain degree of pathology by bequeathing them only two binary identities: whore (Eve) or Madonna (Virgin Mary). Significantly, Eve is the mother of man in the Old Testament and Mary is in the New Testament; the teachings of the church, via the Bible, allow for no in-between female identity other than the ones symbolised by Eve and Mary.

Following Boland's death in 2020, Gerry Smyth wrote an appreciative essay about her, which appeared in the winter edition of *Reading Ireland*. In this essay Smyth wrote: 'Boland's focus has been to challenge the rigid, handed-down concepts of nationhood, to seek newer dispensations of that condition that would widen its boundaries, extend definitions. She has […] through her poetry […] been a powerful advocate of the "new Ireland" that she once recognised on her suburban horizon'.[64] This description of Boland's poetic project encapsulates her desire to forge in the smithy of her poems a version of the Irish nation that would be both inclusive and also, in some ways, provisional and resistant of absolutism. For this reason, among many others, Eavan Boland was deservedly posthumously honoured by having the Trinity College Dublin library named after her in 2024.

The Crying Game

The Crying Game (1992) is Neil Jordan's famous/infamous cinematic exploration of the nature of desire in the context of the Northern Irish Troubles. The first third of the film resembles Frank O'Connor's 'Guests of the Nation' with its focus on the developing friendship between an IRA volunteer, Fergus (Stephen Rea), and his hostage, Jody (Forest Whitaker). The remainder of the film broadens its thematic and geographical scope as it moves from Northern Ireland to England and concentrates on Fergus' relationship with Jody's bereaved partner, Dil (Jaye Davidson).

Maria Pramaggiore succinctly summarises the key concerns of *The Crying Game* and its place in Neil Jordan's cinematic oeuvre:

> In *The Crying Game* (1992), conflicts involving sexuality and Irish nationalism echo postmodern and postcolonial understandings of identity as a process of negotiating claims of gender, sexuality, race, and nationality. As in many of Jordan's previous films, including *In the Company of Wolves* (1984), *Mona Lisa* (1985), *High Spirits* (1988) and *The Miracle* (1991), things are never what they appear to be; any attempt to equate race and nationality, on the one hand, or gender and sexuality on another, meets with disaster. In other words, reading the body's 'natural' attributes as markers of identity fails because vision is unreliable and incomplete because 'nature' is no longer stable.[65]

The revelation halfway through the film that Dil is a transgender female who is biologically male brings issues concerning gender and sexual identity to the fore. The fact that she and Jody are both racially and nationally other to the white, Irish characters allows for the examination of how numerous aspects of identitarian politics are interconnected.

The publicity blurb for the film, 'desire is a danger zone', signals *The Crying Game*'s concern with one of the key aspects of queer theory: how desire is very unstable and cannot be contained by the supposedly 'stable' and 'natural' conception of sexuality. Although

Fergus would consider himself to be definitely heterosexual, he is clearly attracted to the anatomically male figure of Dil. The concealment of all the details of Dil's biology until the moment when they are about to engage in sexual activity means that the audience is just as shocked by the revelation as Fergus.

Earlier in the film, Fergus' relationship with Jody, although not explicitly homoerotic, had several moments of same-sex intimacy. The most obvious of these moments occurs when Fergus is forced to hold the bound Jody's penis as he urinates outside. Fergus' relationship with both Jody and Dil represents a challenge to national, racial and sexual allegiances. As Maria Pramaggiore argues: '*The Crying Game* links problematics of sex and gender, race and nationalism through a crisis of masculinity that is unresolvable through a traditional narrative of wartime heroism and romance'.[66] *The Crying Game* begins and ends with two songs that are revealed to be ironic as the film progresses. The first song heard is Michael Bolton's 'When a Man Loves a Woman' and the last is Dolly Parton's 'Stand by Your Man'. These two avowedly heterosexual songs are given an ironic tinge in the context of *The Crying Game*'s demonstrably 'queer' plot.

The most traditionally female/feminine character in the film is Fergus' fellow IRA traveller and girlfriend, Jude (Miranda Richardson). We first see her at the beginning of the film when she is acting as a honey trap to ensnare Jody. Her hair is blonde and she is wearing a denim mini-skirt. When she reappears in the second half of the film, her hair is dyed black and is cut to make her seem even more like a hypersexual femme fatale. Her adversarial relationship with Dil symbolises the conflict between traditional and queer conceptions of gender that is one of the central themes of the film.

How Jude is treated by the senior IRA figure in the film, Peter (Adrian Dunbar), represents the problematic feminist politics in *The Crying Game*. Every time she attempts to assert herself she is verbally cut off by Peter's command to 'shut the fuck up'. Her main value to her male comrades is largely sexual, as the beginning of the film makes clear. For this reason, whilst the queer politics of the film can be considered as fairly radical, it is a greatly flawed cinematic text in terms of its retrograde attitude towards feminism.

It should also be noted that *The Crying Game*'s 'queer credentials' have not been unchallenged. Celebrated queer theorist Judith (now

Jack) Halberstam has argued that the film's technique of placing the viewer in the heterosexual viewpoint of Fergus by withholding the revelation of Dil's gender identity for so long means that the film refuses a queer perspective and uses that form of identification merely as a piece of narrative pyrotechnics.[67] Halberstam argues that the shocking twist at the heart of *The Crying Game* only serves to alienate an imagined heterosexual audience from the queer perspective. In contrast, Halberstam regards the film *Boys Don't Cry* (1999), which was made nearer the end of the twentieth century, as a film that allows its audience to adopt and sympathise with a non-heteronormative point of view. This argument of Halberstam's also chimes with the central thesis of Laura Mulvey's epochal essay 'Visual Pleasure and Narrative Cinema' (1975), which is that the cinematic camera's gaze is traditionally gendered and sexualised as being male and heterosexual. That symbolic gaze takes on the literal and physical form of Fergus in *The Crying Game*, particularly when he informs Dil: 'I kinda liked you as a girl'.

The character of Dil functions as a perfect example of the power of explicitly performative gender as theorised by Butler. Although Dil seems to play the stereotypical role of an idealised figure of womanhood, particularly at the end of the film when she is literally seen to be standing by her man whilst he (Fergus) is in prison for a murder which she had actually committed (that of Jude), the fact that she is not biologically male explicitly calls to attention how unnatural and performative gender roles are. As Lori Rogers argues extensively:

> Is Dil's safety in heterosexual devotion a reductive politics? Only if it is seen as natural; Dil's bodily construction is constantly working as knowledge that runs counter to a natural reading of her relationship with Jody and/or Fergus. Her safety in heterosexual union is so sharply defined only because of her basic difference. In other words, in a traditional definition of the term, Dil is outside the possibility of heterosexual union because she is not 'really' a woman. Therefore every aspect of her association with Fergus is performative.[68]

The radicality of Dil's gendered and sexualised performativity clearly resides in the fact that body and bodily performance are very much at odds with each other according to the dictates of heteronormativity.

One scene in the film where the queer homosocial bonding that has permeated the plot takes on a distinctly misogynistic turn occurs in the bloody penultimate scene when Dil kills Jude as an act of vengeance for Jody and also, conceivably, as revenge for Jude's 'natural' gendered and sexed identity:

> JUDE: You sick bitch.
> DIL: You was there, wasn't you? You used those tits and that ass to get him, didn't you?
> *(Fergus screams from the bed … Dil shoots Jude in the throat, and she falls dead, covered in blood.)*
> DIL: She was there, wasn't she? … And she used her tits and that cute little ass to get him, didn't she? … Tell me what she wore.
> FERGUS: Can't remember … [69]

'Dil resents Jude for being the perfect white woman who is rewarded by society with attentive, loving men – like her Jody. Jude represents the ultimate whiteness of femininity which Dil must work against yet try to approximate'.[70]

The fact that relations between biological males are privileged in *The Crying Game*, very often violently at the expense of the only 'natural' female character, results in it being a cinematic text that can be read in accordance with Eve Sedgwick's conceptualisation of homosociality and the homosocial triangle.

> The concept of *homosociality* describes and defines social bonds between persons of the same sex. It is, for example, frequently used in studies on men and masculinities, there defined as a mechanism and social dynamic that explains the maintenance of hegemonic masculinity. A popular use of the concept is found in studies on male friendship, male bonding, and fraternity orders.[71]

Sedgwick's theorisation of homosociality is characterised by a triangular structure in which men have bonds with other men and women serve as the conduits through which these bonds are expressed. However, this triangle may portray as rivalry what is actually an attraction between men. The argument and the idea that there is an underlying continuum between different kinds of male homosocial desire open up a potential arena for research on the fragile boundaries and lines between different masculinities and hetero-/homosexuality.

The consistent, soft focus visions that Fergus has of the dead Jody in his cricket gear signals an implicit homoeroticism existing in Fergus' minds-eye for his dead friend. Fergus' obsessive searching out and then romancing Dil can conceivably be interpreted as his attempt to continue his relationship with Jody via the mediating 'female' presence of Dil. The resulting revelation concerning the reality of Dil's anatomy provides a queer twist to this particular homosocial triangle.

Near the end of the film, Fergus attempts to hide Dil from the sinister intention of his former IRA comrades by cutting her hair and dressing her in Jody's cricket clothes. This act on Fergus' part results in Dil symbolically becoming the lost romantic object of Jody. This again provides a metaphorical queer twist to the film *Vertigo* in which the main character, Scottie (James Stewart), tries to recover his lost object of desire by making over a stranger (Kim Novak) in her image.

Eve Sedgwick argues that homosocial bonding and triangles very often result in the violent removal of the female element in that triangle so that the men can come together unmediated by the feminine. This happens in the climax of *The Crying Game* when Jude is murdered by the anatomically male transgender figure of Dil. Before Fergus leaves the scene of Jude's murder, he gazes affectionately at the picture of Jody. This moment signals the continuing importance of Jody to the matrix of desire that exists for Fergus.

The fact that Fergus can't remember what Jude wore when she was with Jody is a reminder of just how unimportant Jude really was in this tale of male homosocial/homoerotic bonding. Pramaggiore implies that *The Crying Game* culminates in a pyrrhic victory for progressive identitarian politics – a victory for a certain version of queerness but a defeat for feminism. According to Pramaggiore, queer male bonding in this piece of cinema succeeds because of its erasure of sexual, gendered and 'racial difference, [but] it still requires that women be disallowed from the bastions of male power, notably the military and the prison. Yet in the character of Dil, the film offers a model where the classical invert is invited to be a member of the fraternity and thus provide the masculine world with difference and sameness'.[72] This reading of *The Crying Game* illuminates how it is a film that prioritises an identity politics of queerness which is firmly grounded in masculinity and all the while representing feminism and female emancipation as an agenda which queerness must overcome in order that it may fully realise itself.

Asking for It

Louise O'Neill's *Asking for It* (2015) was one of the most talked about Irish novels of the 2010s. It themes of sexual violence, gender politics and the politics of consent proved extremely topical in an age that was soon to be rocked by the Hollywood scandals involving Harvey Weinstein and Jeffrey Epstein, which would then lead to the rise of the MeToo movement in 2018. The novel would then spawn a highly successful stage adaptation that premiered at the Abbey Theatre in 2018.

Asking for It begins with the following passage, which can be read as encapsulating many of the texts key themes, issues and concerns:

> My mother's face appears in the mirror beside my own, bright red lips on powdered skin. Her hair is still in its neat bob despite the sticky heat. She gets it done every Saturday. 'I deserve a treat,' she says as she leaves the house. 'I don't care how expensive it is.'
>
> Karen Hennessy gets her hair blow-dried three times a week. She never mentions the cost. I'm flushed, patches of red breaking out on my cheeks, the greying vest top I wore to bed sticking to me. I look from her face to mine. You're so like your mother, people always say. You're the image of her. 'Morning,' she says. 'What are you doing, just staring at yourself in the mirror?' She frowns at my chest, at where the nipples are outlined through the sweat-stained fabric. 'Nothing,' I say as I wrap my arms over them. 'What do you want?'[73]

Here, we are introduced to Emma O'Donovan and her mother and the themes of female sexuality and its dependence on male and, sometimes, other females' approval for validation. As Eugene O'Brien argues, these women 'ideologically enculturate to look their best in order to receive the male gaze'.[74] How gender is performatively constructed, in accordance with Judith Butler's theories, will be a key theme throughout the novel and it is raised in this opening passage where both mother and daughter prepare themselves to perform their best version of femininity during their day. The issue of mother-and-daughter relations and how standards and codes of behaviour can change across the generational divide shall also be of significance as the novel progresses.

The play of *Asking for It* utilises a dramatic style that emphasises artifice and unnatural performances. For much of the first half, many of the characters seem to be performing for an obvious or imagined audience, either in their 'real world' or in the '(virtu)real' realm of various online platforms such as Facebook. Thus, Butlerian performativity manifests itself in the play at the level of both content and style. This is also apparent in the source text through the numerous quotes from online messages, which remind us that the (virtu)real represents a plane of existence in which these young people regularly perform their gendered subjectivities for the purpose of approval from their known or sometimes unknown audiences.

We are given an early example of the female characters' need to perform for approval and to frame these performances through the lens of social media: 'Ali has tagged me in a photo on Instagram, a selfie of the four of us at the match captioned "Me and my girls, fresh as fuck"' (57). Emma and her friend had been performing femininity for the male gaze and the GAA match and now wished to have that performance shared with a wider audience – a desire that is made possible via the online medium of Facebook.

The character of Emma and the traumatic sexual encounter that is inflicted upon her by several of her male peers whilst she is under the influence of alcohol and drugs are the two things that drive the plot of the text. Significantly, Emma is far from a likeable person. She is arrogant, often snobbish, and frequently a disloyal friend. This is a brave narrative decision on O'Neill's part because she relies on her readers to never think that Emma was 'asking for it' no matter how much they personally dislike her as an individual. This characterisation invokes Cixous' insistence in 'The Laugh of the Medusa' that women should be forced to conform to an idealised version of feminine behaviour prior to being granted societal approval. It is certainly clear that Emma's mother feels that her daughter should behave in that approved manner. Hence the reason she keeps on defending Emma's character by constantly reciting that she is 'a good girl'. The manner in which Emma is condemned both nationally and locally in the aftermath of the assault also reminds the readers of Catholic Ireland's prescriptive attitude towards female behaviour, particularly as regards sexual activity. This was an attitude (as discussed above) that certainly contributed in some way to the death of Anne Lovett. We are told during the course of the book that Emma attempted suicide because she could not bear the constant condemnation that was being forced upon her, either vocally or silently.

It is ironic that the figure of the rebellious and independent young Irish woman is a staple of Irish literature and culture. One obvious example of this is the character Glorvina in the novel *The Wilde Irish Girl*, written by Sydney Owenson (later Lady Morgan) in 1906. However, there are always limits imposed on the extent of the wildness allowed for these characters and it is assumed their story will conclude with them being tamed and brought into conformity by the presence of a man. Emma refuses to conform to such societal limits regarding expressions of sexuality and this is one of the reasons for her being ostracised by her community. The book also shows the communal double standards concerning what behaviour is permissible for men and what is permitted for women. Despite the fact that Emma's rapists have definitely committed a crime and she was certainly the victim, their village wants to forgive the young men and condemn the female 'temptress'.

Asking for It's depiction of heterosexuality and the various behaviours it can engender, particularly in men, is represented often throughout the work as being monstrous. Passages such as the following reinforce this reading:

> Now Dylan has two thumbs up to the camera. In the next photos his fingers are inside the body, the girl (me, me, oh God I'm going to be sick) but she doesn't move. Her head and shoulders have fallen off the edge of the bed. He spreads her legs, gesturing for the camera to come closer, the next few photos of pink flesh, and I think of the hundreds of likes, of all the people who have seen this, who have seen her like this … (88)

The act of heterosexual sex, as described in this quote, is clearly horrific, predatory and humiliating for Emma. She feels so traumatised by these images that she is compelled to refer to herself in the third person, despite the fact that she knows that the girl in the pictures is her. This is her only self-defence mechanism and only way of disassociating herself from an event that she cannot bear to confront.

Arguably, moments such as this in the novel are part of O'Neill's strategy of 'queering' heterosexuality and making it seem monstrous and unnatural: This is, of course, a strategy of representation that heteronormativity frequently utilises against that which is considered as being outside its normative confines.

The violent (hetero)sexual encounter that was inflicted upon Emma has clearly had the monstrous and unnatural effect of physically and mentally tearing her apart. This is clear from the following passage that is a recording of Emma's interior consciousness: '"You could be a model. You could be a model. You could be a model." I make my mind go blank. I am not that girl any more. I am an It. I am a collection of doll parts, of pink flesh, of legs spread open for all to see' (121). The effect of this non-consensual (hetero)sexual encounter has clearly had the effect of making Emma feel alien from a body that she now views dispassionately as being unnatural and monstrously alien to her.

A lot of the condemnation and ridicule that Emma suffers is frequently communicated to her via mechanised, disembodied sources such as the radio, the television and the internet. This is a potent and stark comment on our postmodern existence in which communication and approval is easily and widely achievable but so are their opposites. The fact that the book is set in a small Cork village and never leaves its confines, except via excerpts from TV, radio and social media, offers an image of Ireland as being a fractured and disunited nation, consisting of micro-communities that very often fail to cohere as a national whole. It also suggests that Ireland is still quite an insular society that retains its old, repressive codes of normativity, particularly as regards gender and sexuality.

The depiction of some of the darker aspects of online spaces in this novel proved to be very topical because of the suicide in 2018 of a 21-year-old woman named Nicole 'Coco' Fox. Coco took her own life because of years of abuse she had suffered online. Her tragic death led to the passing into Irish law of the Harassment, Harmful Communications and Related Offenses Act in 2021. That piece of legislation is also known as 'Coco's Law'.

Whilst it is certainly true that *Asking for It* is a book which is immersed in the world of postmodernity, it is a text that can also be viewed as containing aspects of literary modernism. As Paige Reynolds argues, many contemporary Irish literary works written by women contain the kind of stylistic experimentations and thematic concerns surrounding gender identities and relations that characterised many of the modernist works written in the early twentieth century by authors such as James Joyce and Virginia Woolf.[75] I would argue that *Asking for It* is one such work of contemporary Irish women's writing.

Like many modern/modernist Irish literary texts, *Asking for It* is invested in depicting Irish rurality and its social mores. It is certainly the case that the book's depiction of rural Ireland and its inhabitants is unrelentingly bleak. The repression, judgement and double standards of the micro-rural community in which *Asking for It* is set, is on display from the very outset and remains a major focus of the novel until its final pages. Thus, it is a work that has more in common with Counter-Revival representations of Irish rurality than it does with the Revivalist works written by Yeats and (to a lesser extent) by Synge.

Asking for It is also a novel that shows how far that literary form has strayed from its stylistic and narrative roots in the nineteenth-century 'realist novel'. Most of those works emphasised growth, education and a narrative that is going towards a fulfilling and satisfactory climax. This book does not follow that narrative trajectory. The book ends on a very downbeat note with Emma planning to withdraw her allegation of rape, and the scene that closes the book is a dark and uncanny repetition of its opening:

> 'Emma?'
>
> My mother's voice floats up from downstairs. 'Emmie, where are you?'
>
> 'In my bedroom.'
>
> 'Come down, will you? I want to talk to you.'
>
> I take a deep breath, then another one. In. One. Two. Three. Out. One. Two. Three. I get dressed, covering that body up. I stare at my reflection. I look normal. I look like a good girl. 'Emmie?' My mother calls again.
>
> 'I'm coming,' I say. 'I'll be down now.' And I walk downstairs, dragging my mouth into a smile so that I can look normal. It's important that I look normal now. It's important that I look like a good girl. (196)

Like the beginning of the work, the novel ends with a focus on strained mother-daughter relations and on the reliance of female subjects on the implied gaze of the (male) Other. Whilst this ending can certainly be read as mirroring how traumatic events repeat themselves inside the psyche of those who experienced them,[76] it can also be read as an anti-traditionally novelistic conclusion because no progress has been achieved and Emma has not been allowed either a moment of triumph nor a moment of insight as a result of the awful events that happened to her.

Study questions

1. **Analyse the repeated use of the female body as emblem for the condition of Ireland in twentieth century writing and/or film.**
2. **Consider the impact of globalisation on contemporary Irish culture**
3. **How is feminist theory and activism a radical departure from some of the theoretical and critical orthodoxies of Irish postcolonial theory?**
4. **What are the similarities and/or differences between feminist theory and queer theory?**
5. **Consider the significance of some of the concepts that have evolved in feminist and queer theory (*ecriture feminine*, gender performativity etc.)**

Notes

1 See Graham Price, 'Quite an Other Thing: Recent Texts in Irish Queer Studies', *Irish University Review* 42:1 (2013), *Special Issue on Queer Theory*, pp. 222–233.

2 Quoted in Lori Rogers, *Feminine Nation* (New York: University Press of America, 1998), pp. 25–26.

3 Ibid.

4 Quoted in Tim Pat Coogan, *De Valera: Long Fellow, Long Shadow* (London: Arrow Books, 1995), p. 620.

5 Fintan O'Toole, 'Foreword', in Margot Backus and Joseph Valente (eds), *The Child Sex Scandal and Modern Irish Literature: Writing the Unspeakable* (Indiana: Indiana University Press, 2020), p. xi.
6 See Helene Cixous, 'The Laugh of the Medusa', *Signs* 1:4 (1976), pp. 879–880.
7 Declan Kiberd, *Inventing Ireland: The Literature of the Modern Nation* (London: Vintage, 1996), p. 355.
8 Gerardine Meaney, *Gender, Ireland, and Cultural Change* (New York: Routledge, 2010), p. 106.
9 Kim McMullen, 'Decolonizing Rosaleen: Some Feminist, Nationalist, and Postcolonialist Discourses in Irish Studies: Winner of the 1995 Senior Scholars Essay Award Women's Caucus for the Modern Languages/ Midwest', *The Journal of the Midwest Modern Language Association* 29:1 (1996), p. 35
10 Patricia Coughlan, 'Feminism and Literature in Postmodernity', *Hungarian Journal of English and American Studies (HJEAS)* 10:1–2 (2004), p. 195.
11 Linda Connolly, 'The Limits of "Irish Studies": Historicism, Culturalism, Paternalism', *Irish Studies Review* 12:2 (2004), p. 148.
12 Ibid., p. 149.
13 Quoted in ibid., p. 90.
14 Quoted in ibid., p. 97.
15 Ibid., p. 151.
16 Elizabeth Butler Cullingford, *Ireland's Others* (Cork: Cork University Press, 2001), p. 104.
17 Edna Longley, *From Cathleen to Anorexia* (Dublin: Attic Press, 1990), p. 17.
18 Ibid., p. 16.
19 Alan Finlayson, 'Towards a Radical Empiricism?', *Irish Review* 28 (Winter 2001), p. 141.
20 Gerardine Meaney, *Sex and Nation: Women in Irish Culture and Politics* (Dublin: Attic Press, 1991), p. 14.
21 Ibid., pp. 14–15.
22 Kim McMullen, 'Decolonizing Rosaleen: Some Feminist, Nationalist, and Postcolonialist Discourses in Irish Studies: Winner of the 1995 Senior Scholars Essay Award Women's Caucus for the Modern Languages/ Midwest', *The Journal of the Midwest Modern Language Association JSTOR* 29:1 (1996), pp. 32–45. https://doi.org/10.2307/1315256
23 Margaret Kelleher, *The Feminization of Famine: Expressions of the Inexpressible* (Cork: Cork University Press, 1997), p. 230.
24 Claire Bracken, *Irish Feminist Futures* (London: Routledge, 2015), p. 51.

25 For a broader list of what feminist critics do in more general term, see Peter Barry, *Beginning Theory: An introduction to Literary and Cultural Theory*, second edition (Manchester: Manchester University Press, 2009), pp. 128–129.
26 Eve Kosofsky Sedgwick, *Tendencies* (London: Routledge, 1994), p. 2.
27 Judith Butler, 'Performative Acts and Gender Constitution: An Essay in Phenomenology and Feminist Theory', *Theatre Journal* 40:4 (December, 1988), p. 519.
28 Sedgwick, *Tendencies*, p. 7.
29 Kate O'Brien, *The Land of Spices* (London: Virago, 1988), p. 157.
30 Quoted in Richard Ellmann, *Oscar Wilde* (London: Penguin, 1988), p. 352.
31 Judith Butler, *Bodies that Matter* (Oxon: Routledge Classics, 1993), p. 173.
32 See Noreen Giffney, 'Quare Theory', in Wanda Balzano, Anne Mulhall and Moynagh Sullivan (eds), *Irish Postmodernisms and Popular Culture* (London: Palgrave Macmillan, 2007), p. 197.
33 See Eoin O'Broin, 'Queer Nation', *Fortnight*, 363 (July–August 1997), p. 25.
34 Joseph Valente, 'Self Queering Ireland', *Canadian Journal of Irish Studies* 36:1 (Spring 2010), pp. 25–27.
35 Robyn Wiegman, *Object Lessons* (Duke: Duke University Press, 2004), p. 334.
36 See Frank McGuinness, 'Foreword', in Fintan Walsh (ed.), *Queer Notions: New Plays and Performances from Ireland* (Cork: Cork University Press, 2010), p. vii.
37 See Chris Morash, *A History of Irish Theatre 1601–2000* (Cambridge: Cambridge University Press, 2002), p. 256.
38 Fintan Walsh, 'Introduction', in Walsh (ed.), *Queer Notions*, p. 14.
39 For a thorough analysis of queer theory's debt to Derrida, see Michael O'Rourke, 'Queer Theory's Loss and the Work of Mourning Jacques Derrida', http://www.rhizomes.net/issue10/orourke.htm (accessed 20 May, 2025).
40 1 Ibid., 6.
41 See Eibhear Walshe, *Oscar's Shadow: Wilde, Homosexuality and Modern Ireland* (Cork: Cork University Press, 2011), p. 7.
42 Ibid., p. 25.
43 Eibhear Walshe, *Oscar's Shadow: Wilde, Homosexuality and Modern Ireland* (Cork: Cork University Press, 2011), p. 68.
44 See Giffney, 'Quare Theory', pp. 197–210.
45 Oscar Wilde, 'The Soul of Man Under Socialism', in *Collins Complete Works of Oscar Wilde*, third edition (Glasgow: HarperCollins, 1994), p. 1184.

46 Jennifer Redmond and Mary McAuliffe, 'Introduction, in Jennifer Redmond and Mary McAuliffe (eds), *The Politics of Gender and Sexuality in Modern Ireland* (Dublin: Four Courts Press, 2024), p. 1.
47 Ibid., p. 2.
48 Lloyd (Meadbh) Houston, *Irish Modernism and the Politics of Sexual Health* (Oxford: Oxford University Press, 2023), p. 31.
49 Anthony Roche, 'An Interview with Frank McGuinness', *Irish University Review* 40:1 (2010), p. 18.
50 David Cregan, 'McGuinness' Dramaturgy and Queer Resistance', *Irish University Review* 40:1 (2010), p. 24.
51 Frank McGuinness, *Carthaginians, Plays 1* (London: Faber & Faber, 1996), p. 332. All future references refer parenthetically to this edition.
52 Claire Gleitman, '"Isn't It Just like Real Life?" Frank McGuinness and the (Re)writing of Stage Space', *The Canadian Journal of Irish Studies* 20:1 (1994), p. 71.
53 Quoted in Meaney, *Sex and Nation*, p. 17.
54 Carmen Zamorano Llena, 'Overcoming Double Exile: (Re)construction of "Inner-Scapes" in Contemporary Irish Women's Poetry', *Nordic Irish Studies* 3 (2004), p. 165.
55 Lucy Collins, 'Lost Lands: The Creation of Memory in the Poetry of Eavan Boland', *Contemporary Irish Women Poets: Memory and Estrangement* (Liverpool: Liverpool University Press, 2015), p. 23.
56 Quoted in ibid., p. 25.
57 Ibid.
58 https://www.blueridgejournal.com/poems/eb2-mise.htm (accessed 20 May, 2026).
59 See Longley, *From Cathleen to Anorexia*, p. 17.
60 See Clutterbuck, 'Mise Eire', p. 289.
61 Quoted in Longley, *From Cathleen to Anorexia*, p. 17.
62 Clutterbuck, 'Mise Eire', p. 289.
63 Eavan Boland, *New Collected Poems* (London: Carcanet, 2005), p. 75. All future references refer parenthetically to this edition.
64 Gerry Smyth, 'Eavan Boland: An Appreciation', *Reading Ireland* (Winter 2023), p. 31.
65 Maria Pramaggiore, '"I Kinda Liked You as a Girl": Masculinity, Postcolonial Queens, and the Nature of Terrorism in Neil Jordan's *The Crying Game*', in James McKillop (ed.), *Contemporary Irish Cinema: From The Quiet Man to Dancing at Lughnasa* (Syracuse: Syracuse University Press, 1999), p. 85.
66 Ibid., p. 96.
67 Judith Halberstam, *In a Queer Time and Place: Transgender Bodies, Subcultural Lives* (New York: New York University Press, 2005), p. 81.

68 Rogers, *Feminine Nation*, p. 102.
69 Neil Jordan, *The Crying Game*, in *A Neil Jordan Reader* (New York: Vintage International, 1993).
70 Rogers, *Feminine Nation*, p. 100.
71 N. Hammarén and T. Johansson', Homosociality: In Between Power and Intimacy', *Sage Open* 4:1 (2014), https://doi.org/10.1177/2158244013518057. Emphasis in original.
72 Pramagiorre, 'I Kinda Liked You as a Girl', p. 96.
73 Louise O'Neill, *Asking for It* (London: Quercus, 2015), p. 8. All future references refer parenthetically to this edition.
74 Eugene, O'Brien, '"That's Because of the Trauma": Repetition, Reflection and Refraction in Social Media in Louise O'Neill's *Asking for It*', *Journal of Franco-Irish Studies*: 7:1, Article 9 (2023), p. 96.
75 See Paige Reynolds, *Modernism in Irish Women's Contemporary Writing: The Stubborn Mode* (Oxford: Oxford University Press, 2024), pp. 1–28.
76 See O'Brien, '"That's Because of the Trauma"', p. 100.

5
Memory, trauma and imagination

Introduction

If the rise of gender and sexuality theory in Irish Studies was particularly dominant in the late 1990s and early noughties, succeeding years have seen an increasing interest in applying the memory and trauma theories of critics and thinkers such as Sigmund Freud, Paul Ricoeur and Pierre Nora to the study of Irish literature and culture. This became most evident during the 'decade of commemoration'. During much of the second decade of the twenty-first century, and into the third, Ireland was engaged in what came to be called 'a decade of commemoration' in which events such as Easter 1916, the War of Independence, and the Irish Civil War were remembered and commemorated via a series of events and documentaries spanning exactly ten years.

Following on from Stephen Dedalus' assertion in *Ulysses* that 'history is a nightmare from which I am trying to awake', Irish literature and culture has attempted to do justice to its traumatic history of colonialisation and famine by writing and creating texts and events that combine remembrance, mourning and commemoration. The ethicality of these works and events has always been of primary concern to their creators. Academics' utilisation of the works by the aforementioned memory theorists has helped them to create nuanced literary and cultural analyses; these consider the extent to which such acts of remembrance, mourning and commemoration have been successful in doing justice to the memories of those gone. In more recent times, the revelations of clerical and other forms of institutionalised abuse have spurred various artists to write, stage and film versions of those traumatic events in Ireland's recent history.

The relationship between individual and collective memory via the examination of specific examples of events (literary or purely historical) is important in this chapter. The literary and cinematic texts examined in detail are Neil Jordan's *Michael Collins*, Anne Enright's *The Gathering*, Sebastian Barry's *The Secret Scripture* and Ellen McWilliams' *Resting Places*. Because of its discussion of the Magdalene Laundries and various other abuses visited upon Irish women in the recent past, the chapter follows on naturally from the previous one.

Memory and trauma theory

Constanza del Rio defines trauma and traumatic memory thus:

> A traumatic event can be defined as a painful occurrence, but so intense that it exceeds our capacities to experience it in the usual ways. It disrupts time and history, breaks through the categories we use to take in the world, and seems to be registered in our memories in forms that are unlike those used to register conventional experience. This atypical memory is sometimes called traumatic memory to differentiate it from our usual narrative memory.[1]

In Freud's landmark text, *Beyond the Pleasure Principle* (a text from which del Rio is clearly drawing), Freud notes the tendency of traumatised veterans of World War I to psychologically re-enact the horrors that they witnessed and suffered during that conflict. Freud theorised that this repetition compulsion was a means to gain mastery of an event that they could not properly process at the time of their original happening.

Ruth Leys makes a similar point concerning the psychological effects of trauma:

> [The mind] cannot register the wound to the psyche because the ordinary mechanisms of awareness and cognition are destroyed. As a result, the victim is unable to recollect and integrate the hurtful experience in normal consciousness; instead, she is haunted or possessed by intrusive traumatic memories. The experience of the trauma, fixed or frozen in time, refuses to be represented as past, but is perpetually re-experienced in a painful, dissociated, traumatic present.[2]

'This temporal structure is based on Freud's concept of *Nachträglichkeit*, translated as "deferred action" or "afterwardsness", a concept which describes a complex and ambiguous temporal trajectory whereby the past, unrecognised as such, surfaces in the present'.[3]

A precursor to Freud's theory of (traumatic) repetition compulsion is the Anglo-Irish politician and thinker Edmund Burke's conceptualisation of the Sublime, which is discussed in his remarkable text on aesthetics, his first book, *A Philosophical Enquiry into the Origin of Our Ideas of the Sublime and the Beautiful* (1757). In this work, Burke argues that the experience of the Sublime is bound up with the experience of the pleasurable terror of pain avoided. Something terrifying and potentially painful came close enough to us to be apprehended but not so close as to totally overwhelm and take possession of us.[4] Similarly, Freud argues that we relive traumatic experiences to celebrate the fact that we survived these terrible events.[5]

As Freud would later argue, Burke sees the drive towards pain and possibly death as being far more powerful within humanity's psyche than that towards life and pleasure. For this reason, we can argue that the Anglo-Irish Burke laid some important ground work for the development of the discipline that would become known over a hundred years later as psychoanalysis and which would then act a catalyst for the growth of memory and trauma studies.

Paul Ricoeur, in his seminal text *Memory, History, Forgetting*, acknowledges that a totality of memory or a totality of forgetting is never good; rather, it is necessary for a dialectic between memory and forgetting to take place, which enables a healthy psychological space to be created and a reconciliation on the psychic level between the past and the present moments. As Ricoeur argues:

> Forgetting is the challenge par excellence put to memory's aim of reliability. The trustworthiness of memory hangs on the enigma constitutive of the entire problematic of memory, namely, the dialectic of presence and absence at the heart of the representation of the past, to which is added the feeling of distance proper to memories, unlike the simple absence of the image, which it serves to depict or to simulate. The problematic of forgetting, formulated at the level of greatest depth,, intervenes at the most critical point of this problematic of presence, of absence, and of distance, at the opposite pole from that

> minor miracle of happy memory which is constituted by the actual recognition of past memories.[6]

At the core of the dialectic that Ricoeur is theorising is the assertion that memory needs forgetting in order that ethical and authentic versions of a traumatic past can be preserved and its victims can be responsibly remembered. Pierre Nora writes similarly of the French Revolution as being a decisive and traumatic break with the past which enabled a certain amount of collective historical and cultural forgetting.[7] For theorists of memory such as Ricoeur and Nora, amnesia needs to be thought of as much in relation to collective as to individual memories in order that a productive relationship between past, present and future can be constituted.

Paul Ricoeur is heavily invested in theorising the problematics of memory when it comes to creating authentic and ethical narratives of history and lived experience: 'Under history, memory and forgetting. Under memory and forgetting, life. But writing life is another story. Incompletion'.[8] Ricoeur is acknowledging that any attempt to give full and complete narratological testimony to the past and also the present is always going to result in a less than total or perfect narrative. Therefore, the best one can do is to try and be as ethical and responsible a witness as possible.

The author Tim O'Brien perfectly encapsulates the problem of bearing witness to trauma in his great narrative of the Vietnam War, *The Things They Carried*:

> What seems to happen becomes its own happening and has to be told that way. The angles of vision are skewed ... When a guy dies ... you look away and then look back for a moment and then look away again. The pictures get jumbled; you tend to miss a lot. And then afterward, when you go to tell about it, there is always that surreal seemingness, which makes the story seem untrue, but which in fact represents the hard and exact truth as it seemed.[9]

As with Ricoeur, there is an acceptance in O'Brien's text that life, particularly traumatic occurrences in life, can never be narrated perfectly and therefore trauma narratives carry incompletion and gaps within their very form. As Cathy Caruth argues, trauma theory is a narrative of 'the failure of the mind to return to an experience it has never quite grasped, the repetition of an originary departure from the moment that constitutes the very experience of trauma'.[10]

Remembering Irish Studies

In Oscar Wilde's *The Importance of Being Earnest*, the character of Cecily responds to her governess' observation that 'memory is the diary that we all keep' by asserting: 'Yes but it usually chronicles the things that have never happened and couldn't possibly have happened'.[11] Irish memory and trauma theorists have devoted much time over the decades to considering the implications of this seemingly glib proto-modernist assertion and interrogating the reliability and unreliability of memory, particularly as it relates to traumatic events. Another important concern in Irish Memory studies is the emphasis on the fictionality of communal memory as a shaper of creative practice. Sebastian Barry's *The Secret Scripture* is a recent exploration and representation of individual and collective trauma in the context of literary writing.

In Emilie Pine's text *The Politics of Irish Memory: Performing Remembrance in Contemporary Irish Culture* (2010) Pine makes the following assertion:

> Irish culture is obsessed with the past. From the commemoration of historic events to the memoirs of childhood, we cannot escape the remembrance of things past in newspapers and books, on stages, on screens, in museums and on the streets of major cities, and in the spaces of public galleries. While representations of the past have always been an integral element of Irish culture, they are now one of its most compelling subjects. And the tone that characterises this subject is trauma.[12]

In this passage, Pine connects history, memory and trauma as being inextricably linked with Irish culture and key components within Irish Studies in the twenty-first century.

Similarly, Luke Gibbons has argued that:

> to reclaim the memory of those who have been forgotten or written out of history … is not to indulge in the self-absorption of victim culture but the opposite: to engage in an act of ethical imagination

> in which one's own uneven development becomes not just a way in, but a way out, a means of empathising with other peoples and societies in similar situations today … If Irish people find it difficult to identify with those parts of their own history that carry the stigma of poverty, there is little likelihood that they will be able to relate to those who come to the Ireland of the Celtic Tiger reminding them of their own unrequited pasts.[13]

The publication in the first few decades of the twenty-first century of various reports into the numerous incidents of clerical abuse that took place in many religious-run institutions such as schools and mother and baby homes in Ireland have also provoked a large debate concerning how justice can be done for those who suffered and, in some cases, died in these institutions. Again, issues concerning commemoration and memory were paramount in these discussions.

If there is one terrifying narrative that towers over all others in the recent traumatic history of the Irish, it is that surrounding the Magdalene Laundries and the abuses that were rampant behind their walls. Ireland's first such institution, the Magdalen Asylum for Penitent Females in Dublin, was founded by the Protestant Church of Ireland in 1765. At the time, there was a worry that sex work in Irish cities was on the rise and that 'wayward' women who had been seduced, had sex outside of marriage, or gotten pregnant out of wedlock were susceptible to becoming sex workers. Soon, parents began to send their unmarried daughters to the institutions to hide their pregnancies.

Initially, the majority of women entered these institutions voluntarily and served out multi-year terms in which they learned a 'respectable' profession. The idea was that they would employ these skills to earn money after being released; their work supported the institution while they were there. But over time, the institutions became more like prisons, with many different groups of women being routed through the system, sometimes by the Irish government. There were inmates imported from psychiatric institutions and jails, women with special needs, victims of rape and sexual assault, pregnant teenagers sent there by their parents, and girls deemed too flirtatious or tempting to men. Others were there for no obvious reason. Though the institutions were run by Catholic orders, they were supported by the Irish government, which funnelled money toward the system in exchange for laundry services. Various investigations and enquiries have been established to investigate the running of the Laundries and Mother and Baby Homes in an effort to facilitate reparation to the inmates and their descendants and also to provide them with a forum in which their traumatic ordeals could obtain acknowledgement via the telling of their stories.[14]

The concept of ethical memory has been crucial when deciding how these various historical events should be enshrined in Ireland's collective consciousness. As Pine argues:

> The goal of ethical memory is a form of justice that recognises the political nature of remembering and forgetting. The political focus of historical memory means that what is remembered of the past is what serves the needs of the present, reflected in the maxim that 'History is written by the victors'.[15]

A good example of an event that was perceived by many as constituting unethical commemoration occurred in 2020 when a public furore was provoked after it was proposed that a commemoration of the RIC (Royal Irish Constabulary, the British run Irish police force during the War of Independence) should take place. This was perceived by many members of the Irish public as being disrespectful to those who had suffered at the hands of the colonial force. The proposed commemoration was abandoned but it continued to be a controversial issue during the general election that was held that year.

Eoin Flannery and Eugene O'Brien have argued:

> In this, the decade of commemorations, one of the core tropes of Irish thinking in the socio-political and cultural spheres is coming to the fore. In some ways, Irish history can be seen as a dialectical process of crises and then commemoration of those crises. Moreover, as the ensuing collection of diverse interventions attest it is timely and enlightening to dwell upon the continuum of Irish historical commemorations and crises as part of an exercise in meta-historical self-reflection.[16]

The remembering and commemorating of history and trauma are thus being described as a mixture of both individual and communal/cultural memory.

The year 2018 saw the important publication of Miriam Haughton's *Staging Trauma*, which examines how British and Irish trauma performs remembrance and commemoration for various victims of abuse in private or public settings. Of paramount concern in Haughton's text is female bodies that have been literally and metaphorically removed from many patriarchal theatrical narratives in theatre and history. In the same year as Haughton's text was published, Kathleen Costello-Sullivan's *Trauma and Recovery in the Twenty-First-Century Novel* was released. This study focusses on hidden narratives of trauma and how they are represented in twentieth-century Irish prose fiction.

Edward Casey has made the salient connection between commemoration and remembrance:

> In its most ancient acceptation 'commemoration' means an intensified remembering. Further, two of its oldest meanings are the deliverance of a formal eulogy and participation in a liturgical service (wherein a 'lesser feast' is observed by being included, in parts, in a 'greater feast'). Taken together, these early senses of the word imply that in acts of commemoration remembering is intensified by taking place through the interposed agency of a text (the eulogy, the liturgy proper) and in the setting of a social ritual (delivering the eulogy, participating in the service).[17]

The importance of memory and commemoration in Irish Studies was further illustrated by the publication of a special issue of the academic journal *Irish Studies Review* in 2022 titled 'Critiquing Crisis and Commemoration', edited by Eoin Flannery and Eugene O'Brien.

Constanza del Rio's theory concerning the Irish need to revisit Ireland's traumatic past is comparable to Freud's theory of repetition compulsion in relation to traumatic events: 'The cultural and psychological need to revisit the historical past can also be founded on the frequent perception of Irish history as a violent, conflicting, fragmented, chaotic and discontinuous terrain. Deprived of the comforting and reassuring sense of closure and completion provided by linear progress, Irish history has been and is repeatedly recounted in an attempt to make it understandable.[18] Faced with a traumatic past that is not completely knowable or graspable, the Irish may feel a great need to revisit and, sometimes, to re-enact it as a means of coming to terms with, and making sense of, their gothically nightmarish history.

An important genre within Irish Studies that testifies to the importance of history, memory and trauma within Irish culture is that of the 'trauma novel'. This is a novelistic form that has at its core the experience of traumatic repetition and the forms that re-enactment can take. An important example of this genre is Ernie O'Malley's seminal, inter-generic memoir/novel *On Another Man's Wound* in which he recounts his life as an IRA soldier during the War of Independence. The title of the work is from the bible and it encapsulates the book's central themes of guilt and trauma: 'It's easier to sleep on another man's wound'.

Significantly, O'Malley was very interested in James Joyce's 'trauma novel' *Ulysses* and wrote a series of lectures on that text, which he delivered in South America. *Ulysses* is also an important text in the history of Irish trauma novels because at its core are two men – Stephen Dedalus and Leopold Bloom – who are both struggling with traumatic memories of loss. Dedalus is still haunted by the ghost of his dead mother and Bloom by the spectre of his dead son Rudy. In the case of Dedalus, he is also plagued by feelings of guilt because of his anti-Catholic refusal to pray for his mother as she lay dying. Many of the passages in *Ulysses* that O'Malley looks at include descriptions of loss, guilt and traumatic memories. Luke Gibbons has also noted how the modernist writing of someone like Joyce would have appealed to someone like O'Malley who was haunted by a nightmarish past from which he wished to awake: 'The appeal of the modernist turn in art towards formal innovation [for someone like O'Malley] was that while rejecting passive or mimetic representation, the "slavish" reproduction of reality in politics as well as art [meant that the modernist texts very often] acted on history, refusing to accept an oppressive past as a given'.[19] O'Malley's *On Another Man's Wound* can thus be interpreted as a traumatic repetition of a traumatic and oppressive past but written using some of the formal devices of the novel, O'Malley is signalling that such a past can be redeemed via artistic re-imaginings that escape mere prosaic recounting in the form of the narrating of a succession of dates and events. For this reason, *On Another Man's Wound* can be read as one of the supreme examples of Irish modernism to emerge from the traumatic events of Ireland's revolutionary period.

One famous Irish author who has written most perceptively on O'Malley and his works is John McGahern, a novelist who wrote another example of an Irish trauma novel *Amongst Women*. This book centres on Michael Moran whose life is haunted, like O'Malley's, by his experiences as a Republican fighter during the War of Independence and the Irish Civil War. Robert Garrat argues that *Amongst Women*, to a large extent, answers yes to the following aesthetic questions: 'Can novels, which are interested in how they report subject matter as much as the subject matter they report, be reliable windows onto the past? When the representation of the past involves trauma or human suffering and emotion, does the novelist have an advantage over the historian who seeks factual objectivity?'[20]

Garrat goes on to argue that the reliving of trauma via imaginative remembrance is a crucial act for all the main characters in the novel:

> The presence of the past in *Amongst Women* is made possible by the notion of revival, first as an active part of the action of the story, and then as an overarching fictive strategy to establish meaning; things that are forgotten need to be remembered in order to connect the future with the past. In *Amongst Women*, the idea of revival works effectively but ironically. There is a sense that before one can get on with the future one must dig up the dead. For Moran this means uncovering and exposing the trauma moment or event to give it some kind of airing, as he does in his recollections associated with Monaghan Day; the recollections, in turn, become a story for his daughters. In the final scene of the novel the daughters, having buried their father, now become themselves the agents of memory, ready to tell stories about him to each other and to the next generation.[21]

As is the case for Joyce and O'Malley, McGahern (as evidenced in *Amongst Women*), feels that the traumatic wounds of the past can only be redemptively exorcised via the process of Freudian repetition through the merging together of both memory and imagination. One notable critic of John McGahern and, occasionally, Ernie O'Malley, is Ellen McWilliams whose memoir/history/trauma novel *Resting Places* shall be examined later in this chapter.

The genre of what could be called the cinema of Irish trauma and commemoration began to emerge in the late 1990s, arguably with the film *Michael Collins* (which shall be examined shortly). One particularly memorable example of this Irish cinematic sub-genre is *The Magdalene Sisters* (2002) which focusses on (partially fictionalised) female residents of the Irish Magdalene Laundries in the 1960s. This film can be regarded as being part of an older tradition of Irish cinema. James Smith notes:

> *The Magdalene Sisters* joins recent films that represent Irish life in the post-independence era emphasizing the repressive aspects of the Irish condition, the stifling eradication of individuality in the face of an indomitable church and state politics, and the relentless but often arbitrary cruelty that enforced social conformity (e.g., *The Field* 1990; *The Butcher Boy* 1997; *Angela's Ashes* 1999).[22]

Unlike these films, however, *The Magdalene Sisters* is explicitly concerned with remembering and commemorating a bleak Irish past rather than just passively representing it as a means of driving a strong cinematic narrative. As Diarmuid Ferriter argues, *The Magdalene Sisters* 'created a demand for a certain type of history that cannot be satisfied, raising troubling questions about the relationship between history, memory, representation and moral outrage'.[23]

Although demonstrably an 'Irish film', *The Magdalene Sisters* is also a piece of cinema that follows a lot of mainstream cinematic conventions:

> This composite story of three girls, generically framed as a prison movie in the tradition of *One Flew over the Cuckoo's Nest* (1975) and *The Shawshank Redemption* (1994), insured its wider appeal to mass audiences rather than simply an earnest localised social realist problem-film. Like all engaging historical stories, events have been fictionalised and the dramatics heightened to create a powerful emotional effect on the audience.[24]

The film's ending, which depicts two of the central characters escaping their confinement in the Magdalene Laundry is undoubtedly a 'happy ending' in the best Hollywood, crowd pleasing tradition, even though one of the final images of the film is of an inmate still in the laundry who had suffered a mental breakdown.

The Magdalene Sisters can be regarded as being an example of an Irish 'anti-nostalgic' text. Emilie Pine defines this type of textual product thus:

> Anti-nostalgia distinguishes the recent trend for remembrance from the standard need of modernity to define itself from what came before. It also shifts away from the nostalgic strategy of using the past as a welcome break from the demands of the present. In the Irish context, the anti-nostalgic narrative of the Irish past is characterised by trauma [...] [T]he implication of anti-nostalgia is that the values of the present are more liberal, more inclusive, more productive than those of the past.[25]

Pine regards *The Magdalene Sisters* as being quite a conservative film because its anti-nostalgia allows its audience to feel that the past, as awful as it was, can be safely consigned to the past tense whilst modern Ireland is far more liberal and tolerant: 'Though *The Magdalene Sisters* makes the point in a postscript that the last laundry in Ireland only closed in 1996, a fact which invariably provokes a gasp from the audience, nevertheless there is relatively little connection being made [...] between the modern audience and the subject'.[26] Thus, a comfortable distance is created between the film's viewers and its events and characters, which can facilitate a sense of superiority for young people living in modern Ireland. They are allowed to feel far more progressive than their 'backward' and intolerant forebears.

However, it should be said that *The Magdalene Sisters* did have a positive impact in terms of raising awareness in contemporary Ireland about its traumatic past and the need to both remember and make reparation to its victims and survivors. As James Smith notes:

> [An] encouraging development [following the appearance of the *Magdalene Sisters* in cinemas] is the appearance of a relatively new Web-based listserv, Justice for Magdalenes. It too emerged in light of Mullan's film and is actively working on a series of related initiatives, including fund-raising, increasing public awareness, and issuing press releases that respond to political and church inaction, as well as disseminating information to support research focusing on these institutions. These diverse initiatives, while fragile and perhaps vulnerable, evince the power of popular cultural representation to generate meaningful social responses.[27]

Thus, *The Magdalene Sisters* can be viewed as having performed a valuable act of remembrance that has led to action being taken in the contemporary moment. It also reminds us of the power and necessity of storytelling. As Smith argues:

> Telling stories of Ireland's architecture of containment fulfils not just a duty to remember but also a duty to tell. Stories ensure that the traces and archives of the past are preserved. And they contribute to what Hannah Arendt calls a continuation of 'action'. Such action involves the ability to forgive the traumas inflicted in the past and to learn from the past in order to effect better practices for future generations.[28]

An important example of a non-fiction text that spurred the Irish state and its citizens into a collective act of memory and reparation was the *States of Fear* documentary that was broadcast on RTÉ between April and May 1999. The programme detailed abuse suffered by children between the 1930s and 1970s in the state childcare system of Ireland, primarily in the Reformatory and Industrial Schools. As a result of this series, Irish Taoiseach Bertie Ahern apologised on behalf of the State; a commission to investigate the abuse of children in these institutions was established in 2000 and delivered its damning report in 2009.

In the second decade of the twentieth century, a multi-volume collection of essays titled *Memory Ireland* (2011–2014), edited by Oona Frawley and Katherine O'Callaghan, was published over a three-year period. This project featured articles by renowned Irish Studies scholars such as Declan Kiberd, Luke Gibbons, P.J. Matthews, Robert Garrat, Vincent Cheng and many more. The project's contribution to the field of Irish memory and trauma studies, ranging from discussions of tradition and modernity to James Joyce and Irish memory, offered convincing proof that this field of academic inquiry was truly a fruitful one in the context of Irish literary, cultural and political studies.

Additionally, 2020 saw the publication of a very significant collection of essays titled *Trauma and Identity in Contemporary Irish Culture* edited by Melania Terrazas Gallego. This is an extremely useful selection of academic essays, which is balanced by contributions from Emer Martin and Pat Boran as creative writers. The collection also has an international spread of contributors, which is important as evidence of the purchase that Irish Studies now has outside Ireland.

What Irish memory and trauma theorists do:

1. **They examine representations of Ireland's traumatic past through the lens of theorists such as Sigmund Freud, Paul Ricoeur, Pierre Nora and Cathy Caruth.**
2. **They consider similarities and/or differences between historical and literary writings in terms of how they represent past events and people.**
3. **They attempt to suggest ways that the past can be ethically and responsibly remembered and commemorated via various acts of representation.**
4. **They endeavour to break down binary distinctions between literary, historical and theoretical texts in the context of acts of remembrance.**

Ireland's theatre of memory

If one were to cite a specific literary genre in Ireland that has been used – possibly more than any other – to effectively create some of the processes of memory and commemoration, it is undoubtedly theatre. The theatre of memory has been dominant in Ireland for more than fifty years and has proven extremely fruitful for the feminist project of recovery, remembrance and commemoration on both a personal and a national level. Following on from Oscar Wilde's assertion that 'The one duty we owe to history is to rewrite it',[29] Irish dramatists since the 1960s have explored the power and tyranny of memory as a tool for sometimes dictatorial and sometimes reparative interventions into historical narratives. Christopher Morash acknowledges how contemporary Irish drama is very much concerned with history, memory and the potential for forgetting or misremembering as a result of the trailblazing example of Brian Friel:

> In the plays of Ireland's most successful dramatist since the 1960s, Brian Friel, the condition of being suspended between past and present provides the occasion for a series of theatrical meditation on the extent to which the past can be known. Usually presented in the context of apparently naturalistic plays (which owe an acknowledged

> debt to Chekhov), Friel's characters typically find that only the living present is knowable and solid, while the past mediated by the vagaries of language, is shifting and constantly revised. Friel would eventually crystallise his concerns with the ontology of the past in what is arguably his best play, *Faith Healer* (1979), composed entirely of monologues in which three characters present conflicting versions of the same set of events.[30]

In this groundbreaking play, Friel draws upon the structure of Akira Kurosawa's film *Rashomon* and William Faulkner's novel *The Sound and the Fury* to probe the relationship between memory 'reality', 'fact' and 'truth', and the extent to which the individual mind and the communal consciousness need to be brought together via the staging of reparative encounters. The extent to which misremembering of events is an unconscious act or an intentional strategy is also of paramount importance to this complex and nuanced 'memory play'.[31]

Samuel Beckett's *Krapp's Last Tape* (1958) can also be viewed as an important, originary text in Ireland's memory theatre. This is particularly apparent in the moment when the younger version of Krapp is heard on the titular tape talking about the remembered moment when his (again younger) self was in the hospital where his mother was dying and heard the news just when he was offering a ball to a dog. Krapp verbally asserts that this moment of remembrance on his part encapsulated 'Moments. Her moments, my moments [...] The dog's moments'.[32] This statement encapsulates something true about the act of memory on the part of one person. It very often represents not just one person's life but that of others as well. Thus, private/individual memory can often bleed into public/ collective/cultural memory also. To bear witness for the Self can often inevitably mean doing the same for the Other(s).

A notable example of an Irish theatre of memory text is Anne Devlin's radio play *The Forgotten* (2009). This somewhat (ironically) forgotten radio play was first broadcast on BBC Radio 4 on 16 January 2009 and centres on the character of Bee, a female Irish emigrant. Bee is experiencing inexplicable bouts of amnesia which take the physical form of the character The Forgotten, a new and novel version of the many spectres that have haunted Irish drama for over a century. Significantly, The Forgotten is a tree with a West

Indian accent which signifies various types of otherness – colonial, gendered and so on – which are important for the play's general thematics. Anne Devlin's essay on *The Forgotten* (published in the *Female Lines* anthology) contains a lengthy and informative paragraph that links various types of otherness to the Afro-Caribbean voice of the character of The Forgotten:

> My personal experience of diaspora and that of the Windrush Generation became entwined; visible to me only as I was leaving England. I felt in returning to my native city I had to keep faith with them. There were in 2007 no representatives of the Windrush Generation in the North I returned to. I came from a society that couldn't tolerate difference. So when we came to casting, I knew the voice of The Forgotten was that of an Afro-Caribbean man. And then other things confirmed this strand for me: I discovered there was a tree of forgetting which slaves planted at the spot where they were abducted from the west coast of Africa.[33]

The voice of The Forgotten symbolically connects all the major concerns of this play, such as outsiders, exile, and memory and forgetting.

In *The Forgotten*, Anne Devlin has created a drama in which the trauma of Irish history is symbolically and surreally conveyed in the intimate and fictional textual narrative of a woman struggling with her own traumatic past. Thus, *The Forgotten* can be said to testify to the truth of Ricoeur's arguments concerning the intimate connection between individual and collective memory which is often denied by those working the field of memory studies:

> In this intensely polemical situation, which opposes a younger tradition of objectivity to the ancient tradition of reflexivity, individual memory and collective memory are placed in a position of rivalry. However, they do not oppose one another in the same place, but occupy universes of discourse that have become estranged from each other.[34]

In a country currently engaged in trying to ethically remember and redress past traumas such as the Magdalene Laundries and clerical sex abuse, the story contained within *The Forgotten* concerning personal trauma, memory, and the abuse of women could not have a greater significance within an Irish context.

The Horatio Complex

In the final scene of Shakespeare's *Hamlet*, the titular character, just before dying, demands that his friend Horatio not take his own life so he can follow Hamlet to the other world. The reason Hamlet gives for why Horatio should not end his life is because it is his duty to live and tell Hamlet's story. Essentially, Horatio is being told that his life has value primarily because he must bear witness to the life and death of Hamlet. His own individual existence has less value than that of his friend because he was only a secondary character in the drama of Hamlet, Hamlet's father, mother and uncle.

This section considers that many works of Irish literature feature examples of Horatio figures and that they are used to reflect on the ethics of remembrance and commemoration. This is particularly the case when the survivors of private and/or public moments of trauma are asked to subordinate the rest of their lives to the recalling and commemorating of these moments from the past and essentially, like Marlow in Joseph Conrad's *Heart of Darkness*, are forced to be the caretakers of the memories of others. The question to be asked is whether this constitutes an unethical form of memorialisation because it gives unfair priority to the Other at the expense of the self.

The concluding stanza of Yeats' 'Easter 1916' (examined at length in Chapter 1 above) has the poetic voice – after avoiding doing so for the whole of the poem up to this point – act as commemorator of the martyrs of the Rising and utters their names like a mother names her child. The poet begins this recitation with the lines 'I write it out in a verse …'. One can almost discern a sigh and a tone of resignation at this point as if he is being forced by public demand to do something that he did not wish to do, that is, to subordinate his art and artistic identity to the popular act of public commemoration and remembrance. Unlike the Joycean artist who wishes to forge within the smithy of his soul the uncreated conscience of his race, this poem foregrounds a poet who ultimately is forced to forsake the creative act of subjective, artistic representation/creation (which was what he had been engaged in up until that final section of the poem) for one that essentially amounts to the passive action of 'naming name upon name'. Like Horatio, this poetic voice feels the need to subordinate their life (albeit briefly in this case) to the telling of a story that he doesn't feels he completely owns.

In Brian Friel's *Faith Healer* (1979), the character of Teddy is the one who is cast in the role of secondary/Horatio character whose function in the play is largely to bear witness to the lives and deaths of the Faith Healer/Frank Hardy and his wife/mistress Grace. It is significant that Teddy is the only one of the three characters in the play who appears on the stage as a living person rather than as a ghost. His identity and dramatic function is very much that of 'the one who lived'.

One moment near the end of Teddy's monologue clearly represents an act of both memory and commemoration on his part. Teddy is remembering the last night of Frank Hardy's life in a bar just outside the town of Ballybeg:

> And the way he's [Frank] gazing at me and the look he has on his face is exactly the way he looks into somebody he knows he's going to cure … It's a look that says two things. It says: No need to speak – I know exactly what the trouble is. And I'm going to cure you of that trouble. That's the look he gave me. He held me in that look for – what? – thirty seconds. And then he turned away from me and looked at her [Grace] – sort of directed his look towards her so that I had to look at her too. And suddenly she is this terrific woman that of course I love very much, married to this man that I love very much – love maybe even more.[35]

With the exception of Frank's monologue that closes the play, the above-quoted passage is probably the most powerful and lyrical one in the whole of *Faith Healer*. It is very clearly an act of imaginative remembrance on Teddy's part and it serves to transform both Frank and Grace into something more than they might otherwise have been at this moment in time. As Richard Rankin Russell argues: 'What Teddy sees that night [and which his memorialisation of the event then renders to his audience] is an idealised vision of Frank and Grace's union without the material sordidness of their existence'.[36] Earlier in this monologue, Teddy makes it clear that the linguistic picture he is painting of Frank and Grace is filtered through imaginative memory: 'It was like I was seeing them for the first time in years and years – no! not seeing them but *remembering* them'.[37] Thus, via the process of memory becoming imagination, Teddy artistically transforms the two people with whom he seems to share a romantic attachment.

Significantly, although Teddy is present during this scene in the bar, his role is that of passive observer and then recounter. He is therefore another Horatio-like narrator of another's story. What we learn about Teddy from the very beginning of his monologue is that his role as the caretaker of the memories of Frank and, to a slightly lesser extent, Grace, has left him an alcoholic, emotional and psychological wreck. Ultimately, what Teddy bears witness to is the truth of an assertion that Friel wrote in the very next play he penned following *Faith Healer – Translations*: 'To remember everything is a form of madness'.[38] By being forced to remember and continually narrative memories that do not fully belong to him, Teddy has been driven into a state of madness and is cursed to merely exist as opposed to live out his own story.

Frank McGuinness' *Observe the Sons of Ulster Marching Towards the Somme* (1985) is a play that also features a Horatio-like figure, Pyper, who struggles to inhabit his own story and extract himself from the traumatic remembrance of his comrades who died at the battle of the Somme. At the beginning of the drama, Pyper is railing, not unlike the poetic voice in Yeats' 'Easter 1916', against the demands from unseen but compelling forces that he continues to tell the stories of these dead Ulstermen: 'I do not understand your insistence on my remembrance. I'm being too mild. I am angry at your demand that I continue to probe'.[39] From this opening monologue, the play's central themes are of trauma, remembrance, imagination, and the ethicality or otherwise of the demand that an Other bear witness to a traumatic past.

Near the end of *Observe the Sons of Ulster*, Pyper's friend and lover, Craig, plays the role of Hamlet to Pyper's Horatio when he insists that Pyper survive the battle and constantly perform acts of remembrance and commemoration for his fallen comrades: 'Don't die. One of us has to go on'.[40] Ironically, it is Pyper who is the main character in this play rather than Craig and yet he is the one who is being asked to play a role equivalent to that of a secondary character from Shakespeare's *Hamlet* and subordinate his individual story to the communal one of the Sons of Ulster who marched towards the Somme.

Observe the Sons of Ulster is not the only one of McGuinness' plays that features a character who feels that they must survive traumatic horrors in order that they can bear witness to that which has been lost. *In Dolly West's Kitchen*, the titular character recollects her time in Ravenna during World War II and her fears that this beautiful place might not survive the horrors of that conflict: 'I believe in Ravenna. I remember it – there would be one [person] in this country who would not forget in case Ravenna is destroyed. I think it's my life's purpose to say I saw it'.[41] In this statement, Dolly West is clearly saying she feels that her life needs to be subordinated to the act of remembering in an archival fashion the beauty and the glory that is the city of Ravenna. Her personal, individual existence is not nearly as important as her role of Irish caretaker for the memory of Ravenna in case it is destroyed.

In Anne Enright's *The Gathering* (which shall be examined in greater detail presently), the female narrator is driven by the same repetition compulsion. In her case, she constantly returns to the story of her brother's abuse at the hands of their grandmother's friend – a traumatic event that would eventually lead to her brother's suicide. The narrator's imprisonment in this traumatising process of remembering and repetition results in her finding it difficult to positively connect with her own life and the people with whom she shares her existence. Her struggle to assert her right to productively inhabit her own life story becomes a central focus of this novel as it proceeds towards its memorable conclusion.

The compulsion to remember and tell the story of another can be linked to Freud's theorising in *Beyond the Pleasure Principle* (1920) of memory, trauma and the death drive. Freud notes two primary examples, one macro and one micro, of the repetition compulsion which he links to the death drive. The first is the tendency of World War I veterans to mentally repeat (like Pyper in *Observe the Sons of the Ulster*) the traumatic feelings they associate with the death and destruction they experienced in the trenches. The other example, on a much smaller scale, is a particular baby boy playing lost and found with his toys. Freud interprets this game as being the baby boy's repetition, not just of the feelings of loss that he experiences when his mother leaves him, but also the positive feelings associated with her return as symbolised when the ball is found again. Marina

Carr's *Audrey or Sorrow* (2024) is one notable Irish text in which traumatic memory and repetition compulsion – specifically with respect to the loss of a child – is thematically and formally central to the theatrical work. Thus, style and content can be said to exist symbiotically in that particular literary example.

Significantly, the child whose game Freud is analysing is his grandson and the mother is his beloved daughter Sophie whose death in 1920 left Freud devastated. Therefore, Freud's analysis of his grandson coping with loss is also a way for him to deal with the traumatic loss of his daughter which occurred in the same year that *Beyond the Pleasure Principle* was published. Thus, Freud is inserting himself and his grief into the narrative and analysis surrounding his interpretation of the grandson's game.

Cathy Caruth interprets these various acts of repetition as being as much connected with a life drive as a death drive. The repetition of trauma is also an acknowledgement by the person who is remembering that they have survived the traumatic event, that their life story is continuing even in the shadow of death: 'As such the theory of trauma does not limit itself to a theoretical formulation of the centrality of death [whether that be of life or of identity] in culture, but constitutes [...] an act of parting that itself creates and passes on a different history of survival'.[42] Thus, the challenge for those who are being asked to play the role of Horatio-esque narrators is to incorporate their story of life and survival into the one of death and commemoration of the Other.

The climax of *Observe the Sons of Ulster* can be interpreted as a moment where the Horatio character (Pyper in this instance) learns to affirm his survival and continuing life story even as he commemorates his fallen comrades: 'Observe the sons of Ulster marching towards the Somme. I love their lives. I love my own life. I love my home. I love my Ulster.[43] In this moment of affirmation and commemoration, Pyper acknowledges the death of his friends, pays tribute to their lives, and also asserts that his life, which he is able to live as a result of surviving whilst his friends perished, is also worthy of narration. Thus, his life and story is one that encompasses the death of others but also the survival of the self.

Equally, the climax of *Carthaginians* involves a moment of naming those who died during Bloody Sunday by those who survived. Unlike the poet in 'Easter 1916', this act of naming name upon name does not preclude the namers from affirming their love of the lives they have been spared to live and the stories they are being allowed to act out in their lives. Similarly, *Dolly West's Kitchen* concludes with Dolly embracing the life she will have with her English lover. No longer does she believe that her life has value only as a caretaker of memories that are not really her own in so far as she is not from Ravenna and its people are not hers.

One other example of this positive version of traumatic repetition occurs in Claire Keegan's novella *Small Things Like These* (2021) and in the cinematic adaption starring Cillian Murphy. In that story, the character of Bill Furlong is condemned to constantly remember his mother's death and the fact that she had given birth to him outside of wedlock. Bill suffers the guilt of surviving whilst his mother died and also regrets not being able to help her in her last few moments. Although he is constantly forced to repeat her loss in his memories, the work climaxes with him rescuing a young woman from a Magdalene Laundry. Like his mother, this woman – also named Sarah – has given birth to an illegitimate child who has been essentially abducted by the nuns. By rescuing Sarah, Bill affirmatively asserts his survival by the act of making a difference in his present moment.

In what is possibly the keynote passage in *Small Things Like These*, Bill recollects his mother's hard life, her death, and the life that he lived in the wake of that traumatic event:

> He thought of Mrs Wilson, of her daily kindnesses, of how she had corrected and encouraged him, of the small things she had said and done and had refused to do and say and what she must have known, the things which, when added up, amounted to a life. Had it not been for her, his mother might very well have wound up in that place. In an earlier time, it could have been his own mother he was saving – if saving was what this could be called. And God knew what would have happened to him, where he might have ended up.[44]

It is clear from this quotation that his compulsion to relive his mother's death and the life that he lived in the immediate aftermath of her passing has a profound impact on his present day existence and begins to influence actions that will shape an undecidable future that has yet to come and over which he does not exert total ownership.

Small Things Like These concludes with an undecidable ending since we do not know the ultimate fate of either Billy or Sarah. However, the living Bill has used his life to ensure that a young person will have the chance of a better life than his mother was able to. Thus, his present life has somewhat redeemed his traumatic past and suggests the possibility of a better future, albeit one of which he does not have full ownership. Thus, Bill has used the spectres of the past in a manner of which Derrida would have approved. Although Bill may feel compelled to relive his mother's traumatic story, he is also able to use it as an inspiration to take partial, positive ownership of his present story. Despite the fact, as Joseph Valente argues, the rescue is incomplete because Sarah's child has been left behind and its story will never be even slightly told, one has to accept that the hope for a better future to come often relies on small acts such as the one undertaken by Bill Furlong – the survivor a traumatic past and active participant in a dynamic present and uncertain future.

Ultimately, the task facing Irish writers and theorisers of memory is that of trying to conceive of memory as not always bound up with debilitating trauma and traumatic repetition. It is important that the remembrance of the past, whether that be a traumatically nightmarish one or otherwise, is used as a reparative tool for the shaping of better, as yet unrealised presents and futures for its survivors and descendants.

Representative textual analyses

Michael Collins (film)

The film *Michael Collins* (1996), although not a particularly successful film internationally, was a massive success in Ireland. The charismatic and physically imposing Irish actor Liam Neeson's heartfelt performance of the titular character struck a great chord with Irish audiences of all ages. Adults wanted the cinematic treatment of a history with which they would be very familiar, and younger viewers flocked to see an exciting and, for some, appealingly violent version of a story about which they would only have known, if at all, from secondary school history lessons. Indeed, many Irish schools would take their students, following the receipt of written permission from their parents, to see the film. The film also drew an enthusiastic audience of supporters of the Irish political party Fine Gael because Michael Collins has always been associated with that party due to his leadership of a political grouping that would eventually become Cumann na nGaedheal (founded in 1923), the precursor to Fine Gael, which was founded in 1933.

In Donald Clarke's review of *Michael Collins*, which he wrote to commemorate the tenth anniversary of its release, Clarke perfectly encapsulated the importance of the film as an Irish cinematic event:

> Nothing better communicates the strange hysteria that, 20 years ago, gathered around the release of *Michael Collins* than the behaviour of the censor (as he was then still known). A 15 cert was originally awarded, but this was lowered to PG because of the film's historical significance. Before its release, Neil Jordan's picture already occupied an officially sanctified status that no mortal entertainment could hope to attain. The film smashed all domestic records and generated a thousand conversations about 'historical accuracy'.[45]

The success of *Michael Collins* in Ireland can be partly attributed to its subject matter but also to its deployment of American cinematic techniques that were very popular in a 'globalised' Irish marketplace. As Lance Pettitt argues: 'Exemplifying the process of postcolonial mimicry [...] Jordan appropriates the epic biopic, film noir, and the gangster movie [...] Visually, the desaturated colour palate and lighting by Chris Menges may be seen to borrow from *The Godfather* and noir lighting, making silhouetted figures a 'signature for the film'.[46] This argument highlights how *Michael Collins* is a cinematic text that looks backwards in terms of content but is very contemporary in terms of its cinematic style. Therefore, it is a film that can be regarded as performing the act of 'excavating the present'.

Brian McIlroy has analysed the famous Bloody Sunday scene in *Michael Collins* – during which Collins' 'boys' kill several members of the British Secret Service – from the perspective of how its style is explicitly indebted to American gangster films, particularly those of Martin Scorsese:

> The way in which the assassinations are choreographed alerts us to the makeshift, awkward nature of murder. The style used for the killings is circumspect, not in a Sam Peckinpah or Quentin Tarantino

> mode of representation, where blood and gore are either aestheticized or parodied, but much more in the vein of Martin Scorsese's *Mean Streets* (1973) in which the act of shooting people is shown to be painful and frequently haphazard.[47]

The appeal of *Michael Collins* to an Irish audience illustrates how Ireland at the turn of the century was a nation that was at once invested in its own specific history but was also deeply immersed in the globalised cultural marketplace of which America was at the vanguard.

One criticism of *Michael Collins* when it first was released, largely from Irish historians, was how the historic Treaty negotiations were not given any screentime. It was felt that this was a momentous juncture during the time in which the film was set and therefore should have been afforded some cinematic representation. However, this omission makes considerable sense from a box office perspective. Long drawn out scenes of politicians arguing about legal, political and diplomatic nuances and niceties would have been alienating for an audience who were looking for a story that dealt with exciting and painfully human moments from recent Irish history.

Emilie Pine has argued that *Michael Collins* is a film that is not just about history, but is actively engaged in commenting upon the process of memory making itself:

> *Michael Collins* became, perhaps unintentionally, almost a deconstruction of history, the anachronisms drawing attention to the performance and construction inherent in historical epics. Certainly, the opening sequence of Jordan's film suggests the fallibility of his version of Collins. The film begins after Collins's death, as Joe O'Reilly (Ian Hart), Collins's aide, speaks almost directly to the camera, exhorting Kitty (Julia Roberts) to 'think of him. The way he was.' This short scene – and thus the status of the film as one long flashback – foregrounds the role of memory and personality in remembering or thinking of 'him'.[48]

The film begins, not with an image of Michael Collins, but with two of the people closest to him who must live, Horatio-like, to remember Collins and tell his story.

One of the most controversial aspects of *Michael Collins* was its portrayal of the character of Eamon De Valera, the future leader of the Irish state and its most significant political figure for the first half of the twentieth century. De Valera is portrayed emphatically as the villain of the film and it is strongly suggested that he was behind the assassination of Collins at the film's conclusion.

> Commenting on Neil Jordan's *Michael Collins*, [Elizabeth Butler] Cullingford notes Jordan's production diary entry that de Valera was 'a father who will betray' Collins: 'If de Valera was the symbolic father and Collins the son, their encounter replicates a theme that has considerable resonance in Irish culture: Cuchulainn's killing of his only son, Connla, and his subsequent battle with the waves'.[49]

By casting Alan Rickman as De Valera, Jordan was clearly making a statement regarding the villainy of the future father of the Irish nation. Ever since playing the memorably slimy Hans Gruber in *Die Hard* (1988), Alan Rickman had been consistently cast as either an outright villain (such as the Sheriff of Nottingham in *Robin Hood Prince of Thieves* (1991)). The portrayal of De Valera is not just a commentary on that historical figure and his legacy, it is also a signal that Jordan believes that modern 1990s' Ireland was ready to reject the republican violence that De Valera advocated during the Irish Civil War in the 1920s and also the IRA republican violence that was still a presence in Northern Ireland, even though the peace process in that part of the island was ongoing at the time.

One of the most famously inaccurate moments in the film occurs when a car bomb kills some British agents outside Dublin Castle, despite the fact that car bombs were not used during the Irish War of Independence. This seemingly unnecessarily inaccurate scene, however, does make sense when one considers that car bombs were a common feature of life in Troubles-era Northern Ireland. Thus, the film is signalling its awareness of modern historical violence and wishes to argue that it exists on a line of historical continuity with the traumatic violence from which modern independent Ireland would emerge.

Luke Gibbons argues that the decision to end *Michael Collins* whilst the Irish Civil War was still ongoing suggests that the film has a far from happy outlook on contemporary Irish history as it existed in the last decade of the twentieth century: 'Instead of sealing off the legacy of the Civil War in the past, as would be possible if it marked the belated coming of age of the Free State, *Michael Collins* suggests that the past is far from over and done with, and that we still await a painfully deferred [peace]'.[50]

In the penultimate scene of the film in which Collins appears, he says 'it's [the total achievement of a 32 county Irish Republic] not worth fighting for any longer. We've got to learn to build with what we have'. The audience watching the film more than seventy years after the events depicted in its narrative would have felt a pang of regret that not enough Irish, Northern Irish and British people in power had, at that time, come to that same conclusion. As Elizabeth Butler Cullingford also argues: '[The] oversimplified portrait of Collins as a reformed revolutionary appealed to a modern Irish nation weary of the Troubles, hopeful about the ongoing peace process and willing to make do with the truncated Republic that De Valera never accepted'.[51]

The casual and often sexist treatment of women in *Michael Collins*, particularly the character of Kitty Kiernan (Julia Roberts), can be interpreted as a commentary on the treatment of Irish women more generally in both the Irish Free State and the Irish Republic. Like the female character Jude in Jordan's earlier film, *The Crying Game* (discussed in the previous chapter), Kiernan is used by Collins and his close friend Harry Boland merely as something to be fought over. Through their romantic rivalry, their male homosocial bonding can be enacted. Kiernan's own relevance in their lives and in the narrative of the film more broadly is thus portrayed as limited at best, and at worst largely irrelevant.

Gibbons argues that the gender politics in the film, particularly in the film's closing scenes, can also be connected with the failure of liberatory politics in independent Ireland for decades after the Irish state was formed:

> Suspended between the (private) maternal and the (public) paternal, with no possibility of return but unable to progress further, Collins's fate tragically allegorizes the incomplete narratives of the nation itself. Had Collins been able to bring the nation with him and make it co-terminus with the state, post-treaty Ireland might not have been so easily transformed into the patriarchal order it became; and there would be less reason to resort to the imaginary of Hollywood to put the past into perspective.[52]

The moment after Collins is shot dead by a Republican soldier's bullet, the camera cuts to a shot of Kiernan having a veil placed on head, which makes her resemble the Virgin Mary, a common image used to symbolise the connection between the maternal and the Irish nation. This abrupt intercutting between male/state violence and the quiet bliss of the symbolically maternal/Irish nation suggests the inequality between the Irish nation as woman and the Irish state as patriarchal that would lead to many of the traumatic events in twentieth-century Ireland that have never been forgotten and for which ethical remembrance and recompense is still being sought.

One of the reasons that *Michael Collins* is an important piece of Irish cinema is because it does emphasise how cinematic and other textual genres can engage in the process of making as opposed to merely recording history. The film acknowledges its creative and also subjective attitude towards historical narratives in its closing moments when it puts a quotation from De Valera on the screen just before the credits roll: 'It is my considered opinion that, in the fullness of time, history will record the greatness of Michael Collins, and it will be recorded at my expense'. By ending the film with that observation, Jordan implicitly recognises that his film is engaged in the performative process of shaping historical narratives rather than merely passively describing a succession of events. Brian McIlroy, in his analysis of *Michael Collins*, argues for the importance of examining such cinematic texts in terms of what they tell us about how history is 'made'. 'Little is to be gained by too closely comparing a film to received written history, yet it seems equally limiting to isolate history from film representations and to view them as separate activities'.[53] The creation of a binary opposition between the process of creating historical and cinematic narratives would be impossible and also self-defeating in the case of a film such as *Michael Collins*, as this chapter has consistently argued.

The Gathering

Anne Enright's *The Gathering* (2007) is one of the archetypal trauma novels in the annals of contemporary Irish literature. As a result of having won the Booker Prize, it is also the most successful and well known.

> A mixture of family history, crisis diary, and fantasy, *The Gathering* is a testimonial written by protagonist Veronica Hegarty following the suicide of her brother. She is driven to 'bear witness' to a childhood molestation. She believes the event was a key event contributing to his despair and she produces, as she moves along, a searing document of deep feeling and an uncertain locating of blame that attests more to her own trauma than to her brother's.[54]

The book's opening passage makes it very clear that *The Gathering* will be a novel intimately concerned with the vagaries of memory and the challenges of ethically bearing witness to past events: 'I would like to write down what happened in my grandmother's house when I was eight or nine, but I am not sure if it really did happen. I need to bear witness to an uncertain event. I feel it roaring inside me. This thing that may not have taken place'.[55]

Significantly, Diarmuid Ferriter opens his history text *The Revelation of Ireland: 1995–2020* with a discussion of the opening passage of *The Gathering* (quoted above):

> There was great deal of 'roaring inside' during the period this book covers, as many people attempted to make sense of deep grievances and hurt and the degree to which the Irish social contract had failed them. Some of that roaring also became external as demands for answers became louder.[56]

A historian such as Ferriter would understandably have felt a connection with the sentences that open *The Gathering* because it is the job of historians to 'bear witness' in an ethical fashion to events that they may not have been present to physically witness when they were actually unfolding.

> As it happens, Veronica does not divulge the nature of this 'event' until her narrative is well underway, and when she does, she states once more that it 'may be a false memory' [*The Gathering*, 144]. She qualifies her statement yet again soon thereafter, saying that it is not the molestation itself but her memory of where and how precisely it took place that is in doubt.[57]

Veronica memorialises various events and people from different times and places. As to some of these events, such as her time in college, she can be said to be a fairly reliable narrator when it comes to recounting them. On other occasions, such as when she is recounting the early life of her grandmother Ada, Veronica is far more in the vein of an unreliable narrator because her stories are at best speculative and, very often, active fictionalisations. For example, it is not clear why Veronica spends so much time telling a constructed narrative about her grandmother's relationship with Lambert Nugent until the revelation of how Nugent molested Liam is recounted. Once it is revealed that Veronica is an aspiring writer, we as readers begin to become even less likely to believe her account of certain events.

However, 'Veronica never lies; as readers, we believe in Veronica even if we might not necessarily believe the truth of her statements: she never asks us to believe that her speculations are true and the force of her conviction and the depth of her pain and suffering carry us along'.[58] Because of the traumatic nature of the events being narrated by Veronica, and the effect they clearly had on her, we never condemn her for not being a totally reliable narrator as we are encouraged to treat this work as a text in which the processes of traumatic repetition are played out for its readers. It is an open question whether or not Veronica may have been abused herself by Nugent but she certainly 'demonstrates all of the textbook symptoms of a post-traumatic or "hysterical" subject who is suffering the effects of sexual abuse or violence'.[59] Veronica's account of her own abuse by Nugent is admitted by her to be more likely a fantasy than a memory but it does demonstrate how traumatised she personally was as a result of witnessing the sexual abuse of Liam by Nugent.

Margot Backus' and Joseph Valente's analysis of how Veronica narrativises Liam's abuse speaks very clearly to the effect that traumatic witnessing can have on the person who has been forced into playing this role of witness against her will:

> As a witness, Veronica stands outside the event; yet she feels it 'roaring inside her'. And while her phraseology certainly signifies her internalization of her brother's plight, a common effect of traumatic witnessing, it also indexes how the event taps into and amplifies stirrings interior to Veronica's affective and libidinal constitution. Indeed, her initial paragraph [describing the abuse] is entirely self-reflexive; no mention is made of Liam, only of the continued life of the event within Veronica's body [...] The result is an identification, amounting almost to a conflation, of inside and outside of her brother's shattering and her own, and, most acutely, of his and her coerced desire.[60]

This powerful and provocative reading of one of the key moments in the novel draws attention to the effect that the role of witness can be an immersive experience that can be as damaging to the person who is witnessing (and will continue bearing witness into the future) as it will inevitably be to the direct and explicit victim of the traumatic experience. This inevitably brings to our attention the issue (discussed above) of how remembrance, witnessing and commemoration need to be ethically handled for the benefit of the witness, as much as for the victim, of a traumatic and nightmarish past.

It is undoubtedly true that the memory of her brother's abuse has damaged Veronica's life considerably, particularly concerning her familial relationships. This is particularly apparent when one observes the very fractious relationship she has with her husband. The novel concludes with Veronica vowing to return to her family and forget (at least to some extent) the traumatic events of the past. However, it is an open question whether or not this will actually transpire.

The character of Liam in *The Gathering* has been interpreted as being representative of Ireland's suffering people whose past has been too often denied public remembrance and commemoration. As Carol Dell'Amico argues: 'In reading Veronica's story we are, in turn, reading part of Ireland's, *The Gathering* is a parable of a nation with the choice either to face or ignore a disturbing past, so as to become, with the right choice, a bit of that which "Tiger hood" narratives were already trumpeting was the case' (64).

In the case of Liam, it can be argued that attention has been paid to the victim of a nightmarish Irish past. However, there is one figure in the novel whose story does not receive the same degree of recognition: Veronica's uncle Brendan who had been placed in a nursing home for the mentally ill and was visited very infrequently by members of his family. His erasure from the dominant narrative in the novel does point to something quite unpleasant about Irish cultural memory and public discourse concerning trauma narrative. As Backus and Valente argue:

> The society of Irish journalists (lifestyle or otherwise), opinion makers, authority figures, professionals, churchgoers, job holders, and similarly classed subjects (from the upper to the lower range of 'middle') have had, on average, greater familiarity and engagement with those who

> are known, supposed, or imagined to be child sexual abuse victims than with the mentally or psychosocially disabled once thought to require commitment to asylums like St Ita's.[61]

As is the case with many works of James Joyce, Anne Enright wants us to pay attention whilst reading *The Gathering* to so-called 'unimportant' or 'peripheral' narratives operating within the text and asks us to question on whose authority some stories and memories are elevated to the status of 'important' and some are denied such distinction. Such questioning can help us to identify the existence of a 'politics of Irish memory' and goes some way to shedding light on how it operates in twenty-first century Ireland.

The Secret Scripture

Following on from *The Gathering*, Sebastian Barry continued the contemporary Irish novel's investment in probing the recesses of collective/cultural and private/personal memory in relation to Ireland's traumatic past. Like the film *The Magdalene Sisters*, *The Secret Scripture* shines a light on the sufferings of the Irish women inhabitants of state run institutions (in this case it is a mental institution) and that of their children. *The Secret Scripture* utilises various literary techniques such as stream of consciousness and free indirect discourse to examine the relationship between collective and individual memory and their roles in shaping a national consciousness more broadly. Like *The Gathering*, *The Secret Scripture* was the recipient of many literary awards, both within Ireland and outside. Significantly, the books were published within a year of each other (2007 and 2008 respectively) and cover similar thematic and stylistic grounds.

The main character, Roseanne McNulty, is a hundred years old and has spent most of her life incarcerated in a mental institution. Half of the novel is narrated via her 'personal testimony', which she is writing in secret as a means of coming to terms with her traumatic past. The other half of the text is told through the diary of Dr Grene, Roseanne's psychiatrist. The fact that Rosanne's life spans the entire history of the Irish state means that the text can consider themes of historical and personal traumas and the intersections of individual and cultural memory.

The undoubted villain in *The Secret Scripture*, Father Gaunt, represents a villainy in the life of not just Roseanne but in the life of the Irish state. His cruel misogyny and dogmatic moralising make him an archetypal version of the type of priest that Irish history has documented as being at the fore in terms of influencing the culture and politics of the Irish state for the vast majority of the twentieth century. For this reason, Dr Grene's description of this priest in the second half of the novel frequently departs from a discussion of his influence on Roseanne and talks about the greater influence that such men had on Catholic Ireland, particularly during the time of Eamon De Valera. Gaunt's constant persecution of Roseanne stems largely from her refusal to convert to Catholicism, and this serves as a reminder of the intolerant aspect of the Irish Catholic Church which led to so many abuses over a protracted period of time.

Dr Grene's description of Father Gaunt makes it clear that Gaunt represents not just an individual but many of the Catholic clergy who held sway in Ireland during the twentieth century:

> He betrays at every stroke an intense hatred if not of women, then of the sexuality of women, or sexuality in general. For him it is the devil's cloak and hood … It is also crystal clear that he regards her Protestantism as a simple, primal evil in itself. His anger that she would not let herself be made a Catholic … is absolute, long before she married her Catholic husband, and likewise remained what she was. This in itself for Father Gaunt is a real perversion.[62]

The misogyny and bigotry displayed by numerous servants of Catholicism ever since the foundation of the Irish state account for much of Ireland's recent, traumatic history.

By having two narrators relate the story, *The Secret Scripture* is able to consider the vexatious character of narrative truth in a fashion that can be compared with William Falkner's *The Sound and the Fury* and Brian Friel's *Faith Healer*. By calling Roseanne's book her 'testimony', the theme of bearing witness and offering the signature of personal testimony to the traumatic events of a national and private past is foregrounded. In many ways, Roseanne's writing of this narrative account offers her a therapeutic writing cure that is more beneficial for her than the talking cure her psychiatrist endeavours to provide.

During an interview which Frank McGuinness conducted with Rebecca Pelan as part of the Abbey Theatre's 2014 conference The Theatre of Memory, McGuinness asserted that 'if memory is anything, it is a fight against mortality'. *The Secret Scripture* narrativises Roseanne's efforts to use her memory as a means of ensuring that her life story will survive after her death. Importantly, in a very Wildean move, she also acknowledges at several points during the novel that her memory will often record that which could not possibly have happened, which means we as readers must be willing to cast a critical eye over the story we are consuming.

The quotation from the Preface to Maria Edgeworth's *Castle Rackrent* that begins Barry's novel neatly encapsulates its attitude towards the relationship between memory, history and narration: 'Of the numbers who study, or at least read history, how few derive any advantage from their labours! … Besides, there is much uncertainty even in the best authenticated ancient and modern histories, and that love of truth, which in some minds is innate and immutable, necessarily leads to a love of secret memoirs and private anecdotes'.[63] *The Secret Scripture* deconstructs historical metanarratives' claim to objectivity and accuracy and privileges the uncertain and often silenced voices of memory that emerge. Whilst these voices may be able to lay no greater claim to accuracy than historical texts, their personal nature very often contain nuggets of truth even if the facts are at best inconclusive.

The character of Dr Grene will express a similar opinion to Edgeworth's about the truth of historical narratives and their claim to absolute accuracy:

> I am beginning to wonder strongly what is the nature of history. Is it only a memory in decent sentences, and if so, how reliable is it? I would suggest, not very. And that therefore most truth and fact offered by these syntactical means is treacherous and unreliable. And yet I recognise that we live our lives, and even keep our sanity, by the lights of this treachery and this unreliability, just as we build our love of country on these paper worlds of misapprehension and untruth. Perhaps this is our nature, and perhaps unaccountably it is part of our glory as a creature, that we can build our best and most permanent building on foundations of utter dust. (304–305)

Like Paul Ricoeur, Grene argues that reparative narratives of subjectivity and nationhood need to be crafted via the dynamic process of memory, forgetting and sometimes misremembering.

The Secret Scripture is not just a trauma novel but a meditation on the evolution of the novelistic form from the nineteenth century onwards. The multiplicity of narrative voices, styles and the use of various tenses makes it seem like a perfect example of a modernist novel from the early to mid-twentieth century. Equally, the story's focus on social injustice, intolerance and gender persecution reminds one very much of the realist novels from the nineteenth century written by authors such Charlotte Brontë Thomas Hardy and Charles Dickens. Roseanne's numerous references to 'Dear Reader' is a clear invocation of the address to the reader by the titular character that occurs at the conclusion of Brontë's iconic feminist novel *Jane Eyre*: 'Reader, I married him'. Thus, the role of trauma, real or imagined, in the creative process is a key theme in *The Secret Scripture*.

This novel also reminds its readers of the numerous Others and minorities that can get left out of the official narratives of Irish history. Roseanne's traumatic life is symbolic of that of many Irish women who were literarily and metaphorically shut away out of the sight of the puritanical, dominant Irish gaze that can be regarded as being male/masculine and Catholic (certainly until relatively recently). Also, the fact that Roseanne and her parents are not Catholic represents an attempted recovery of a religious otherness from the cultural amnesia of post-independence Ireland.

The book's title implies that this is a significant narrative that expresses important truths concerning Ireland and Irishness but also that it is an unofficial narrative that will often find itself in conflict with official national and personal narratological versions of independent Ireland's 'National Tale'. The inclusion of the Edgeworth quote from the Preface to *Castle Rackrent* at the beginning *The Secret Scripture* also draws ones attention to the vexed question of what constitutes a truly ethical and authentic version of a National Tale in an Irish context. This is because of the irony that the slippery and often undecidable narrative in *Castle Rackrent* is often referred to as an archetypal example of an Irish National Tale despite its stylistic resistance to both certainty and clarity at the level of story and character.

One part of Roseanne's story that is left ambiguous until very near the end is whether or not her father had been in the RIC (Royal Irish Constabulary), the police force of colonial Ireland and whether or not he had been murdered in the years following the Irish War of independence because of his former profession. Roseanne vehemently denies this as being true whenever it is mentioned to her by any other character in the novel. Her wilful repression of this memory serves as reminder of what Ricoeur refers to as the dialectic between memory and forgetting, which results in the creation of personal accounts of selfhood, giving individual subjects a sense of themselves as stable, of their lives as being liveable and traumatic memories bearable. Roseanne's refusal to acknowledge that her father had been an 'unpatriotic Irishman' because of his membership of the hated RIC may have been a result of shame but it may also have been because of the trauma she experienced by being present when members of the IRA were attempting to murder him. She was spared witnessing his final moments only because she was knocked unconscious by a hammer thrown from the window of the room where her father was being murdered and from which she had been barred. It is the case with many trauma novels (and certainly in *The Secret Scripture*) that both grief and guilt are portrayed as being powerful forces in the determining of what is related to the reader, how these events are told, and what is withheld.

Ultimately, the most the reader can say is that it is the balance of probability that Roseanne's father was in the RIC. A man with his name is listed as having served in the 1910s and his name was quite rare. However, that is all the evidence that exists to corroborate Father Gaunt's assertion that Rosanne's father was a policeman and was murdered for that reason. The exact circumstances concerning his death are also contested by Roseanne and Gaunt.

By writing her 'testimony', Roseanne also gains an attitude of quite calm and stoicism in relation to the myriad of injustices that had been inflicted on her throughout her life. This is in contrast to the feeling of extreme rage that she admits to feeling when she is informed that she will never be with her husband again (234). So great was her rage that she freely admits to having very real murderous thoughts concerning Father Gaunt.

David Lloyd has written about the damaging effects that rage can wreak on the subjecthood and sense of self of person experiencing this extreme emotion:

> To be enraged is to be outside oneself, out of oneself; it is to be possessed of a force that is indifferent to the subject in oneself and to the subject in another by a force that is in another. Hence the one who witnesses rage witnesses the enraged as a lack of subject and knows that in the absence of subjecthood [...] Rage, therefore, can be neither founding nor destructive, though it may give way to either [...] It is sheer manifestation, but of nothing.[64]

By writing her testimony, Roseanne transcends paralysing rage; she regains her narrative and her dynamic subjectivity, which enables her to experience a sense of calmness and joy concerning her being in the world. Dr Grene, when he finally reads her testimony, notes the celebratory and joyful tone in her accounts of the world around her. This description makes Roseanne, as a writer, sound like John McGahern when he was writing later works such as *That They May Face the Rising Sun*. The effect that writing her testimony has had on Roseanne can be described, in another context, by Dori Lamb in her theorising of testimony writing: 'the testimony is [...] the process by which the narrator (the survivor) reclaims his [or her] role as a witness: reconstitutes the internal 'thou', and thus [claims] the possibility of a witness or a listener inside himself [or herself]'.[65]

Kathleen Costello-Sullivan's reading of *The Secret Scripture* through the lens of trauma studies encapsulates the narrative strategy and attitude towards 'truth' that governs the novel's representation of memory, trauma and imagination:

> Ultimately ... the novel suggests that questions of which account [of Roseanne's life] is 'true' are largely ancillary to the main point, which is instead fundamentally the process of *telling*. Roseanne's narrative in *The Secret Scripture* not only echoes the workings and omissions characteristic of traumatic memory but through its metanarrative consideration of what constitutes a 'story' also highlights the cathartic and healing properties of narrativizing trauma. Although such healing comes regardless of claims to authenticity or validated 'truth', the novel's provocative awareness of its own, highly crafted conclusion simultaneously challenges the reader to consider what 'recovery' means in light of traumatic and personal and cultural experience.[66]

Although some critics have argued that the revelation at the end of the novel that Dr Grene is Roseanne's long lost son is too convenient and an unrealistic an example of a 'happy ending', it can be interpreted symbolically as offering hope that, through gaining control of the means of representing one's life, intergenerational trauma can be transcended and a reparative reconciliation and coming together of past and present might possibly occur. This temporal event is metaphorically achieved at the end of *The Secret Scripture* via the reunion of mother and son, although the novel ends before Grene tells Roseanne that he is her son. Like Costello-Sullivan, I read 'the [undecidable] ending of *The Secret Scripture* as an acknowledgement of a wished-for but in some respects unattainable happy ending, which nonetheless holds out hope for the future'.[67]

In his reading of John McGahern's writing as a reparative act that enables the calming of inner rage that exists because of injustices inflicted, Joe Cleary asks the following rhetorical question that could be equally applied to *The Secret Scripture*: 'Whether in a world as outrageously violent and self-destructive as ours is, this stoic ethos, this association of wisdom with "quiet" and "calm", is an achievement or a form of reversion from conflict, or a mixture of both, we may wonder'.[68] Whilst a Marxist-postcolonial critic such Cleary would understandably prefer that trauma novels retain a sense of anger and outrage about the injustices inflicted on many Irish people over the last hundred years and longer, it is also arguable that novels such as *The Secret Scripture* offer a corrective vision of the reparative powers of memory that is the opposite of many trauma texts, which generally connect memory constantly with trauma.

Resting Places: On Wounds, War and the Irish Revolution

Resting Places is Ellen McWilliams' fourth book. Her previous three have been very firmly within the academic writing genre: *Margaret Atwood and the Female Bildungsroman* (2009), winner of the Margaret Atwood Society Best Book Prize; *Women and Exile in Contemporary Irish Fiction* (2013); and *Irishness in North American Women's Writing: Transatlantic Affinities* (2021). McWilliams' career has been defined by a commitment to the examination of female writers from America, Ireland and England from a variety of theoretical contexts, most prominently those of feminism and new materialism. *Resting Places* marks a new departure in McWilliams' writing career. It is a work that is firmly ensconced in the genre of memoir but it can also lay claim to being partly a work of history and partly one of novelistic influences. Therefore, it is a truly intergeneric text. The subtitle of the book (*On Wounds, War and the Irish Revolution*) invokes Ernie O'Malley's *On Another Man's Wound*, another work that utilises the memoir genre to examine the psychological wounds that were wrought by the Irish revolutionary period on those who fought in that conflict. Like O'Malley, McWilliams' book is one that sits comfortably in the annals of the Irish trauma novel. Indeed, McWilliams points out that she is not a historian even though she cites the works of historians, journalists and political scientists. The work is a memoir.

Sally Bar Ebest's review of *Resting Places* explains the book's relationship to the genre of memoir:

> As Helen Buss explains in *Repossessing the World: Reading Memoirs by Contemporary Women* (2002), memoirs are 'highly individual, experience-based, and personally invested. The memoir persuades not by logical argument but through a constructed narrative that depends on reflection and the interpretation of experience.' Its purpose is 'to reveal the hidden thing, the forbidden knowledge, the shameful and guilty secret, and to make what was formerly a private matter into public knowledge,' thus melding the personal with the political. Increasingly, women have used memoir to interrogate their relationship to a culture from which they have been excluded. In the process, they reveal their political commitment to expose injustice, explore their personal values, and divulge their political stance. In this way, both the author and the memoir instantiate change. *Resting Places* does just that.[69]

This description of *Resting Places* encapsulates the text's focus on what could be called a feminist-memoir-trauma narrative that seeks to excavate the past for the purposes of purging unspoken but not totally forgotten pain from both a private/personal and national psyche. The above quote from Helen Buss shows how a memoir can be stylistically linked to the novel in terms of how it artfully constructs a life-narrative and that is certainly the case in McWilliams' work. Her memoir was published quite soon after Emilie Pine's *Notes to*

Self, which is another work from the same genre by a female academic. Pine's memoir follows the same formula for that genre as Ebest outlined above but is less concerned with national memory and politics and more immersed in her personal life and narrative McWilliams'. However, one of the remarkable aspects of McWilliams' book is the way she clearly narrates how, for her certainly, the personal can be intimately bound up with the political, particularly when it comes to tackling national narratives.

As well as being a reference to O'Malley's memoir, the use of the word 'wounds' in the subtitle of *Resting Places* links the text to other narratives of trauma. As Richard Kearney notes, works such as *The Odyssey*, *Oedipus Rex* and *Hamlet*, which deal with the legacy of traumatic events and memories, often feature literal wounds to complement the metaphorical psychic wounds and the wounds of history that are key thematic touchstones of those texts.[70] Thus, McWilliams is signalling her awareness of the literary tropes and devices that feature prominently in the literature of trauma from the classical period to the contemporary moment.

McWilliams makes her background as a literary critic abundantly clear in the book's first chapter when she talks about the role that authors of literature have played in helping Irish people remember Ireland's traumatic past in an ethical and calm fashion: 'We can count ourselves lucky to have writers such as Elizabeth Bowen, Sean O'Faolain, Julia O'Faolain, John McGahern and William Trevor to guide our way in coming to terms with this [traumatic] history and its aftershocks'.[71] To this list of literary memorialists can now be added Ellen McWilliams.

Resting Places has its roots in McWilliams' essay 'Dunmanway Fields', published in the *Irish Times* on 15 April, 2022. It focusses on a historical event from McWilliams' own family history which became known as the Dunmanway massacre. This event resulted in the murders of thirteen men (whose ages ranged from sixteen to eighty) by the IRA. These occurred simultaneously in Bandon, Enniskeane and Clonakilty, Ireland, between 26 and 28 April, 1922. All of the victims were of the Protestant faith. As the IRA admitted, the area of Cork in which this atrocity was committed was under a truce at the time and it was on a scale that was atypically ferocious in nature.

Charles Duff, one of the descendants of the Dunmanway massacre victims has written the following description of Ellen McWilliams as a writer of commemorative and ethical memory, which is attached to the beginning of her book: 'empathy – always being able to know the vulnerability of the other – and sensibility, that gift of accessing deep feelings and expressing them lucidly and articulately, are Ellen McWilliams's core characteristics as a writer'.[72] McWilliams talks about the importance of empathy when engaged in acts of remembrance and it is certainly a quality that is present in abundance in her writing. This description of McWilliams' gifts as a writer also marks her out as being an ideal historian. As Dominick LaCapra argues, historical analysis should involve 'both an objective (not objectivist) reconstruction of the past and a dialogic exchange with it and other inquirers into it wherein knowledge involves not only the processing of information but also affect, empathy, and questions of value'.[73] Thus, *Resting Places* can be viewed as being a portrait of the academic as memoirist/historian/novelist.

Neale Jagoe, another descendent who wrote a piece for the beginning of *Resting Places*, has correctly highlighted the importance of acts of remembrance in whatever forms when it comes to trying to understand and come to terms with traumatic pasts, whether they be personal or collective: 'It is only by confronting our problematic pasts that we can hope to achieve understanding and accommodation'.[74]

McWilliams acknowledges the risky venture upon which one embarks when one decides to bear witness to other people's tragedies:

> In trying to write about this [the events of April 2022 in Cork], I have asked myself: who am I to speak? In examining these agonising histories who speaks matters and I traded one south-west for another 20 years ago and this is not my story. But the silence, between families and close-knit communities, in this case, although it might seem to serve the dignified and honourable purpose of self-preservation, can also be painful and inflict further pain and injury on people who have already suffered enough. (2)

In this passage one gets a clear picture of how seriously McWilliams takes the role of caretaker of the memory of others. She wishes to bear witness and do honour to the victims and their descendants but in a way that would be responsible and would never seem in any way exploitative. Significantly, McWilliams links these old histories with her own upbringing in Cork and her later life working in English Universities and thus refuses the role of Horatio subordinating her life and history to that of other. Rather, McWilliams links all these pasts and histories together in a movingly cohesive manner.

Returning to her background as an academic specialising in literature, McWilliams acknowledges the tradition of caution and refusal to speak directly about difficult topics in Irish writing: 'The value of silence is something Irish writers have always appreciated, from James Joyce's holy trinity of 'silence, exile, and cunning' to Seamus Heaney's gentle commandment in one of his best-known poems: "Whatever You Say, Say Nothing". Looking back, I better understand the nature of such silence and the knowledge gained early on that to ask too many questions, to ask too much, was to risk causing hurt to the people you cared about' (2). One important recent example of a book written in this style of evasion is Anna Burns' *Milkman* (2018), which many critics and reviewers (invoking a famous quote from the poems of Seamus Heaney) have described as being written in the 'whatever you say, say nothing' style.

As a scholar of John McGahern, McWilliams has learnt the value of writing in a way that treads the fine line between distance and closeness and writes eloquently about the need to feel connected and somewhat immersed in the events she was seeking to recount but also about the importance of some critical distance: 'It may be that in the intimate details of the local history there was too much that was too close to home – the familiar family names that appear in this story of Irish Republican Army ambushes, the troubling history of civilian harassment' (4). Later on in the work, McWilliams talks about how one of the things she admired about her future husband was his ability to write about the violent history of his own (English) people in the detached and more objective style of the historian. This was something that McWilliams admits to having always found challenging: 'Perhaps I can be forgiven for failing to see what was always in plain view, because if you grow up in those fields it is sometimes impossible to see higher than the ditches that break up the canvas of the land' (120). This admission by McWilliams is a perfect metaphor for the difficulty that will be encountered when trying to memorialise and interpret a history to which you feel too close. For this reason, one could argue that McWilliams' aim in writing *Resting Places* is to do what Emily Dickinson would call telling the truth but telling it slant.

As Emily Lawless did more than a century before, McWilliams writes of an Irish Famine Road as a physical space in which the past is preserved. 'Famine Roads extracted forced labour from the starving Irish population in exchange for food and were built without any concern for direction of the hands that toiled on them' (111). There is a Famine Road in McWilliams' local area of Cork but the rawness of its proximity to her has meant that she has always been reluctant to 'examine it, to cross the sloping field that leads down the road and then into the woods that eventually take you to the banks of the Bandon River in all its glassy, dark-stoned beauty' (111).

In one of the most probing and perceptive passages in *Resting Places*, McWilliams argues that the Cork Famine Road offers a truth about the cycles of tragedy and violence that comprise much of Irish history:

> It can be no accident that this part of the world that was home to some of the most violent and dramatic events of the Irish War of Independence and Irish Civil War was also home to some of the worst losses of the Great Irish Famine. The suffering of one generation produced another that was forged in steel and had nothing to lose. (111)

Thus, the Irish Famine Road in McWilliams' home area of Cork exists as both a physical monument and a symbolic representation of the nightmare of Irish history in which violence and death have always begotten more of the same.

In McWilliams' opinion, acts of remembrance must always involve, to some extent, acts of forgiveness, otherwise learning and redemption cannot be gained from the process. As McWilliams bluntly asserts, 'There is nothing much intelligent to say about the burning of a house when you can only think about the people inside it' (118). Forgiveness in the context of Anglo-Irish relations is, as far as McWilliams is concerned, an act of pragmatism as much as one of humanity: 'Forgiveness is all we [the Irish] have when the British will always be on our doorstep and we are so practised in forgiving ourselves and each other for the killing cycles of Irish history' (116).

Like Jacques Derrida, McWilliams is invested in the futural potential that is present in acts of remembrance or what Derrida would call speaking with ghosts. Both McWilliams and Derrida see acts of memory as being productive of ethical, possibly undecidable, futures to come that will not be prescriptively utopian, but will be better at least in some ways than the past which it has temporally succeeded. This is apparent in the concluding section of *Resting Places* in which McWilliams writes about the plans she has for herself and her son. In this concluding chapter, it is significant that McWilliams writes in the tense that John McGahern regarded as being the most linguistically hopeful: the simple future tense: 'I will take him blackberry picking [...] I will teach him how to lift a briar [...] I wish for him and for others, in times to come on the other side of history, where in spite of all that has been lost there are hopeful possibilities of things yet to be regained' (172). At the conclusion of a book in which McWilliams has grappled with the ghosts of history, she is now ready to look hopefully towards a future to come.

Ultimately, *Resting Places* is a text that bears witness and gives powerful testimony to the value of texts that engage thematically and often formally with acts of traumatic remembrance and commemoration. Implicitly, McWilliams asserts that the value of such works lies in the reality that 'We cannot change what happened [in the past] ... we can only try to find the courage to look history in the face if we can bear it. Staring down the barrel of history comes at a cost, but it is a price worth paying' (170). Narratives of history, memory and trauma involve communing with 'ancestors brought together by the collisions of a deeper past, who somehow and against impossible odds, stone upon stone, found a way of rebuilding a place blown apart by history for the sake of their children' (171).

Study questions

1. **Consider how Irish history has been 'filmed' and ask what do these cinematic texts tell us about how the nightmare of Irish history is being remembered and commemorated in contemporary Ireland?**

2. **What is the relationship between trauma and certain acts of memory?**
3. **What events in Ireland have spurred on an interest in memory studies?**
4. **How does the figure of the Ghost function as an appropriate metaphor for memory and remembrance?**
5. **In what ways can memory enable the imagination of futures that are not fully owned or totally grasped?**

Notes

1 Constanza del Rio, 'Trauma Studies and the Contemporary Irish Novel', in David Clarke and Ruben Jarazo (edes), *In the Wake of the Tiger: Irish Studies in the Twenty-First Century* (A Coruña: Netbiblo, 2010), p. 5.
2 Quoted in ibid.
3 Ibid.
4 See Edmund Burke, *A Philosophical Inquiry into the Sublime and the Beautiful* (Oxford: Oxford World's Classics, 2015), pp. 28–30.
5 See Siegmund Freud, *Beyond the Pleasure Principle* (New York: Dover Publications, 2015), pp. 12–17.
6 Paul Ricouer, *Memory, History, Forgetting*, trans. Kathleen Blamey and David Pellauer (Chicago: University of Chicago Press, 2004), p. 414.
7 See Pierre Nora, 'Between Memory and History: Les Lieux De Mémoire', *Representations*, 26 (1989), p. 7.
8 Ricouer, *Memory, History, Forgetting*, p. 506.
9 Tim O'Brien, *The Things They Carried* (New York: Broadway, 1998), p. 71.
10 Cathy Caruth, *Literature in the Ashes of History* (Baltimore: Johns Hopkins University Press, 2013), p. 15.
11 Oscar Wilde, *The Importance of Being Earnest*, in *Collins Complete Works of Oscar Wilde*, ed. Merlin Holland, fifth edition (Glasgow: HarperCollins, 2003), p. 376.
12 Emilie Pine, *The Politics of Irish Memory: Performing Remembrance in Contemporary Irish Culture* (London: Palgrave Macmillan, 2011), p. 3.
13 Luke Gibbons, 'The Global Cure? History, Therapy and the Celtic Tiger', in Peadar Kirby, Luke Gibbons and Michael Cronin (eds), *Reinventing Ireland: Culture, Society, and the Global Economy* (London: Pluto, 2002), p. 104.

14 See www.history.com/news/magdalene-laundry-ireland-asylum-abuse (accessed 20 May, 2025).
15 Emilie Pine, *The Politics of Irish Memory: Performing Remembrance in Contemporary Irish Culture* (London: Palgrave Macmillan, 2010), p. 14.
16 Eoin Flannery and Eugene O'Brien, 'Introduction: Critiquing Crisis and Commemoration', *Irish Studies Review* 30:4 (2022), p. 376.
17 Quoted in ibid., p. 379.
18 Del Rio, 'Trauma Theory and the Contemporary Irish Novel', p. 7.
19 Luke Gibbons, *James Joyce and the Irish Revolution: The Easter Rising as Modern Event* (Chicago and London: University of Chicago Press, 2023), p. 196.
20 Robert Garrat, 'John McGahern's *Amongst Women*: Representation, Memory, and Trauma', *Irish University Review* 35:1 (2005), p. 123.
21 Ibid.
22 James M. Smith, 'The Magdalene Sisters: Evidence, Testimony … Action?' *Signs* 32:2 (2007), p. 433.
23 Diarmuid Ferriter, *The Revelation of Ireland: 1995–2020* (London: Profile Books Limited, 2024), p. 302.
24 Pat Brereton, 'Religion and Irish Cinema', *Studies: An Irish Quarterly Review* 97:387 (2008), p. 325.
25 Pine, *The Politics of Irish Memory*, p. 8.
26 Ibid., p. 43.
27 Smith, 'The Magdalene Sisters: Evidence, Testimony … Action?', p. 458.
28 James M. Smith. 'Remembering Ireland's Architecture of Containment: "Telling" Stories on Stage, Patricia Burke Brogan's Eclipsed and Stained Glass at Samhain', *Ireland's Magdalen Laundries and the Nation's Architecture of Containment* (Notre Dame: University of Notre Dame Press, 2007), p. 90.
29 See Oscar Wilde, 'The Critic as Artist', in *Collins Complete Works of Oscar Wilde*, ed. Merlin Holland, fifth edition (Glasgow: HarperCollins, 2003), p. 1121.
30 Christopher Morash, 'Irish Theatre', in Joe Cleary and Claire Connolly (eds), *The Cambridge Companion to Modern Irish Culture* (Cambridge: Cambridge University Press, 2005), p. 334.
31 For further discussion of the role of memory and forgetting in *Faith Healer*, see Graham Price, 'Memory, Narration and Spectrality in Brian Friel's *Faith Healer* and Frank McGuinness' *Observe the Sons of Ulster Marching Towards the Somme*', *Irish Studies Review* 23:1 (2014), pp. 33–47.
32 Samuel Beckett, *The Complete Dramatic Works* (London: Faber & Faber, 1986), p. 220.

33 Anne Devlin, 'Waking the Forgotten', in Linda Anderson and Dawn Miranda Sheratt-Bado (eds), *Female Lines: New Writing by Women from Northern Ireland* (Stillorgan and Oregon: New Island Books, 2017), p. 142.
34 Ricouer, *Memory, History, Forgetting*, p. 95.
35 Brian Friel, *Plays 1* (London: Faber & Faber, 1996), p. 368.
36 Richard Rankin Russell, *Memory, Community, and Place in Brian Friel's Drama*, second edition (Syracuse: Syracuse University Press, 2022), p. 160.
37 Friel, *Plays 1*, p. 367. Emphasis in original.
38 Ibid., p. 445.
39 Frank McGuinness, *Plays 1* (London: Faber & Faber, 1996), p. 97.
40 Ibid.,
41 Frank McGuinness, *Plays 2* (London: Faber & Faber, 2002), p. 219.
42 Caruth, *Literature in the Ashes of History*, p. 17.
43 McGuinnes, *Plays 1*, p. 196.
44 Claire Keegan, *Small Things Like These* (London: Faber & Faber, 2021), p. 43.
45 Donald Clarke, Review of *Michael Collins*, *Irish Times*, Friday 18 March, 2016 – 09:56, https://www.irishtimes.com/culture/film/michael-collins-review-nowhere-near-as-historically-inaccurate-as-we-once-supposed-1.2576150 (accessed 20 May, 2025).
46 Lance Petitt, *Screening Ireland* (Manchester: Manchester University Press, 2000), p. 258.
47 Brian McIlroy, 'History without Borders: Neil Jordan's *Michael Collins*', in James McKillop (ed.), *Contemporary Irish Cinema: From The Quiet Man to Dancing at Lughnasa* (Syracuse: Syracuse University Press, 1999), p. 24.
48 Emilie Pine, 'Memory & Legacy in Irish Theatre & Film', *Éire-Ireland* 43:1–2 (Spring/Summer 2008), p. 227.
49 Gerardine Meaney, 'The Sons of Cuchulainn: Violence, the Family, and the Irish Canon', *Éire-Ireland* 41:1 (2006), p. 243.
50 Luke Gibbons, 'Engendering the State: Narrative Allegory and *Michael Collins*', *Eire Ireland* 31:3–4 (Winter 1996), p. 263.
51 Elizabeth Butler Cullingford, *Ireland's Others* (Cork: Cork University Press, 2001), p. 216.
52 Luke Gibbons, 'Engendering the State: Narrative, Allegory, and Michael Collins', *Éire-Ireland*, 31:3–4 (Autumn/Winter 1996), p. 269.
53 McIlroy, 'History without Borders', p. 24.
54 Carol Dell'Amico 'Anne Enright's "The Gathering": Trauma, Testimony, Memory', *New Hibernia Review* 14:3 (2010), p. 59.

55 Anne Enright, *The Gathering* (London: Vintage, 2007), p. 1.
56 Ferriter, *The Revelation of Ireland*, p. 2.
57 Dell'Amico 'Anne Enright's "The Gathering": Trauma, Testimony, Memory', p. 60.
58 Ibid., p. 62.
59 Sarah C. Gardam, '"Default[ing] to the Oldest Scar": A Psychoanalytic Investigation of Subjectivity in Anne Enright's The Gathering', *Etudes Irlandaises* 34:1 (2009), p. 100.
60 Margot Backus and Joseph Valente, *The Child Sex Scandal and Modern Irish Literature: Writing the Unspeakable* (Indiana: Indiana University Press, 2020), p. 219.
61 Ibid., p. 238.
62 Sebastian Barry, *Secret Scripture* (London: Faber and Faber, 2008), p. 230.
63 Kevin Barry, *The Secret Scripture* (London: Faber & Faber, 2008), front page.
64 David Lloyd, 'Rage against the Divine: In Memoriam Jacques Derrida', *South Atlantic Quarterly* 106:2 (Spring 2007), pp. 353–354.
65 Dori Laub, 'Truth and Testimony: The Process and the Struggle', in Shoshana Felman and Dori Laub (eds), *Testimony: Crises of Witnessing in Literature, Psychoanalysis, and History* (New York: Routledge, 1992), p. 70.
66 Kathleen Costello-Sullivan, *Trauma and Recovery in the Twenty-First-Century Irish Novel* (Syracuse: Syracuse University Press, 2018), p. 74. Emphasis in original.
67 Ibid., p. 88.
68 Joe Cleary, 'McGahern's Rages', in Derek Hand and Eamon Maher (eds), *Essays on John McGahern: Assessing a Literary Legacy* (Cork: Cork University Press, 2019), p. 180.
69 Sally Barr Ebest, Review of *Resting Places: On Wounds, War, and the Irish Revolution*, *New Hibernia Review* 28:1 (Spring 2024), p. 147.
70 Richard Kearney discusses literal and symbolic wounds in the literature of trauma in a lecture given at the Abbey Theatre in 2014. The paper was titled 'Writing Trauma: From Memory to Fiction'. See https://www.youtube.com/watch?v=EW3W-6CwXWc&t=1081s (accessed 20 May, 2025).
71 Ellen McWilliams, *Resting Places: On Wounds, War and the Irish Revolution* (Belfast: Beyond the Pale Books, 2023), p. 1. All future references refer parenthetically to this edition.
72 Charles Duff, 'Reflections', in Ellen McWilliams, *Resting Places: On Wounds, War and the Irish Revolution* (Belfast: Beyond the Pale Books, 2023), p. xxv.

73 Dominick La Capra, *Writing History, Writing Trauma* (Baltimore and London: Johns Hopkins University Press, 2001), p. 35.
74 Neal Jagoe, 'Reflections', in Ellen McWilliams, *Resting Places: On Wounds, War and the Irish Revolution* (Belfast: Beyond the Pale Books, 2023), p. xxv.

6
Irish ecocriticism

Introduction

The influence of ecocriticism in an Irish Studies context has grown in recent years. In a plenary address to the IASIL conference in Gothenburg in 1997 Neil Sammells correctly asserted that 'Ecocriticism would help determine the shape of Irish literary studies in the next decade or so'. Considering the ongoing, worldwide environmental crisis and the rise of the Anthropocene, it is perhaps inevitable that ecocriticism should have begun to attain a certain position of influence within academic classes and research. This chapter draws and expands upon these critics' theories and considers the recent trend in Irish literature and theory to explore the relationship between various texts and their environments. The representative texts chosen for analysis shall be drawn from both older and more recent Irish literature. They are: some of Emily Lawless' eco-essays, John McGahern's *Memoir* and *That They May Face the Rising Sun*, selections from Paula Meehan's poetry, and Éilís Ní Dhuibhne's *The Dancers Dancing*. Attention shall be paid to how ecocritical analysis can be productively connected with the insights supplied by postcolonial theory and gender and sexuality studies. These issues that have been discussed in previous chapters, thus this chapter shall provide a line of continuity with earlier sections of this book. The concluding questions will centre around what changes are needed in the world order concerning politics and human behaviour to make a positive difference in the climate situation and what role literature and theory might have in influencing such changes.

Ecocriticism/ecocritical theory

The central contention at the heart of ecocriticism/ecocritical theory in the twenty-first century (although, as shall be discussed, there were ecocritical thinkers prior to this) is the contention that the planet is currently existing in what is called 'the Anthropocene'. This refers to the current historical and cultural moment that is characterised by the powerful – and predominantly negative – influence of humanity on the natural world. In other words, the cultural and the natural are no longer two distinct entities. As Fintan O'Toole has argued, we are now living in a world that could be best described as one that is extremely Uncanny (drawing upon Freud's influential concept) in which events that would have once been considered the product of an over active, Gothic-inflected imagination, such as the planet either being completely flooded or burnt up, are now discussed as very possible future occurrences. In essence, the distance between imagination and reality has been erased. This is the essence of an Uncanny event according to Freud. Ecocriticism is concerned with analysing and critiquing this Uncanny/Anthropocentric moment in the affairs of ecology, humanity and non-humanity.[1]

The term Anthropocene can be traced back to the essay from 2000, 'Anthropocene', co-authored by atmospheric scientists Paul J. Crutzen and Eugene F. Stoermer in the newsletter of the *International Geosphere-Biosphere Programme*. In their essay, Crutzen and Stoermer trace the beginning of this phase of earthly existence to the beginning of the Industrial Revolution:

> We proposed the latter part of the 18th century [...] we choose this date because, during the past two centuries, the global effects of human activities have become clearly noticeable. This is the period when data retrieved from glacial ice cores show the beginning of a growth in the atmospheric concentrations of several 'greenhouse gases', in particular CO2 and CH4(7). Such a starting date also coincides with James Watt's invention of the steam engine in 1784. About at that time, biotic assemblages in most lakes began to show large changes.[2]

'Motivated by the tangible acceleration of anthropogenic degradation of the non-human world, and by their accumulated scientific evidence of the irreparable scars inflicted on the global environment by humanity, Crutzen and Stoermer diagnosed that humanity has, in fact, ascended to the role of geological agent'.[3]

Ecocriticism arguably has its roots in the philosophical project of Gilles Deleuze in the late 1980s. Philosopher and self-confessed 'Deleuzian', Manuel DeLanda argues for Deleuze's philosophy as positing a radical departure from social constructivism in its focus on the relationship between men, the non-human, temporality, and the natural world; these are concerns that have been at the core of the discipline of Irish Studies for more than twenty years:

> unlike social constructivism, which achieves openness by making the world depend on human interpretation, Deleuze achieves it by making the world into a creative, complexifying and problematizing cauldron of becoming. Because of their anthropocentrism, constructivist philosophies remain prisoners of what Foucault called 'the episteme of man', while Deleuze plunges ahead into a post-humanist future, in which the world has been enriched by a multiplicity of non-human agencies, of which metallic catalysts, and their acts of recognition and intervention, are only one example.[4]

Claire Bracken also notes how Deleuze's philosophy is very much concerned with materiality, nature and embodiment and how this distinguishes it from the linguistic and cultural preoccupations of the majority of twentieth-century philosophy and cultural theory:

> Differing from deconstruction, Deleuze's work posits a space that exists in excess of language and discourse, a heterogeneous material force that is always virtual – meaning that it cannot be captured within discourse / representation / language. Furthermore, this space is positive and productive, as it is generative of the actual – discourse / representation/language.[5]

Whilst poststructuralism/Deconstruction focussed its philosophical lens on the primacy of language, Deleuzian thought/ecocriticism focussed more on the dynamic relationship between humanity and ecology. This would continue to be a preoccupation of Deleuze's critical project during his extensive writing projects with Felix Guattari, especially in their magnus opus *A Thousand Plateaus* (1980).

Deleuze was to express his ecocritical desire for worldwide existence in the following lines from *Difference and Repetition* (1966):

> A single and same voice for the whole thousand – voiced multiple, a single and same Ocean for all the drops, a single clamour of Being for all beings: on condition that each being, each drop and each voice has reached the state of excess – in other words, the difference which displaces and disguises them and, in turning upon its mobile cusp, causes them to return.[6]

What Deleuze is envisioning is a state of existence that can accommodate all things because of the fact that everything on planet earth is united by what Judith Butler would call a 'shared precarity'.[7] Equally, Deleuze in this passage is privileging a conception of time that is more cyclical and therefore more ecological than the human conception of modern temporality, which is predicated on notions of linearity and progress.

Deleuze was to argue for this ecocritical notion of perpetually recurring, cyclical/seasonal time in *Difference and Repetition* as being what he called a succession of 'present presents':

> The succession of present presents is only the manifestation of something more profound – namely, the manner in which each continues the whole life, but a different level or degree to the preceding, since all levels and degrees coexist and present themselves for our choice on the basis of a past which was never present. What we call the empirical character of the presents which make us up is constituted by the relations of succession and simultaneity between them, their relations of contiguity, causality, resemblance and even opposition.[8]

Irish ecocriticism, it shall be argued, is supremely invested in excavating within chosen texts the ways that new modes of non-anthropocentric existence and conceptions of temporality are contained within their form and thematic content.[9]

In his text *Foucault*, Gilles Deleuze argued that: 'The world is made up of superimposed surface, archives, and strata. The world is thus knowledge'.[10] Deleuze is asserting that our world has a history and a memory in the same way that humanity has and thus should be considered as being similar to human-made societies and their narratives.

Ecocriticism as a concept first officially appeared in the late 1970s, at meetings of the WLA (Western Literature Association, a body whose field of interest is the literature of the Americas). In his introduction to a series of brief position papers (all entitled 'What is Ecocriticism?') Michael P. Branch traces the word 'ecocriticism' back to William Ruecker's 1978 essay 'Literature and Ecology: An Experiment in Ecocriticism'.[11]

'The point repeatedly made by ecocritics is that for the first time in human history, no true wilderness exists on the planet, every region is affected by global warming, and other "anthropocentric" problems, such as toxic waste and nuclear fallout'.[12] Whilst the discourse of various theoretical practices have sought to diagnose and, to some extent, propose solutions to the inequalities and injustices related to gender, race and class, ecocriticism asserts that the problems related to ecology in an anthropocentric world must also be examined. Also, many ecocritics propose alliances and highlight similar concerns as existing between their theoretical methodology and that of feminism, postcolonialism and Marxism.

The works of certain ecocritical practitioners have given rise to the recognition of a certain strand of poetry that has now become known as ecopoetry. In Jonathan Bate's *The Song of the Earth*, Bate's defines Ecopoetry in the following terms:

> Ecopoetry is not a description of dwelling with the earth, not a disengaged thinking about it, but an experiencing of it. By 'poetry' here I mean poiesis, making [...] Ecopoetry is not synonymous with writing that is pragmatically green: a manifesto for ecological correctness will not be poetic because its language is bound to be instrumental, to address questions of doing rather than to 'present' the experiences of dwelling.[13]

As was referenced in Chapter 1 of this book, W.B. Yeats asserts in his poem 'The Municipal Gallery Revisited' that his art and that of his fellow Revivalists (Synge and Lady Gregory especially) came from 'contact with the soil'. Later Irish writers, especially poets such as Seamus Heaney, Derek Mahon and Paula Meehan have found their inspiration in the natural world and have written memorable works about the experience of 'being with' nature and ecology. Poetry is not the only artistic form that is productive of an ecological subtext, though it does possess certain qualities that are conducive to the creation of such works. As Bates argues: 'the rhythmic, syntactic and linguistic intensifications that are characteristic of verse-writing frequently give peculiar force to the *poiesis* [making]: it could be argued that poiesis in the sense of verse-making is language's most direct path of return to the *oikos*, the place of dwelling'.[14]

Timothy Clarke has encouraged literary critics, when analysing specific texts, to take into account necessary 'derangements of scale' when engaging with particular cultural products. According to Clarke, a person's individual actions, whilst seemingly trivial, can cause massive impacts on the climate and environment, and therefore textual analysis should take into account the connection between human action and global impact:

> Climate change disrupts the scale at which one must think, skews categories of internal and external and resists inherited, closed economies of accounting or explanations [...] scale effects in particular defy sensuous representation or any plot confined, say, to human-to-human dramas and intentions, demanding new, innovative modes of writing that have yet to emerge.[15]

Irish ecocritics have taken up the challenge posed by Clarke (some before it was even posed) and examined various cultural and textual products (literary and others) that move beyond a purely humanist analysis and consider how various texts represent the linkage between all forms of existence, living, planetary, temporal and so on.

Ecocritical Irish Studies

A very early example of an (Anglo-)Irish literary text that can be partially read as an example of 'ecocritical literature' is Oscar Wilde's dramatic masterpiece *The Importance of Being Earnest* (1895). At the centre of this play are two characters, Jack/Ernest and Algy/Bunbury, who change their names and whole aspects of their identities depending on whether they are residing in the town or the country. Whilst the line 'I am Ernest in town and Jack in the country' can be easily played for laughs, it also makes the proto-ecocritical point that humanity's existence can, to a certain degree, be determined by the environment in which they reside. Indeed, prior to *The Importance of Being Earnest*, a character in *Lady Windermere's Fan* gave the following reason for leaving London: 'London is too full of fogs and serious people. Whether the fogs produce the serious people or the serious people produce the fogs I cannot tell, but the whole thing rather gets on my nerves'.[16] The question about the exact nature of the relationship between humanity and ecology is one that exists at the heart of ecocriticism. Thus, Wilde can be read as having anticipated the ecological and pastoral concerns of the Irish Revival.

Ireland's growing interest in its ecology and natural history was made obvious in 1857 with the opening of the Dublin Natural History Museum (which is also humorously called 'The Dead Zoo'). This interest in natural history was accentuated at that time by the rise of the movement known as the Irish Revival (examined in detail in Chapter 1). 'Both movements sought to distinguish the nation as a unique and culturally valuable entity, and also to reject imposed Anglo-centric models'.[17]

Lucy Collins has acknowledged the long history of ecologically invested works in Irish literature in her 2014 article 'The Frosty Winters of Ireland, Poetry and Climate Crisis 1739–41':

> These poems of pronounced political engagement affirm the importance of the weather to the present and future of all human beings, regardless of nationality or station. In the Irish context, where agriculture has played such a role in both the economic and social development of the country, climate is an especially pivotal dimension. As an island nation Ireland's weather is subject to continuous fluctuation, though rarely to climate crisis, yet it has also played a role in the country's experience of war, of conquest and of civil unrest. Constantly changing weather is a marker of vulnerability that the passage to modernity cannot quite overcome. Centuries after these powerful poems were written, the close connections between the weather and human behaviour continue to challenge and engage us.[18]

Ireland's traumatic experience of famine made it people acutely aware of the precarious nature of human and ecological existence and the fragile but important relationship between the two. Margaret Kelleher's 1997 text The *Feminisation of Famine: Expressions of the Inexpressible* (discussed in Chapter 4) offers a valuable ecofeminist reading of Irish literature and the famine; this version of ecocriticism shall be examined in greater detail in this chapter's analysis. Lucy Collins and Andrew Carpenter's collection *The Irish Poet and the Natural World: An Anthology of Verse in English from the*

Tudors to the Romantics showcases the extent to which Irish writers have engaged with ecological representation for centuries before ecocriticism emerged as a recognisable academic mode of analysis and representation.

The application of ecocriticism to an Irish Studies theoretical context was always going to be quite an obvious move. Arguably, the non-fiction writings of Emily Lawless and J.M. Synge (as argued in greater detail shortly) provide good examples of a nascent ecocritical approach to the examination of nature and landscape in Ireland. Thus, they could be christened as proto-ecocritics in the same way that Roger Casement can be viewed as a proto-postcolonial theorist.

One of the earliest examples of an Irish Studies critical text that adopts something of an ecocritical approach to the examination of various texts from Ireland is Oona Frawley's *Irish Pastoral: Nostalgia and Twentieth-Century Irish Literature*. In this study, Frawley argues that, in a literary context, nature and landscape 'become signifiers, lenses through which it is possible to examine cultural and historical development'.[19] Frawley's extensive and expansive textual analyses span several centuries, from the 1600s up to the end of the twentieth century, and focus on writers such as Yeats, Joyce, Synge, Beckett, Seamus Heaney and Eavan Boland.

Crucially, however, Frawley's critical methodology is avowedly that of cultural materialism. At the beginning of the book, she quotes Simon Shama extensively as way of framing the approach she is going to take in relation to the consideration of the representation of landscape in her chosen texts:

> Landscapes are culture before they are nature, constructs of the imagination projected onto wood and water and rock [...] But it should also be acknowledged that once a certain idea of landscape, a myth, a vision, establishes itself in an actual place, it has a peculiar way of muddling, categorizing, of making metaphors more real than their referents; of becoming, in fact, part of the scenery.[20]

Frawley's central argument, developed throughout *Irish Pastoral*, is that representations of nature and landscape exert a prescriptive power upon an individual's perception of the natural, physical world. Thus, the signifier begins to exert an influence over the signified and its tangibility. In contrast, ecocriticism is often used to explore how nature controls humanity and human-made culture with the result that both states of existence are treated as equals in this theoretical way of seeing the world. Indeed, it is sometimes the case that the natural is presented as being more powerful than the cultural.

Perhaps fortuitously, during the mid-1970s, at the same time that ecocriticism began to gain a foothold in, particularly, academic discourse and debate, Seamus Heaney's seminal poetic collection *North* was published (in 1975). In this volume, Heaney evokes the bogs of Northern Europe and the secrets, both human and natural, that they contain. Heaney uses these bogs as a poetic image through which he can engage with the horrific violence that was raging in Northern Ireland at that time and the toll it was taking on both humanity and nature. The title *North* thus takes on a double meaning just as the poems represent, almost simultaneously, contemporary Northern Ireland and ancient Northern Europe.

The collection was preceded by the volume *Wintering Out*, which contained the poem 'Tollund Man' in which a bog body is asked to 'make germinate' the bodies of four brothers who had been killed in 1921 in Northern Ireland by a Unionist-controlled police force and their bodies dragged along the railway lines. This request implies the need for a greater connection between humanity and the environment if the sterility of human violence is to be transcended and its victims given some meaning even if only in death. Germination is not something of which humans are capable; only nature can achieve this state of growth and rejuvenation.[21] The poems in *North* are arguably continuing this plea for greater ecological connection on the part of the anthropocentric world.

If Heaney's poem, 'Punishment', provided some of the impetus for the rise of postcolonial theory in Irish Studies (as discussed in Chapter 3) then the collection as a whole very conceivably spurred on the rise of ecocriticism in an Irish context. Heaney's example also inspired the poet Derek Mahon to write poems such as 'A Disused Shed in County Wexford' (published in 1975), which consider the tangled relationship between humanity, ecology and history. The poem certainly contains many images that represent humans' misuse of the natural world and the ravages of anthropocentricism, calling for a counter-narrative to that of anthropocentric modernity and 'progress':

> deep in the grounds of a burnt out hotel,
> Among the bathtubs and the washbasins
> A thousand mushrooms crowd to a keyhole.
> This is the one star in their firmament
> Or frames a star within a star.
> What should they do there but desire?
> So many days beyond the rhododendrons
> With the world waltzing in its bowl of cloud,
> They have learnt patience and silence
> Listening to the rooks querulous in the high wood.[22]

This stanza anthropomorphises the mushrooms described and suggests that they too have feelings that should be recognised and represented, even in the context of an anthropocentric world.

The poem ends with the mushrooms speaking in a manner comparable to Keats' Grecian Urn: '"Save us, save us," they seem to say,/ "Let the god not abandon us/ Who have come so far in darkness and in pain./ We too had our lives to live./ You with your light meter and relaxed itinerary,/ Let not our naive labours have been in vain!"'[23] Mahon acknowledges that the poet's vocation should be to bear witness to the whole world – both human, natural and otherwise. Significantly, the poem is dedicated to J.G. Farrell whose novel *Troubles* (1970) depicts the decline of a Wexford Anglo-Irish family during the Irish Revolutionary period in tandem with the physical decay of their Big House and the land around it. Human and natural tragedy were thus portrayed as being inextricably linked as is indicated by the title of the novel, which suggests the book's concern with more than one specific form of distress. This is also the case in Mahon's poem in which the cries of the distressed mushrooms are compared to the tragic demise of the humans who perished at Treblinka and Pompei.

Lucy Collins' extensive analysis of 'A Disused Shed in County Wexford' elucidates the powerful ecological concerns and imagery contained within the poem:

> In this poem, the ability of nature to take over from human habitation, to mature and die and be renewed while the world of human objects crumbles to insignificance, offers a different emphasis on the speaker's discovery. In such a scheme, the dynamic between the mushrooms and their human observer loses metaphorical ground in favour of a

> more actualized account; likewise the questioning of the value of a human-orientated, mechanized life against the organic persistence of a world of nature grows in prominence.[24]

Similarly, as Collins notes, Mahon's collection *Life on Earth* emphasises 'that human and creaturely experience must find a way of existing together within the same landscape'.[25]

James McElroy's reading of 'A Disused Shed' is also firmly grounded in ecocriticism:

> 'A Disused Shed in Co. Wexford' makes clear that, even after years and years of isolation in a cenobitic environment of uncelestial shade, 'there is life yet in their feverish forms'. More, it is 'their feverish forms' that beg us, in their 'wordless way', to rethink the poem's mycological species in terms other than our own and so withstand the temptations of species-ism in both theory and practice.[26]

Both McElroy and Collins point to the centrality of the natural, non-human world in Mahon's work and how it argues for various forms of compromise and sometimes alliance between the Anthropocene and ecology.

In the ensuing decades, ecocriticism has only grown in relevance and importance in Irish academic and cultural discourse and debate. Eoin Flannery asserts that the post-Celtic Tiger period in Ireland has proven a most fertile hunting ground for ecocritical thinkers because many Irish people are

> now scrambling for a new set of codes by which to live their lives and with which to engage with the altered landscape of the country. Having been disabused of the long term tenability of copious wealth, fevered accumulation, and high-value property, it seems appropriate to consider and to endorse a renewed sense of eco-conscious within the Irish context.[27]

The publication in 2016 of Flannery's important study *Ireland and Ecocriticism: Literature, History, and Environmental Justice* provided a valuable survey of the growth of ecocritical literature and thought in Ireland over the previous century.

In 2014, John Brannigan's study *Archipelagic Modernism* was published. The book considers works of modernist literature from the late nineteenth century until the late twentieth century and examines how the chosen texts represent encounters between humanity, land and sea. The central argument of this text is that the anglophone works of literature from this period offer new ways of thinking about political geographies and about humanity's relationship with the environment. Some of the Irish authors examined are J.M. Synge, W.B. Yeats and James Joyce.

As John Brannigan argues in his introduction to *Archipelagic Modernism*:

> We use the term 'archipelago' to denote a group of islands, and to stress in neutral and plural terms the relationship between those islands. In the historical and political contexts of relations between the various nations, islands, and peoples in the Irish and British archipelago, this has obvious advantages in avoiding terms that are offensive, misrepresentative, or inaccurate.[28]

The consideration of an 'archipelagic modernism' has obvious progressive, anti-absolutist potential because islands are neither wholly land nor sea, and to consider modernism in such liminal terms highlights that literary movement's rejection of absolutism in any form; national, racial, gendered or stylistic.

Brannigan encapsulates the central argument in *Archipelagic Modernism* in the following passage:

> During the period examined in this book, from 1890 to 1970, many writers from the Irish and British archipelago began to write as if the dominant narratives of political identity in these islands were already exhausted, and they sought to explore their peripheries – their seas, coastlines, and islands – for the cultural resources with which to reimagine and re-calibrate their identities, cartographies, and ecologies.[29]

Brannigan's central argument is that his chosen authors and texts sought to reimagine the identities and physical realities of both the human and non-human worlds in which the works were set.

When discussing J.M. Synge's travel novel *The Aran Islands*, Brannigan focusses on how the Aran Islands and their inhabitants represented for Synge a space and race of people more in tune with the natural world and less with that of the modern, anthropocentric land of Europe from which Yeats had advised him to distance himself. As Brannigan notes via the use of the following quotation, Synge seemed to almost regard the Aran Islanders as belonging to an older version of humanity, that has a greater connection with the wild sensuality of nature than their more modern fellow humans: 'These strange men with their receding foreheads, high cheek-bones and ungovernable eyes seem to represent some old type found on these few acres at the extreme border of Europe, where it is only in wild jest and laughter that they can express their loneliness and isolation'.[30] Ironically, Synge's description of how these pre-modern peasants found solace from and insight concerning their unhappy lives actually anticipates the postmodern observation in Beckett's *Endgame* that 'there is nothing funnier than unhappiness'.[31] This implies a link between the worldview and behaviour of the pre-modern, ecologically entwined peasant and some of the insights that were to emerge from the literature of postmodernity, which was supposed to have embraced the cultural completely at the expense of the natural.

It is important to note that one of the most influential ecocritics to write about the land of Ireland is actually not Irish but English – Tim Robinson. This writer's groundbreaking work of cartography and essays, spreading out over a number of decades, rendered the Aran Islands and Connemara both tangibly physical and magically non-static. When writing about Robinson, Brannigan argues that 'The formal patterning of [Robinson's] narrative attempts, in lithe prose, to efface the presence of the narrator as barely more than a witness. The naming of the landscape is always understood in its contingency, as a temporary human mark upon the landscape as any sculpture, any field boundary, any furrow'.[32] 'It is in this rich flowering of the offshoots of late modernism that we can see the earlier modernist preoccupations with anthropology, primitivism, and evolution become more discernibly part of an ecological imagination of localities and environment'.[33] This comparative analysis of the environmental concerns and emphasis of high and late modernism is one of the most original aspects of Brannigan's study.

Nicholas Allen's obituary for Tim Robinson, who died in 2020, describes the Robinson's importance to the history of Irish ecocriticism in a manner that is comparable to Brannigan's analysis of Robinson:

> His [Robinson's] maps of the Aran islands, the Burren and Connemara – places he referred to as the 'ABC of earth wonders' – are little

> miracles of collective assembly, combining topography, language, geology, myth and physics. Robinson was acutely conscious of the damage, both representative and real, that centuries of conflict over land and language had caused. [34]

Allen has also made his own important contribution to the development of Irish ecocriticism with his 2020 study *Irish Literature and the Coast: Seatangled.*

The year 2022 saw the publication of a significant collection of essays edited by Malcolm Sen and titled *A History of Irish Literature and the Environment.* This should be considered one of the most important recent publishing events in the history of Irish ecocriticism. It contains essays by prominent critics such as John Brannigan, Margaret Kelleher and Sharae Deckard which examine the representation of ecology and humanity in Irish literature. Kelleher's essay continues her examination of Irish ecofeminism in relation to the Irish famine. Brannigan's piece can be read as a valuable companion to his aforementioned study *Archipelagic Modernism.* The scope of the work enables a clear sense of how important ecocriticism has become to the discipline of Irish Studies in recent times. This is made even clearer when one reads Sen's introduction to the volume, which provides a coherent and broad evaluation of the climate crisis and how Irish Studies is responding to this world emergency. It emphasises how Irish academics use interdisciplinary and multidisciplinary tools to asses Ireland's relationship to ecology.

Another notable essay from the collection is Katherine O'Callaghan's 'Solastalgic Modernism and the West in Irish Literature, 1900–1950':

> The term 'solastalgia', coined by philosopher Glenn Albrecht, refers to the lived experience of negative environmental change so that one might feel homesickness even when *at home*. Solastalgia alludes to both the notion of comfort in the face of distressing forces (solace) but also to desolation, *abandonment*, and *loneliness*. Experiencing solastalgia is knowing that our local and planetary ecologies are in the process of extreme change, and the solace of our place within them is being removed from us.[35]

O'Callaghan examines a variety of Irish modernist writers ranging from the Irish Revival to Joyce's *Finnegans Wake* and considers their representation of the disorientating and vertiginous effects of solastalgia:

> For most Irish artists in the first half of the twentieth century, the West of Ireland was a place encountered not through personal visits or deep study but through the paintings, sketches, and accounts of others. Nevertheless, it had a systemic influence on their texts, culminating in an exploration of its felt history and the manner in which it had previously been depicted, in Joyce's last work *Finnegans Wake* (1939)'.[36]

Another important Irish literary work that acutely represents this experience of solastalgia is Patrick Kavanagh's 'The Great Hunger' (examined in Chapter 2 on Counter-Revival) in which an actual representative of the Irish Catholic farming class (so often written about but rarely seizing control of their own representative powers) gives voice to the simultaneous feeling of intimacy and alienation from the land to which they were wedded in an Oedipal bond.

Malcolm Sen has himself written an important ecocritical reading of Yeats' poetry, which was published in 2022 in the journal *International Yeats Studies*. The essay is titled '"Dragon-Ridden" Days: Yeats, Apocalypse, and the Anthropocene' and explores the symbolic significance of dragons in Yeats' poetry. Sen argues that the figure of the Dragon is an uncanny figure rooted in myth and cultural memory, reflecting both the destructive forces affecting humanity and the complex interplay of history, biology, ecology and the Anthropocene. An important line from Yeats that reflects this view of anthropocentric culture is from 'Nineteen Hundred and Nineteen': 'Now Days are dragon ridden'. That line is regularly read as a description of the apocalyptic time of the Irish War of Independence in the second decade of the twentieth century but can also be interpreted as a commentary on the anthropocentric phase in history during which we are still living.

Sen argues in relation to the interconnectedness between the Dragon, apocalypse and the Anthropocene:

> If, as has been proposed, one of the markers of the Anthropocene is an irradiated planet after the first nuclear tests were carried out in the 1940s, then mass extinctions have become an ontological signifier of this geological epoch in the twenty-first century. Dragons, in

> this scheme of things, are avatars of dinosaurs, the iconic species of the extinction narrative (although subversively, they do not die out themselves). Dragons emerge in the contemporary moment from the abyssal depths of modernity not through biological adaptation or resilience, but because of their archetypal alterity; they are an iconic reminder of existential ends and the slow violence of species extinction.[37]

In this reading, the uncanny figure of the Dragon represents both human monstrosity and the assured destruction of humanity, ecology and the non-human as a result of the combined excesses of anthropocentric history. In this respect, Sen's essay accords with Judith Butler's conception of a 'shared precarity' as what unites earth and everything that exists within its atmosphere.

Sen's reading of 'Nineteen Hundred and Nineteen' speaks very strongly to a strand in ecocriticism titled 'the Ecogothic'. Sharae Deckard has written extensively on this version of ecocriticism and describes it thus:

> If gothic is understood as often turning around a 'return of the repressed' or as revealing the buried social truths of a 'political unconscious', ecogothic turns around the uncanny manifestation of the 'environmental unconscious', particularly those forms of environmental violence or crisis that have been occulted. Whether this revelation is a cause for fear or for triumph, depicting the return of the repressed as a horrifying confrontation or as a resistant recuperation, is a question of the politics of the text.[38]

Deckard goes on: 'If gothic is characterized by excess, in ecogothic, land- and waterscapes are themselves extreme sites of monstrous fecundity that seemingly threaten human civilization, where vines and vegetation run rampant, where decay ferments and festers, or where plagues and vermin spread deliriums'.[39]

A very important example of Irish Ecogothic is Mike McCormick's novel *Solar Bones* (2016), a text in which an inhospitable ecology and temporal, spectral dislocations are placed in conflict with the anthropocentric world of Irish Celtic Tiger modernity. The novel's view of that period in Irish history is filtered through the hyper-critical lens of the Ireland that existed following the economic crash of 2008.

Considering the times in which we are all living, both globally and nationally, ecocriticism could not be more relevant to an analysis of our 'Dragon ridden days'. The state of geopolitics across the globe has resulted in our having to confront the possibility of annihilation on a daily basis. Ecocriticism and its thinkers have the ability to critique our anthropocentric age and also to endeavour, however tentatively, to imagine possible, as yet unrealised, alternative futures and modes of existence. Rather than being a simplistically 'utopian' or 'dystopian' way of thinking, ecocriticism is one of the supreme theories of what Derrida would call the 'to come' (*avenir*).

In Eoin Flannery's comparative analysis of John McGahern's *That They May Face the Rising Sun* and *Memoir*, Flannery argues that ecocriticism's primary value lies in its 'capacity to see through and beyond the necessary attachments of local rootedness to the ways in which we are implicated in the immense scalar preoccupations of deep historical time and global spatiality'.[40] Irish ecocritics and artists have developed an antidote to the Anthropocentric world by exposing the ways we (human and non-human) are all simultaneously local and global, specific and universal, as a result of our shared precarious connectedness to a planet whose resilience should not be taken as a given.

What Irish ecocritics do:

1. **They read various Irish texts, paying particular attention to the representation of the natural world.**
2. **They consider alternatives to a purely anthropocentric view of existence. In particular, they interrogate the possibility of a more equitable relationship between humanity and ecology in the world today.**
3. **They pay particular attention to literary writers such as Derek Mahon, Paula Meehan and John McGahern who foreground nature as a major part of their subject matter.**
4. **Rather than looking at purely 'literary works', they extend their range of examination to genres such as travel writings, essays and memoirs. In this respect, the works of Emily**

Lawless, John Millington Synge and Tim Robinson have been especially fruitful hunting grounds.

5. **They turn away from the 'social constructivism' and 'linguistic determinism' of dominant literary theorists (with their emphasis on the linguistic and social constructedness of the central world) and instead emphasise ecocentric values of meticulous observation, collective ethical responsibility, and the claims of the world beyond ourselves.**[41]

Representative textual analyses

The essays of Emily Lawless

As an Anglo-Irish Unionist, Emily Lawless could not be expected to be a natural ally of the Irish Literary and Cultural Revival. However, as Sean Hewitt has argued: 'If, increasingly, the cultural imagination of the Irish landscape as "enchanted" during the Revival brought forward the immanence and importance of "the soul of things", this made it the ideal setting for Lawless' exploration of the potential meeting points and divergencies between natural history and apparently anti-scientific thought'.[42] Lawless' writing, especially her novels and essays, depict landscape and natural history as something that can be apprehended by both human rationalism and apparently illogical, non-scientific thought. Her essays can be regarded as ripe for ecocritical analysis. Equally, they can be read as examples of proto-ecocritical theory in and of themselves.

In her essay, 'A Note on the Ethics of Literary Forgery' Lawless depicts the Atlantic as an anthropomorphised entity that does not exist merely for the convenience and betterment of humanity:

> The Atlantic is perhaps of all still extant and surviving magicians the most potent in this art of conjuring up and rejuvenating a world which has never entirely ceased to rustle and whisper along his shores. Place yourself also there, and listen with sufficient docility to his rather inarticulate teachings, and there is no [telling] important secrets he may not someday murmur suddenly into your ears. Emanations with the very thinnest of white misty finger-tips may be seen to flit silently out of the seaweeds, as you crunch your way homeward towards

> evening over the rocks. Incorporeal presences – which can be perfectly well seen so long as you do not look directly at them – peer suddenly at you from behind some glittering rock, or glide away into deeper water as you run your boat inshore.[43]

In this remarkable passage, Lawless depicts the natural world as one that is autonomous, powerful and mysterious. As Hewitt argues in relation to the representation of nature in the above quotation: 'Rather than the natural world being a tool for the exploration of the psyche of the speaker, or being merely emblematic or metaphorical, it is framed as autonomous, imminent with knowledge, and able to act independently of the human observer'.[44] Equally, Lawless suggests that the tools of human-made scientific analytics would be, on their own, insufficient when it comes to attempting to understand ecology. Importantly, Lawless never depicts the relationship between the world of nature and that of humanity as one that is capable of being totally benign and hospitable. She acknowledges that there will always be moments in history when the two spheres of existence will be engaged in conflict and that nature never considers itself to be the benign servant of man.

Lawless also casts Ireland's relationship with nature in terms that are relevant to its colonial condition:

> To be told that we lag behind England – flat, fat, prosaic England – in the number of our 'mountain' or 'highland' plants is already sufficiently trying, but when it comes to being gravely assured by Mr. Watson that out of what he calls his 'Atlantic type' we have but a miserable thirty four plants, to Wales and England's sixty-two – well, I can only say that I consider such a statement to be an outrage! Are we going to put up with such an invasion of our few prerogatives? Can any patriotic, any commonly self- respecting Irish botanist accept for a moment so palpably prejudiced and hostile a judgement? Let us, I say for my part, not accept it. Arise, botanic Celts, and glut your ire! Let us have an entirely new botany, based upon an entirely new system and classification, and let not the name of the hostile and anti-Irish botanist be so much named in it![45]

By invoking the colonial-tinged word 'invasion' and marshalling the nationalistic term 'Celt', Lawless is drawing battle lines between Ireland and England in terms of which can boast the most amazing ecological landmarks. Lawless regards a nation's natural landscape as being a sign of the deep soul of that place and certainly considers Ireland to be superior to its colonial master in that regard. In this respect, Lawless displays a greater loyalty to her Irishness than her Unionist background would have suggested possible. In the concluding chapter of Heidi Hansson's valuable book-length study of Lawless titled *Emily Lawless 1845–1913: Writing the Interspace* (2007), Hansson argues that the contradictory aspects of Lawless' identity enabled her work to evade insertion into any stable categories and to occupy a nuanced space of liminality.

In an 1898 essay, titled 'Famine Roads and Famine Monuments' Lawless was to lament the extent to which physical remnants of those lost in the famine, in particular many cabins in Co. Connemara, are being covered over by the ravages of time: 'There they stand, those poor perishing memorials, and yearly the slope on which they rest crumbles a little nearer to the sea, and yearly the rain batters them a little more down [...] and the bog will overtake them, and the last trace of what was once a popular village will have disappeared'.[46] In essays such as 'Famine Roads' and 'North Clare: Leaves from a Diary', as Katherine O'Callaghan argues, 'Lawless emphasized the need for a specific language to "describe our own mountains and our own sea", calling for an "entirely new system and classification"'.[47] As Declan Kiberd and P.J. Mathews assert: 'one of the recurring motifs in her [Lawless'] writing is the idea that Ireland has been misrepresented by modes of scientific description that have been derived elsewhere and do not take into account the specificities of indigenous flora and local ecosystems'.[48]

Lawless powerfully notes that the Irish famine had left its mark on the language as well as on the landscape of Ireland:

> Certain words and certain combinations of words seem to need an eminently local education in order to adequately appreciate them. These two words, 'Famine road', are amongst the number. To other, larger minds than ours they are probably without any particular meaning or inwardness. To the home-staying Irishman or Irishwoman they mean only too much. To hear them casually uttered is to be penetrated by a sense of something at once familiar and terrible. The entire history of two of the most appalling years that any country has ever been called upon to pass through seems to be summed up, and compendiously packed into them.[49]

This passage encapsulates how even the most seemingly harmless linguistic constructs can be charged with retroactive meaning and powerful affect if they are linked with the cultural memory of a terrible trauma. As Margaret Kelleher notes: 'The immediacy and relevance of famine for those writing in the last years of the nineteenth century was further underlined by the recurrence of hunger, disease and starvation in the years after the 1840s'.[50]

Lawless' essays anticipate some of the travel writings of writers such as J.M. Synge and also many of the theories and concerns of ecocriticism that were only to gain academic and cultural prominence nearly a hundred years later. Although her background would naturally make her a decrier of many works of Revivalist writing and much of its politics, some of her work has rightly been included in Declan Kiberd and P.J. Mathews' *Handbook of the Irish Revival* (2015) since her texts are very much of a piece with the zeitgeist of that literary and cultural period in Irish history.

The Dancers Dancing

Éilís Ní Dhuibhne's novel *The Dancers Dancing* was first published in 1999, a year after the epochal moment in Irish history which was the signing of the Good Friday Agreement in 1998. The document gave the residents of Northern Ireland the opportunity to establish a local power-sharing government on that part of the island instead of being governed from Westminster. It also gave them the right to identify as Irish, British or both. From a geographical perspective, this agreement was highly significant because it allowed for a shifting of the balance of political power from England to Northern Ireland. Equally, from a psychological perspective, it gave each individual Northern Irish citizen the right to decide whether they identified more with the United Kingdom or Ireland.

Importantly, *The Dancers Dancing* is not set at the time when it is written. Instead, its story takes place in 1972, one of the infamous years in the history of the Northern Irish Troubles because that was the year members of the British army opened fire on a civil rights march in Derry in Northern Ireland and killed 14 people. This event is now known as Bloody Sunday. The events of Ní Dhuibhne's novel, however, occur in a place removed from such traumatic events. The story is set just across the border in the rural heartland of Co. Donegal, in a part of that county that is known as a Gaeltacht area because it is a part of Ireland where Irish is almost exclusively spoken. School children spend holidays in these Gaeltacht parts of Ireland in order to improve proficiency in Ireland's native language.

The novel has been correctly described by Declan Kiberd as a *Female Bildungsroman* (coming of age narrative). This literary genre focusses on the growth to maturity of its central character(s). As a result of the shadow that James Joyce's *Portrait of the Artist as a Young Man* has cast over Irish literature, most examples of this literary form have tended to focus on male protagonists and their development into adults. *The Dancers Dancing* is a notable exception (as are the works of Edna and Kate O'Brien). The text depicts the growth to personal and sexual maturity of some young school children – particularly the Dublin girl Orla – and is set against the backdrop of a wild and beautiful rural Irish landscape that symbolises their burgeoning sexualities.

The novel's title, *The Dancers Dancing*, invokes the famous rhetorical question from Yeats' 'Among School Children' (quoted in Chapter 3 above): 'How can we know the dancer from the dance'? In the context of *The Dancers Dancing*, the reference to that quote reminds the readers not only of the performative nature of gender and sexual desire but also that a performance requires a stage on which it can be enacted and in this context that stage is the wild and beautiful natural landscape of Donegal, which enables the *Bildung* that runs through the entire work.

In Ní Dhuibhne's essay that accompanies recent editions of *The Dancers Dancing*, she describes how her holidays to rural Donegal inspired her to write the book. Thus, the natural landscape acted as her muse and aided her in the development of the novel:

The inspiration for it came in the summer of 1997 when the IRA initiated its first ceasefire which eventually led to the Good Friday Agreement and the cessation of the Northern Ireland conflict. I began to think of the summers I had spent in Irish college in Donegal in 1965 and 1966 when I was eleven and twelve.[51]

She goes on to say that what she remember most about her time spent in the Donegal Irish college was the river she played in. Thus, in Éilís Ní Dhuibhne's artistic mind, the politics and violence of man and the natural world are intertwined. The fact that this novel is set in 1972 rather than 1965 or 1966 when the author had actually been to Irish college makes the point made above concerning the book's oblique reference to the 1972 Bloody Sunday tragedy even more plausible.

The Dancers Dancing begins with a short chapter which describes what the author regards as being the best and truest forms of maps: 'When the lines of latitude and longitude were in place, the tables and compasses painted in the corner, they [the mapmakers] set to work with brush and paint: little men plough and hunt; wolves and bears and – yes – unicorns and griffins gambol in the forests' (2). Like the descriptions given of this ideal map, the novel attempts the 'all but impossible … [it tries] to show the woods and the trees, the whole world and the people in it' (2). In terms of style, this novel oscillates between the objectivity of a traditional map and the subjectivity of an archetypal modernist novel in a manner that is definitely comparable to the aforementioned description of an ideal mapmaking exercise.

The Dancers Dancing wishes to evoke a fully whole world in which humanity and nature exist side by side in something like harmony. Like William Butler Yeats in 'The Municipal Gallery Revisited', Ní Dhuibhne is also of the opinion that great works of art need to emerge from at least some contact with the soil: 'Every picture tells a story. A truism. Half true like all truisms. Half false. The rest of the story is in the mud. Clear as muddy old mud' (3).

From very early on in the novel, the young girls from Dublin begin to show the influence of the natural landscape that surrounds them. This is apparent when we are given a description of one of the native Galway girls, Sava, via the hybrid narrative style of free indirect discourse in which third and first person narrative styles are mixed to give the impression that it is from the perspective of the Dublin girls that this view of Sava is emanating. 'Her [Sava's] hair is black, black as a river at night' (48): this image is not one which urban Dublin dwellers such as Orla and her friends would have had much first-hand experience of but their time in the ecology of rural Donegal has clearly impacted upon their minds' eyes already.

The chapter titles are often very ironic which evokes comparisons with those in the 'Aeolus' episode of *Ulysses*. They remind us that they emanate from an authorial mind that is looking back on a natural world that has undergone much change in the times between those described in the book and that of its publication. One stand-out example of this style is the following chapter title: 'The Truce is Over (But Not to Worry it's 1972)' (116). This chapter title clearly indicates to the reader that two dual temporalities, past and present, are in existence in the page of *The Dancers Dancing*. As is the case with the micro-sections in 'Aeolus', the chapter titles in Ní Dhuibhne's novel often have very little relation to the succeeding incidents that are described, which suggests that the ecological narrative that exists in the book can sometimes overpower and outdistance the powers of the human artists who wishes to represent this world.

One word place name that continually appears in the chapter title is 'The burn', this is a secluded, often deserted river in the Donegal Gaeltacht that Orla constantly visits in order that she might renew a sense of connection with both herself and nature. The natural world of the burn's influence on even the physical movements of Orla is made apparent in the following passage:

> Her feet keep going, however, as if they have a life of their own. They take longer and braver leaps, but they never miss. Even when she lands on a sharp pointed stone, or on a big round stone that wobbles terrifyingly, like a loose tooth, she remains upright. Her feet are sure and practised, they can cope much better than she would have given them credit for. (83)

It is as if Orla's body has become one with the ecology of the burn and it is enabling a sureness of foot that surprises her considering how unaccustomed she would be to traversing such terrain. As Declan Kiberd argues: 'It is here [in the burn], in the presence of the female divinity of the river, that much is resolved, so that the Euclid Theorems may be cast aside to make way for real dancers really dancing' (296). Thus, whilst much learning might be done in the classrooms of Donegal, it is only in its natural environs that true *Bildung* (personal, cultural, local and national) can take place.

Patricia Coughlan's consideration of *The Dancers Dancing* from the perspective of postmodern feminism makes the following ecocritical argument in relation to Orla's time in the burn:

> In exploring the burn, officially out of bounds, Orla finds a hidden place that fills her with completeness and peace: the flowing stream suggests ceaseless natural process. Behind a luxuriant screen of wild

> natural growth, she discovers a green tunnel and follows it beyond a little waterfall. All this symbolises Orla's interiority, specifically the mystery of her developing selfhood and her own strength, of which she has been unconscious. Along these hidden banks, she feels more intensely herself.[52]

Through her contact with the soil and water of the natural world, Orla's development into a fully formed, authentic female subject is enabled.

Susan Cahill has noted the connection between human body and landscape in *The Dancers Dancing*:

> Orla's reaction to her transformation experienced at the burn are generally described in physical terms. For instance, her body reacts in a profound way to the discovery of the skulls in the burn; she begins to menstruate. The moment before she discovers the skulls 'she begins to feel tired, and the damp greenness of the burn seems to be seeping into her stomach.[53]

Éilís Ní Dhuibhne has herself written about the symbolic importance of the river in the context of *The Dancers Dancing*: '[The river] is a symbol of life and a metaphor for eternity [...] The river is also a place of beauty and mystery: to me it seemed that anything could be hiding in there, in that little country. It represented the great potential of the world to yield astonishing treasures' (289). This passage is a perfect example of a human being contemplating from the outside the astonishing mysteriousness and power of the ecological phenomenon that are rivers.

Importantly, although the world of rural Donegal is evoked with an intimate immediacy and intimacy, Ní Dhuibhne still acknowledges that it is a world in decline and its past is about to make way, at least partially, for a more human-made space that privileges violence and division: 'The myth of the last is strong here. The last monoglot, the last Irish speaker, the last horse-drawn plough, the last fisherman. While people mourn the last of everything and have not accustomed themselves to observing the new firsts, the myth of the IRA, heroism, bravery, recklessness, lawlessness, sustains them' (82). That this natural world has now become at least a partial repository of a dead past is encapsulated by Orla's falling over the cluster of skulls during one of her visits to the burn.

The final chapter of the novel, titled 'Now', takes place in the present with Orla visiting Galway with her children and husband. Whilst on the beach she encounters Micheál, who she had met and had a brief relationship with as a young girl in Donegal. The site of him provokes a moment of involuntary memory that transports her back to the landscape of 1972 Donegal: 'I have not looked at him for years. But he is in my head, he is in my dreams, he is in my body, forever, along with Elizabeth, who died three years ago, and my father, who is in a home in Dalkey. Micheál is more active in my dreams than either of them, or than anyone else, perhaps because he featured in my reality for such a short time' (277). Orla's relationship with Micheál was enacted almost entirely in the burn and by remembering him she is also recapturing the time she spent in that ecological space and thus ensuring its survival in the circular temporality of her memory. It is ironic that the title of the chapter is 'Now' since its subject is as much 'Then' as 'Now'. In Orla's mind's eye, the past and the present converge in a form of natural, cyclical time.

Writing about the structure of *The Dancers Dancing*, Paige Reynolds made the following argument concerning the 'scene' chapters in the novel that are devoted to natural descriptions of the burn: 'These chapters, with their freeze-frame returns to the burn, interrupt the novel's overarching progressive narrative'.[54] These chapters insert a purely ecological narrative into *The Dancers Dancing*, which exists independently of the book's ongoing, human-centred story concerning the personal growth of Orla. Reynolds also recognises that *The Dancers Dancing* is set in an era before human-made tech had all but made the concept of privacy extinct. This means that Orla is allowed to experiment with various forms of privacy such as communing with nature free from the culture of surveillance that the anthropocentric realm of the VirtuReal has facilitated in recent decades.

Ní Dhuibhne herself, when writing about how she composed the beginning of *The Dancers Dancing* in rural Kerry, has described the natural world as having a temporality and pace that are different to those that one experiences in a human-made urban setting such as Dublin:

> In this place writing is not work – in Dublin, it can begin to be that, to be a chore. In the country, even if there is a deadline, and there

> often is, it is easy, it is play, it blends into the daily pattern, it is an essential component of that tapestry of walking, listening to music, swimming, cooking dinner. It is a part of life, and fun, as it should be. I often start my novels in this place, in the field of long grass, where ideas flow into my head without any effort on my part. (292)

By removing herself to this natural landscape of peace and slowness, Ní Dhuibhne is able to escape being tormented by what Beckett referred to in *Waiting for Godot* as 'accursed time' and to write at a leisurely pace that that she finds to be greatly conducive to creativity. Thus, ecological time can be viewed as the temporality of the artist.

In *The Dancer's Dancing*, Ní Dhuibhne celebrates the beginning of the end of the conflict in Northern Ireland by representing a mode of existence that transcends the brutality of human-made, anthropocentric life and offers a vision of a future to come in which humanity and ecology might potentially peacefully coexist. Thus, it is a work that is more oriented towards the future than to a nightmarish past. This is made clear in the final line of the novel: 'Since then, I have not seen him [Micheál]' (279). This sentence serves as a reminder that *The Dancers Dancing* was written in an unrepresented, as yet unrealised future that might be a better version of the past and present from which it sprang.

John McGahern's *That They May Face the Rising Sun* and *Memoir*

Martin Ryle has written an in-depth comparison between John McGahern's *That They May Face the Rising Sun* (2002) (his last novel) and *Memoir* (2005) explicitly through the lens of ecocriticism:

> Throughout Europe for some time now, the multiple crisis of 'the environment' has been moving the question of remembered, surviving, and threatened pleasures, in places at the edge of modernisation, to the centre of metropolitan consciousness. McGahern's last two books, through and beyond their scrupulous naturalism, give a compelling sense of remembered and still surviving landscape that embodies the cultural dream-memory of pastoral. If ever we made it central to the terms of our politics as well as of our aesthetics, this sense of what is being lost but could be saved 'might amount to a positive alternative'. Its evocation makes these last works as readable and as significant in

> a wider international context as in the local and national setting that all McGahern's fiction commemorates.[55]

John McGahern famously wrote about the importance of the creation of a dynamic relationship between physical reality and imaginative art:

> Art is an attempt to create a world in which we can live: if not for long or forever, still a world of the imagination over which we can reign, and by reign I mean to reflect purely on our situation through this created world of ours, this Medusa's mirror, allowing us to see and to celebrate even the totally intolerable.[56]

Art is seen by McGahern as the vehicle for the creation of alternative eco-systems that are both deriving and separate from those in the contemporary world of the Anthropocene.

It could be argued that an attempt at an ecocritical reading of the supposedly non-fictional *Memoir* is a mistaken endeavour because it is, by nature of its genre, supposed to be a prosaic recitation of events that occurred in real life and the style is therefore supposed to be realist rather than imaginative. However, as Eoin Flannery rightly contends:

> Though autobiography [and memoir] may be infused with the affective power of recalled events, place and people – all familiar and revisited – there are inescapable fictions braided into all efforts at historical veracity at the personal level. And this 'literary' trace of invention, this residue of artifice, is a matter of contention when we consider the relationship between autobiographical life-writing and an author's ecological vision.[57]

In other words, McGahern's *Memoir* can be read as his attempt to turn his life and world into an aesthetic zone via the use of literary devices.

The opening of *That They May Face* describes a world in which humanity and nature exist in something approaching harmony: 'The morning was clear. There was no wind on the lake. There was also a great stillness. When the bells rang for Mass, the strokes trembling on the water, they had the entire world to themselves'.[58] The reference to the 'entire world' in this quotation can be read as an implicit reference to the world of art in the previous citation and implies that the world by the lake is both physically real and imaginatively constructed.

In an interview with Eamon Maher in 2003, McGahern explicitly rejected the notion that there was always an inherent opposition in the relationship between humanity and nature:

> We are part of nature, like the animals and the trees, and we are all part of that passing world we learn to love and to leave. Naturally it is described with care and attention, as everything else should be, and it is also seen through a certain vision, maybe fallible and flawed, but mine or those of my characters.[59]

Both *That They May Face* and *Memoir* represent examples of McGahern's artistic project, which is aimed at creating, via art, a union between the natural and the human that can be read as acting as an escape from the anthropocentric world of reality.

Without directly invoking ecocriticism, Denis Sampson's reading of *That They May Face* suggests that the book is written in a style which represents the natural flowing of the seasons during the course of a year: 'The absence of plotting or chapter divisions, the lack of dramatic build-up, the transparency of narrative point of view, the emphasis on description and dialogue with minimal analysis, the presentation of character without interior monologue or development during the novel's timespan: in so many ways, McGahern's poetic narrative appears to discard many conventions of novelistic tradition and to simply present in an impersonal way a year in the life of a closed, rural community'.[60] Rather than adhering to the conventions of a linear, realist narrative, *That They Face* follows a cyclical, almost circular rhythm that reminds one of the repetitive flow of the seasons from one year to the next.

The importance of natural repetition to the world of this novel is also apparent in the following description of the auctioneer's voice at a cattle market: 'Once it started, the selling went very quickly. The auctioneer's voice took on the incantation of prayer; it was the rhythm and repetition that indicated its simple purpose more than any words or numbers' (234). The reader is again reminded that the natural rhythms and repetitions of existence are important constituent parts of this novel's style.

Similarly, Eoin Flannery has argued at length concerning the differing speeds and flows that exist in *Memoir*:

> As Jeremy Miller and Michael Schwart suggest: 'to possess speed is to be modern; to control speed rather than be controlled by it is perhaps the most important form of contemporary power'. Yet surely this is part of the action evident in *Memoir*, in, firstly, its ecological vision, and, secondly, in the generic form that the narrative assumes. The slow deliberation of the local news without concern for regional or national matters stands in juxtaposition to the incessant flow of irrelevant news and sound bytes. Likewise the formal 'reflexiveness' of the memoir as a variety of life writing and memory work, requires time, contemplation, and deceleration in order to compose itself and to engage with and avail of the retrieval of memories, and to allow the imagination to act upon these half remembrances, impressions, and clear-cut recollections. Thus, there is a circuit of literary form, individual remembrance, and geographical rootedness that combines to produce McGahern's ecological vision in *Memoir*.[61]

At the level of both content and style, *Memoir* allows for the speed of ecological and modern time to flow simultaneously through its pages.

The main character in *That They May Face*, Joe Ruttledge, is a strong believer in life following the slow pace of the natural world rather than being conscripted into the hurried temporality of modernity:

> As he [Ruttledge] listened to the two voices he was so attached to and thought back to the afternoon, the striking of the clocks, the easy pleasant company … he felt this must be happiness. As soon as the thought came to him he fought it back, blaming the whiskey … [H]appiness could not be sought or worried into being, or even fully grasped; it should be allowed its own slow pace so that it passes unnoticed, if it ever comes at all. (192)

The reference to the striking of the clocks creates a distinction between ordered, linear time and the pace of natural time in which Ruttledge believes that happiness should be allowed to exist.

Near the end of the book, there is an exchange between Ruttledge and the local IRA activist, Joe McKiernan, with McKiernan acknowledging that his life of inhumane, toxically masculine violence is actually at odds with the life of Ruttledge, which involves embracing the natural, the everyday, and a slow, non-linear focussed temporal existence. McKiernan feels himself and his outmoded approach to life to be almost outside of time:

> McKiernan took him [Ruttledge] by surprise by asking, 'You don't believe in our cause?' 'No', Ruttledge said. 'I don't like violence'. 'You don't believe in freedom then'? 'Our country is free'. 'A part of it is not free'. 'That is a matter for that other part. I don't think it is any of our business' … 'Do you have the time [said McKiernan]?' 'My time is plainly untrustworthy'. (302)

At this moment, McKiernan seems almost as much a fish out of water in the world by the lake as the character of Johnny, the returning immigrant who likes to view life as an ordered, modern existence in which everything worked entirely 'alphabetically' and whose funeral formed the backdrop to the encounter between Ruttledge and McKiernan. This funeral can also be read as symbolically representing the past world of linearity and modern order that both Johnny and the ruthlessly efficient terrorist McKiernan represented.

Similarly, *Memoir*, as its genre makes inevitable, foregrounds the process of remembrance as a way of breaking free from temporal linearity and embracing one of cyclicality and repetition. As the novelist Milan Kundera argues:

> There is a secret bond between slowness and memory, between speed and forgetting … In existential mathematics, that experience takes the form of two basic equations: the degree of slowness is directly proportional to the intensity of memory; the degree of speed is directly proportional to the degree of forgetting.[62]

The opening of *Memoir* brings together the themes of memory and slowness as McGahern recollects the morning routines he had as a child walking the lanes of Limerick:

> In good weather we always walked. There was a drinking pool for horses along the way, gates to houses, and the banks were covered with all kinds of wild flowers and vetches and wild strawberries. My mother named these flowers for me as we walked, and sometimes we stopped and picked them for jam jars.[63]

These slow, languid walks are idyllic but are also not unproductive. This means they do not stand outside the world of capitalist modernity, which dictates that life should consist of a series of productive activities.

That They May Face is somewhat unique in the literary oeuvre of John McGahern and in the human-made genre of the novel more generally, in that it allows a greater degree of happiness for its characters and the world they inhabit than is usual for the novelistic form. As Declan Kiberd observes:

> Novels, it is often said by those who remember their Tolstoy, can only be written about unhappy persons: the happy family seems proofed against any kind of narrative. Yet in this book McGahern sets himself the task of writing an interesting account of people who are almost all utterly at one with their world.[64]

The implication is that by allowing themselves to reach a harmonised relationship with the landscape in which they reside, these characters achieve a state of existence that could be said to approach grace.

If humanity is at one with nature in this novel, then it is also fair to say it enters into a kind of creative dynamic with the natural world also. When Joe Ruttledge is working on a new shed he notices something about the rafters reaching out to the sky: '[Look at] how the rafters frame the sky. How the squares of light are more interesting than the open sky. They make it look more human by reducing the sky, and then the whole sky grows out from that small space' (71). The image that Ruttledge conjures up by this word picture is of a landscape that is enriched rather than corrupted by the incorporation of human-made architecture.

However, McGahern is not so naive as to present this world by the lake as being completely immune from the negative interference of the technological modernity that constitutes the age of the Anthropocene. The image that suggests this interference most strongly is that of the telephone poles springing up around the lake and obstructing the natural, beautiful view: 'As they [Ruttledge and Jamesie] passed the new line of telephone poles, Jamesie counted them silently. "Fourteen in one day. In no time at all they'll be up"' (*RS*, 305). The natural world by the lake, as it is artistically represented in this work, may represent an improved living space in the age of the

Anthropocene but it is by no means completely immune from its more nefarious aspects.

In *Memoir*, McGahern also acknowledges the presence of human-made modernity in the natural world where he spent his childhood:

> We walked to Ollarton's with a can for milk. We wore coats, as the night had turned cold under a clear, pale moon. We passed Brady's pool where the horses drank … In the corner of the meadow below Brady's was a deep, dark quarry … An avenue of great trees led up to Ollarton's, and in front of the house was a small lake ringed with reeds, still and clear as a mirror, reflecting the pale moon. When we entered the yard behind the house, we could hear them milking, which they interrupted when they saw us waiting with our can in the doorway.[65]

In this passage, McGahern's memory's eye offers us an image of an anthropocentric landscape in which human-made technology is actively interacting with nature. Like James Whyte has argued concerning *That They May Face*, *Memoir* 'is as much about how we see and represent nature as it is about nature itself'.[66] In this respect, both *That They May Face* and *Memoir* can be interpreted as modern examples of Romantic literature in the manner of works by William Wordsworth such as the poems 'Tintern Abbey' and 'The Prelude'. These poems are deeply invested in the artistic vision that produces certain kinds of natural images rather than pretending that they are realistic, objective representation of natural landscapes.

That They May Face ends with a symbolic folding together of the human and the natural in a very powerful final image: 'At the porch, before entering the house, they [Joe and Kate] both turned to look back across the lake, even though they both knew that Mary and Jamesie had long since disappeared from the sky' (314). Although this moment only really signifies that Jamesie and Mary had walked out of view, the language that is used implies that they had disappeared, Christ-like into the natural realm of the eternal sky.

Derek Hand has argued that this book differs from traditional Irish novels in that it, for the most part, embraces the natural, universal world and identities associated with it and ignores the potentially treacherous obsessions with national specificity and difference: 'There are no stereotypes here, no representative types who embody national or political or historical currents, only the elusive complexities of people as they are – inconsistent and contradictory'.[67] For this reason, it is arguable that *That They May Face* represents a moment when the Irish novel reached a certain level of maturity and achieved an awakening from Joyce's nightmare of history by embracing the natural world of the pastoral.

Similarly, the concluding moments of *Memoir* loop back – in cyclical/seasonal fashion – to the beginning scene of the work in which McGahern and his mother are walking the lanes of Leitrim. What is acknowledged by ending the work in this way is that the two identities of McGahern – son and artist – that are expressed in this text are interlinked via his embeddedness in the landscape of Leitrim. As Denis Sampson argues: 'These overlapping experiences of returning to childhood places and experiences, in actuality, in memory, and in the writing of this book, are all given depth by the fact that his mother died here. While she was the most intimate image of arrested time, she was also the image of 'unrelenting change'.[68] In the same way, *Memoir* and *That They May Face* represent a timeless world of nature that also coexists with the changing world of linear modernity.

John McGahern had himself already expressed a love for representations of man at one with nature and landscape and escaping linear, temporal modernity when he wrote approvingly of Tomás Ó Criomhthain's memoir *An t'Oileanach* (*The Islandman*):

> I think that the strange sense of timelessness that the book has, of being outside time, comes from the day, a single day breaking continually over the scene and action … If the strong sense of the day, the endlessly recurring day, gives to the work its timeless quality, this is deepened still more by the fact that people and place seem to stand outside history. There is no sense of national pride. The distant rumblings of a new Ireland are brushed aside.[69]

The character of Jamesie in *That They May Face* expresses his belief that the rejection of modern, linear temporality, in favour of a more natural focus of cyclicality symbolised by living in the recurring rituality of 'the day' is actually quite an Irish instinct: 'The greatest country in Ireland was always the world to come […] And all we have is the day' (210). As is the case with living season by season, to live day by day is to embrace the eternal/recurring being folded into the specific/immediate that constitutes ecological, slow time.

In 2023, a brilliant film was made of *That They May Face*, which managed to render visual many of the literary effects and themes that are discussed above. The use of music in this film is highly effective, particularly in one moment near the end that involves the laying out of a body. Irene and Linda Buckley's original score permeates scenes and shots involving both natural and human-made environments and helps to create a pantheistic sense of a divinity invisibly existing because of the serene flow of worldly existence. The ultimate impression one takes away from this cinematic experience is that of having watched the work of a supremely humane artistic utiliser of medium of cinema.

Both *That They May Face* and *Memoir* utilise a post-Romanticism aesthetic to depict humanity's relationship with landscape and ecology. They suggest alternative ways of being in and with nature that are not solely reliant on human-made technologies and modern conceptions of temporality and speed. They testify to how, at the end of his career, John McGahern had come to terms with both his own traumatic past and also that of the human-made violence that constituted Ireland's nightmarish history. This history is very much bound up with the institutional abuses conducted by men in the Catholic Church – a faith that McGahern acknowledges near the end of *Memoir* (via the use of an ecological metaphor) as being as being integral to his sense of self: 'It [the Catholic Church] was the sacred weather of my early life, and I could no more turn against it than I could turn on any deep part of my own life' (222). Via the use of this ecocritical metaphor, McGahern acknowledges a calmness and sense of peace having being attained by himself in relation to his attitude towards his life and world around him.

The poetry of Paula Meehan

Paula Meehan's poetry has always been concerned with representing a liminal space that might be created between the world of nature and that of the Anthropocene. In an interview with Anne Karhio, Meehan made the following assertion concerning her view of spatiality:

> But I don't actually see the city and the human beings and non-human beings in the city as apart from nature. That nature ends where man-made material looms. I'm interested too in the liminal zones between the city and the countryside. Ireland is such an intensely worked landscape, to talk about wilderness in relation to Ireland becomes difficult, yet there are these extraordinary forests, and these extraordinary and vulnerable habitats on the edges of the cities and towns and suburbs, that have to negotiate with the urban development. But also within the city itself.[70]

For Meehan, humanity and nature, city and countryside, are entities that must exist together and part of her poetic project is the imagining and representing of such sites of compromise and communality. Meehan's poems merge form and content to express a profoundly *humane* concern with all aspects of existence and a refusal to prioritise one aspect of life over another.

In her poetry, Meehan also brings a gendered dimension to her representation of landscape, which gives her poetry the feel of ecocritical feminism. Meehan's poetic vision is partly a result of her admiration for the poetry of Eavan Boland. '[Both Eavan Boland] and Paula Meehan share a desire to tell women's stories, to redefine what it means to write the political poem, to find, as Boland notes in her poem "The Singers," a voice where they found a vision'.[71] Meehan writes about an even wider range of female figures, whether a poem becomes a prayer offered to an unknown woman walking home alone in 'Night Walk' or an homage to former Irish president Mary Robinson in 'She-Who-Walks-Among-The-People'.[72]

Rosi Braidotti has written about the hybrid theoretical discourse of Ecofeminism in the following terms:

> Ecofeminism raises the issue of the structural interconnections between the domination of women, natives and the domination of nature. This leads to a critique of patriarchal power in two specific forms: firstly, the idea of progress, modernization and development and, secondly, the dominant notions of science and technology. Both of them involve epistemic and physical violence over the structural 'others' and are related to the European Enlightenment ideal of 'reason'. This is a world view which equates mastery with rational scientific control over 'others'.[73]

Paula Meehan's poetry deconstructs grand narratives of the kind that Braidotti speaks of – narratives that render ecology, women and various other minority groups as second-class 'others'.

Pilar Vilar-Argaiz argues that

> Meehan's work acknowledges a pervading sense of rupture between past and present, ancestral knowledge and rational modernity. An important aspect of her poetry is to draw our attention towards the perils that a global world may present for cultural identities, by emphasizing the fragility of myth and local stories in danger of disappearing or being forgotten in modern times.[74]

For Meehan, modernity is symbolised by humanity and the human-made. The temporality of the pre-modern and the mythical is more ecological. Lucy Collins argues that 'While both the concentration of poetic language and its ability to express complex interior states makes it highly suited to investigations of identity politics, the lyric emphasis on the individual perspective engages with core issues of ecological debate in both subtle and intense ways'.[75]

The most demonstrably ecocritical of Meehan's poems is undoubtedly 'Death of a Field'. In this poem, Meehan laments the demise of a local field in order that a building site can be created: 'The field itself is lost the morning it becomes a site/ When the Notice goes up: Fingal County Council – 44 houses/ The memory of the field is lost with the loss of its herbs'.[76] This poem is a classic example of pastoral elegy in the tradition of Oliver Goldsmith's 'The Deserted Village' and Patrick Kavanagh's 'The Great Hunger'. Meehan is mourning not just the loss of a natural landscape but also the memories of times past that she feels are embedded in its soil:

> And the memory of the field disappears with its flora:
> Who can know the yearning of yarrow
> Or the plight of the scarlet pimpernel
> Whose true colour is orange? ...
> [...]
> The end of the field is the end as we know it is the start of the
> estate
> The site to be planted with houses each two or three bedroom
> Nest of sorrow and chemical, cargo of joy. (13)

Meehan attributes human feelings and emotions to the flora and fauna that existed in that field and which will now be totally erased in the name of human accommodation.

The poet describes the destruction of the field as intrinsically linked to the brutal rise of a human-made environment that is represented in this poem – human-created products that will fill the house that will be built where the field once existed: 'The end of dandelion is the start of Flash/ The end of dock is the start of Pledge/ The end of teazel is the start of Ariel/ The end of primrose is the start of Brillo/ The end of thistle is the start of Bounce' (14).

In 'Death of a Field', Meehan's poetic voice expresses a desire to bear witness to the partial death of the natural world as symbolised by the destruction of the field: 'That – before the field becomes solely map memory/ In some archive of some architect's screen/ I might possess it or it possess me/ Through its night dew, its moon white caul/ Its slick and shine and its profligacy/ In every wingbeat in every beat of time' (14). Although the field may no longer exist, the poem in which it is elegised will endure and thus act as a guarantor of the field's immortality. The world of art is thus figured as one in which the ecological and the anthropocentric can to some extent coexist.

Meehan's poetry also performs a demythologising function through which female identity is connected with a non-anthropocentric, ecological existence. This is apparent in the poem 'Not Your Muse': 'I'm not your muse, not that creature, in the painting, with the beautiful body/ Venus on the half-shell. Can you not see I'm an ordinary woman/ tied to the moon's phases, bloody six days in twenty-eight? Sure'. This woman does not belong in the idealising realm of human representation, she is a real person whose existence is tied to the natural cycles of moon.

'Not Your Muse' also exhibits a realism concerning the prevailing power of patriarchal mythmaking which this poetic voice is content to leave undisturbed: 'But if it keeps you happy who am I to charge into battle dressed to force you test your painted doll against the harsh light, I live by, against a brutal merciless sky'. In this poem, patriarchal anthropocentrism is portrayed as fragile and in need of protection from the harsh realities of the natural world with which the female poet feels a connection.

Du Jun has correctly described the importance of Meehan's poetry to the literary style of feminist ecopoetics:

> A salient feature of our anthropocentric age is that nonhuman lives are not recognized – they are regarded as 'ungrievable' or less grievable [to quote Judith Butler] – and public grieving for their loss is implicitly prohibited. In this context, Meehan's public mourning of ecological loss in her poetry resists the normalized unrecognition and ungrievability of other-than-human lives. The exploration and negotiation of the relationship between humans and nonhumans have also been an important dimension of Meehan's artistry; she subtly integrates a quest for the interrelationship between human and nonhuman beings into the process of open mourning of ecological loss.[77]

Paula Meehan's poetry is deeply engaged with the genre of ecocritical poetry. It critiques patriarchal anthropocentrism and its tendency to craft totalising narratives of progress that render the natural world and femininity as secondary to the primary concerns of human-made modernity and its notions of what constitutes 'progress'. Her work represents a profound examination of our current, Butlerian world of 'shared precarity', which is also one of the great achievements of ecocriticism more generally.

Study questions

1. **What is the Anthropocene?**
2. **Why has ecocriticism generally, and Irish ecocriticism specifically, developed in the historical moment that it has?**
3. **How can ecocriticism be productively connected to other theoretical disciplines?**
4. **How has Ireland's colonial past influenced its relationship with nature and landscape?**
5. **What is the relationship between ecocriticism and activism?**
6. **How can ecocriticism offer insight into the relationship between the human and the non-human?**
7. **How is the relationship between humanity and nature problematic and potentially hostile in essence?**

Notes

1 See 2024 Annual Edmund Burke Lecture | Fintan O'Toole, 26 November, 2024, https://www.youtube.com/watch?v=UMqVplXzQeU (accessed 15 June, 2025).
2 Paul J. Crutzen and Eugene Stoermer, 'The Anthropocene', *International Geosphere-Biosphere Programme Newsletter* (2000), np.
3 Eoin Flannery, *Ireland and Ecocriticism: Literature, History, and Environmental* Justice (New York: Routledge, 2016), p. 9.
4 Manuel DeLanda, 'Deleuze and the Open-Ended Becoming of the World', *Dialogues*, np.
5 Claire Bracken, 'Queer Intersections and Nomadic Routes: Anne Enright's "The Pleasure of Eliza Lynch"', *The Canadian Journal of Irish Studies* 36:1 (2010), p. 124n.
6 Gilles Deleuze, *Difference and Repetition*, trans. Paul Patton (London, New Delhi, and New York: Bloomsbury, 1994), p. 378.
7 See Judith Butler, *Precarious Life: The Powers of Mourning and Violence* (London and New York: Verso Books, 2006).
8 Gilles Deleuze, *Difference and Repetition* (London: Continuum, 2004), p. 96.
9 For a fuller consideration of Gilles Deleuze and ecocriticism in relation to Irish Studies, see Graham Price, '"Accursed Time": Gilles Deleuze's *Difference and Repetition* and John McGahern's *That They May Face the Rising Sun*', *Etudes Irlandaises*, 44–2 (2019), pp. 95–111.
10 Gilles Deleuze, *Foucault* (Minneapolis: University of Minnesota Press, 1988), p. 98.
11 See Peter Barry, *Beginning Theory: An Introduction to Literary and Cultural Theory*, third edition (Manchester: Manchester University Press, 2009), p. 40.
12 Eoin Flannery, *Ireland and Ecocriticism* (London: Routledge, 2015), p. 23.
13 Jonathan Bate, *The Song of the Earth* (Cambridge, MA: Harvard University Press, 2000), p. 42.
14 Ibid., pp. 75–76.
15 Timothy Clarke, 'Scale: Derangements of Scale', in Tom Cohen (ed.), *Telemorphosis: Theory in the Era of Climate Change* (Ann Arbor, MI: Open Humanities Press/University of Michigan Library, 2012), pp. 150, 156.
16 Oscar Wilde, *Lady Windermere's Fan*, in *Collins Complete Works of Oscar Wilde*, ed. Merlin Holland, fifth edition (Glasgow: HarperCollins, 2003), p. 457.

17 Sean Hewitt, 'Emily Lawless, Natural History, and the Possibilities of Enchantment', *Irish University Review* 54:2 (Autumn/Winter 2024), p. 229.
18 Lucy Collins, 'The Frosty Winters of Ireland: Poems of Climate Crisis 1739–41', *Journal of Ecocriticism* 5:2 (2014), p. 11.
19 Oona Frawley, *Irish Pastoral: Nostalgia and Twentieth-Century Irish Literature* (Dublin: Irish Academic Press, 2005), p. 1.
20 Quoted in ibid, p. 2.
21 For an extended version of this ecocritical-adjacent analysis of Heaney, see Fintan O'Toole's lecture 'Political Heaney', which was delivered at Boston College in November 2023, https://www.youtube.com/watch?v=YL7kTjtohHQ (accessed 15 June, 2025).
22 Derek Mahon, 'A Disused Shed in Country Wexford', *Selected Poems* (London: Faber & Faber, 2016), p. 34.
23 Ibid., p. 35.
24 Lucy Collins, '"A Disused Shed in Co Wexford", Derek Mahon', *Irish University Review* 39:2 (2009), p. 263.
25 Ibid.
26 James McElroy, 'Eco-Criticism and Derek Mahon's "A Disused Shed in County Wexford"', Studies*: An Irish Quarterly Review* 107:426 (2018), p. 222.
27 Flannery, *Ireland and Ecocriticism*, pp. 2–3.
28 John Brannigan, *Archipelagic Modernism: Literature in the Irish and British Isles, 1890–1970* (Edinburgh: Edinburgh University Press, 2014), p. 9.
29 Ibid.
30 Ibid., p. 46.
31 Samuel Beckett, *Endgame* (London: Faber and Faber, 1958), p. 51.
32 Ibid., p. 253.
33 Ibid., p. 252.
34 https://www.theguardian.com/books/2020/apr/27/tim-robinson-obituary (accessed 18 June, 2025).
35 Katherine O'Callaghan, 'Solastalgic Modernism and the West in Irish Literature, 1900–1950', in Malcolm Sen (ed.), *A History of Irish Literature and the Environment* (Cambridge: Cambridge University Press, 2022), p. 159. Emphasis in original.
36 Ibid., p. 152.
37 Malcolm Sen, '"Dragon-Ridden" Days: Yeats, Apocalypse, and the Anthropocene', *International Yeats Studies* 4:1 (2022), p. 122.
38 Sharae Deckard, 'Ecogothic', in Maisha Wester and Xavier Aldana Reyes (eds), *Twenty-First Century Gothic: An Edinburgh Companion* (Edinburgh: Edinburgh University Press, 2019), p. 174.
39 Ibid.

40 Eoin Flannery, 'Ecology, Time, and Scale in *That They May Face the Rising Sun* and *Memoir*, in Derek Hand and Eamon Maher (eds), *Essays on John McGahern: Assessing a Literary Legacy* (Cork: Cork University Press, 2019), p. 111.

41 Much of this section of the chapter draws heavily on the 'What Ecocritics Do' section of Peter Barry's *Beginning Theory*, third edition (Manchester: Manchester University Press, 2009), pp. 254–255. This is especially the case with regards to point five.

42 Hewitt, 'Emily Lawless and Natural History', p. 244.

43 Emily Lawless, 'A Note on the Ethics of Literary Forgery', *The Nineteenth Century* (January 1897), pp. 91–92.

44 Hewitt, 'Emily Lawless and Natural History', p. 240.

45 Emily Lawless, 'North Clare – Leaves from a Diary', *The Nineteenth Century*, 36:272 (2015), p. 603.

46 Emily Lawless, 'Famine Roads and Famine Monuments', in Declan Kiberd and P.J. Mathews (eds), *A Handbook of the Irish Revival: An Anthology of Irish Cultural and Political Writings* (Dublin: Abbey Theatre Press, 2015), p. 37.

47 O'Callaghan, 'Solastalgic Modernism', pp. 157–158.

48 Quoted in ibid., p. 158.

49 Lawless, 'Famine Roads and Famine Monuments', p. 37.

50 Margaret Kelleher, *The Feminization of Famine: Expressions of the Inexpressible* (Cork: Cork University Press, 1997), p. 114.

51 Éilís Ní Dhuibhne, *The Dancers Dancing* (Belfast: Blackstaff Press, 2010), p. 186. All future references refer parenthetically to this edition

52 Patricia Coughlan, 'Irish Literature and Postmodernity', *Hungarian Journal of English and American Studies (HJEAS)* 10:1/2 (2004), p. 191.

53 Susan Cahill, *Irish Literature in the Celtic Tiger Years, 1990–2008: Gender, Bodies, Memory* (London: Continuum, 2011), p. 52.

54 Paige Reynolds, *Modernism in Irish Women's Contemporary Writing: The Stubborn Mode* (Oxford: Oxford University Press, 2024), p. 138.

55 Martin Ryle, 'John McGahern: Memory, Autobiography, Fiction, History', *New Formations* (2009), p. 45.

56 John McGahern, 'The Image', *Canadian Journal of Irish Studies* (July 1991), p. 12; previously published as 'The Image: Prologue to a Reading at the Rockefeller University', *Honest Ulsterman*, 8 (1968), p. 10.

57 Eoin Flannery, 'Ecology, Memory, and Speed in John McGahern's *Memoir*, *Irish University Review* 42:2 (2012), p. 274.

58 John McGahern, *That They May Face the Rising Sun* (London: Faber & Faber, 2003), p. 3. All future references refer parenthetically to this edition.

59 Quoted in ibid., p. 276.

60 Denis Sampson, '"Open to the World": A Reading of John McGahern's *That They May Face the Rising Sun*', *Irish University Review* 35:1 (2005), p. 136.
61 Flannery, 'Ecology, Memory, and Speed in John McGahern's *Memoir*'.
62 Quoted in Flannery, p. 281.
63 John McGahern, *Memoir* (London: Faber, 2005), p. 1.
64 Declan Kiberd, 'Fallen Nobility: The World of John McGahern', *Irish University Review* 35:1 (2005), p. 171.
65 McGahern, *Memoir*, p. 71.
66 James Whyte, 'The Nature of Imaginative Sympathy', in John Kenny (ed.), *The John McGahern Yearbook 1* (Galway: NUI Galway, 2008), p. 35.
67 Derek Hand, *A History of the Irish Novel* (Oxford: Oxford University Press, 2011), p. 289.
68 Denis Sampson, 'The "Sacred Weather" of County Leitrim: John McGahern's "Memoir", *The Irish Review* 36/37 (2007), p. 121.
69 John McGahern, '*An tOileanach/ The Islandman*', *Canadian Journal of Irish Studies* 13:1 (June 1987), p. 9.
70 Anne Karhio and Paula Meehan. '"Imagined Domains": A Conversation with Paula Meehan', *Nordic Irish Studies* 8 (2009), p. 75.
71 Batten Guinn, 'Eavan Boland, History and Silence', in A. Darcy and D. Wheatley (eds), *A History of Irish Women's Poetry* (Cambridge: Cambridge University Press, 2021), p. 360.
72 Eileen O'Halloran, Kelli Maloy and Paula Meehan, 'An Interview with Paula Meehan', *Contemporary Literature* 43:1 (2002), p. 3.
73 Rosi Braidotti, *Transpositions: On Nomadic Ethics* (Cambridge: Polity Press, 2006), p. 112. This quote is examined in greater detail in Flannery, *Ireland and Ecocriticism*, p. 59.
74 Pilar Vilar Argaiz, 'The Enchantment of Myth in Paula Meehan's Poetry', *Journal of Irish Studies* 24 (2009), p. 91.
75 Lucy Collins, 'Clearing the Air: Irish Women Poets and Environmental Change', in John Strachan and Alison O'Malley-Younger (eds), *Ireland: Revolution and Evolution* (Bern: Peter Lang, 2009), p. 196.
76 Paula Meehan, 'Death of a Field', in *Painting Rain* (Manchester: Carcanet, 2009), p. 13.
77 Du Jun, '"A Stern Language of Beauty": Ecological Grief and Ecofeminist Ethics in Paula Meehan's Poetry', *Contemporary Women's Writing* 16:1 (March 2022), p. 99.

Coda: waiting for the 'Irish Studies to come'[1]

This Coda considers the possible futures that might one day take shape for the discipline of Irish Studies. Taking as a starting point the Derridean concept of the *avenir* (the 'to come'), the chapter considers what intersectional Irish Studies futures might align to create an 'Irish Studies to come'. Such a future will not be prescriptively utopian but will, rather, be desirable due to its undecidability and democratic openness to various Others: Multicultural Others, Traveller Others, Queer Others, and as yet unknown Others. Works of literary and cultural analysis will be mined for their insights into some of these potential futures to determine what forms of theoretical hospitality are needed to fully embrace these encounters with new forms of Irishness and Irish Studies. Some of these may already exist and may merely need the correct critical vocabulary to appreciate them and bring them to proper fruition.

The recently published volume *New Irish Studies* (2019) edited by Paige Reyolds will provide useful signposts for the futural quality of Irish Studies in the twenty-first century. Equally, the theoretical concept of transnationalism shall be considered as offering valuable and as yet not totally tapped potentialities for an Irish Studies to come. The literary text chosen for representative textual analysis in this chapter is Melatu Uche Okorie's *This Hostel Life*. The reasons for including this collection of short stories in the consideration of an as yet not fully realised Irish Studies to come are as follows:

1. They offer a vision of new versions of Irishness that have not yet fully come into being but whose potential exists in a somewhat embryonic form at the level of literature and culture.

2. The stories resist assimilationist and totalising versions of multiculturalist Irishness and instead offer the as yet unrealised potential for a trans-nationalist Irishness/Irish Studies is to come. The open-ended attitude that these stories display towards futurity means that they resist, to some extent, the danger of seeming dated to readers of various kinds in the foreseeable future.
3. The fact that these stories end, like many of those stories in Joyce's *Dubliners*, with a sense of goals unachieved, means they remind their readers that the project of a Roguish Irish Studies to come still has a long way to go before it reaches completion. They also allow for a sense of a future that is open-ended and may yet result in failure. Thus, they resist the programmatic tendencies of some utopic, future-oriented texts. Arguably, a Roguish Irish Studies to come should also strive to avoid these utopian, simplistic urges.

Democratic, undecidable futurity

In chapter forty-one of his history-memoir, *We Don't Know Ourselves* (2021), Fintan O'Toole argues that one of the negative aspects of the Celtic Tiger era of Irish History (spanning the mid-1990s until approximately the late noughties) was its total disavowal of futurity. History had officially ended in the minds of many of the business people and politicians who drove the Tiger economy, and the state of affairs that existed at that time would continue unchanged in perpetuity. O'Toole asserts that one word which was off limits at that time, if it was used as part of a question, was 'sustainability'. Whether it was at all sustainable for Ireland to live in a continuous Celtic Tiger present was only contemplated by a few select people – those who the then Taoiseach Bertie Ahern regarded as being so depressed it was a wonder 'they did not commit suicide'.[2]

In the conclusion to *We Don't Know Ourselves*, O'Toole argues for an Irish futurity that will be open and therefore radically democratic. He invokes the poet John Keats' concept of 'negative capability', which means that uncertainty and undecidability can lead to creativity by virtue of the fact that one is contemplating something – whether that be a country, a future, or an art object – that is not fully known and therefore not closed off in advance of our being faced with that something. Approaching the 'Ireland to come' in this way could lead to the creation of a nation that is positively 'weak' because it refuses to define itself totally and therefore is leaving itself open to various forms of otherness, whether that be racially, sexed, gendered or an as yet unanticipated form of otherness. This would be taking heed of Oscar Wilde's aphorism, 'To define is to limit'. Thinking about Ireland as being yet 'to come', as will be argued presently, would also lead to the thinking of an 'Irish Studies to come'. Like Godot, its ultimate arrival is always deferred and therein can lie its radically democratic potential.

Seamus Heaney's poem, 'Clearances', can be interpreted as being a metaphor for the contemplation of negative capability:

> The space we stood around had been emptied
> Into us to keep, it penetrated
> Clearances that suddenly stood open.
> High cries were felled and a pure change happened. [3]

Words such as 'emptied', 'open' and 'pure change' suggest that Heaney is challenging his readers to take responsibility for this undefined, cleared space and ensure that it remains open, part of us, and used to facilitate change that is real rather than essentially an imitation of what existed before. Arguably, what 'Clearances' is representing is akin to what Walter Benjamin called a 'weak messianism', a concept that promotes the notion of a 'mystical stranger – the Weak Messiah – who may break open the continuum of history at any time: what Benjamin calls the irruption of a mystical "now"'.[4] 'Clearances' asks that we remain open to those events that disrupt temporality and tradition and restore an openness to things and people that existed prior to their concretisation. To be open to that which is to come can be described as a quasi-religious experience, what Oscar Wilde called in 'De Profundis' the 'confraternity of the faithless'.[5] That openness, I would argue, is what can lead to an Irish Studies to come, the work on which will never be totally finished and which will never be wholly defined, yet it is that undecidability and negative capability at its core that can lead to its radicalism.

Although O'Toole does not invoke Jacques Derrida in the concluding section of his book when he suggests that Ireland's future should lie in incompleteness and uncertainty, what he is advocating does certainly echo Derrida's conception of the *avenir* ('to come') as being the ideal way of conceiving of institutions and events such as democracy or 'the University'. In one of the significant texts from Derrida's later period, *Rogues*, he proposes the 'to come' as an unanticipatable event that cannot be known or planned for in advance:

> If an event worthy of this name is to arrive or happen, it must, beyond all mastery, affect a passivity. It must touch an exposed vulnerability, one without absolute immunity, without indemnity; it must touch this vulnerability in its finitude and in a non-horizontal fashion, there where it is not yet or is already no longer possible to face or face up to the unforeseeability of The Other. In this regard, autoimmunity is not an absolute ill or evil. It enables an exposure to the other, to what and to who comes –which means that it must remain incalculable.[6]

When democratic elections in Algeria were suspended in 1992 due to the fear of an Islamic fundamentalist government being elected, Derrida greeted the news with jubilation. For Derrida, democracy must always be deferred, must always be *avenir*, if it is not to be perverted and corrupted by human forces as was often the case when communist leaders gained power in countries such as Russia and Cambodia.

For this reason, Derrida did not like using the word 'programme' when it came to talking about revolutions to come:

> I would hesitate to use the word 'program' [...] it implies a knowledge of norms, a pre-established authority that, using this knowledge, would dictate the decisions and the responsibilities (thus annulling them in advance and in the same gesture). There is a necessity for programs, for the secondary effects of programs, for a programmatic economy and strategy, but in the first or last instance, what is to be done is invented or inaugurated, and therefore it comes about without a program.[7]

The role of surprise and undecidability in relation to creating radical and revolutionary futures to come is something that Derrida championed for a large part of his philosophical career.

However, Derrida does acknowledge that events such as democracy cannot be put off indefinitely: 'in the necessarily finite time of politics and thus of democracy, the democracy to come certainly does not mean the right to defer, even if it be in the name of some regulative

Idea, the experience or even less the injunction of democracy'.[8] Derrida's philosophy is thus one of realism even if it does sometimes sound unrealistically utopian. He does acknowledge the political realities of the world in which we live even as he tries to think them into an improved version.

Derrida's friend and fellow philosopher, Jean Luc Nancy, also spoke of the need to think of the *avenir* in terms of the discipline of philosophy: 'Of course: philosophizing always turns itself towards the "to-come" (*avenir*) of philosophy. But this coming is not exactly the future. A future is predictable, calculable, appreciable, or imaginable. A "coming" is incalculable and inappreciable. In a sense, philosophy, is always, in essence, "to-come"'.[9]

Michael O'Rourke's valuable theoretical work has made important connections to the Derridean *avenir* and what O'Rourke calls a 'queer theory to come':

> This unconditionally hospitable queer theory to-come inhabits the time of the promise, the weak force of the perhaps, the what if (another world were possible?). But, a queer theory premised on a kind of irreligious faith in the justice to-come, always marked by its own contestability and resignification, an unforeclosable, khoral deontology, all according to Butler in 'Critically Queer', must itself relentlessly be queered.[10]

According to O'Rourke, Derridean figures such as 'the Rogue', 'the *monstrous arrivant*', and 'the spectre' are the encapsulation of the disruptive 'queer' presences that are championed by both Judith Butler and Eve Kosofsky Sedgwick. O'Rourke's vision of a 'becoming Derridean' queer theory couches itself in the language of spectral futurity and envisages an undecidable queer theory to come. Judith Butler, in their engagement with Chantelle Mouffe and Ernest Laclau's conceptualisation of 'the radical democracy to come' has argued for a similar vision of the 'queer theory to come'.[11] It is my contention that the idea which Butler and O'Rourke have for the future of queer theory is equally desirable for the 'Irish Studies to come'.

O'Rourke describes what he feels the 'Roguish queer theory to come' might conceivably look like. This is a vision that, I would argue, is highly desirable for the 'weak Irish Studies to come': 'A roguish, unconditionally hospitable, weak queer studies would open up its borders, render itself porous (this would involve of course an openness to other languages and a critique of the sovereignty of any given language, of English as the lingua franca of Queer studies)'.[12] In a time when Ireland is becoming a very multicultural, multiracial and transnational country as a result of rising migration, an Irish Studies that is hospitable to the various kinds of otherness that Michael O'Rourke mentioned is extremely important.

Roguish Irish Studies

Irish Studies has always been willing to adapt to broadening conceptualisations of Irishness(es). A notable example of this occurred in 1997 when the International Association for the Study of Anglo-Irish Literature changed its name to the International Association for the Study of Irish Literature. This was done so that the organisation could be said to reflect the varying interests and diversity of its members. A year before this occurred, in the concluding passage of *Inventing Ireland*, Declan Kiberd wrote an impassioned plea for a conception of an ethical Ireland and Irish Studies that is now probably more relevant and urgent than when he wrote these words in the late 1990s:

> If the notion of 'Ireland' seemed to some to have become problematic that was only because the seamless garment once wrapped like a green flag around Cathleen ni Houlihan had given way to a quilt of many patches and colours, all beautiful, all distinct, yet all connected too. No one element should subordinate or assimilate the others: Irish or English, rural or urban, Gaelic or Anglo, each has its part in the pattern.[13]

It is now the case that there are many more versions of identity that can be claimed to be a part of 'Irishness' than were listed above by Kiberd. People that are both distinct and yet should also be considered as being distinctly Irish. Baruch Spinoza once asserted that the divine could be most clearly identified in the individual. I would argue that the divine in Irish Studies manifests itself in those who are clearly individualistic but who also are connected to bigger communities – the first person singular encountering the first person plural, in essence.

In the introduction to her timely collection of essays, *The New Irish Studies*, Paige Reynolds argues that contemporary Irish writing is enabling what Derrida and O'Rourke would call a 'Roguish Irish Studies': 'Contemporary Irish writing strips us of our knowing authority, unsettling us, even as it reminds us of certain familiar and elemental aspects of life, ones that might be lost in the rush and distraction of the present moment'.[14] Eamon Maher has said of this collection: 'Readers of *The New Irish Studies* are alerted to avoid falling into the trap of inattention. For example, we are reminded that the terms "Irish writer" and "Irish literature"', once linked to the author's nationality or the setting of the work, are now moving targets that reflect the durability and adaptability of Irish writing in the present moment'. Long-accepted canons are being challenged by emerging voices, be they writers, literary critics, or other interested parties'.[15] The 'weak Irish studies to come' is certainly shown to be in good hands in the various texts (literary and academic) that have emerged in the twenty-first century. The democratic grammatical tool that is the quotation mark is becoming more in vogue now than ever (as evidenced by its constant usage in this text by the author and those who are quoted).

The New Irish Studies collection has done the discipline an invaluable service by showing how Irish literature, drama and film are roguishly opening up Irish Studies and Irishness in general to an incalculably undecidable world of permanent contestation. It can only be a matter of time before a similar volume emerges that demonstrates the same for works of Irish historical, political and cultural criticism.

The 'Irish Studies to come' is beginning to demonstrate a strong epiphanic quality because it sometimes involves retrieving past potentials and actualising them in a future moment. In his study *Anatheism: Returning to God after God*, Richard Kearney treats moments of epiphany thus: 'In repeating a past moment, epiphany gives a future to the past. It somehow transubstantiates the empirical thisness of a particular lived event onto something sacred and eschatological'.[16] Kearney argues that the final moments of *Ulysses*, which involve Molly Bloom remembering the moment she emphatically said 'Yes' she would marry Leopold Bloom, is filled with an epiphanic charge:

> Molly's final cry blends and balances past and future tenses in a typically kairological way – 'I *said* yes I *will* yes'. As she lies in her bed in Eccles Street with Bloom curled by her side, her scatological memories of all-too human eros are repeated forward to the rhythm of eschatological time. I said. I will. Yes. Word becomes flesh as flesh becomes word. The secular and sacramental traverse each other.[17]

An epiphanic Irish Studies returns to its past and seek for as yet unknown potential from well-known historical, literary and cultural texts. The past need not dictate what Irish Studies is, but it can be productively part of the incalculable future that awaits the discipline. O'Rourke makes a similar point when he argues for what we could term an 'epiphanic queer theory to come': 'I am saying that queer theory needs to reactivate or return to its past [...] in order to open up its virtual, potential future or to, as Deleuze would say, actualize the absolutely new, to tap into what Bernard Stiegler might call its "tertiary memory"'.[18]

The 2025 Abbey Theatre production of Mary Manning's *Youth's the Season-?* enacted a moment of retrospective recovery by explicitly staging what was only implicit in the play's first production in 1931 – an openly gay male interacting with someone who is probably his same-sex romantic partner. If the play had been performed back then the way it was in 2025 it would have been the first Irish drama to stage a gay man and a homosexual partnership. The history of Irish drama states that the first gay character appeared in Thomas Kilroy's *The Death and Resurrection of Mr Roche* (1966) and the first gay couple in Brian Friel's *The Gentle Island* (1972). This is an example of how those who wish to create an 'Irish Studies to come' can reactivate the energies from the past and use them to animate the democratically undecidable future for Ireland and Irish Studies that will happily embrace all forms of otherness.

Audiences at the time of the first production were well aware of the queerness of the characters in *Youth's the Season-?* In Dublin this remained largely unmentionable while in London, critics responded with distaste at the characters' 'unnatural' inclinations. What has mainly changed is our willingness to embrace and even celebrate the gayness, which then of course also changes how it is portrayed on stage.

Another term that could be productively applied to a Roguish Irish Studies to come is 'plastic'. Catherine Malabou, the foremost theoriser of plastic/plasticity, defines this philosophical concept thus. Plasticity denotes both the capacity to 'take form (as in the plasticity of clay) and to give form (as in the plastic arts and plastic surgery)'.[19] Malabou also acknowledges plasticity's power to destroy form. In Malabou's 1996 study *The Future of Hegel: Plasticity, Temporality, Dialectic* (a book that grew out of her PhD thesis, which she did under Derrida's supervision and a book for which he wrote the preface), Malabou argues that, for the nineteenth-century philosopher Georg Wilhelm Hegel, the future was not something to be thought of as moments in time but, rather, as something that is endlessly malleable, re-inscribable and reinterpretable – in short, perpetually plastic.[20] It is in terms of plasticity that the roguish future for Irish Studies can certainly be conceptualised.

A memorable description of what Derrida would call messianic time and Malabou would term temporal plasticity is to be found in Colum McCann's *Let the Great World Spin* (2009):

> I know that I will return to this day whenever I want to. I can bid it alive. Preserve it. There is a still a point where the present, the now, winds around itself, and nothing is tangled. The river is not where it begins or ends, *but right in the middle point, anchored by what has happened and what is to arrive* [my italics]. You can close your eyes and there will be a light snow falling in New York, and seconds later you are sunning upon a rock in Zacapa, and seconds later still you are surfing through the Bronx on the strength of your own desire. There is no way to find a word to fit around this feeling. Words resist it. Words give it a pattern it does not own. Words put it in time. They freeze what cannot be stopped.[21]

These words, which are being thought by one character in the novel, neatly encapsulate the work's representation of temporality and how the various individuals in the text experience time. Equally, the text can be used as a blueprint for the temporality of the Roguish Irish Studies to come – an Irish Studies of 'the middle' for which past, present and futures exist simultaneously and in mutual dependence.

The 'transnational turn' in Irish Studies is becoming a valuable route that the Irish Studies to come can take, and its further development can only further add to the Roguish future of Irish Studies As has been written in the abstract for the volume of essays *Transnationalism in Irish Literature and Culture* (2024), which appears on the book cover: 'Nation and territory have long been central to cultural production in Ireland, especially as both remain significantly contested, but a continued focus on these inherited scales has hindered critical attention to transnational routes and roots that exist alongside and challenge the nation'. The volume offers a wide-ranging number of essays from a diverse group of leading Irish Studies academics, which examine the works of Irish writers such as Maria Edgeworth and James Joyce from a transnationalist rather than a nationalist perspective. They also examine some of the future directions that transnational Irish Studies could take, allowing the collection to take both a backward and a forward look in relation to this as yet incalculable methodology.

The editor of *Transnationalism in Irish Literature and Culture*, Cóilín Parsons, has written in the introduction to the volume that Irish Studies must embrace a 'weak transnationalism', a phrase that clearly echoes the theory of weak messianism proposed by Benjamin and the weak theory advocated by Derrida, Butler and O'Rourke. Parsons writes:

> One way to 'depart from the national paradigm' [in Irish Studies] would be to start with the fact of the rapid expansion in the movement of goods and services across the world that we call 'globalization,' along with the migrations of people and transformations of culture that go along with it. The future study of Irish literature and culture will necessarily involve the interrogation of the continued relevance of something called 'Ireland' in the face of such global and planetary challenges as financialization and economic crisis, widespread and increasing unsettlement of millions of people within and beyond the borders of their places of origin, and climate collapse.[22]

The Irish Studies to come, according to Parsons, is one that by necessity will be continually open to contestation and renegotiation.

Parsons is by no means dismissive of postcolonial theory, which is arguably the dominant theoretical paradigm in Irish Studies (especially in the latter part of the twentieth century). However, he is willing to acknowledge its shortcomings and accept a need for a more open direction for Irish Studies going forward:

> To its advocates, including me, postcolonial studies promised an *engagé* articulation of a relationship between Ireland and the world, and between nation and the transnational. It rapidly became the default theoretical position for thinking about Irish literature and culture in transnational terms, offering a ready-made set of comparators for Irish culture throughout the colonial world. At the same time, Irish postcolonial studies was often marked by a paradoxical exceptionalism, given its turn to the centrality of the nation and the exemplarity of the Irish experience. It borrowed paradigms from elsewhere that in the end often served to bolster the special status of Ireland, a move seen in Declan Kiberd's influential *Inventing Ireland*, for example, or in the ways that a phrase by Luke Gibbons that was in its time revelatory (and controversial) was taken up by other critics: 'Ireland is a first-world country, but with a third-world memory'. In this early work, the question of Ireland's place in the global economy of racial violence was frequently overlooked in favor of a forced equivalence with other sites of colonization (though there were notable exceptions, especially in the work of David Lloyd).[23]

Whilst it can be argued (as in Chapter 3 on postcolonial Ireland above), that the work of Irish postcolonial theorists, including Kiberd and Gibbons, has endeavoured to avoid the trap of arguing for Irish exceptionalism, it is certainly the case that transnationalism offers a way for Irish Studies to avoid the worst excesses of cultural and political nationalism.

Another theoretical and activist movement that is becoming increasingly used in Irish Studies is intersectionalism. Kimberlé Crenshaw theorises 'intersectionalism as the "process of recognizing as social and systemic what was formerly perceived as isolated and individual" with regard to the "broad-scale system of domination that affects women," in addition to other multiply oppressed groups such as "people of color, and gays and lesbians, among others'.[24] Dawn Sharrat Bado makes the following important distinction: '"intersectionalism" as a critical framework is not to be confused with "intersectionality," as the latter term denotes the intersecting systems of oppression which the former analyses'.[25] intersectionalism should thus be interpreted as being more actively interrogative whilst the word intersectionality is more passively (but usefully) descriptive.

The 2017 special issue of the Irish Studies Journal *Breac*, titled *Gender, Sexuality, and Intersectionality in Irish Studies*, highlights a rich collection of articles that showcased intersectional potential in Irish Studies via literary, political and cultural analysis. Intersectionalism allows for the alignment of various Others (gendered, sexed, racial etc.) in a theoretical and activist context in which they can coalesce rather than compete in their struggle for personal and political recognition.

Anne Mulhall, a critic who often uses feminist and queer theory in an Irish Studies context, has written extensively on the migrant crisis in Ireland and the need to resolve the direct provision problem whereby asylum seekers are detained in direct provision centres, sometimes for years, whilst their application is being processed. Mulhall has studied the representation of the 'Migrant Other' in literature by actual migrant writers. Mulhall argues:

> The categorisation of people as 'migrants' and of writers as 'migrant writers', particularly by those of us who do not carry the burden of such designations ourselves, can be racialising, dehumanising, and ghettoising. The category 'migrant writer' threatens a confinement that the writer may find difficult to escape, a segregated silo adjacent to the literary mainstream. Özgecan Kesici, a poet who grew up in Turkey and is now living in Ireland, emphasises the importance for writers not to be curtailed within 'that migrant frame' and of 'allowing spaces for migrants to be represented beyond their migrant identity'.[26]

This is one example of an academic utilising the approach of intersectionalism in the study of Ireland and issues of Irishness. It is an approach that brings the gendered, sexual and racial Other into close alliance.

The current interest in issues of race and ethnicity in Irish Studies was made apparent by the publication of the volume *Race in Irish Literature and Culture* (2024). The collection brought together a large number of Irish Studies academics to examine how Irish literature and culture represent and to some extent produce an explicitly racialised versions of Irishness. It covers a vast historical terrain from the sixteenth century to the present.

To conclude: a Roguish Irish Studies would be endlessly democratic in its openness. It would be absent a telos in the sense that it would never have a prescribed set of outcomes. It would embrace multiplicity in terms of its conceptualisations of Irishness(es). It would always be waiting in hospitable readiness for the event that Diarmuid Ferriter would call 'the revelation of Ireland' whilst accepting that such an event (like Godot) may never arrive, and if it does it will probably not take an anticipated form.[27] It would embrace a futurity of perpetual undecidability and deferral. Roguish Irish Studies, like the golden bird in Yeats' 'Sailing to Byzantium' exists in what Derrida called messianic (non-ordered/non-linear) time and (to quote Yeats' poem) shall sing 'Of what is past, or passing, or to come'.[28]

Representative textual analysis

This Hostel Life

Melatu Uche Okorie's short story collection *This Hostel Life* gives an example of an Irish migrant representing themselves rather than being represented by native Irish writers or commentators. The collection was begun during her eight years living in the direct provision system in Ireland. Okorie describes direct provision at the beginning of *This Hostel Life* as 'like being in an abusive relationship. Abuse in itself is homogenous, no matter what race, class, or in this case, the hostel of the abused'.[29] The first story ('This Hostel Life') is set in a direct provision centre, the second ('Under the Awning') centres on a migrant's experience of living in an Irish community outside the direct provision system. The final story ('The Egg Broke') is set back in the author's native Africa. In essence, these stories represent different facets and lived experiences of the evolving identity we can call 'new Irish' that migrants in Ireland represent. Although 'Under the Awning' is the story within this volume that habitually receives the most attention, the collection certainly has something approaching the unity of Joyce's volume of short stories, *Dubliners* and all three are worthy of consideration. Although only one of Okorie's stories is set in a direct provision centre, they all focus around places of cruelty and exploitation that create the conditions for which Okorie terms the 'hostel life'. The word hostel can be read as intending to remind readers of the word 'hostile', which also describes the life that many migrants have to endure in Ireland.

The story 'This Hostel Life' is written in the first person and the voice comprises a hybrid African and Transatlantic English dialect:

'From the window, me I can see everybody is here, and me I can see the place is also full. Mercy voice reach my ear before me I even go outside' (1). Okorie insightfully describes the narrative voice that exists in the first story of 'This Hostel Life': 'I told this story from the point of view of a Congolese woman for whom I created a language, a mixture of Nigerian pidgin English and some American slang words which she speaks in a strong Kinsala. The idea was born from my observation of how the different nationalities in the direct provision hostel were reconstructing language in order to communicate with each other' (xiv). What Okorie is predicting in this story is no less than a new way of speaking in the Ireland to come as its migrant population expands. For example, if you look at other countries with historically large immigrant populations, you see that communities may have or develop their own ways of speaking, and that some words or phrases may enter the language at large. This may eventually occur in Ireland if Okorie's prediction comes true.

The life that the narrator of 'This Hostel Life' lives whilst in the direct provision system is one of deadening habit and repetition. An existence that is nothing short of Beckettian. Interestingly, one of the characters in the collection's second story, 'Under the Awning', is at one point actually named as 'Didi'; a very definite allusion to the shortened name of the character of Vladimir in *Waiting for Godot*. This story also represents the kind of distance and alienation from one's world, landscape and fellow inhabitants that is habitually depicted in Beckett's texts. Okorie obtained a degree in English before she left Nigeria. Perhaps she came across Beckett even then. It would certainly complicate her relationship with Ireland/Irishness if Irish literature was already part of her background when she arrived in the country.

As Okorie acknowledges, a large amount of the narrative in 'Under the Awning' is told through a 'story within a story' that the narrator has written and is reading out to her writing class. Texts within texts – whether that be 'plays within plays', 'films within films', or 'stories within stories' – are used to depict something about the inner life and feelings of a character in the main body of the narrative. This dates back to *Hamlet* in which the titular character uses the strategy of obliquely dramatising the events that he believes led to his father's murder in order to attempt to 'catch the conscience' of his uncle who he believes committed fratricide. In 'Under the Awning', the 'story within the story' depicts the inner turmoil the narrator feels as she undergoes subtle and sometimes very explicit racism on a daily basis. The narrator uses the second person narrative voice ('you') to tell her 'story within a story'. This helps convey both her sense of subjective uncertainty and that of her main character.

After finishing her story, our unnamed narrator (a device which again contributes to a sense of how uncertain she is about her own identity as a migrant living in Ireland) is receiving a critique of her writing from the other members of the class:

> B –… 'I think the story could have a bit of light and shade to it, so that it's not all bleak and negative.
>
> E – 'I saw it as a kind of paranoia on the part of the character. Like the scene at the cinema where a woman was being nice and she completely misread it. (37–38)

Most of the comments centre around wanting the writer not to depict all white people in the story as racists and several want the second person narrator to be abandoned. Although the story does not explicitly state that these other class members are not immigrants and not people of colour, their very paranoid response to the narrator's story does suggest that this is the case.

As Deirdre Flynn argues:

> For the narrator of 'Under the Awning', there is [what Lauren Berlant would call] a 'cruel optimism' in her actions, as within the framed narrative she is caught in the repeated dismissal of her experiences. She is outside, unnamed and impeded by the liminality of her existence within the Irish state. She is locked out of being Irish, a fact highlighted further by the colour of her skin. The structural inequality of both her temporal space in the writing group and the fictional space of her story is unfamiliar to those outside the state of exception. Okorie details the plurality of our contemporary state, and the precarious position of those locked out of Ireland through citizenship laws [which state that your parents must be born in Ireland in order for you to be entitled to the identity category of 'Irish'].[30]

In essence, the other members of the class want the writer to A) write a narrative for a traditional white Irish audience, and B) create a more conventional narrative and structure. The latter comment really irritates the narrator who wonders to herself: 'Does every story have to have a traditional plot trajectory?' This question alerts the reader to the fact that the 'New Irish' will have new forms of narrative that they will wish to use to represent their identities and experience and this will have consequences in terms of the development of the Ireland, Irishness and Irish Studies 'to come'.

Eventually, the writer softens some of the more overt instances of racism that occur in her story but, significantly, retains the second person narrative style. This form of narration is very rare in Irish writing (John McGahern's *The Dark* and J.P. Donleavy's *The Ginger Man* are two of the texts that do deploy that voice) and gestures towards the formal radicalism that will possibly emerge from 'New Irish' writing in the decades to come. That this writing could prove disruptive to literary and cultural norms is signalled at the end of the story when we are told that the class member who really did not like the use of the second person in the story refuses to give feedback. Similarly, the music of the Nigerian descended Denise Chaila whose work combines both African and Celtic styles and rhythms can be said to orientate itself towards a 'new Irish style' that may have profound cultural and identity consequences for the 'Ireland to come'.

The question concerning the extent to which the teller of this story is a somewhat unreliable narrator arises when she seems to suggest that non-immigrant Irish writers use (only) conventional narrative and structure. We know that that is patently not true; as Anna Burns' stylistically radical *Milkman* (2018) – among other recent Irish literary texts – makes abundantly clear. Also, the members of the writing class in Okorie's story seem particularly rigid in their attitude; the suggestion seems to be that the narrator is open-minded while the others are closed-minded. This raises all sorts of questions about the perception of one group by another group.

Flynn asserts that 'The [writing] group's response to her [Didi's] changes [to her story] only serves to prove their lack of understanding and denial of the racism so obvious in Ireland, so tied to the legal exclusion of certain bodies to membership of the nation'.[31] It is clear from 'Under the Awning' that new narratives of identity and experience, and the forms needed to ethically express them, are needed if there is to be a truly transnational and intersectional Ireland and Irish Studies 'to come'. Okorie describes the act of reading literature (and this can apply to other artistic forms) as an encounter with the event of newness (xiv) and *This Hostel Life* enables the staging of just such an encounter.

Parsons offers a similar assessment concerning how *This Hostel Life* offers a view of an as yet undecidable literary and cultural futurity: 'The packaging and marketing of Okorie's writing offers an opportunity to reflect on the necessary and ongoing work of interrupting, creating, and regenerating Irish literature that will result from a diverse writing and reading population in Ireland, drawing on a wide array of literary archives and cultural lexicons'.[32] Parsons also acknowledges the importance of Skein Press who undertook to publish *This Hostel Life* and also the works of many other 'minority authors':

> *This Hostel Life* is emblematic of a much larger landscape: it is caught in a trap of its own limited set of possible representations. Its place in the Irish literary field is, by virtue of its publication history, inescapably contingent and dependent on the hospitality of the industry, an issue that Skein Press is working to overcome. (13)

The opening up of the Irish literary and publishing establishment to a greater hospitability in terms of publishing new works from 'new Irish' authors should certainly be a priority for Ireland's futural imaginings.

The final story in *This Hostel Life*, by virtue of its being set in the Africa where Okorie was born, acknowledges the country of origin and the past that is still part of Okorie's identity. However, the story refuses to glorify or romanticise this past because it centres on the possible killing of twins, 'A practice that was abolished in the 1990s after religion was introduced to my [Okorie's] village' (xiii). Past traditions and customs can be acknowledged without being wholeheartedly embraced for a people's present or incalculable future, which is very much akin to what the 'Roguish Irish Studies to come' should be doing now and in its undecidable future.

In the 2021 edition of *This Hostel Life*, Dr Liam Thornton (Associate Professor, School of Law, University College Dublin) published an expanded version of his essay in the original, 2018 edition. Thornton outlines some of the changes he hopes will come into being in Ireland's asylum seeking process and direct provision system: 'The task of Irish society, if as a society we are truly sorry for creating and supporting this system for over twenty years, is to hold whatever government is in power to a key promise: end direct provision' (80–81). Thornton is not sure if this will come to pass but he says he remains optimistic. Essentially, he is making a wager on an undecidable Irish future that will hopefully be more hospitable to the migrant other. Arguably, Thornton is being a bit unrealistically optimistic. Anyone can hope, but actually, the current realities in the world suggest that the migrant other is going to have an increasingly difficult time, including in Ireland. I would argue, however, that this is a necessary hope; much like how it was necessary for Vladimir and Estragon to keep hoping for the arrival of Godot. Maybe literary and cultural texts such as *This Hostel Life* won't solve or change anything, but they can act as the canary in the coalmine in alerting us to what is occluded in official narratives. As Oscar Wilde put it succinctly: 'The future is what artists are'.[33]

The reasons why *This Hostel Life* cannot be considered a perfect example of a new type of Irish literature suggests goals and aspirations for that future form of Irish literature and how it could be interpreted. Okorie is one of the writers who are too often neatly siloed and bracketed into the category of non-Irish migrant writers; her work also views herself and people like her as being Others to Irishness. A Roguish Irish Studies to come would ensure that a narrative of Irishness(es) would be grown which would ensure that writers like Okorie would not be reduced to a narrow category such as 'non-Irish migrant writer' and her future work might reflect her sense of being a part of an evolving version of an Irish identity.

The publishing story of *This Hostel Life* offers a line of flight for both Irish literature and the Roguish Irish Studies academic discipline that will examine both the literary works and the history, politics and culture from which they sprang. As Parsons (quoted above) has asserted, the future of Irish writing and publishing must reside with the mainstream publishers adopting the approach of Skein Press. These more commercial publication houses must be willing to embrace and publish marginal and minority voices and allow their stories and identities to become part of what Declan Kiberd might call the 'patchwork quilt(s) of Irishness'.

Study questions

1. **What possible future directions could Irish Studies take?**
2. **What are the differences between utopian and undecidable futures?**
3. **What are some of the features of intersectionality?**
4. **What are some of the features of transnationalism?**
5. **Consider Derrida's conceptualisation of the *avenir* (the 'to come')**
6. **What's Queer about the 'queer theory to come'?**

Notes

1 The title of this Coda is derived from my friend and former mentor Michael O'Rourke's PhD thesis, 'A Passion for the Impossible: Waiting for the Queer Theory to Come'. I owe him a huge debt for opening my eyes to so many of the intellectual and humanitarian wonders with which I have engaged in this book.
2 See Fintan O'Toole, *We Don't Know Ourselves* (London: Head of Zeus Press, 2021).
3 https://www.poetryfoundation.org/poems/57042/clearances (accessed 18 June, 2025).
4 Richard Kearney, *Anatheism: Returning to God After God* (New York: Columbia University Press, 2010), p. 65.
5 For a full analysis of Wilde's conception of agnostic faith, see Simon Critchley, *The Faith of the Faithless: Experiments in Political Theology* (New York: Verso Press, 2012).
6 Jacques Derrida, *Rogues: Two Essays on Reason* (Stanford: Stanford University Press, 2005), p. 152.
7 Jacques Derrida and Elisabeth Roudinesco, *For What Tomorrow: A Dialogue* (Stanford: Stanford University Press, 2004), p. 96.
8 Ibid., p. 29.
9 Jean Luc Nancy, 'Interview: The Future of Philosophy', in B.C. Hutchens (ed.), *Jean-Luc Nancy and the Future of Philosophy* (Chesham: Acumen, 2005), p. 162.
10 Michael O'Rourke, 'The Roguish Future of Queer Studies', *SQS – Suomen Queer-tutkimuksen Seuran lehti*, 1:2, p. 30.
11 See Judith Butler, 'Further Reflections on Conversations of Our Time', *Diacritics* 27:1 (1997), pp. 13–15.

12 O'Rourke, 'The Roguish Future of Queer Studies', p. 33.
13 Declan Kiberd, *Inventing Ireland: The Literature of the Modern Nation* (London: Vintage, 1996), p. 653.
14 Paige Reynolds, 'Introduction', in Paige Reynolds (ed.), *The New Irish Studies* (Cambridge: Cambridge University Press; 2020), p. 3.
15 Eamon Maher, 'Review of *The New Irish Studies*', *Irish University Review* 51:2 (2021), p. 389.
16 Kearney, *Anatheism*, p. 105.
17 Ibid., p. 110. Emphasis in original.
18 O'Rourke, 'The Roguish Future of Queer Studies', p. 35.
19 Catherine Malabou, *Changer de difference: Le féminin et la question philosophique* (Paris: Galilée: 2009), p. 75.
20 This book was translated into English in 2000.
21 Colum McCann, *Let the Great World Spin* (London: Bloomsbury, 2009), pp. 278–279.
22 Cóilín Parsons, 'Introduction', in Cóilín Parsons (ed.), *Transnationalism in Irish Literature and Culture* (Cambridge: Cambridge University Press, 2024), p. 4.
23 Ibid., p. 7.
24 Kimberlé Crenshaw, 'Mapping the Margins: Intersectionality, Identity Politics, and Violence against Women of Color', *Stanford Law Review* 43:6 (July 1991), p. 1241–1242.
25 Dawn Miranda Sharratt Bado, 'Living as the "Cuckoo's Mother": Feminism, Interculturalism, and Intersectionalism in Linda Anderson's Cuckoo', *Breac: Gender, Sexuality, and Intersectionality in Irish Studies* (17 July, 2017), np. https://breac.nd.edu/articles/living-as-the-cuckoos-mother-feminism-interculturalism-and-intersectionalism-in-linda-andersons-cuckoo/ (accessed 18 June, 2025).
26 Anne Mulhall, 'Arrivals: Inward Migration and Irish Literature', in Eric Falci and Paige Reynolds (eds), *Irish Literature in Transition: 1980–2020* (Cambridge: Cambridge University Press; 2020), p. 183.
27 This refers to the title of Diarmuid Ferriter's book *The Revelation of Ireland, 1995–2022* (2024).
28 William Butler Yeats, 'Sailing to Byzantium', in *Selected Poems* (London: Penguin Classics, 2000), p. 129.
29 Melatu Uche Okorie, *This Hostel Life* (Dublin: Skein Press, 2018), pp. vii–viii. All future references refer parenthetically to this edition.
30 Deirdre Flynn, '"Where Are You From Originally": The Cruel Optimism of the Precarious Irish Public Sphere in Melatu Uche Okorie's "Under the Awning"', *The Wayback Machine* (21 March, 2021), https://web.archive.org/web/20220311163716/ (accessed 18 June, 2025).

31 Ibid.
32 Parsons, 'Introduction', p. 13.
33 *Collins Complete Works of Oscar Wilde*, ed. Merlin Holland, fifth edition (Glasgow: HarperCollins, 2003), p. 1194.

Selected readings

1 The Irish Revival: the birth of a discipline?

Bruna, Giulia, *J.M. Synge and the Travel Writing of the Irish Revival* (Syracuse: Syracuse University Press, 2017).

Cleary, Joe, and Connolly, Claire (eds), *The Cambridge Companion to Modern Irish Culture* (Cambridge: Cambridge University Press, 2005).

Conrad, Kathryn, Parsons, Cóilín, and McCormack, Julie (eds), *Science, Technology, and Irish Modernism* (Syracuse: Syracuse University Press, 2019).

Gibbons, Luke, *Transformations in Irish Culture* (Cork: Cork University Press, 1996).

Grene, Nicholas, *The Politics of Irish Drama: Plays in Context from Boucicault to Friel* (Cambridge: Cambridge University Press, 1999).

Hand, Derek, *A History of the Irish Novel* (Cambridge: Cambridge University Press, 2011).

Kiberd, Declan, *Inventing Ireland: The Literature of the Modern Nation* (London: Vintage, 1996).

Kiberd, Declan, *Irish Classics* (London: Granta Books, 2001).

Killeen, Jarlath, and Morin, Tina (eds), *Irish Gothic: An Edinburgh Companion* (Edinburgh: Edinburgh University Press, 2023).

Mathews, P.J., *Revival: The Abbey Theatre, Sinn Fein, The Gaelic League and the Cooperative Movement* (Cork: Cork University Press, 2000).

Mathews, P.J., and Kiberd, Declan (eds), *Handbook of the Irish Revival: An Anthology of Irish Cultural and Political Writings 1891–1922* (Dublin: Abbey Theatre Press, 1915).

Meaney, Gerardine, *Gender, Ireland, and Cultural Change* (New York: Routledge, 2010).

Roche, Anthony, *Synge and the Making of Modern Irish Drama* (Dublin: Carysfort Press, 2013).

Valente, Joseph, and Howes, Marjorie (eds), *The Irish Revival: A Complex Vision* (Syracuse: Syracuse University Press, 2023).

2 The Counter-Revival: revising a discipline?

Brannigan, John, *Brendan Behan, Cultural Nationalism and the Revisionist Writer* (Dublin: Four Courts Press, 2002).

Brown, Terence, *Ireland: A Social and Cultural History 1922–1985* (London: Fontana Paperbacks 1985).

Coogan, Tim Pat, *Michael Collins* (London: Arrow Books, 1991).

Corkery, Daniel, *Hidden Ireland* (Dublin: Gill & Macmillan, 1967).

Corkery, Daniel, *Synge and Anglo-Irish Literature* (Cork: The Mercier Press, 5th impression, 1966).

Knowlson, James, *Damned to Fame: The Life of Samuel Beckett* (London: Bloomsbury, 1996).

Knowlson, James, *Damned to Fame: The Life of Samuel Beckett* (New York: Grove Press, 1997).

Matthews, Kelly, *The Bell Magazine and the Representation of Irish Identity: Opening Windows* (Dublin: Four Courts Press, 2012).

May, Charles E. (ed.), *Short Story Theories* (Ohio: Ohio University Press, 1976).

O'Connor, Frank, *The Big Fellow* (Dublin: Poolbeg Press Ltd, 1996).

Price, Graham, '"Idle Talk, Idle Talk, Idle Talk": Samuel Beckett, Anglo-Ireland, and Heideggerian Thought', *Estudios Irlandeses* 16 (2021), pp. 13–27.

Richards, Shaun (ed.), *The Cambridge Companion to Twentieth-Century Irish Drama* (Cambridge: Cambridge University Press, 2004).

Roche, Anthony, *Contemporary Irish Drama: From Beckett to McGuinness*, second edition (London and New York: Palgrave Macmillan, 2009).

van der Ziel, Stanley 'John McGahern, Post-Revival Literature, and Irish Cultural Criticism', *New Hibernia Review* 21:1 (Spring/Earrach, 2017), pp. 123–142.

3 Postcolonial theory and Irish Studies

Bixby, Patrick, *Nietzsche and Irish Modernism* (Manchester: Manchester University Press, 2025).

Cairns, Richard, and Richards, Shaun, *Writing Ireland: Colonialism, Nationalism, Culture* (Manchester: Manchester University Press, 1988).

Carroll, Clare, and King, Patricia (eds), *Ireland and Postcolonial Theory* (Cork: Cork University Press, 2003).

Cleary, Joe, *Modernism, Empire, World Literature* (Cambridge: Cambridge University Press, 2021).

Deane, Seamus, *Celtic Revivals: Essays in Modern Irish Literature, 1880–1980* (London: Faber & Faber, 1987).

Flannery, Eoin, *Ireland and Postcolonial Studies: Theory, Discourse, Utopia* (Basingstoke and New York: Palgrave Macmillan, 2009).

Gibbons, Luke, *James Joyce and the Irish Revolution: The Easter Rising as Modern Event* (London: University of Chicago Press, 2023).

Graham, Colin, and Hooper, Glenn (eds), *Irish and Postcolonial Writing: History, Theory, Practice* (Basingstoke: Palgrave, 2002).

Kearney, Richard, *Transitions: Narratives in Modern Irish Culture* (Manchester: Manchester University Press, 1988).

Kiberd, Declan, *Inventing Ireland: The Literature of the Modern Nation* (London: Vintage, 1996).

Lloyd, David, *Anomalous States: Irish Writing and the Postcolonial Moment* (Dublin: Lilliput Press, 1993).

McGrath, F.C., *Brian Friel's (Post)Colonial Drama: Language, Illusion, and Politics* (Syracuse: Syracuse University Press, 1999).

Pine, Richard, *The Disappointed Bridge: Ireland and the Postcolonial World* (Newcastle: Cambridge Scholars Publishing, 2014).

Price, Graham, 'Spectrality and Hospitality in Brian Friel's *Translations*', *Irish University Review* 55:2 (2025), pp. 359–377.

Richtarick, Marilyn J., *Acting Between the Lines: The Field Day Theatre Company and Irish Cultural Politics 1980–1984* (Oxford: Clarendon Press, 1994).

Richtarik, Marilynn, *Acting Between the Lines: The Field Day Theatre Company and Irish Cultural Politics 1980–1984* (Oxford: Oxford University Press, 1995; Washington, DC: Catholic University of America Press, 2001).

Said, Edward, *Orientalism* (New York: Vintage Books, 1979).

Tracey, Robert, *The Unappeasable Host: Studies in Irish Identities* (Dublin: UCD Press, 1998).

Wilder, David (ed.), *Literature in the Modern World* (Oxford: Oxford University Press, 1990).

4 Gender, sex and sexuality

Backus, Margot, and Valente, Joseph, *The Child Sex Scandal and Modern Irish Literature: Writing the Unspeakable* (Indiana: Indiana University Press, 2020).

Balzano, Wanda, Mulhall, Anne, and Sullivan, Moynagh (eds), *Irish Post-modernisms and Popular Culture* (London: Palgrave Macmillan, 2007).

Bracken, Claire, *Irish Feminist Futures* (London: Routledge, 2015).

Coughlan, Patricia, 'Feminism and Literature in Postmodernity', *Hungarian Journal of English and American Studies (HJEAS)* 10:1/2 (2004).

Houston, Lloyd (Meadbh) *Irish Modernism and the Politics of Sexual Health* (Oxford: Oxford University Press, 2023).

Kelleher, *The Feminization of Famine: Expressions of the Inexpressible* (Cork: Cork University Press, 1997.

Longley, Edna, *From Cathleen to Anorexia* (Dublin: Attic Press, 1990).

Meaney, Gerardine, *Gender, Ireland, and Cultural Change* (New York: Routledge, 2010).

Price, Graham, *Oscar Wilde and Contemporary Irish Drama: Learning to be Oscar's Contemporary* (London: Palgrave, 2018).

Price, Graham, 'Quite an Other Thing: Recent Texts in Irish Queer Studies', *Irish University Review* 42:1 (2013), *Queering the Issue*, pp. 222–233.

Redmond, Jennifer, and McAuliffe, Mary (eds), *The Politics of Gender and Sexuality in Modern Ireland: A Reader* (Dublin: Four Courts Press, 2024).

Reynolds, Paige, *Modernism in Irish Women's Contemporary Writing: The Stubborn Mode* (Oxford: Oxford University Press, 2024).

Valente, Joseph, 'Self-Queering Ireland?', *The Canadian Journal of Irish Studies* 36:1 (2010), pp. 25–43.

Walshe, Eibhear, *Oscar's Shadow: Wilde, Homosexuality and Modern Ireland* (Cork: Cork University Press, 2011).

5 Memory, trauma and imagination

Caruth, Cathy, *Literature in the Ashes of History* (Baltimore: Johns Hopkins University Press, 2013).

Costello-Sullivan, Kathleen, *Trauma and Recovery in the Twenty-First-Century Irish Novel* (Syracuse: Syracuse University Press, 2018).

Ferriter, Diarmuid, *The Revelation of Ireland: 1995–2020* (London: Profile Books Limited, 2024).

Flannery, Eoin, and O'Brien, Eugene (eds), *Irish Studies Review: Critiquing Crisis and Commemoration* 30:4 (2022).

Gallego, Melania Terrazas (ed.), *Trauma and Identity in Contemporary Irish Culture* (Oxford: Peter Lang, 2020).

Gibbons, Luke, *Joyce's Ghosts: Ireland, Modernism, and Memory* (Chicago: University of Chicago Press, 2017).

Haughton, Miriam, *Staging Trauma: Bodies in Shadow* (London: Palgrave, 2018).

Kirby, Peadar et al. (eds), *Reinventing Ireland: Culture, Society, and the Global Economy* (London: Pluto, 2002).

La Capra, Dominick, *Writing History, Writing Trauma* (Baltimore and London: Johns Hopkins University Press, 2001).

Petitt, Lance, *Screening Ireland* (Manchester: Manchester University Press, 2000).
Pine, Emilie, *The Politics of Irish Memory: Performing Remembrance in Contemporary Irish Culture* (London: Palgrave Macmillan, 2010).
Pine, Emilie, *The Memory Marketplace: Witnessing Pain in Contemporary Irish and International Theatre* (Indiana: Indiana University Press, 2020).
Ricoeur, Paul, *Memory, History, Forgetting*, trans. Kathleen Blamey and David Pellauer (Chicago: University of Chicago Press, 2004).

6 Irish ecocriticism

Braidotti, Rosi, *Transpositions: On Nomadic Ethics* (Cambridge: Polity Press, 2006).
Brannigan, John, *Archipelagic Modernism: Literature in the Irish and British Isles, 1890–1970* (Edinburgh: Edinburgh University Press, 2014).
Cohen, Tom (ed.), *Telemorphosis: Theory in the Era of Climate Change* (Ann Arbor, MI: Open Humanities Press/University of Michigan Library, 2012).
Deleuze, Gilles, *Difference and Repetition* (London: Continuum, 2004).
Flannery, Eoin, *Ireland and Ecocriticism: Literature, History, and Environmental* Justice (New York: Routledge, 2016).
Frawley, Oona, *Irish Pastoral: Nostalgia and Twentieth-Century Irish Literature* (Dublin: Irish Academic Press, 2005).
Kelleher, Margaret, *The Feminization of Famine: Expressions of the Inexpressible* (Cork: Cork University Press, 1997).
Kerridge, Richard, and Sammells, Neil (eds), *Writing the Environment: Ecocriticism and Literature* (London: Zed Books, 1998).
Price, Graham, '"Accursed Time": Gilles Deleuze's *Difference and Repetition* and John McGahern's *That They May Face the Rising Sun*', *Etudes Irlandais* 44:2 (2019), pp. 95–111.
Sen, Malcolm (ed.), *A History of Irish Literature and the Environment* (Cambridge: Cambridge University Press, 2022).
Sen, Malcolm, *Irish Anthropocene: Literature, Climate Change, Sovereignity* (Syracuse: Syracuse University Press, 2026).

Coda: waiting for the 'Irish Studies to come'

Derrida, Jacques, *Rogues: Two Essays on Reason* (Stanford: Stanford University Press, 2004).
Kearney, Richard, *Anatheism: Returning to God After God* (New York: Columbia University Press, 2010).

O'Rourke, Michael, 'The Roguish Future of Queer Studies', *SQS – Suomen Queer tutkimuksen Seuran lehti* 1(2).

O'Toole, Fintan, *We Don't Know Ourselves* (London: Head of Zeus Press, 2021).

Parsons, Cóilín (ed.), *Transnationalism in Irish Literature and Culture* (Cambridge: Cambridge University Press, 2024).

Reynolds, Paige (ed.), *The New Irish Studies* (Cambridge: Cambridge University Press; 2020).

Index